The Peabody Sisters
of Salem

Books by Louise Hall Tharp

CHAMPLAIN
Northwest Voyager

COMPANY OF ADVENTURERS
The Story of the Hudson's Bay Company

THE PEABODY SISTERS OF SALEM

UNTIL VICTORY
Horace Mann and Mary Peabody

THREE SAINTS AND A SINNER
Julia Ward Howe, Louise, Annie and Sam Ward

TORY HOLE

ADVENTUROUS ALLIANCE
The Story of the Agassiz Family of Boston

LOUIS AGASSIZ
Adventurous Scientist

THE BARONESS AND THE GENERAL

MRS. JACK
A Biography of Isabella Stewart Gardner

SAINT-GAUDENS AND THE GILDED ERA

THE APPLETONS OF BEACON HILL

The Peabody Sisters
of Salem

by

LOUISE HALL THARP

INTRODUCTION BY LOUIS AUCHINCLOSS

Little, Brown and Company
Boston   *Toronto*

Library of Congress Cataloging-in-Publication Data

Tharp, Louise Hall, 1898–
  The Peabody sisters of Salem.

  Originally published 1950.
  Bibliography: p.
  Includes index.
  1. Peabody family. 2. Peabody, Elizabeth Palmer,
1804–1894. 3. Mann, Mary Tyler Peabody, 1806–1887.
4. Hawthorne, Sophia Amelia Peabody, 1811–1871.
I. Title.
CT274.P43T46 1988   929'.2'0973   88-9262
ISBN 0-316-83920-5
ISBN 0-316-83919-1 (pbk.)

        HC: 10 9 8 7 6 5 4 3 2 1

        PB: 10 9 8 7 6 5 4 3 2 1

FG

Published simultaneously in Canada
by Little, Brown & Company (Canada) Limited

PRINTED IN THE UNITED STATES OF AMERICA

To the Hawthorne descendants

Ah me! the years go swiftly by . . .
—EUGENE FIELD

Contents

Illustrations appear following page 180.

Introduction

by Louis Auchincloss

PERHAPS no caste in American history has taken itself more seriously than the intellectuals of the greater Boston area in the middle of the last century. They had little doubt that the "hub" was the equal of ancient Athens and that from their midst would spring the spiritual philosophers who would guide the nation to a better life. But always snapping at the heels of their bounding idealism were the nagging hounds of duty and guilt. One had to wonder at times if heaven would be worth it, with the coexistence of hell as the price. Channing, Alcott, Hawthorne, Mann, Webster, Sumner, Howe agonized over abolition, Transcendentalism, Unitarianism, evolution, even spiritualism. Emerson sometimes seems the only man of his time to have attained serenity.

Louise Hall Tharp limns this era of seething intellects in the vision of three sisters, each unlike the other two. The result is a brilliant assessment of the role of women in that time and place. As two of them had to patch a life out of the material left them by demanding mates, Tharp provides us with a study in depth of the New England husband. He resembled no other, before or since. He did not, like a peasant, treat his spouse as a beast of burden, or, like a capitalist, as the subject of "conspicuous consumption," or, like a sensualist, as a bauble. No, he took her much too seriously for any such nonsense. For she had to play a vital role in his life. She had even to be stronger than he, though her strength would be derived from her lesser sensitivity. She had to sustain and console him in his black moments of depression and despair, agonies from which her coarser nature would exempt her. For the highest genius had to be male and, by reason of the burden, neurotic. It was a woman's glory to be the adored junior partner.

Two of the Peabody sisters, Mary and Sophia, were the perfect wives of the time, to very different but equally exigent men. The third and oldest, Elizabeth, offers a gallant and touching picture of the most that could be made of the life of a single woman.

Horace Mann, Mary's husband, like his friend Samuel Gridley Howe, whose wife, Julia, wrote "The Battle Hymn of the Republic," was a grimly dedicated public servant who believed that it was his wife's privilege to share his backbreaking tasks. He loved her well enough in his craggy way, but his love was expressed in his continual apprehension that disaster would befall her. Mary battled with near poverty and the constant ailments of her children and spouse in her struggle to sustain the latter in his granite resolution to maintain, against terrible opposition, Antioch, a liberal college for men and women in Yellow Springs, Ohio. And although she never had to cope with infidelity on Mann's part (the New England husband was ineluctably faithful), she was always jealous of his dead first wife whose fate Mann was gloomily convinced she was about to share. But she was still the indispensable partner in a noble enterprise. Public education may owe her as much as it owes her husband, for it seems more than possible that that dour, neurotic man would have gone to pieces without her.

The same is true in a very different field with Sophia. When she married Nathaniel Hawthorne, he was a shy, reclusive, impecunious bachelor of thirty-seven, probably still a virgin, whom, with only *Twice-Told Tales* and some children's stories to his credit, no critic would have picked as America's first great novelist. But Sophia saw precisely what he needed: a quiet, isolated home in the country and a wife willing to dedicate all her waking hours to building up his confidence and shielding him from troubles and distraction. So completely did she throw herself into this mission that, when her abolitionist sisters expressed their dismay at Hawthorne's adoption, in his campaign biography of his old friend, Franklin Pierce, of the latter's position that slavery should be tolerated in the southern states as the price of preserving the Union, she defended him fiercely. But of course she knew that her husband was never going to have any real influence on the fate of the slaves. What did it matter if he was unenlightened on the issues of abolition? Let him stick to the one thing he knew how to do peerlessly: the writing of beautiful tales. And out of the happiness of his nuptial state came, in fairly rapid succession, *The Scarlet Letter*, *The House of the Seven Gables*, *The Blithedale Romance*, and *The Marble Faun*.

However distasteful such a conception of a woman's role may appear to modern eyes, it seems uncomfortably clear that Sophia was as much of a partner in the post-marital explosion of her husband's genius as was her sister Mary in the founding and development of Antioch College.

Perhaps we could modify modern doctrine to allow the spouse of a genius (male or female) to give up his or her career to further the other's. The trouble is that one cannot be sure that the beneficiary of one's sacrifice *is* a genius.

Elizabeth Peabody, the oldest and only unmarried sister, was constantly the victim of a burstingly generous heart and an intellect that had too wide a range for its limited discrimination. She threw herself into cause after cause, with the altruism of a saint and the egotism of a passionately possessive friend. One can see why William Ellery Channing had to back away from her rapturous discipleship, why Hawthorne could not endure her suggestions for "happy endings" to his tales, and why the governor of Virginia, when she rushed down to Richmond to plead for the lives of John Brown's adherents, should have regarded her as the very essence of everything he loathed in the north. In a long life of mild errors and undoubted achievements, of teaching, lecturing, bookselling and book writing, of the advocacy of many unpopular and ultimately successful causes, this wonderful old lady, whose most notable achievement was the spreading of kindergartens throughout our land, excites our liveliest admiration, even when we find her a bit ridiculous.

And it is right here that I find my only bone to pick with Louise Hall Tharp. She does not like the picture of Miss Peabody as Miss Birdseye in Henry James's novel *The Bostonians*, and indeed James's brother William took him severely to task for unkindness to the very much still living model. But I insist that Miss Birdseye is one of James's greatest characters and the novel in which she appears one of the finest of his middle period. Of course, he depicts the silly and fatuous side of the Boston world of multiple causes, and of course it existed. But even when he pokes his slyest fun he sees the virtue in his target. Here, for example, is Miss Birdseye encountering the hero as she descends from a tram car on her indefatigable round of conferences. She immediately embarks on the defense of women's rights, knowing that he is a staunch anti-feminist, and he exclaims that it is not the function of women to be reasonable.

"His companion turned upon him, slowly and mildly, and each of her glasses, in her aspect of reproach, had the glitter of an enormous tear. 'Do you regard us, then, simply as lovely baubles?' The effect of this question, as coming from Miss Birdseye, and referring in some degree to her own venerable identity, was such as to move him to irresistible laughter."

And I do not see how the most ardent admirer of Elizabeth Peabody could ask for a more eloquent tribute than James's description of the passing of Miss Birdseye:

"Miss Birdseye's voice was very low, like that of a person breathing with difficulty; but it had no painful nor querulous note — it expressed only the cheerful weariness which had marked all this last period of her life, and which seemed to make it now as blissful as it was suitable that she should pass away. Her head was thrown back against the top of the chair, the ribbon which confined her ancient hat hung loose, and the late afternoon-light covered her octogenarian face and gave it a kind of fairness, a double placidity. There was, to Ransom, something almost august in the trustful renunciation of her countenance; something in it seemed to say that she had been ready long before, but as the time was not ripe she had waited, with her usual faith that all was for the best; only, at present, since the right conditions met, she couldn't help feeling that it was quite a luxury, the greatest she had ever tasted. Miss Birdseye had given herself so lavishly all her life that it was rather odd there was anything left of her for the supreme surrender."

The Peabody Sisters
of Salem

CHAPTER ONE

Cuba Journey

ON the sixth of December, 1833, the newspaper-reading public of Boston and Salem was informed that Masonic organizations constituted a secret menace to government. The *New England Palladium and Advertiser* devoted most of its space to this subject. The *Salem Gazette*, on the other hand, regarded as still more dangerous the preaching of Boston's great Unitarian, Dr. William Ellery Channing. Had Dr. Channing miscounted, when he told how few were the allusions to hell and damnation in Holy Scripture? In the *Gazette*'s opinion, he had indeed! On a day such as this, when six vessels cleared Boston harbor for foreign ports, no item so personal as a passenger list was usually considered worthy of publication. There was, however, one notable exception. Just below the shipping news, the *Boston Advertiser* printed a small notice:

PASSENGERS

In the *Newcastle* for Havana, Misses Sophia and Mary Peabody and servant, Madam Girault, Mrs. Hull, Messrs. Jas. Burroughs, Cleveland, L. Stockwell, J. Humphrey and Henry Gilmer.

It was actually on Wednesday, December 4, that the Peabodys of Salem made their way along Central Wharf, Boston. Among the confusing waterfront crowd of passengers, porters, dock hands and seamen, they presented a compact family group united against the world. Mother Peabody, her face pale with a stoic New England effort to restrain her tears, led the way. But also in the vanguard strode her daughter Elizabeth, oldest of the Peabody sisters. There was no telltale swelling around Elizabeth's eyelids; her blue eyes shone with triumph as she too tried to take the lead. Behind the two women came Dr. Peabody, giving his arm to his youngest daughter, the frail Sophia. His wife and his oldest daughter succeeded in blocking Sophia's path fully as often as they cleared it, and the Doctor loudly expressed his annoyance. His remarks went un-heeded as usual — save for a few pacifying words from Mary, second of the sisters, who brought up the rear. Although also bound for Cuba, Mary shared none of the attention lavished upon Sophia. Withdrawn and self-contained, she walked with the family — yet alone.

Dr. Peabody glanced curiously at his daughter Sophia, whose hand rested so lightly on his arm. She had been an invalid for most of her twenty-four years. Recently, her life had been despaired of, and this voyage upon which she and her sister Mary were bound was a journey for health. Yet here was Sophia, small-boned and fragile to be sure, but walking with a gay rhythm that was almost dancing. She had a delicate flush in her cheeks and her wide gray eyes were alight with anticipation. If she had one of her chronic headaches, she had certainly forgotten it for the moment at least.

This Cuba journey had been all Elizabeth's doing. "Impossible," her father had said, mindful of his pitifully small practice as physician and dentist. But Lizzie had managed. She had found a place for Mary as governess in a wealthy planter's family. Mary's salary would be negligible, since Sophia was to live at the hacienda and be treated as a guest as part of the bargain. No wonder there was a victor's gleam in Lizzie's eye as she shouldered her way along the wharf, her bonnet all askew, and her shawl, too hastily pinned, threatening to come loose from its moorings. Mary observed with mortification that strangers cast amused glances in Elizabeth's direction. But Mary misunderstood. Elizabeth's vitality was so immense, her enthusiasm so infectious, her plain face so friendly, that strangers were attracted to her. If they smiled, it was with tolerance. If they did not know her name, they asked; and so wide was Elizabeth's acquaintance in Boston that, wherever she went, there was someone to say, "Why, that's Miss Peabody!"

Automatically, Mary stooped to pick up a glove that Lizzie had dropped. Elizabeth was always looking after other people, forgetting herself, her appearance and her belongings. In marked contrast, not a hair of Mary's head was out of place. Her Quaker-gray traveling cloak, though far from new, was put on with care and worn with distinction. Mary was a little person, exquisitely well made, with hands that were quick and sure. A fine forehead, eyes of an intriguing gray-green color and abundant dark brown hair gave her friends good reason to call her the beauty of the family. There was a hint of subtle humor in her smile. Mary could laugh a little even when family situations became tense. But lately, Mary Peabody had seemed to try to escape attention, even to appear less charming than she really was.

The Peabodys passed the schooner *Volunteer*, also Havana bound and taking on freight with all possible speed. The tide would soon be high and the wind, although fitful, was in the right quarter. They reached the *Newcastle*, a "first-rate coppered brig for freight or passage," according to the newspaper advertisements. Mary stepped forward to take Sophia's arm. But now it was discovered that the boy with their baggage was missing! He had been trundling his barrow along behind them, and had last been seen as they crossed the current of traffic eddying toward the *Volunteer*. Dr. Peabody, Mrs. Peabody and the masterful Elizabeth all tried to take charge of finding him at the same time. Each gave conflicting orders to the others — to Mary and Sophia, and to any dock hand who would listen.

The invalid Sophia sank down upon a packing case. Mentally, she began to count over their lost belongings, beginning with the "Volante box." "Three nightgowns, four nightcaps, our riding dresses, my cambric spencer, the corded petticoats . . ." Elizabeth and her father had lost their tempers by this time, and Sophia's headache returned with shattering force. She moaned faintly and her mother sat down beside her, remarking that it was all Father's fault. As a rule, the very real agony that Sophia suffered during family altercations brought a temporary armistice if not a permanent peace. This time, however, it was Mary's quiet, "Do let Father manage, Lizzie," that had the best effect. During the momentary ensuing calm, the boy appeared of his own accord, whistling, trundling his barrow, and taking his own good time.

Mrs. Peabody now prepared to take a last farewell of Sophia. Although still tearless, she made it clear that she never expected to see her beloved child again. Even if there were no shipwreck, Sophia could not be expected to survive the voyage. Or if she did, she would surely die in a strange land, with no one near to close her eyes in death — except Mary, of course. But — the Lord's will be done!

Dr. Peabody angrily cleared his throat. They had been all over this, not once but many times, and he began urging the girls to go aboard ship. As a matter of fact, there was now only time for a last quick embrace. Mary handed Elizabeth her glove and admonished her not to lose it again. Then Mary and Sophia boarded the *Newcastle*.

On the deck of the brig they found Mr. James Burroughs. His sister, wife of the wealthy importer Henry Rice, was a friend of Elizabeth Peabody's. Mr. Burroughs traveled frequently to Cuba as agent for some of the big sugar plantations and he had agreed to keep an eye on "the traveling Miss Peabodys," as he called them. Burroughs was not overenthusiastic at the prospect. Elizabeth Peabody he knew by reputation as a brilliant, somewhat eccentric young woman, much admired by certain highly intellectual men but not by men about town such as he considered himself to be. Miss Mary was more quiet, better-looking, and said to have a pretty wit, if you got to know her. Miss Sophia was, of course, the invalid. James Burroughs detached himself languidly from his companions and came forward. Henry Cleveland, old friend and an admirer of Sophia's, made the introductions.

Sophia put her hand out. She was an artist of more than average ability and subconsciously she saw in every face a potential portrait. This interested glance of hers was intensely flattering, although she was unaware of it as she gave James Burroughs a friendly smile. Suddenly it occurred to Burroughs that he might have a very pleasant voyage. With considerable show of solicitude he found a place on deck for Mary and Sophia where they could see their family and wave good-by.

Mechanically, Mary thanked Mr. Burroughs and turned her eyes toward the shore. It was understood in the family that if Sophia did not die at once she might have to live in Cuba always, in order to be well. Therefore the sister who was chosen to go with her might have to support her through many years of voluntary exile. Should Elizabeth have been the one? She loved Sophia dearly. Or should it be Mary, with whom Sophia was happiest? After sleepless nights of debate within herself, Mary had chosen to go, but the reason for her decision she kept hidden deep in her heart. It was not a taste for martyrdom as her mother supposed, nor devotion to Sophia as Elizabeth assumed.

In Mary Peabody's day no woman ever admitted that she loved a man until he had "declared himself." Mary had felt safe, therefore, in the friendship of a man much older than herself who had never professed anything but friendship for her. Then one day he looked down at her and smiled, and love had struck her like a blinding light. An additional cause of suffering was the fact that Mary felt certain that her sister Elizabeth loved the same man — although Elizabeth was perhaps not ready to acknowledge it even to herself. Mary had been happy in Boston, living with Elizabeth; but now she was in mortal terror lest her secret be discovered. She might have gone home to Salem, where Sophia lived with her parents and three younger brothers. But Elizabeth would never have let her go without some explanation — needing her as she did, to help run a little private school. This journey for Sophia's health seemed providential — if Mary accepted the fact that Providence is not always kind.

Unable to stifle a faint hope, Mary looked along the wharf for a brisk figure with a springing step — an air not of haste but of liveliness — a youthful face contrasting curiously with prematurely white hair. But Horace Mann was not there. He was at this time a lawyer and a member of the Massachusetts House of Representatives, and it was not to be supposed that he would take half an hour of his time to watch the *Newcastle* set sail. Elizabeth could tell him all about it in the evening at Mrs. Clarke's boardinghouse. Mary decided not to think about that.

Perhaps Mary ought to have thought about Mr. Lindsey. He was a man she had met in New Bedford a year or two previously and who had frequently sought her society in Boston. Hearing of her intended journey, Mr. Lindsey had startled her by asking her to marry him. But her heart was given away and she had refused him as gently as she could. Given the slightest encouragement, Mr. Lindsey would have been at the wharf to see her off.

Activity increased aboard the brig. Orders were shouted and repeated; ropes creaked; seamen sprang up the masts with practiced ease. Up forward, a jib was set, while high on the mainmast a square topsail opened like a white flower blossoming miraculously against a winter sky. The brig gave a sigh like a sleeper awakening, and slid outward with the tide. Mary became aware of a widening gap between ship and shore. . . . It seemed as if death might be like this.

Turning, Mary forced herself to think of her duty to Sophia. But Sophia had borrowed a fine cambric handkerchief from the increasingly attentive Mr. Burroughs, and was waving it gaily to three figures still identifiable on the wharf. Her light brown hair, arranged in side ringlets, was blowing about her face; even in a sister's eyes, she looked distractingly pretty.

"Shouldn't you go to the cabin and lie down?" Mary asked. "How is your head?"

But Sophia thought the fresh air was doing her good and James Burroughs offered his arm for a turn about the deck. She took it with the confiding air of one who had always been looked-after. James Burroughs was over forty. If his sister's opinion of him was to be trusted, he had known many women, white, brown and black, in America and in Cuba, but he had never cared for anyone except himself. Sophia, with her look of trustfulness and truth, was a new experience. She made him feel strong, protective — and almost as virtuous as she assumed he was.

They left Mary standing at the rail. She watched the city of Boston as its rose-red brick faded to lavender, then to blue; as the pale gray of the State House dome flickered against a gray sky and disappeared. A voice behind her startled her. It was the "servant" of the newspaper notice. The Peabody resources could have stood no such extravagance, but her presence was one more testimony to Elizabeth's executive genius. Inquiring among friends, Elizabeth had heard of a negro slavewoman who had been sent from Cuba with two planters' children coming to Boston to be educated. The woman would be delighted to care for an invalid young lady on the voyage back to Cuba. She spoke now, with a strong Spanish accent which sounded strange from her lips. Which of the Peabody ladies was the invalid, she wanted to know.

"Why, it is Miss Sophia," said Mary in surprise.

The slavewoman looked at her with wise old eyes. She made no comment save to suggest that Miss Mary, then, would do well to come to the cabin for a rest.

The brig *Newcastle* was now well down Boston Harbor. Dr. Peabody, with his wife and his daughter Elizabeth, turned and walked slowly away from the wharf.

Elizabeth had been waiting to speak a word to her father in behalf of her younger brother Nathaniel, who was twenty-two and in love with a girl by the name of Elizabeth Hibbard. But Nathaniel had been involved in a scrape at Harvard ending in expulsion. He was deeply in debt and the family did not approve of marriage at this time. Mother Peabody had warned Lizzie to say nothing to Father about the matter, but it took more than a warning to make Lizzie hold her tongue if she thought she was doing good by speaking out.

Elizabeth began by talking of wonderful opportunities "at the West," of great tracts of land to be acquired for almost nothing from a generous government — of friends she knew who had been as far west as Cleveland. James Freeman Clarke, for example, was a young minister going "West" — to Louisville, Kentucky. Her father thought there might indeed be missionary work for the young Unitarian in such a place. But he would be taking his life in his hands. This led Dr. Peabody to unhappy reflections concerning Andrew Jackson, whose brand of democracy he distrusted. Elizabeth came a bit hastily to the point. Her brother, Nathaniel, wanted to go West with a bride and take up land.

Dr. Peabody turned upon Elizabeth with one of his sudden gusts of anger. Did she not know that equipment for a trek westward would put them all still further in debt? Could she not see, moreover, that Nathaniel would be accused of running away from debts already incurred? As to land — Dr. Peabody's people had been land poor, and he had escaped that environment by means of hard work. His son was to be an apothecary, since he had thrown away his chance to become a doctor; and in Salem, under the parental eye, Nathaniel was to live. Mrs. Peabody had been shaking her head at Elizabeth all through the tirade. She maintained one of her exasperatingly noble silences, when she and her husband left Elizabeth at the next cross street and set out for the Jennings Hotel to wait for the Salem stage. As a parting shot, Dr. Peabody suggested that Lizzie mind her own business, just for a change.

Elizabeth watched the two retreating figures. Her father had been a fine-looking man, but anxiety had stooped his shoulders and now her mother was almost the taller of the two. Elizabeth loved her father dearly, yet they always quarreled, his anger against her increased by the suspicion that his wife was on her side always and that he would probably have to give in. It was not that Elizabeth failed to understand this. After an argument, she could always see where she should have shown more consideration for her father's point of view.

But as to minding her own business — Elizabeth Peabody had at the moment no business to mind. Mary was not the only one to make a personal sacrifice by going to Cuba with Sophia. Elizabeth had given up her school because, with Mary gone, she could no longer handle enough pupils to pay for a schoolroom and her own room and board at Mrs. Clarke's. She would give lectures. But one never knew how many women and girls would come — and remember to pay. Then there were the history books of course, two slim volumes full of questions and answers to help a student study history, alone, since classes in it were practically nonexistent. The function of history was "to deliver the mind from the thralldom of the present, and to prepare it to comprehend the future," so wrote Elizabeth with all the ardor of a crusader. But so far the books had never delivered her from the thralldom of financial insecurity.

Key to History. Part III: The Greeks — by E. P. Peabody — would soon be finished, however. It contained not only questions but translations from Homeric hymns by Chapman and poems from *Blackwood's Magazine*. Elizabeth felt a surge of optimism as she wended her way toward Mrs. Clarke's boardinghouse at Number 3 Somerset Court, close under the shadow of the State House.[1] She would not be able to live there more than a week or two longer, and she loved the place. But the new history books would sell. . . . She began to think what she would do with the money — not for herself, but for her family.

CHAPTER TWO

"I Hear the Drums"

THE family which so absorbed Elizabeth's affections was her
own. The Peabodys of Salem were sufficiently distinguished; yet
when Mother Peabody was called upon to set anyone straight as
to ancestry, she always began with the fact that she herself was a
Palmer, and so were her children. In the words of her oldest
daughter, Mrs. Peabody's was a "life of proud poverty." The
reasons for her poverty were for the most part beyond her control.
The source of her pride lay in the fact that she was General Joseph
Palmer's granddaughter.

Born in 1778, Elizabeth Palmer — the future Mrs. Peabody —
was the third of nine children. Her mother's father, John Hunt,
had been a minister but had left the pulpit to become a distiller.
The Lord had smiled upon his efforts and considerable wealth was
his reward; so Mrs. Peabody's mother, Betsey Hunt, had been
brought up in luxury. But it was John Hunt's belief that "boys
ought to be educated for the good of their country but that girls
knew quite enough if they could make a shirt or a pudding." Betsey
Hunt had learned to read in secret, and had fallen in love with
young Joseph Palmer, a Harvard undergraduate, because he brought
her forbidden fruit from the tree of knowledge in the form of
books to read.[1]

On November 2, 1772, when Betsey Hunt was "one month after
seventeen," she set out in a coach with her sister for Hampton,
New Hampshire. She wore a riding habit "of silk calumet trimmed
with silver lace, the little spencer set close to the body, turned over
as to lapels with blue satin." It was her wedding gown. Galloping
alongside the coach were Joseph Palmer, Foster Candy, Israel Keith
and Paul Revere. This whole gay, galloping wedding party was
practically an elopement, since Betsey's father had not been able to

bring himself to approve of a young man who would let his wife read and write.

After her marriage, Betsey took to writing in good earnest, keeping a journal all her long, eventful life. The young couple had gone to live in Shrimpton Lane, Boston, where their first child was born, in August 1773. "In the month of November following," Betsey wrote in her journal, "one evening at ten o'clock I was sitting rocking the baby when I heard the gate and door open. I supposed my husband was just returning from his club, so I opened the parlor door and there stood three stout Indians. I screamed out and would have fainted for very fright had I not recognized my husband's voice saying 'Don't be afraid, Betsey. We were only making a little salt water tea.'"

The Indian disguise was but a thin one. Young Joseph Palmer was known to have been a member of the Boston Tea Party, and the Colonial Governor ordered him to leave Boston. His father had given him a partnership in an importing business with two warehouses on Long Wharf. The warehouses were burned, their stock of "spermacetti candles" making a fine white blaze by which to see red-coated soldiers — and citizens with angry faces.

Forgetting all past differences, John Hunt then invited his daughter and her husband to live with him, in Watertown.

"On the night of the eighteenth of April, I heard the drums beat," wrote Betsey Hunt Palmer. "I wakened Mr. Palmer and I said, 'My dear, I hear the drums.'"

The year was 1775 — and Joseph Palmer rode off to the Battle of Lexington.

Betsey heard the guns on Breed's Hill. She saw the burning of Charlestown. On February 25, 1778, her third child was born, and named Elizabeth. If little attention could be spared for this child who was to become Mrs. Peabody, it was not surprising.

Soon after the birth of his daughter Elizabeth, Joseph Palmer was given "the farm house" — part of old General Palmer's estate on a point of land overlooking the Neponset River. Here the future Mrs. Peabody spent her most impressionable years in an atmosphere of quiet elegance. There were servants, a carpet for the parlor and muslin curtains for the bed and at the windows of her mother's room overlooking the water. By her husband's orders, a bowl of chocolate was brought to Betsey Hunt Palmer's bedside every morning whenever she was pregnant or when she was nursing a child. As Mrs. Palmer bore her nine children in as rapid succession as possible, Mrs. Peabody was to remember this as a regular routine. But the person in Mrs. Peabody's early life who awakened her imagination most was her dynamic, awe-inspiring grandfather, General Palmer. He ruled a feudal realm, a seeming anachronism in American life, but by no means unusual for the period. Mrs. Peabody was eight years old before this was all swept away, leaving only memories like scenes in a fairy tale. She was always to remember the wide flight of stone steps in front of the manor house, the entrance hall with its buck's horns whereon reposed the tricorn hats of gentlemen guests and Grandfather's gold-headed cane. There was a room with wall coverings of crimson velvet flowered in black and bordered with gold. Grandfather, with his heavy-set figure, florid face and powdered wig, was a person to be obeyed. He was wonderfully kind nevertheless, with ideas about the education of girls diametrically opposite from those of Grandfather Hunt. General Palmer spread beautiful books out upon the carpet in the book-lined library so that a little granddaughter could lie upon her stomach and try to read Spenser's *Faerie Queene,* and *The Works of William Shakespeare.* Only in later years did Mrs. Peabody realize how rare and valuable these volumes must have been.

Coming from England in 1746, General Palmer had been a successful Boston merchant, and had then bought a tract of land in what is now Quincy. He built a curious circular stone factory and imported German artisans to make glass bottles "of all capacities." Because of these workers, the place became known as "Germantown." And "Friendship Hall" they called the manor house, with its three stories, four great rooms to a floor with, on the second floor, "a boudoir at the south and west corners" for each of General Palmer's two daughters.

It was General Palmer's daughter, Elizabeth, who fascinated Mrs. Peabody as a child. This girl had been, once, a daring horsewoman, a crack shot, and the pride of her father's heart. She was afraid of nothing, boasted General Palmer; and he had consented when her cousin and fiancé, Joseph Cranch, proposed to test her nerve by firing a pistol close above her head as she lay on the grass in the garden reading a book. . . . The shot rang out. Elizabeth leaped up, saw who had played the trick and went into a series of fainting fits. Then she broke her engagement and took to her bed. . . . Any loud sounds, particularly gun fire, threw her into hysterics. General Palmer blamed himself and was overcome with grief. He ordered that nothing must ever again disturb Miss Elizabeth, and the whole household crept on tiptoe past her door. The little granddaughter who would someday become Mrs. Peabody felt that an invalid daughter must be a source of distinction, and that her aunt's room and corner boudoir were like the castle of an enchanted princess.

Mrs. Peabody was still a child when all this ended, but old enough to remember with passionate regret the fading of the whole idyllic dream.

Grandfather Palmer was wealthy one day, unable to pay his debts the next — because of the depreciation of Continental currency. It is said that General Palmer had made an enemy of his old friend, John Hancock, by declaring publicly that government should secure individuals against loss from worthless paper money. The family story carries a strong suggestion of Naboth's vineyard, throughout. In order to pay the men in his command during the Revolution, Palmer had borrowed money from Hancock, pledging Friendship Hall. He sold valuable lands in Connecticut, filling his saddlebags with paper money with which to pay his debt. But John Hancock gave notice that he would take paper money at the rate of twenty-four dollars for one, and set a deadline — after which devaluation would go still further. Delayed by floods upon his return journey from Connecticut, General Palmer arrived half an hour too late to save his Germantown estate. Hancock's lawyer was with the sheriff when the Palmer family was put out of doors. Mrs. Peabody never forgot the sight of her grandmother, crippled by rheumatism, being helped down the broad stone steps of Friendship Hall.

With the loss of the family money, however, General Palmer's invalid daughter recovered her health! She forgave her fiancé, Joseph Cranch — who had very fortunately remained faithful all this time — married him and went to West Point to live.[2] In her new home she heard constantly the sound of practice gunfire, but it never bothered her at all.

Mrs. Peabody's parents moved to Boston. They brought their cow with them, salvaged from the Germantown disaster, and pastured her in the Park Street Burying Ground, along with the other neighbors' cows. Mrs. Peabody's father attempted to establish himself as a merchant; but times were cruel, and he failed.

Far from accepting defeat, old General Palmer had started life over again with a project to make salt from sea water. He had acquired some marsh land on Boston Neck, and some capital from friends to put with the last vestige of his own. Now, taking his son into partnership, he built dykes and tidegates, tramping about all day in icy mud to supervise the work. Mrs. Peabody later could remember how, when night fell, he would come to their house, take his ease before the fire — and tell his granddaughter about some new method he had contrived for his salt works, "worth hundreds of dollars." General Palmer was over seventy at this time, and when death suddenly overtook him he was sure that he had re-established the family fortune.

But with the death of the old general, investors lost faith and called their loans; the salt works failed. The rest of the story is one of courage and persistent ill-fortune. The Hunt brothers did what they could for Betsey; when one of them received a farm in Framingham in unexpected payment of a debt, the farm was given to the Palmers. Studious, impractical Joseph Palmer was ill-fitted to be a farmer, however. Life was far different from what it had been at Germantown where profits from the factory had paid for houseservants, grooms and gardeners, and the estate had seemed to run itself — one assumed at a profit. Betsey and Joseph Palmer had nothing, now, but a large family of children, five out of nine of them being girls. The oldest boy ran away to sea. It humiliated their father to see his daughters milk the cows and he insisted that they dress themselves in silk each afternoon, however faded and frayed their dresses might be. "Tea" was served — never a country-style supper — and guests were bidden in the old Friendship Hall manner and fed bountifully, even though the family lived on short rations for days afterwards. The girls were constantly reminded that they were born to a high station and that they must be ladies at all cost.

Mrs. Peabody often told her daughters of the day when "Mother took her carpet from the parlor" and Joseph Palmer started a school. The farm was a failure, but the school was a success; and rather late in life, Joseph Palmer found what he was suited to do. Since the neighborhood of Framingham could not supply enough scholars, he set out for Vermont, the frontier of his time. He had heard that around Bennington there were young families growing up, hungering and thirsting for education. With a spark of his father's courage and optimism, he determined to start an academy.

There was one vital flaw in Joseph Palmer's plan. However hungry for learning the Vermonters might be, they had no money to pay for it. Palmer never doubted that someday his handful of students would grow into a school, where his sons and daughters could come to learn, to teach, and eventually to carry on his work. But in 1797, while helping his pioneer neighbors to build a bridge, Joseph Palmer fell and was killed, with all his dreams unrealized.

At the age of sixteen, Betsey's daughter Elizabeth Palmer began a career of schoolteaching which she interrupted only once — to travel over a hundred miles on horseback in order to care for her sister Mary Tyler's family when another child was expected. All she could possibly spare from a meager salary went to help younger brothers and sisters. By the time she was twenty-four years old, she seemed to have become the typical maiden aunt. And then, in 1802, Elizabeth fell in love.

Nathaniel Peabody was teaching at Phillips Andover Academy and Elizabeth Palmer was "preceptress" at the North Andover academy for young ladies, when they met. If Palmers prided themselves upon being descended from leaders of the American Revolution, they were mere newcomers to the country compared to Peabodys. Francis Peabody had arrived in Salem on the ship *Planter* in 1635. In 1657 he took out a large grant of land around Topsfield, Massachusetts, and Nathaniel was a member of the fifth generation from Topsfield. Born in 1774, he graduated from Dartmouth in 1800, the only one out of six brothers to achieve a higher education. Although there was a medical school at Dartmouth at that time, there is no record that Dr. Peabody took any medical courses. When Elizabeth Palmer met him, he was a mild, absent-minded man who could draw pictures, whittle little objects out of wood, and who seemed to enjoy the society of his students. He was a fine Latin scholar and liked to teach Latin to small boys.

By this time, Elizabeth Palmer's brothers and sisters were able to look after themselves, but here was a man much in need of a firm hand! Unless someone took charge, it looked as if Nathaniel Peabody would be content to end his days quietly teaching school! On November 3, 1802, Elizabeth and Nathaniel Peabody were married. "My heart was at rest and my hopes all of happiness," wrote Mrs. Peabody as she recalled the birth of her first child. Elizabeth Palmer Peabody was born in Billerica, Massachusetts, on May 16, 1804. She was named for her mother, for her grandmother Betsey Hunt, and for her great-aunt, the mysterious and lovely invalid, Elizabeth Palmer.

After the Peabodys had moved to Billerica, only a few miles from Andover, Mrs. Peabody opened a boarding school for girls with about thirty pupils. This should have absorbed all her energies; but memories of Friendship Hall made her long to regain a high social position. Nathaniel, therefore, discovered that he was to be a doctor, content with schoolteaching though he might be. To his own surprise he found himself accompanying the local doctor on his rounds, then the usual way in which a man, in a short time, acquired the right to call himself a physician. It was no part of Mrs. Peabody's plan that her husband should be an ordinary country doctor, however; and soon the family moved to Cambridgeport so that Dr. Peabody could attend medical lectures at Harvard. Here was a fine medical education indeed, and Mrs. Peabody saw herself the wife of a city physician, second only in social importance to the minister's wife. How proud she would be of her Nathaniel, in his smart doctor's gig, driving a fast horse on some dramatic life-and-death endeavor! And then — at Harvard Dr. Peabody became interested in dentistry, with its opportunity for him to use his clever hands. Where was the dignity, where the drama in making false teeth? Mrs. Peabody took the whole thing as a personal affront and felt that Nathaniel became a dentist just to spite her.

There was now little rest in Mrs. Peabody's heart and no particular joy at the prospect of a second child. In Cambridgeport on November 16, 1806, her second daughter was born and named Mary Tyler Peabody. Obligingly enough, Mary resembled her Aunt Tyler,[3] her mother's oldest sister, who was considered a beautiful woman. As she grew older, Mary's delicate features would be redeemed from mere prettiness by an aristocratic Roman nose like her aunt's — and like that of the dashing Betsey Hunt Palmer, now "witty, cheerful and conversational" as a grandmother.

Mrs. Peabody said with pride that she never left her children with ignorant servants but always with some genteel woman who liked to read Shakespeare. At a time when so many avenues of employment were closed to women, there was no trouble in finding an unmarried lady or a widow, both cultured enough, and hungry enough, to be glad to stay with two little girls in return for food and shelter. Mrs. Peabody was free to become head of the Lynn Academy soon after Mary was born.

Although invariably referred to by his wife as a physician, it was as a dentist that Dr. Peabody established himself in Salem, the home of his ancestors. On the twenty-first of September, 1809, the Peabodys' third successive daughter was born.[4] Sophia Amelia was named for not just one of her mother's sisters but two of them at a time. She was, however, very much a Peabody, with wavy blond hair, gray eyes, soft features and a round face that would always make her look young and appealing. According to Mrs. Peabody, Sophia's "delicate constitution" was the result of her mother's anxiety before her birth and while nursing her. Certainly the first year in Salem was terrifyingly lean. Mrs. Peabody sincerely believed that she had sacrificed everything to further her husband's career, but somehow not only wealth but happiness had escaped her. She searched her own soul in vain for the reason why Dr. Peabody, physician and dentist, was not as happy as plain Mr. Peabody had been — nor even as successful financially.

The Peabodys seemed to have taken root in Salem now, and Mrs. Peabody managed to add to the family income by teaching. It is hard to see where she could have found the time. In 1811, Nathaniel Cranch Peabody was born and in 1813, George Francis. By 1815, the victory at Waterloo was ringing joyfully in the ears of the English-speaking world, and in a burst of enthusiasm the youngest Peabody son was named Wellington.

During their childhood, the Peabody children lived upon the story of bygone Palmer splendor. It made present hardships easier to bear to have such a glorious family past upon which to feed one's dreams. Grandmother Palmer was often a visitor and always delighted in recalling happier days for such an appreciative audience as her three little granddaughters. Each sister interpreted the story for herself, and each drew different conclusions. These differences were unobservable at first; but, as radii of the same circle are often far apart when they reach the circumference, so the sisters were setting a pattern of divergence even while they started from the same point of departure.

In Sophia's romantic imaginings, she and her sisters were like members of an exiled nobility. She felt that she had been born in the upper strata of society, a position which suited her very well indeed — and so she would wage no war against social inequalities. Claims to distinction for no better reason than the accident of birth would always seem valid to her.

Mary listened with glowing eyes at her grandmother's knee as she seemed to hear for herself the drums of Lexington. She liked to think of past glories as lost in the cause of freedom — whether they were or not. The sensitive Sophia was afraid of her grandmother's sharp tongue, but Mary's laughter always greeted some sally on the part of the spirited old lady. She even answered in kind now and then, and Grandmother Palmer would overlook the impertinence.

The drums and banners of a cause stirred Elizabeth, most of all; but they stirred her to action rather than to dreams. She could hardly wait for the day when she herself would go out into the world to right wrongs. The world was a wicked place, her mother assured her; and this, to Elizabeth, seemed good news — for she would soon set things straight. Too much a part of her, for conscious thought, was old General Palmer's inability to recognize defeat.

Sometimes Dr. Peabody felt that he had heard about as much of the Palmer family as he could stand. He knew a family folk tale of his own that could silence even Grandmother Betsey herself. The name "Peabody" had once been "Paybodie," he informed his children. "Men of the Mountain" it meant, since the Peabodys of old had taken refuge in the Welsh mountains, fleeing before Caesar's legions. But they had not fled without a battle. Dr. Peabody found it amusing, yet slightly alarming, to observe how seriously his three little daughters took the news that they were directly descended from Boadicea, Queen of Britons!

CHAPTER THREE
Kennebec Kingdom

THE Peabody sisters were children in Salem when the stately mansions of the East India Merchants were new and when Samuel McIntire, the great artist who designed them, was still alive and at work. The play of light and shade upon carved doorways, the proud perfection of Greek orders rendered in wood and miraculously reborn with a New England accent — all this had had its effect upon the little girls. While they would grow to consider Salem mansions more old-fashioned than beautiful, they would always love high ceilings, spacious rooms. The charm of a simple country farmhouse would escape them forever and Europe, with all its palaces, might please these Salem girls — but not surprise them. Foreign objects of art they would have seen before, since Salem sailing ships brought such things to their own home town with every voyage; and if Queen Victoria had more silver on display at Windsor castle, the Peabody sisters would still feel that the Derbys' silver was better chosen.

The doors of the wealthy were open to Dr. Peabody and his family, and Mrs. Peabody entered all the best drawing rooms, her head held high as became a Palmer. But appropriate costumes for formal appearances were not easy to come by, and more often than not the girls and their mother sent "regrets" with real regret in their hearts. Toward Peabody relatives who were wealthy merchant-adventurers, Mrs. Peabody preserved an attitude of armed neutrality, believing, probably with reason, that they were purse-proud and overcritical. There were other homes, however, where real friendship flourished, wealth or no wealth. Miss Burley, sociable, talkative, and a great patron of the arts, was always cordial to the Peabodys, and it was here that Sophia had acquired her passion for Greek sculpture — as portrayed in Miss Burley's books of engravings. Miss Guild was another Salem maiden lady of wealth fond of Mrs. Peabody and of her three daughters. But Mrs. Richard Cleveland was Mrs. Peabody's most cherished friend. Married to her cousin, a Salem merchant-adventurer who had brought home a fortune of seventy thousand dollars from his first voyage, she was perhaps the wealthiest in the Peabodys' Salem circle. As far as the girls were concerned, she was their patroness and also the bane of their existence with her gossiping tongue and her talent for jumping to wrong conclusions.

Mrs. Peabody would not have been human if she had not envied her more fortunate friends, and if she had not tried just a little too hard to remind them that she was at least as well-born as they. As time went by she became excessively "genteel," a word of which she was fond; and Sophia, who was the daughter most often with her, was quick to copy the attitude.

But whatever her faults, Mrs. Peabody never let envy or gentility stand in the way of action. The only way in which she could help with the family finances in Salem days was by teaching, and the only way to teach was to keep school at home where she could have an eye on her brood of little children. Her father had "taken up the parlor carpet" to start a school, and so did she, but in her case the action was even more of a symbol of self-sacrifice. The carpet was no Aubusson, like those Mrs. Peabody saw in the homes of friends, but without it she had no proper home. Without a parlor she could not "receive," or be "at home," or even offer a cup of tea with the elegance her heart desired. Mrs. Peabody had wasted no time in vain regret, however. She listed the neighbors' children and called upon their parents.

Across the back fence, in a house as gaunt and gray as the Peabodys', lived a Mrs. Hathorne,[1] whose son and two daughters could be seen playing in the garden. Maria Louisa was but a baby, and Nathaniel did not interest Mrs. Peabody for she did not aspire to teach boys. It was "Ebe," as Elizabeth, the oldest Hathorne child, was called, whom Mrs. Peabody wanted for her school.[2] There was a difficulty, however. Since the death of Captain Hathorne in Surinam, his widow had become a recluse. In a town of individualists such as Salem, her behavior was commented upon but respected, and no one ever knocked at her door.[3]

Mrs. Peabody was resourceful and determined, nevertheless. She recalled that her husband's brother John, a sea captain, had married Elizabeth Manning, first cousin to Mrs. Hathorne. She wrote a note claiming kinship and Mrs. Hathorne "asked her to come and see her in her chamber." Mrs. Peabody never forgot this almost legendary lady who seemed, in her dress of an earlier mode, to have stepped down from a family portrait — beautiful, gracious and smiling. Little Ebe was promised for the school and the two "kinswomen" never met again.

Elizabeth Peabody, also, at the age of four, was a pupil in her mother's school. She looked with profound admiration upon Ebe Hathorne who was six and could read Shakespeare. In after years, Elizabeth Peabody spoke of her first childhood impression as one of shame because, at four, she could not unlock the printed word and Shakespeare was too much for her. She remembered vividly her determination to learn, to equal and if possible to surpass her schoolmates. Ambition awoke early. Like her mother, she felt it the duty of a Palmer to excel; but she ignored, even flouted, social customs, setting intellectual superiority as her goal. Words and the subjects they unlocked, such as philosophy and history, soon became her specialty and she easily outdistanced other girls. Men, with their superior opportunities for education, aroused her envy, and unconsciously she strove to outshine them — to put them in their place. Long before childhood ended, Elizabeth was to take over her mother's job of teaching — and for the same purpose: to help out with the family finances. Never to "finish" school, she was to make her whole life into a process of education.

After the War of 1812 maritime Salem had had a brief era of prosperity. Inflation enriched the shipowners and more mansions were built. They had not the exquisite touch of McIntire, for now he was dead; but they made up for it in size and pretentiousness, built of brick and ornamented with the sullen cold of marble where a bit of gracious wood carving had once sufficed. There were more private carriages upon the streets to spatter mud on the still pedestrian Peabodys. But those Peabodys shared the general prosperity, none the less. Shipowners who could afford new mansions could also afford to have Dr. Peabody pull their teeth and make them new ones. Being amateurs of the arts, they could see that Dr. Peabody's work was of the best and so they overlooked some of his radical ideas. He told them that every tooth which ached need not be pulled at once, but might be filled. A few of the more daring Salemites let him try out his ideas. In 1816, Mrs. Peabody found she could afford to give up her school, put back the parlor carpet and enjoy a little well-earned sociability.

Inflation was running its course, however, with its inevitable evil consequences this time taking the form of the first nation-wide bank panic of 1818–1819. Salem's prosperity proved but the last bright flame of a dying fire as merchants saw their fortunes disappearing overnight. Who would pay a doctor or a dentist, when faced with the loss of a mansion and a fleet of sailing ships? The Peabodys suffered severely. Dr. Peabody would not and could not demand his money, but his landlord and his butcher had no such scruples. During this unhappy period, Catherine Peabody was born, to live only seven weeks.[4]

On previous occasions, the little girls had been sent away to visit relatives for reasons not explained, then summoned home again to find a miracle, a tiny infant in their mother's arms. But this time Elizabeth was fifteen and old enough to stay at home and help. She was mature-minded, and her mother confided in her — remaining true to genteel principles, however, and telling only half-truths such as would frighten but not inform a young girl. It would be unreasonable to suppose that Mrs. Peabody wanted a seventh child. She could not help blaming her husband, not only for his ill-success at providing for his family, but for his good success in adding to it. Elizabeth gathered that somehow her father had been unkind although she saw for herself when she went into his now deserted office for her Latin lessons with him that he was the kindest and gentlest of men. It was man in general that must be feared, therefore, and to whom, her mother said, it was woman's duty to submit. Woman, on the other hand, was all virtue. Elizabeth had her mother's word for that, too.

The death of Catherine brought an agony of remorse to Mrs. Peabody. As always, she had loved the baby passionately as soon as it was put into her arms and she felt secretly guilty, this time, since she believed so firmly in prenatal influences. It seemed as if Mother Peabody would never recover. Speaking of her sisters and herself, Elizabeth afterwards wrote, "We three were first drawn together by a common calamity."

Enjoined not to breathe a word abroad about troubles at home, it was the gay little thirteen-year-old Mary who suffered the most. She had been the particular favorite of her mother's friend Miss Guild, but now Miss Guild noticed that the child changed "from extreme talkativeness to reserve." Mary had realized instinctively that Miss Guild might read her mind by means of affectionate understanding, and so the child developed a fear of close friendship entirely alien to her nature. Meant for laughter and easy companionship with others, Mary conscientiously built a wall around her heart to protect, not herself, but her family.

At the time of Catherine's death in 1819, Sophia was ten years old. It was flattering to have her two older sisters confide in her although it always seemed to her that they exaggerated family troubles and that everything would be all right again soon. She found herself more and more the object of her mother's anxiety — lest God should take her, as He had taken Catherine. But Sophia was a healthy, normal child and she turned to her father, sensing his loneliness and finding pleasure in cheering him with her natural optimism. She too was studying Latin, but she often lingered after a lesson with her father to watch his clever hands as he made work for himself when paying work there was none — experimenting further with his ideas about dentistry.

Dr. Peabody knew that he had the beginnings of a good practice in Salem and he believed that business would surely pick up. But Salem had become intolerable to Mrs. Peabody. Her friend Mrs. Cleveland was living on an estate in Lancaster, Massachusetts, purchased for her by her merchant-adventurer husband with one of the several fortunes he made. He had retired to Lancaster, but heavy losses had sent him to sea again to recoup and Mrs. Cleveland occupied herself with establishing a school for boys — Jared Sparks, headmaster. She encouraged Mrs. Peabody to believe that a similar school for girls would be equally successful and the Peabody family moved to Lancaster.

The sisters would always look back upon Lancaster days as among the happiest of their lives. They had acquired an old farmhouse which, according to Salem standards, was not beautiful, but which they found surprisingly comfortable all the same. Off the kitchen ell a spacious schoolroom was built for them — by Mrs. Cleveland, in all probability. Here, when lessons were over, there were games and square dances with the boys from Mrs. Cleveland's school as partners — all properly chaperoned, of course. Kissing games were permitted but Sophia was so often chosen to be kissed that Mrs. Cleveland, at least, looked upon her with suspicion.

There had been a few more years of childhood for Sophia, and for Mary as well — when there was time to go wading in the brook and return home for a scolding; time to hunt for wild flowers in the woods with boys from Mrs. Cleveland's school, to cut their names on trees. Thinking that Mary was following, Sophia went walking alone with Frank Dana, one day. Mrs. Cleveland found it out and complained to Sophia's mother, whereupon the indignant Sophia vowed never to go out with Frank Dana again.

Only for Elizabeth had the Lancaster experience come too late. She would never in her life have a chance to play, for her mother turned the school over to her almost at once. Still "Lizzie" or "dear E." or even "Biddy" to her sisters, at the age of sixteen she became "Miss Peabody" to the rest of the world forever. It was as though she had been so christened in infancy. Her reputation as an unusually gifted teacher was very early established, for she was able to communicate to her pupils some of her own passion for acquiring knowledge. There were those who said that she lacked system and was too little of a drillmaster, but no one ever failed to add that she was always inspirational.

After long hours of teaching, Elizabeth spent her leisure in study. Jared Sparks, head of Mrs. Cleveland's school, was a self-educated man with much the same insatiable thirst for knowledge. He lent books to Miss Peabody which she devoured one after the other without pausing to form more than a casual friendship for the man who owned them. Jared Sparks was thirty-three years old, unmarried, and extremely handsome. If Lizzie noticed his good looks they only made her nervous. As for Sparks, much as he enjoyed Miss Peabody's keen mind, he could not have considered her beautiful and he liked beautiful women, preferably wealthy ones.

Mary was learning to make her own dresses in those days, and Sophia had ideas about style and color — telling Lizzie that a red ribbon would look pretty in her dark hair (and keep it neater). Elizabeth paid no attention to her own appearance. She began the study of Greek.

Boston had become Elizabeth's goal by 1822; and, like young Joshua of old, she set forth to spy out the land for herself and her whole family. Mary could take her sister's place in the Lancaster school, for she had been Elizabeth's assistant during the past year. Sophia could step into Mary's place, and the fact that "Sophie" was only thirteen and hated teaching made no difference. Elizabeth had become an expert in ordering other peoples' lives, but what could her sisters say when she was at work only for their own good? They too longed to live in Boston, and Lizzie promised to manage it by establishing a school which would soon support them all.

Elizabeth saw but did not conquer Boston. She acquired the lasting friendship of Eliza Cabot, however, who helped her to enroll a school from among the socially elect, large enough for her own support but not sufficiently large to employ her sisters and provide for her family. It was as well, perhaps. Elizabeth needed to be free of the family and they, it must be admitted, needed to be free of her. As an unattached young lady with a friendly personality, Miss Peabody now laid the groundwork for her extensive Boston acquaintance. Theological controversy had begun to invade Boston. Elizabeth enjoyed it tremendously and gave herself a course of reading which would have prepared a young man for the ministry. Being a woman, her problem was what to do with the whole armor of God, now that she had put it on. It served her well in her first tentative flights of what would later come to be considered brilliant drawing-room conversation. But at eighteen, Elizabeth had been too serious to consider this a sufficiently worthy field of endeavor.

The probably unregenerate state of her sister Sophia's soul occurred to her. "It has been my feeling ever since I was as old as you are now," wrote Elizabeth, who at eighteen felt older than she ever would again, "that *life* was a serious thing." Elizabeth proceeded through seven closely written pages along this line. "You now have no system, but you doubtless have a strong bias toward Unitarianism," she told Sophia in a third letter. This was true of all three sisters, since their mother, as a child, had been taken to "Stone Chapel," as old King's Chapel was called when the Revolution put an end to kings in America. Mrs. Peabody had listened long ago to the Reverend Mr. Freeman, a young man who was re-writing the prayer book to exclude kings but to ask God's blessing on a new democracy, and so it was their mother who had first become interested in new religious interpretations. But Elizabeth had continued relentlessly to "convert" the already believing Sophia. She commended eight books to the child's attention, beginning with "Middleton's *Letter from Rome*" and ending with "Stewart and Norton's Controversy" and "Wood and Ware's Controversy." . . . "There are many — very many more which I have read," wrote Elizabeth, proud of her mental endurance.

Having attended to Sophia's soul, Elizabeth turned her attention to her sister's cultural development. "I wish you now to read only those poets with whom no one has found fault and which are perfectly moral." This restricted the field! Thompson and Cooper made the grade but Moore, whose *Lalla Rookh* Sophia secretly adored, had "an enervating effect" according to Elizabeth, and Byron was strictly forbidden. But, "I will not exactly say that you should not read Scott," conceded Elizabeth, probably aware that Sophia had already read every word of Scott that had so far appeared in the United States. When she had finished her series of admonitory letters to Sophia, Elizabeth regarded them with such pride that she suggested that they be used by "Sophie" in her schoolteaching. The letters were spelled correctly, Lizzie said. The children could be set to copying them.

"I thank you very much my dearest sister for your excellent advice and the kindness and anxiety you manifest for my happiness," replied Sophia, taking the utmost pains with her penmanship.

With Sophia morally and spiritually taken care of, Elizabeth now had leisure for her favorite pastime, the study of Greek. She heard of a young man, "who teaches in a young ladies' school kept by his brother William in his mother's house on Federal Street." He was available for private lessons, but Elizabeth found the young man so shy he would scarcely speak a word to her as she carefully and accurately translated, day after day. Never a shy person herself, Elizabeth was astonished to find that the teacher's shyness was catching and that she herself was equally tongue-tied. She stole glances at the young man's cavernous eyes, his rugged, abnormally serious face. A feeling of excitement stole over Elizabeth and she told herself that her heart was moved by Greek — it was such a glorious language! She remembered what Sophia had said about a red ribbon and bought one to bind her hair. It was nothing of course but a Greek style suggested by her studies. Since Elizabeth's teacher was nineteen, just a year older than herself, "Waldo" was what she called him. It was the name that, all his life, Ralph Waldo Emerson liked best to hear his old friends use.

When the series of lessons was over, Waldo refused payment. She already knew Greek, he told Elizabeth; he had not needed to help her at all. With that, the ice broke, they began to talk, and Elizabeth saw that wonderful smile which so transformed Emerson's face. It was a smile worth waiting for, thrilling to have evoked. They talked about philosophy, since Waldo would soon enter a theological seminary, and he found himself telling some of his inmost thoughts to this young woman whose ardent blue eyes were all that he could afterwards remember about her. Had she been beautiful? Perhaps not but she had certainly admired him. How pleasant it was that she could read Plato in Greek! They could discuss Platonic Friendship next time they met.

But Elizabeth had been worsted in her first attempt to establish herself in Boston. Too few scholars enrolled for the coming year and she gave up her school, although it never occurred to her to admit defeat. She merely raised the siege temporarily, and beat a strategic retreat to Hallowell, Maine. As she wrote, in the allegorical manner made fashionable by Alcott a few years later, her Boston experience had been "the showery afternoon after the brief morning sunshine of Lancaster."

Except for family migrations such as the journey from Salem to Lancaster, Elizabeth had never traveled. But in the autumn of 1823, when she found herself on the deck of the Kennebec steam packet, her little hair trunk beside her, she had felt nothing but elation. To see new places, to make new people her friends — this was a fine life. She glanced about at her fellow passengers, for the first time in her life unconsciously preferring the men. Very recently she had allowed herself to like a young man and the experience had proved exhilarating. There was Mr. Moses Whittier, already a Boston acquaintance, and Elizabeth bowed. He hurried over and became "so polite to me on the packet" as to warrant that line in a letter home. Mr. Whittier was soon eclipsed, however, after he had introduced a most attractive stranger. Writing in strictest confidence, for Mary's eyes alone, Lizzie called him "Bridge, my steamboat beau."

A member of an old Augusta family, Bridge could tell of the Kennebec,[5] river of hopes and disappointments, artery of a small world as isolated and as self-sufficient as a medieval kingdom. At the mouth of the Kennebec lay wharves, warehouses and a wet dock for masts — all built by Charles Vaughan and now rotting away. Geographically and logically, Jones Eddy, at the mouth of the Kennebec, should have become the port of entry for the Province of Maine, and a great shipbuilding center — or so Vaughan had thought. Settlers, however, showed a very human preference for the security of an established town. The English courts gave to Bath the official sanction and defeated this scheme. Charles Vaughan impoverished himself with grandiose projects. At Hallowell, storehouses, a printing press, gristmill and brewery; all were built by him. He was bankrupt now but still living in his fine old house, thanks to his brother Benjamin. Elizabeth Peabody listened with interest to all that Mr. Bridge could tell her about the Vaughan family, because she herself was on her way up the Kennebec to become a governess in the home of Mr. Benjamin Vaughan.

The steamboat puffed its way slowly up the river. Here and there the Kennebec was joined by a winding stream having natural meadows on either side where still the deer came out of the woods to graze and where the first settlers found grass for their cattle without having to toil against the forest to wrest from it a bit of cleared pasture land. But for the most part, heavy timber crowded close to the water's edge, and some of the great trees still bore the king's mark, impotent now, but once all powerful to reserve them for masts for a royal navy. A faint salty tang from the distant sea mingled with the smell of resin from the pines and made the air a joy to breathe, the blood to run faster in the veins. Yet in spite of the noisy puffing of the steam packet, the pleasant voices of new friends, Elizabeth felt the silence of the river. Where a clearing and a cabin appeared upon the shore, man's efforts seemed trifling against the power of the pines. Some woman must live in that tiny cabin and Elizabeth felt that unknown woman's loneliness touch her heart.

The packet paused at a prosperous town where there was a paper mill, a fulling mill and numerous wood-working mills. Elizabeth's new friends told her that this town was Gardiner and that the owner of all these mills, of all the land and of a fine estate besides, was Mr. Robert Hallowell Gardiner. "The paper mill alone shows a 375 per cent profit," said the knowing Mr. Bridge. But Elizabeth made no comment for neither money nor the lack of it impressed her.

Within a few more miles came a bend in the river, known as "the Hook." The steam packet hugged the east bank in search of a channel while high on a bluff on the west bank shone a jewel of a white house. It was set in the green of wide, well-tended lawns and gardens, a miracle of domestic charm and elegance. The town beyond the Hook was Hallowell, and this lovely house was Salama, home of Benjamin Vaughan and the end of Elizabeth's journey.[6]

Benjamin Vaughan had been born in Jamaica in 1751. He was educated in England but was refused a degree at Cambridge University because he had become a Unitarian. He studied law at the Inner Temple, and had received a medical degree from Edinburgh. Wealthy and well-connected, he exerted all his influence in favor of the American colonists at the time of the Revolution. He became a close friend of Benjamin Franklin, editing Franklin's writings and working with him during peace negotiations between Great Britain and the United States. His work for both governments as a lawyer and a diplomat was excessively confidential, like that of a secret agent.

Vaughan had sympathized so wholeheartedly with the French Revolution that he had been imprisoned in Paris, but was released through the efforts of Robespierre. It was a close call and it had seemed wise to come to the United States. His mother's father had been Benjamin Hallowell, one of the proprietors of the Kennebec Purchase, a tract thirty-one miles wide along the Kennebec. Dr. Vaughan arrived on the Kennebec just in time to buy up the land which his brother Charles had lost through bankruptcy.

At the time when Elizabeth Peabody appeared on the scene, "Uncle Benjamin" was over seventy. He still wore the wig, the hose and the small clothes of Revolutionary style and he presided over numerous progeny with the benevolent tyranny of a Roman paterfamilias. He was still a fine figure on horseback and, at the Unitarian church which he was building, his family would occupy four front pews.

Tutors for the Vaughan boys were young graduates of Cambridge University, while Frenchmen with the purest Parisian accent saw to it that Vaughan children, grandchildren, nephews, and nieces spoke French as beautifully as they spoke English. It was a distinction, then, for Miss Peabody of Boston to have been given a position in this discriminating family. And no situation could have been devised which would have contributed more to Elizabeth's development. The Vaughans were people of the world, but they were not worldly people. They had not the slightest touch of pretentiousness as they welcomed Miss Peabody, made her one of them and became her lifelong friends. They shared freely their knowledge, their ideals, their experience, while much of Elizabeth's provincialism dropped from her.

Coming early to breakfast soon after her arrival, Elizabeth took down one of the books with which the Vaughan breakfast room was lined. She discovered that behind the front row was another and she counted sixty-four volumes of Voltaire alone. Since she knew Latin so well, Elizabeth found French not too difficult as she dipped into one of the vellum-bound books. She explored further, coming across "Laws of Maine," Spanish and Italian works, "Greek and Latin in abundance." Mr. Vaughan came upon her in the midst of her investigations and smiled at her pleasure and astonishment. Yes, indeed, she might read any and all she wished whenever she had time. The attic, too was full of books, he told her. He had carried 10,000 volumes to Maine with him at a time when the Harvard College library boasted only 12,000.

Elizabeth had come to Hallowell to teach the youngest Vaughan descendants, and conscientiously she did so, gathering them into a little school. But she was a rapid as well as a voracious reader, and if she received a still better education than the children, her employers were only the more pleased.

While Elizabeth was at Hallowell, the Peabodys moved back to Salem. The sisters regretted the return; Mary began to long for independence away from home such as Elizabeth now enjoyed. It had already become Mary's habit to say nothing about her own desires, however, so it was for Sophia that Elizabeth showed her first concern. There was an opening for a governess at Oaklands, the great neoclassic mansion belonging to Robert Hallowell Gardiner. Elizabeth proposed that she herself take this position, which was bound to be a difficult one, and that Sophia should come to the Vaughans. The Gardiners and the Vaughans had intermarried, the womenfolk were friends, and all could be arranged.

Sophia's reply should not have been the surprise to Elizabeth that it was. "Don't you think that Mary had better come the first year and let me be older? She wants to go so *very much* and I should think it would be the best way. I guess it will be the first instance of a person going into a school at *fourteen*."

So Sophia had been allowed to remain a child a little longer, and Mary it was who had gone to Hallowell.

At first Mary lived at "Uncle Benjamin's," just as Elizabeth had done. Elizabeth enjoined her to read all the books she could; but Mary loved the gardens better, with their little white summerhouses like miniature Greek temples, flower beds between. She liked to walk across the broad lawns and beyond, where the formal gardens gave way to woodland paths that clung to a high bank along a brook and ended where the "cascade" turned a gristmill. Dr. Vaughan, whose gardens were the pride of his heart, showed

Mary his books on horticulture and botany, which opened a new world to her. She could use this new knowledge someday — meanwhile, she preferred botany to the works of Voltaire.

Mary was more a teacher of a private school here than she was a governess, and she lived sometimes in one house, sometimes in another, getting to know other townspeople as well as the Vaughans. There was a young people's club, meeting each week for the ostensible purpose of reading uplifting literature aloud. Mary and Elizabeth joined it, although Elizabeth complained because it cut down her time for studying Hebrew, a subject she had just embarked upon with the local minister as teacher. On Christmas Day, the sisters attended a dinner party for fifty at Oaklands, Mr. Gardiner's home, where Elizabeth was now living. Young men who were members of the reading club had been invited, and neither Mary nor Elizabeth lacked for partners when the dancing began in the great rooms all decked out with ground pine and spruce boughs.

Elizabeth knew just a little too much Greek, Latin and Hebrew to be popular, however, and for the first time in her life it bothered her. She confided her troubles to the Unitarian minister at her next Hebrew lesson and he told her just what to do. The Reading Club met the very next evening and, in Elizabeth's own words: "I never took so much pains with my person. I rigged myself in my black bombaseen which is trimmed with a very handsome crimson and black merino trimming . . . round the bottom, the sleeves, the waist. I then put on one of those square handkerchiefs fastened each side, and then my mantle on my head done up more tastefully than ever it was before."

It was Elizabeth's turn to read and she selected from "Frisbie's *Fragments*," the "Memoirs — Eulogy — Inaugural Address and the Essay on Moral Taste." After the reading was over, Elizabeth proceeded with her program as outlined by the minister. "The gentlemen were very polite and I took the greatest pains to please them. I went and sat down by each who had formerly considered themselves neglected by me and made myself as agreeable as possible. My friend, Mr. Robinson, had told me the day before, how to do — and I complied with his instructions and he tells me I worked wonders for myself."

Pleased as she was by her success, Elizabeth was unprepared for what followed. She acquired a suitor for her hand in marriage. It moved her strangely to have a man speak to her of love, and part of her emotion was fear. When she walked by his side along the river in the long Maine twilight, she felt herself threatened by something greater than her pride and will. Woman must "submit," her mother had said. How she hated the word even while she thought she understood it now as this man's hand touched hers and a shock of pleasure flashed through her; as tenderness crept into his voice and he begged her to be his wife. "I know what the feeling of love is," Elizabeth realized as she lay awake and lonely in the night, listening to the faint sound of the river.

At first, Elizabeth's letters from Oaklands, the Gardiner estate, were as happy as those she had written from Salama, the home of the Vaughans. She described her pupils affectionately. "Delia, I call 'Daybreak' for the sight of her exhilarates everybody and she has the purity, the freshness, the gayety and the transparent promise of the morning hour. Lucy might be denominated 'Twilight.' She never will charm so generally nor charm all; but the few who are sentimental enough to feel interest in the beauties that must be *sought* will always find delight in her interesting character."

Elizabeth told of spending stimulating hours with Mrs. Tudor, mother-in-law of her employer. She read aloud in French to Mrs. Tudor, who helped her with her accent, having lived in Paris many years. Mrs. Tudor had known Madame de Staël and she was gratified by Elizabeth's interest and talked on and on. "Madame de Staël made no distinction between the sexes. She treated men in the same manner as women. She knew that genius has no sex," so Elizabeth wrote her sister Sophia, retailing Mrs. Tudor's conversation. The young and ardent Elizabeth was profoundly impressed and decided that she must pattern her life as closely as possible after Madame de Staël.

Both Mrs. Gardiner and Mrs. Tudor thought the world of Miss Peabody, but with Robert Hallowell Gardiner, matters were different. In the first place, he was a stanch Episcopalian and he literally believed that there was some special torment in Hell reserved for Dr. Channing for leading so many people astray. Elizabeth was shocked to discover the existence of such bitter opposition to a man she loved and admired. It is to be feared that she said so, for it was always her habit to speak her mind and she could always be depended upon to spring to the defense of a friend. The Gardiner attitude during the Revolution had been in direct contrast to that of the Vaughans. Old Dr. Sylvester Gardiner had fled to Halifax with more haste than dignity when the British evacuated Boston. To the great-granddaughter of General Palmer, Robert

Hallowell Gardiner seemed still a Tory and she was all too prone to fight the Revolution over again every time the subject came up. Elizabeth felt sure of Gardiner's friendship at first, but she soon saw that her democratic ideas disgusted him. "Impractical," he called her. This troubled her, but she never suspected how much he really disliked his young rebel of a governess.

Gradually, under the cold eyes of Robert Hallowell Gardiner, the joy of the Maine adventure began to grow cold for Elizabeth. She longed to go back to Boston where she felt, as is the way of youth, that some high destiny must await her. Was not Boston the equal of Paris? Perhaps, then, Boston stood in need of a Madame de Staël, and Elizabeth felt quite capable of assuming the role.

Nothing had been said in letters to her mother or to Sophia about Elizabeth's love affair. Mary knew all about it; but even to Mary, Elizabeth always referred to her lover guardedly as "L.B." She now told L.B. that she believed she could be happy only in Boston.

There must have been some strong reason why L.B. could not give Elizabeth the home in Boston she so much desired. "I have been wooed and almost won," Elizabeth said — but L.B. had lost her. He took his final refusal in a shocking manner. Open-hearted and "communicative" to a fault, in her letters, there was one thing Elizabeth Peabody never talked about. She mentioned just once, in a letter to Mary, that "poor L.B. found his way, in such a horrid way, out of this world."

It would have taken a strong man to make Elizabeth happy or to be happy with her, and yet it was inevitable that weak men should be attracted to her, needing her strength. She judged her first lover's character as impartially as she could when she decided that "L.B. was not sound-minded nor well-principled." But it seemed as if she never could rid her soul of a sense of guilt and responsibility for the tragedy.[7]

CHAPTER FOUR
Eden in Miniature

IN 1825, after her unhappy experience in Maine, Elizabeth had returned, not to Salem but to lay siege to Boston once more. This time, she and her sister Mary had opened a flank attack upon Beacon Hill by starting a suburban school for girls in an enchanting spot at the end of a country lane beside a brook. There were marshes, fields and pastures — and the place is now the middle of Brookline. Just enough wealthy Bostonians had country homes in Brookline to warrant a good school for their daughters; the Misses Peabody were received with enthusiasm, word of their talents having been spread through the far-reaching influence of the Vaughan family.

Elizabeth was now twenty-one. The gracious living at the Gardiners' and the Vaughans' had softened her manners and given her poise, while those intellectual women in both families, with their foreign education, had broadened her point of view. She still considered Boston the cultural capital of the world, but she was now ready to admit the existence at least of Paris, Rome and London. To have been "sought and almost won," her love affair both sad and secret, lent her a mysterious charm which her young girl pupils were quick to appreciate. Lizzie was always dramatic. Even if she never talked about "poor L.B." she could not resist playing the part of a lady with a past and her young scholars wrote verses to her and crowned her with flowers upon the slightest provocation. This was an admiration Elizabeth felt it safe to enjoy and she gave her pupils all the love she would have lavished upon children of her own. She took great pains with their Latin but still more with their character, writing little notes to them, telling one that she was "unfeminine and indelicate," and another that she was "vain," still another that she was "wickedly passionate." Then

Elizabeth worried herself almost sick lest she had been too severe. She even journeyed to Lancaster to consult her former minister, Mr. Ware, upon the subject. But her pupils responded, also in little private notes, "full of love and gratitude."

With Mary, schoolteaching was a way of earning a living rather than a life in itself. She taught adequately and thoroughly, her pupils doing better perhaps in fundamentals than Elizabeth's did, and she most certainly worried less about their souls. Mary had no use for being crowned with columbine and her pupils would not have attempted it. They brought her flowers though, because somehow she made it seem interesting to know the name and even the Latin name of everything that grew in the fields or by the brook. It was astonishing to discover that Miss Mary was studying German, with a teacher, just so that she could read thick books about plants and flowers.

When school was over, Mary shut the schoolroom door and became a young girl herself — only nineteen after all, and pretty in a delicate, cameo-like way. The Peabody girls were received in the best drawing rooms like the ladies that they were. Mary, with new-found confidence, would sing of an evening whenever asked. She chose the simple folk melodies which the Vaughans had told her were so well suited to her lovely contralto voice. Sometimes a daughter of the house, instructed at great expense, would attempt an aria from an opera and Mary would feel envious because she herself knew no such elaborate music. The feeling would pass almost at once because she was fundamentally so happy. In later years, looking back upon Brookline days, Mary realized that she had perhaps had "beauty" or "if not — it was some subtle thing that used to open doors of sympathy and understanding."

There were young men in Mary's life. "Brigham the Cambridge singer" came to entertain at a Brookline musical evening and afterwards Mary was moved to sit by her bedroom window in the moonlight and dream dreams that it would take "a whole sheet of paper to tell." It was "Brignal banks are fair . . ." that Brigham sang, "not in the fashionable manner but with all the simplicity of nature." Mary left the moonlit window at last but, with characteristic humor, she told Sophia that it was the mosquitoes which drove her to bed and broke up her romantic mood.

In June 1825, Mary "jumped into a chaise" and went to Cambridge to have a look at the nation's hero, a friend of whom Grandmother Palmer had often spoken. "Lafayette kissed our paws" she reported irreverently to Sophia. She thought as she wrote the letter that it would be good to make her little sister laugh if possible — even though Mrs. Peabody had warned that Sophia must do no such thing!

While Elizabeth and Mary were in Maine, Sophia had been at home in Salem, the only daughter available to be the object of Mrs. Peabody's anxieties. Sophia was fifteen when she began to have severe headaches and her mother explained to her that suffering was woman's peculiar lot. It was the will of God, it all had something to do with the fall of Adam, and a woman's duty was to become "resigned." Mrs. Peabody was too good a Unitarian to believe in original sin; but she seemed to have swung to an opposite pole and to believe in saintlike virtue, especially for Sophia. At an age when most girls were thinking about clothes and beginning to feel romantic about boys, Sophia was urged to fix her hopes on heaven. Other parents might attempt to prepare their young daughters for life but Mrs. Peabody felt that she was answering a higher call when she prepared Sophia for an early death!

Sophia resisted her mother's efforts with lively optimism. At first her headaches lasted only a day or two and she was sure that each one would be her last. She loved nothing so much as to go places and see people. Mrs. Cleveland invited her to visit in Lancaster; Elizabeth and Mary arranged an invitation for her from the Vaughans in Maine. Sophia was all agog to go. She went to neither place. It was Mrs. Peabody, in 1825, who wrote explaining about Sophia's delicate health and the impossibility of her leaving home. Only after two months of earnest pleading did Sophia succeed in visiting her Peabody grandparents in New Boston, New Hampshire; and it was her father, finally, who had insisted that she be allowed to go. She traveled a hundred and twenty miles by chaise, swaying over rutted roads, splashing through fords or rattling over precarious wooden bridges — and she never felt better in her life. She wrote home that she loved every mile of the journey and was not tired at all. She wrote of bountiful meals, of hill-climbing excursions, and of long nights of sound sleep. If only she had written of homesickness and ill-health! Word came from her mother that she must come home at once.

Sophia began to resist her mother with torrents of tears. "Thunder-gusts" she called her paroxysms of weeping and she was heartily ashamed of them — although it was hard to believe that she was wickedly resisting God's will, as her mother told her. Naturally, the headaches grew more violent and so much was said about them that Sophia could not help taking more and more interest in them herself. She described the "cannonading of her temples" with gusto and a sympathetic sister Mary sent her leeches. Ever since her early childhood, when Sophia had been given a good deal of paregoric to ease difficult teething, her father had feared that he had given her too much sedative. He gave her sedatives now, at the insistence of her mother, but with increasing reluctance because he had become interested in homeopathy with its theory that "like cures like" and its use of drugs in small doses only. Dr. Peabody was pleased with the "best European leeches" and so was Sophia. She really wanted good health and she was so naturally optimistic that she made much of each slight improvement. It puzzled her that her headaches should be so much more severe when she was at home and she became adept at escaping for short visits and then putting her mother off with excuses to make each visit last a little longer.

In 1824 Sophia had begun to study drawing with "Aunt Curtis," one of the Palmer sisters for whom she was named and who now lived in Salem. The drawing lessons took place only on Saturdays and would not interfere with her other studies, Sophia anxiously told Elizabeth — who was, as always, supervising her younger sister to an astonishing degree. Sophia studied French all day, twice a week, she said, reading in French a sixteen-volume history of literature. (Her friends read French novels, but Sophia dared mention only *Corinne*, certain that Elizabeth would approve since it was by Madame de Staël.) She studied Latin all day on alternate days, learning the rules of grammar by heart to prove, not to herself but to Elizabeth, that a girl could do it as well or better than a boy and was therefore worthy of college. Would Elizabeth make a fuss about those Saturday drawing lessons and insist upon Greek instead? Sophia never could figure out Lizzie's reactions, but she always feared the worst.

As usual, Elizabeth was unpredictable. She brought all the weight of her benevolent tyranny to bear in favor of Sophia's art, rather than against it. She ordered her young sister to take up oil painting at once. Suddenly Sophia, who had been as docile and admiring as one of Elizabeth's best-loved pupils, became not a pupil but a sister and an equal, not a child but a young woman with a mind of her own. She would not try to paint in color yet. She would continue to study perspective and work in black and white, she said. She would take up color when she felt herself ready but not before. But it was nice of dear Lizzie to offer to buy the paints.

Mary understood and applauded the new Sophia, but Elizabeth was too busy to notice or try to understand. The Brookline school was a success and Lizzie was preparing to move upon Boston once more. Beacon Hill was still the most beautiful acropolis of them all, and Miss Peabody was certain that she was now ready to take her place as high priestess in one of the temples on that hill – a temple of learning, naturally. A Golden Age was dawning, like the Golden Age of Athens, Elizabeth thought, and she had no doubt that she was to play an important part in the Athens of America. High priest and prophet of this new age was Dr. William Ellery Channing – or so Elizabeth considered at this particular time, when she was in her twenties. She liked to say that she had fallen under the spell of Dr. Channing when she was eight or nine years old and still living in Salem.

Church bells were ringing then, she remembered, and neighbors from another congregation had come to the door to ask if they might sit in the Peabody pew at Second Church. Dr. Channing was going to preach, they said. Mrs. Peabody had intended to stay at home, but now there were frantic scurryings to and fro as she got herself and her oldest daughter into their Sunday best. Dr. Peabody was already at church, because he sang in the choir; the neighbors expressed surprise at seeing Elizabeth taken along, because she was usually left to look after the younger children. They wondered if there would be room in the pew. "It takes genius to reach a child," said Mrs. Peabody, forestalling argument.

They had been late; but Channing had been later. Elizabeth saw "a small man with rapid, nervous motions, dressed in a traveler's great coat, go into the pulpit, and, without sitting down, take up the hymnbook, turn its leaves quickly and enter the desk; then slowly lifting his large, remarkable eyes with an expression of 'seeing something,' begin to read the devotional hymn." This look, as if speaking face to face with God, was a faculty in Dr. Channing which never failed to communicate a sense of exaltation in Elizabeth. Dr. Channing was frequently the guest of parents of Elizabeth's pupils in Brookline, and it was here that she really came to know him. Her friends sympathized, she said, "in the pleasurable excitement" she felt.

The truth was that now Elizabeth was developing a romantic passion for the "great little man," beginning not at the age of eight or nine but at twenty-one, when she was ready for love yet still fearful of receiving advances from a suitable lover. Channing was twenty-four years older than she, happily married to a wealthy cousin — what had she to fear in giving him her heart and soul — as to a spiritual father, of course? Elizabeth was not by any means the first nor the last young girl to feel romantic about a minister and many of her friends not only sympathized but shared her sentiments. Only Mary had misgivings. Lizzie would get laughed at and she would be hurt, sooner or later. But Elizabeth paid no attention to Mary's warnings.

While she lived in Brookline, Dr. Channing's sermons became the great events of Elizabeth's life. Her enthusiasm carried her on foot through the winter drifts on Sundays when the omnibus refused to run. Now that she was going to live in Boston, Elizabeth would attend every church service and every meeting connected with the church. She would see Dr. Channing in his study every day and there would be long talks. To him alone she would confide her sense of guilt because "poor L.B." had seen fit to "leave this world" on her account; and, in a religion which has no provision for absolution, it was Dr. Channing, nevertheless, who could hold out hope of atonement.

Like Wesley, Wycliffe and Luther, Dr. Channing headed a religious sect, for he was hailed as the "apostle of Unitarianism"; but like his great predecessors, his intention had been not schism but liberalism. He believed in "the goodness of God, the essential virtue and perfectibility of man, and the freedom of the will with its consequent responsibility for action." To many of his contemporaries, this was heresy. To Elizabeth it was light in darkness. No longer need she suffer from a sense of guilt; she needed now only to express her gratitude to the man who had restored her soul. The ideal life was one of service to others, Channing had told her, and he had assured her that teaching was the ideal form of service where she was concerned. But now, in her gratitude, Elizabeth longed to serve the minister personally.

Once established in Boston, Elizabeth was soon acquainted with all of Dr. Channing's parishioners. Everywhere she went, she heard them bemoan the fact that Channing's sermons were never available in print or even in manuscript; that no copy could be found to read to the sick and afflicted. Here was just the service for Lizzie and she appeared in Channing's study with the news that she was going to copy out his sermons and pass them around.

"My handwriting is impossible to read," objected the doctor. "I use abbreviations known only to myself." Known only to himself was something else of more importance. His power lay in his personal magnetism. Much of the inspiration his parishioners drew from him was never on the page of hen-scratchings he held in his hand and referred to once in a while. It was in his voice, his eyes — that wonderful quality he had of seeming to speak with God.

"But I can read the writing and I will divine the abbreviations, intuitively," countered Elizabeth, inexorably determined to serve.

The last objection that Dr. Channing could think of was that copying would take too much of Miss Peabody's time. If she gave him all her leisure, as she proposed, how was she to keep up with her reading? He was interested in her education and there were books he would like to read aloud to her. Elizabeth said that copying would be so easy for her that she could do it and listen to reading at the same time.

Now the doctor thought he had her. Smiling indulgently at the earnestness of his young votary, he went to the bookcase and took down Cousin's French translation of Plato. He was unable to resist showing off a little, as he remarked that he would read *Timaeus* direct from French into English.

While Elizabeth copied the previous Sunday's sermon, Channing read but "kept raising his large, devouring eyes" and asking questions which she somehow answered."

When she had finished writing, he took her copy to read before she could so much as look it over. It was not fair, she protested; but her phenomenal memory had stood her in good stead. She had remembered the previous Sunday's sermon almost word for word, and she already knew Plato both in Greek and in English. There was little wrong with her copy, as Dr. Channing was quick to admit. It did Elizabeth's school no harm when Dr. Channing spread the story of Miss Peabody's almost unbelievably brilliant mind.

Elizabeth copied fifty of Channing's sermons which would never have appeared in print, he said, but for her patient efforts. Hereafter, whenever Channing published anything, it was Miss Peabody who must put the manuscript in shape for the printer. He would send for her, long after she ceased to be his unpaid secretary.

Fortunately, Elizabeth was not always obliged to copy sermons every time Channing read aloud. He delighted in watching her keen mind develop as he introduced her to new intellectual pleasures and let her lay aside the pen when he read her Wordsworth for the first time. He chose "Intimations of Immortality" and saw Elizabeth's whole soul in her eyes, heaven about her — not in her infancy but in her twenty-second year. It troubled him a little to be so much the object of her devotion, but he found her instant acceptance of the idea of pre-existence most diverting and he could not resist experimenting with her mental reactions.

Channing formed the habit of taking a walk with Elizabeth every Saturday morning. He would propound a theory in theology and she would attempt to demolish it if it conflicted with her newly awakened belief in the goodness of God. "Isn't she delightful!" Channing said of the ardent Elizabeth. When next Sunday's sermon proved to be upon the very topic of Saturday's talk, Elizabeth was astonished, utterly unaware of her value to him, but very happy. Again, it was only her sister Mary who sounded a warning. "He is too much your whole happiness," she said.

Mary Channing was a pupil in Elizabeth's school, as were the daughters of many of Channing's parishioners. There were thirty scholars the first year, more the next as the Peabody school became the thing. Elizabeth decided that a man's name should appear with hers and Mary's in connection with the really large private school she seemed on the verge of establishing. Boston was by no means ready to accept two women as heads of a business enterprise; Elizabeth not yet prepared to force the issue. A newcomer to Boston and to Dr. Channing's circle appeared the ideal choice for an associate. Mr. Russell was elegant in his tight-fitting coffee-colored coat, he had an intriguing touch of the actor about him which delighted the ladies — with Elizabeth and Mary by no means the least susceptible to his charms. There was a Mrs. Russell, daughter of a Connecticut minister, but she was always at home with the children while her husband came alone to the Channings' or the Cabots'. In 1826, Russell became the first editor of the *American Journal of Education* and, with a capacity for thinking of himself in capital letters, he was an Educator; while the earnest, unassuming Misses Peabody were content to call themselves simply teachers.

By 1827, William Russell had succeeded in arousing interest in the art of elocution, with himself as the chief exponent thereof. Dr. Channing attended a "Reading Party" at the Cabots', where Mr. Russell had him read certain of Mrs. Hemans's poems — and then made suggestions for improvement in the famous Channing voice and delivery! Mary Peabody was there that night. "It sounded a little oddly to hear him tell Dr. C. that he did not read very well. The Dr. himself seemed hardly to know what to make of it, but on the whole, he bore it very meekly."

Free lessons in elocution might be acceptable enough but few people would pay for them after the series of Reading Parties (for which a fee was charged) was over. Coffee-colored coats came high and a "new-born bliss," as Mrs. Russell put it, was forever being added to the family. Mr. Russell thought he might start a school and it seemed to Elizabeth that she had a solution both to his problem and her own. "We have more pupils than we can take," she told him, proposing partnership. Undoubtedly, Mr. Russell spoke of the school as his; but Elizabeth herself stated that he "was for a while a partner with my sister and myself in our school."

Thus, by 1828, Elizabeth's most cherished dream had been realized and she could afford to bring her whole family to Boston. There is no record as to whether Dr. Peabody wished to leave Salem — probably he was not consulted. To the astonishment of everyone, particularly his wife, he had just written a book. *The Art of Preserving Teeth* was the title, and if it were not exactly entertaining reading, the subject was a new one such as should bring him a reputation and a Boston practice. Not that Dr. Peabody was burning all his Salem bridges. As late as September 10, 1830, he advertised in the *Gazette:*

> DR. PEABODY continues to visit Salem the first and third Wednesday and Thursday of every month — for the purpose of operating upon Teeth. His off. is at Mr. S. S. Page's corner of Essex and Summer streets.
>
> As a report is abroad that Dr. Peabody has raised his fees for operating upon teeth, he takes this opportunity to state that it is not true; his fees are the same as they always have been.

The whole Peabody family, with the possible exception of the Doctor himself, was happy to come to Boston to live; but Sophia was probably the one who felt the keenest joy. Her sisters had asked her to teach drawing in their school. Her mother had forbidden it. Aunt Tyler had invited her to Brattleboro where she had enjoyed mountain climbing, horseback rides and the society of young cousins her own age. Then her mother had written: "The high state of excitement you are in is not exactly the thing for your head. I am glad to see you alive to the simple pleasures of nature, that heart must be least corrupt which can enjoy them most, but you enjoy too fervently. Come home now and live upon the past." Sophia made excuses to stay but finally obeyed and lived upon as much of the past as a sixteen-year-old could muster.

But now she was in enchanting Boston and no one could call her home. In her diary for 1829, she wrote: "I walked along Beacon Street for the first time since we lived in Boston and could but just keep my feet upon the side-walk, so bubble-like and balloony were my sensations. The full, rich foliage, the hills, the water, inflated me. Oh that Common — that Eden in Miniature!" [1]

CHAPTER FIVE
New England Barbizon

SOPHIA at twenty was very pretty, and because of her semi-invalid state, free from the long hours of teaching which kept her two sisters always a little tired and preoccupied. Young men came flocking to Fayette Place, some of them friends of Elizabeth's, some to see Mary, but most of them to call on Miss Sophia. There was Park Benjamin, "overflowing with fun and good spirits," to quote Sophia's diary. He was about to enter Harvard Law School and would one day become a bitter, caustic critic as literary editor for Horace Greeley's *New Yorker*. But the Peabodys made him happy, able to forget his permanent lameness. Then there was George Hillard, senior at Harvard Law School. He had been teaching for two years in Northampton under George Bancroft and he brought Bancroft to meet the Peabody sisters, Miss Elizabeth in particular.

Romance was in the air. Lydia Sears, a beloved former pupil of Elizabeth's, was being married and, as Lydia's parents were dead, she would be married from the Peabodys' home. For several years she had made them long visits and had become a sort of adopted daughter. The Peabody parlor was flooded with May sunshine while Sophia sat by the window, her deft hands busy among yards of soft white lace. She was making Lydia's wedding veil. She raised her serene gray eyes, the sunlight turned her light brown hair to gold, and more than one young man felt something happen to his heart.

Sophia enjoyed attention. Of Harry Cleveland she wrote, "He is a dignified, lofty-minded, noble fellow" — but she added something further in her diary which she afterwards deleted by taking scissors and carefully cutting out the lines. Had Harry proposed? Perhaps. If so, he had most certainly been refused. Harry need not have been discouraged, nor need any young man who found Sophia attractive. It was just that she was seriously interested in becoming a good artist and for the first time in her life she found herself able to study with good teachers. It was Elizabeth who made the teaching possible, as Sophia never forgot.

First came Francis Graeter, a young German who taught drawing in Elizabeth's school. He became interested in Miss Peabody's invalid sister, then in Sophia herself whom he found most charming. No one else had ever listened so pleasantly to his stories of life in Germany. He was a fine draftsman, painstaking and thorough, just the man to develop Sophia's naturally accurate eye and give her the discipline of working in black and white before she experimented in color. Graeter was a popular illustrator, doing, among other things, Lydia Maria Child's *Girls' Own Book*, and he encouraged Sophia to hope that she, too, might someday illustrate.[1]

Lessons in oil painting cost as much as twenty-four dollars each — a staggering sum for the Peabodys even now when things were going well with them. But Elizabeth was undaunted. Her appealing description of the invalid sister, so talented, so "resigned," brought Thomas Doughty to the Peabody parlor, not to give a lesson but to allow Sophia to watch him at work. Doughty, one day to be considered a leader of the Hudson River school, was at the height of his career at this time.[2] He thought Sophia could hardly be more than a sweet young thing taking up art as a genteel accomplishment, and he marveled at Miss Elizabeth Peabody's powers of persuasion as he found himself carrying easel, canvas, palette, paints and brushes to 18 Fayette Place.

Doughty arrived at three and Sophia was all of a flutter. "Ye powers! How my heart beat!" she wrote. "It seemed as if he embodied the Art in some way so that I was in its immediate presence and I felt consequently awe-struck. He looked very smiling and pleasant, however, not in the least fearful, and painted on his own picture an hour and then left me to copy. . . .

"The instant he departed I began my own operations and found that the portion of his art w'ch he had left on the board possessed the same awful power as he brought with him and before I had put my brush to the picture, I trembled from head to foot. Certainly, I never felt so much about anything before. I did not know what to make of it. . . . I was almost afraid to be alone with the — what? I am sure I can not tell."

Doughty was pleasantly surprised when he arrived at nine the next morning. Sophia had caught the silvery tones that were his trade mark. The subject, a medieval castle in moonlight, was just what would most delight her romantic soul and she copied it with all the accuracy that Francis Graeter had instilled into her. "You must learn to compose your own landscapes," Doughty told Sophia, suggesting that while she might copy his technique at first, she should also develop a style of her own. Her sense of color was remarkable, he told her.

"What an intense feeling of delight it gives me to think that I may ever create, too!" wrote Sophia. The pain Sophia suffered was by no means imaginary, some of her sensations suggesting sinus trouble. Her pain had always so disturbed her rest that her dreams were vivid and full of flashing colors. Because of her mother's increasing emphasis on religion, Sophia dreamed of paradise and saw angels ascending and descending. But now, instead of writing in her journal that she was resigned to an early death, she made notes of colors she had seen, sure that someday she would paint these pictures which appeared to her more as visions than as dreams. It seemed to her that she had but to be patient and study hard and soon she would be illustrating Milton. At twenty she knew just what she wanted to do with her life and success seemed just around the corner.

Meanwhile Elizabeth continued to bring to Sophia the best available teachers. Next to appear in the Peabody parlor was Chester Harding, already acquainted with two of the Peabody sisters but new to Sophia. This portrait painter now had as many as fifty visitors a day at his studio while sittings were booked far in advance. The aging Gilbert Stuart remarked with understandable bitterness that Boston was suffering from "Harding Fever." Just back from Washington, Harding had been painting "the hoary-headed old man," Ex-President Madison.[3] His critical view of Andrew Jackson coincided with Peabody political opinion. "He spoke of King Andrew and said his grey hair was the only venerable thing about him. He was very tall and affable — but his manners, in his opinion, extremely vulgar. . . . Mr. Harding thought manners were fast degenerating — all deference, politeness and polish of old times were gone and he thought it the levelling consequence of democracy — it was easier to pull down than to rise up, so everything was pulled down — as there must be equality at any rate."

Harding's own manners were polished to a degree and Sophia admired the thirty-eight-year-old painter, considering him her ideal aristocrat. Yet he was actually an interesting example of the "consequences of democracy," and, far from being a snob, he wrote about his backwoods beginnings and loved to tell anecdotes of his early struggles. Born in Conway, Massachusetts, where his father was spending a lifetime trying to invent a perpetual motion machine, Harding ran away to the War of 1812. Upon his return home, he began to make drums on government contract but the business went so badly that he was arrested for debt upon his wedding day!

After his release or perhaps escape from prison, Harding opened an inn at Caledonia, New York, where, to quote his own words, he "paid off old debts with new." This time he left town ahead of the sheriff and worked his way down the Allegheny. In Pittsburgh he made just enough money as a house painter to return on foot for his wife and child and raft them down the river. They arrived penniless, and Harding borrowed twenty dollars to set himself up as a sign painter. When a traveling portrait painter came along Harding could afford to pay the man ten dollars for a portrait of Mrs. Harding. The likeness was a disappointment and Harding sat down, sign paints in hand, and painted a better one. His neighbor, the baker, saw this first Harding portrait, marveled, and paid five dollars for a portrait of his own wife. Chester Harding's career had begun.

A day came when the proud Harding went home to see his mother with a thousand dollars in cash, a carriage and pair, his wife and four children! It was his idea to leave his wife and children with his mother and go to Europe to study but his mother would have none of it. A thousand dollars was not enough money, she said. So the ship *Albion* on which he had booked passage sailed without Harding — and sank with all hands. Harding painted successfully in Washington, St. Louis; he even traveled to a wilderness cabin to paint a portrait of Daniel Boone.

In 1823 Harding succeeded in reaching Europe, but not as a student like most American artists. Two months of study at the Academy in Philadelphia had convinced him that lessons were a waste of time and he went abroad to paint portraits. The American Minister introduced him to the Duke of Sussex. Harding had good looks, personal charm; he enjoyed making his homespun adventures a source of entertainment for his new friends — and it so happened that he could really paint. London society took him up and he returned to the United States with a glittering reputation, handsome profits which he was quick to spend — and a new-found admiration for "politeness and polish."

Harding's touch was sure, his style natural but a trifle hard. Colors were in a high key, foreshadowing a modern trend. When sentimentality overwhelmed public taste, his popularity waned — for his was an almost photographic record of his times, and if he ever flattered a sitter then some of them must have been hideous indeed! A modern re-evaluation of his work would give him a high place among painters of the Early American school.

It must have been during that Sunday-afternoon call that Harding asked Sophia to sit to him. "I have no features," she always said, and she was astonished at the invitation. But Chester Harding saw something he wanted to put on canvas: a young girl on tiptoe at the threshold of life and sure that sunshine lay before her. Her eyes, which Sophia said were gray, looked blue to Harding. He would have her smiling, of course, but in her smile there would be a hint of mischief for he had divined the sense of humor she usually kept hidden. She must wear the white dress she had on, Harding told Sophia — and bring the transparent green shawl. The dress was cut low off the shoulders but a single layer of muslin veiled shoulders and bosom with an effect demure yet beguiling. Harding would be at his best when painting young flesh under soft muslin.

"Mr. Harding sent for me to be painted at nine, and very loth I went — for the heat and damp together composed an atmosphere w'ch it seemed purgatory to breathe," Sophia said. "I found the mighty man as bright as an eagle. . . . He was as agreeable as he could be while I was doing penance. He spoke of Allston, his beau ideal of a man and a gentleman and his dearest friend."

Sophia received permission to come to the studio to watch Harding at work as she had watched Doughty. A portrait of Allston stood nearly finished by the window. The pose was heroic, hand thrust into coat Napoleon-fashion, the eyes intent with inner vision. But Harding, painting more accurately than he meant, had given Allston's chin the fullness of inertia, the mouth an indecisive sweetness at variance with the fine brow. The portrait was by no means Harding's best, for his sure touch was missing, as though mind and eye were in conflict. Sophia, however, admired the portrait unreservedly. Again the studio was oppressively hot and Sophia took up a fan. Standing behind the painter, she fanned both herself and him and kept away the flies which were tormenting both of them.

Mrs. Harding came into the room carrying an infant son and Sophia asked the baby's name. But this was the seventh or eighth child and they seemed to have run out of names — for the baby had none! "Why don't you call him Allston?" suggested Sophia — with no idea that she would be taken seriously.

But Harding was delighted. "Allston it shall be!" he cried. Sophia was embarrassed but at the same time amused to see that Mrs. Harding looked far from pleased. She had not been consulted nor did she speak a word.

Harding told Sophia that he never under any circumstances gave permission for his pictures to be copied. He had seen her copy of Doughty's landscape, however, and he would make an exception in her case. Sophia took the honor seriously but with confidence. It pleased Harding when she asked to copy his portrait of Allston and she set to work, right at his studio, with the benefit of all the advice he could give her.[4] Sophia next took to making sketches of family and friends, and Harding said she had a knack for catching a likeness.

Although Mary was at work many hours a day helping Elizabeth in her school, she too now fulfilled a cherished ambition. She began singing lessons with Mr. Padden, who advertised that his "mode of instruction in singing belongs to the first European school." Mary had always been willing to make a social evening pleasant by singing upon request. At the Channings' she had been encouraged and praised. But many young ladies of the parish who sang at the Channings were pupils of Padden and embarked upon an aria from an opera without batting an eyelid. Mary longed for the confidence lessons might give. Mrs. Channing loved what she called "the spirit tones of Mary's voice" and said that this popular teacher might make it stronger but that he could hardly make it sweeter. Mary's "low tones were like a summer evening."

Like the breadwinner of the family that she was, Elizabeth had little time to enjoy the pleasures she helped to earn for her family. Her school seemed to be going wonderfully well even though there never was enough money, no matter how many pupils were enrolled. Her chief delight was in enlarging her acquaintance and it was in 1830 that she met Bronson Alcott, who wrote of a first meeting which was a prelude to a stormy association. He had not liked Elizabeth. "She may perhaps aim at being 'original' and fail in her attempt by becoming offensively assertive. On the whole there is, we think, too much of the man and too little of the woman in her familiarity and freedom, her affected indifference of manner. Yet after all, she is interesting."

Quite by accident, the Peabodys were at Alcott's wedding. On May 23, 1830, Sophia was just leaving King's Chapel [5] when she saw Dr. Walter Channing, physician brother of William Ellery. He was an especial friend of hers, so she stopped to talk and he told her that there was to be a wedding and that the wedding party would be pleased if churchgoers lingered for the ceremony. So they all crowded around and the Peabody girls saw old Colonel May give his daughter in marriage to Bronson Alcott.

The Alcott friendship progressed with reservations on both sides. A few days later, "Mr. and Mrs. Alcott spent the evening but Betty talked all the time and I did not have a chance to hear a word from the interesting, contemplative man," Sophia complained. "I liked Mrs. A. much better than I expected from all accounts," she added.

It would be surprising if another adverse opinion had not gone into the Alcott journal, since the "contemplative man" was himself a notable talker. But, "I was much pleased with the thoughts expressed in the course of this interview," Alcott wrote. "Miss Peabody is certainly a very sensible lady. She has a mind of a superior order. In its range of thought, in the philosophical discrimination of its character, I have seldom if ever found a female mind to equal it." Female mind, indeed! Elizabeth would not have liked that if she could have looked over Alcott's shoulder. Madame de Staël's "genius has no sex" was still her ideal. But she could not have quarreled with what Alcott went on to say. "Her [Elizabeth's] notions of character, the nicety of analysis, her accurate knowledge of the human mind, are remarkable, original and just. Her views of morals are very elevated. I was better pleased with her on the whole than I expected to be, and shall repeat my visits at her request."

The Alcotts were asked again and so were many other friends, for the Peabodys liked to keep open house and now at last they could afford it. They dared to hope that they were firmly established on the road to prosperity and Sophia could have spoken for all three sisters when she wrote, "Sometimes it seems to me as if my life were a pathway of peculiar beauty — an indefinable atmosphere of music — a mingling of birds' voices floating round glimpses of endless visions where is heard the distant falling of fountains and the sighing of leaves . . . this is always my life if left to itself."

Sophia and her sisters were to learn that no life is ever left to itself for long. The Peabody sons had been involved in a student scrape at Harvard. This was toward the end of the Kirkland administration, when "student rebellions" were everyday occurrences. Boys were expelled in dozen lots until, in some circles, it was accounted more of a distinction to be thrown out of Harvard than to graduate. The Peabody parents, however, were not the sort to smirk and murmur something about "wild oats" and boys being boys. And now there was worse to come. As soon as the Peabody young gentlemen were no longer at Harvard, here came tailors, tavernkeepers and even acquaintances with unpaid bills to collect.

The whole affair was particularly hard for people like the Peabodys to try to live down. They were notably high-minded; and Elizabeth, at least, was given to advising others on ethical behavior. Mary, who suffered from having the family's keenest sense of humor, could imagine all too well what people were saying behind their backs. "Dandycock" was what Aunt Pickman called her sister's youngest son, and Mrs. Peabody had no defense. She "could not reason about the matter, she could only feel," she said.

The womenfolk seemed to draw together, leaving Dr. Peabody alone with his anxieties and somehow subtly to blame for everything. He was just beginning to succeed in Boston. Until recently, he had depended upon Elizabeth's school to help out with family expenses and now, with the boys' debts to pay, he must ask her for help again. And at this point, the school, which had seemed so successful, proved suddenly insolvent!

It was a pity that some of the law students who frequented the Peabody parlor could not have advised Elizabeth and Mary when they took a partner into their school. As it was, there was nothing but a vague verbal agreement with William Russell and Russell with his actor's airs, which so pleased the ladies, knew better how to spend money than to earn it. His salary was not a stipulated amount, he had a share in the school and took what portion of the profits he needed. Elizabeth had no idea what his needs would amount to until she was faced with an urgent need of her own and attempted to look into the books of accounts. She found that no books had been kept. Elizabeth was "forbearing" for the sake of Mrs. Russell and the children, but her school had failed and, when Russell went off to Germantown with Alcott to make a new start, Elizabeth had nothing left with which to continue. She was too human not to feel satisfaction, however, when Russell ran into debt in Philadelphia very shortly. After all, it was a comfort to know that there were other people in the world as gullible as herself where the plausible Russell was concerned.

"I will not admit that I am impractical," Elizabeth had insisted. But now, in the face of family disaster, she was determined to take one more step in what Mary considered a wrong direction. She had always taken a close personal interest in her pupils and now she believed that she had discovered that two of her girls were being cheated by a relative. The girls' parents were dead, so Elizabeth went to their legal guardian with "revelations" — but with facts hard to prove against people much cleverer than herself in these matters. Even Dr. Channing, when appealed to, was against Elizabeth's quixotism. It troubled him afterwards that he had counseled expediency, for rarely would he meet with anyone who came as close as Elizabeth did to practicing what he preached. But he was wise in the ways of the world. "Do not neglect your own for other peoples' duties," was Channing's advice — to which Mary said a heartfelt amen.

But nothing could stop Elizabeth from going to New Bedford, where it seemed necessary that she stay all winter trying to fight other peoples' battles. The "cold-hearted selfishness" of the very people she tried to help came as a cruel but inevitable experience. She had been so sure that she was right, so uplifted by living according to her highest ideal! "I was unprepared and lost," she said, as she began to learn that there are limits to the amount of help one human being can give, or, for that matter, take from another. "I kept stumbling over realities and still the guiding light was not," Elizabeth said afterwards.

The Peabody parents and their sons were going back to Salem. Mary, once more silent and withdrawn, would go with them to teach a few neighbors' children — if she could find any friends who would pay her for such an enterprise. It was understood that Sophia would go too, and perhaps teach drawing. For the first time in her life, however, Sophia had made plans for herself.

Sophia's new-found courage was not quite equal to the task of laying her plans before her family and then enduring her mother's tearful protest. She fell back upon the old subterfuge of "just visiting" and Mrs. Peabody agreed that it would be a good idea for her to escape the upheaval of moving by visiting Lydia Haven in Dedham; the "dear Lyd" whose wedding veil she had made.

Lydia was more lovely to look at than ever. "My Peri of Lyd," Sophia called her, for this dearest of friends seemed to have stepped out of Moore's *Lalla Rookh* with her black hair and white skin. The visit could have extended almost indefinitely, but instead, Sophia hired a tiny room within walking distance of her friends' houses and set about supporting herself by painting. Board and room cost two dollars a week, while laundry was done for four cents an item.

There was nothing impractical about Sophia's plan. Boston had broken through a Puritan distrust of art and suddenly no drawing room was worthy of the name unless oil paintings of all descriptions elbowed each other for space and competed for attention from floor to ceiling. Dr. Channing's sister-in-law, Mrs. Gibbs, had the great Allston paint her a picture especially for the one and only vacant spot on her dining room wall. Less well-to-do people were content with copies, and, thanks largely to Elizabeth's talents as press agent, Sophia's skill at copying was well known. She could charge fifty dollars a canvas and sell as many pictures as she found time to paint.

One problem was to find paintings suitable for copying. Foreign scenes, preferably French or Italian, were infinitely more popular than anything by an American artist and people owning a genuine Salvator Rosa might be loth to have it copied — particularly when Sophia copied so well. Elizabeth furnished the solution as she did so often. Already she had shamelessly asked to borrow for Sophia almost every picture she saw, good or bad. Letters were full of promises of "Salvator's landscape" or "that sea-piece of Salmon's." There were promises too from people who had "spoken for" copies in advance. It was hard for Sophia to make Elizabeth understand that copying was a slow and careful process and that therefore she could not take numberless commissions and just dash them off. Too many orders made her feel harried and nervous, for Sophia was a perfectionist; it was a quality she could not change and it was part of her success. From the security of her Dedham retreat, Sophia found that she could refuse orders and cope better with Elizabeth's tireless efforts in her behalf.

It was a delight to wake early in the morning in the tiny room, to lie still a few moments savoring the fact that the whole day lay ahead in which to work without interruption at a well-loved task. The window would be tightly closed of course, to shut out the dangerous night air. But Sophia loved to rise early, open the window wide and enjoy the morning sun. Within the room, the fresh air seemed all the sweeter for being mingled with the smell of oil and turpentine, varnish and canvas. These odors filled her with delight in a way the rarest perfume could never do. She set to work as soon as the light was right.

Later in the day might come fatigue, even headaches. The Havens would send their carriage for her then and she would make a round of calls with them or meet their friends at Havenwood for tea. Sophia enjoyed people. She could even paint serenely with friends looking on.

Sophia told herself that she was not ready to "create." Whether she admitted it or not, she knew that the price of her freedom was to copy and keep selling copies of other artists' work. It was highly unlikely that she could have found anyone willing to pay fifty dollars for a landscape by "S. A. Peabody" — even with Elizabeth as salesman. Sophia wrote home often, reporting improved health, ecstatic happiness — and no need for money.

But Sophia Peabody was not enough of a genius to be ruthless to those who stood in her path. She was an affectionate, tender-hearted young girl, and when her mother could no longer bear Sophia's "fervent happiness" she came home. She would spend the winter months in Salem, secretly thinking of them as a visit, while her mother's grudging permission for her to "visit" Dedham in the spring would be the real homecoming at last.

Sophia managed visits even in winter, for in January 1832 she was at Tremont Place, studying Greek — but also drawing many hours a day. There were blinding headaches when she returned home, but visits to and exhibits at the Athenæum and the vision caught in Dedham gave her courage. "What do you think I have actually begun to do?" she wrote Elizabeth. "Nothing less than *create* and do you wonder that I lay awake all last night after sketching my first picture. I actually thought my head would have made its final explosion. When once I began to excurse, I could not stop. Three distinct landscapes came forth in full array besides that which I had arranged before I went to bed and it seemed as if I should fly to be up and doing. I have always determined not to force the creative power but wait till it mastered *me* and now I feel as if the time had come and such freedom and revelry of spirit does it bring!"

By May 1832 Sophia had finished her landscape. It was made up of memories of Dedham and her own young dreams and Elizabeth pronounced it wonderful beyond words. Not but what Lizzie found plenty of words with which to express her loving pride in her sister as she went about among her friends. Sophia came to Boston to visit, bringing her landscape with her; and she found that Elizabeth had given her so much advance publicity that people came calling on her every day, asking to see the painting. Even the great Allston himself, skeptical as he was of what a little nobody like Sophia Peabody could do, promised to call none the less, look at the picture and give Sophia the benefit of his criticism.

At fifty-one, Washington Allston [1] had put his best years behind him. His reputation, however, like his canvases, was still of heroic proportions. In chill, foggy Cambridgeport, Allston could set good food and wine before his circle of admirers and then evoke for them the warm sun, the blue skies, of Rome where, as a student, he had patterned his work upon the then neglected Venetian School. Too much under the spell of the past, Allston had caught some of the dullness age had brought to Titian without being able to kindle a flame of his own to match the golden vitality of Venetian art when it was new. But there was no dullness when Allston talked about painting. He could make his hearers believe in him and see him as the great master he would have given his soul to be; and as perhaps he was — almost.

In London, as a student of Benjamin West, Allston had met with immediate success. His Biblical pictures received prizes and he was talked of as the logical successor to West as President of the Royal Academy. Then Ann Channing, his first wife and sister of Dr. William Ellery Channing, died and Allston's genius seemed to falter. Ann had waited for him eleven years, from the time of their boy-and-girl engagement when Allston was a Harvard undergraduate. Some said that their marriage was but a fulfillment of an obligation, love having grown cold. In any case, Allston went through a period of morbid depression at the time of her death, painting a "Portrait of Judas" which he liked to refer to as his greatest work. He destroyed it, lest, as he said, it should prove an evil influence in the world.

Allston's return to America was considered his fatal step by many of his friends. His very simple reason, that he was tired of Europe and wanted to come home, was incomprehensible to expatriate geniuses like West. A craze for huge canvases such as might cover a wall in the palace at Versailles was in progress, and Allston had conceived a colossal composition, "Belshazzar's Feast." What a picture it was, as he saw it in his mind's eye! It would be his masterpiece, his incontestable proof that he was the equal of Titian. There were money difficulties, however, and Allston accepted a thousand dollars each from ten friends before the picture was completed. Then once more his mental torment began, for the picture in his mind would not go down on canvas. Hiding from himself the specter of failure and hopeless indebtedness, Allston began to talk about his picture instead of working on it. This was a fatal evasion but in Boston talk was better understood than art. Allston grew in reputation as he decreased in stature as an artist. He married Martha Dana, who helped to make his home a meeting place for the intellectual.

It was only for diversion, when not at work upon his masterpiece, that he painted other pictures, Allston said. In 1832 his "Diana on a Chase," "Florimel," "Storm" and "Tuscan Maiden" were on display in the May exhibit at the Athenæum. Allston himself was also on exhibition at the gallery. It was really a miracle of condescension that moved him to call upon Miss Sophia Peabody and look at a picture she had painted.

Sophia was properly overcome.

"Elizabeth, Mary and Amelia Greenwood came to announce him. He had come to Boston, he told Betty, almost on purpose to see my picture and so we confidently expected him.

"Every ring of the bell made my heart leap and it leapt three times to no purpose, once for a strange lady, once for the *Transcript* (which so often comes instead of an expected person, you know) and once for a whole bundle of manifold newspapers.

"At length, as I was looking out of the window, the very man appeared with an inquiring attitude which seemed to wonder whether this was the house. I then jumped in good earnest, in uncontrollable tumult. I felt unutterable things. He took down the poor pic – and looked very attentively and long at it. I stood behind him trembling like a sinner. Mary whispered, 'Tell him you painted it in perfect ignorance,' and like a perfect parrot, said I, 'Mr. Allston, I painted it in perfect ignorance.'

"He hummed and replied, 'But you have not painted it ignorantly. It does you great credit. I have no fault to find with it. I am very much surprised at it for it is superior to what I expected, although I have heard it so much spoken of!' I was relieved and breathed without panting. They seemed like the words of an oracle."

Sophia was working on a copy of a French picture that she admired and could readily sell, for it was in the popular taste. The original was in the house where she was visiting so "we carried him up to the drawing room to see Sappho," she wrote. "He did not like it *at all*, said it was ill drawn, poorly colored and badly put together and that it was of the ancient French school before the revolution! Alas Me! He then said that if I had commenced copying it I might as well go on as I should learn to handle colors and that whenever I felt inclined to *alter*, I had better do it. He thought I might find pictures enough to copy but he wished I might copy nature."

Allston went on to tell Sophia that she should study from sculptures, from casts and from living models. As was so often his custom, he recreated for her the glamor of his student days abroad and described the long discipline an artist must undergo. Sophia would have loved nothing better but he might as well have described the planet Mars as Europe — for all the chance Sophia had of going there. (Not but what Elizabeth would arrange it if she could, however!)

Had Allston any objection to having his own work copied? Elizabeth wanted to know. "Not the least in the world, if your sister should," was the reply. And Elizabeth promptly asked for "Jessica and Lorenzo," Allston's very latest work which she had just seen in his studio. The paint was not dry yet, he told her — but he promised the picture.

Allston sent Sophia to his nephew, George Flagg, a boy of sixteen. "Tell him to repeat to you all the lectures on art I have ever given him," said Allston. "The boy has great talent and I have taught him all I know." [6]

Within three days, Sophia was at Flagg's studio, where she found him painting "the beautiful Marian Marshall, like a princess in her white satin robes." Marian's sister Charlotte was by her side and the picture was in the popular neo-Gothic manner, with a minstrel boy looking up at the sisters, "an elegant greyhound caressing Marian's hand." Sophia was enchanted by all this affectation and asked Flagg why he did not paint himself as the minstrel.

" 'Oh, I cannot,' he earnestly replied. 'I want a *beautiful* head.' I smiled in my sleeve and spoke not a word," said Sophia, "since his reason against happened to be my reason *for*."

Flagg returned the call to look at Sophia's work. "Your pictures are all remarkable for correct drawing," he told her. " 'You have a correct eye.' " The boy spoke in perfect imitation of his uncle's pontifical style.

Back home in Salem, Sophia's mood of exaltation lasted through September, while she composed what she called "fourth picture," writing this identification carefully on the wooden stretcher back of the canvas. It seemed miraculous to her when she finished it in 70 hours, and so she made a note of that, too, behind the canvas — adding with pride a neatly printed S. A. Peabody and the year, 1832.[7]

Sophia had a right to be proud, for her landscape was a lovely thing: a matter of tender blue sky, a sunny plain whereon a distant town was delicately suggested. That it was an Italian town borrowed from some picture she had seen bothered nobody. In the foreground was a river, its depth and reflections handled admirably, while directly behind it rose a cliff with again just the suggestion of an ancient watchtower. On the right, a path overhung with trees led along the river, and a boy walked on the path, charming touches of red in his costume bringing to life a canvas dominantly blue and lavender. The boy was badly drawn but the red of his coat was repeated with subtlety in tiny flowers on the riverbank. The foliage of the high trees was of the stilted, feather-duster type so much in vogue, and the whole picture had a smooth lacquered look, with not a brush stroke to be seen — also a fashionable style. No wonder Sophia's picture was found worthy of a broad gold frame; no wonder it hung in a fashionable Salem drawing room. It could not be called original — perhaps if it had been she would not have been able to sell it. But Sophia's landscape expressed her own personality, it was beautifully painted, it had charm.

Just at first, during the winter of 1832 in Salem, Sophia could say, as she had said a year ago in Dedham, "Each separate little Sophie had wings on shoulders and feet."

CHAPTER SIX
"Dear Mr. M"

ELIZABETH had returned to Boston sadder but not much wiser after her attempts to fight other people's battles in New Bedford. She found Miss Dorothea Dix installed as Channing's secretary, doing, for a salary, the work which Miss Peabody had delighted to do for nothing. Lizzie hated Miss Dix at sight.

"You want order, method, arrangement," Dr. Channing told Elizabeth severely. He said she was not to rely so much upon "the principle within" to help her "intuitively" when need arose. Having preached his little sermon, Dr. Channing gave Elizabeth his daughter Mary to teach — as proof positive of his continued faith in her. Dr. Channing's powerful friendship had not been withdrawn, and once more Miss Peabody's school was the thing. Mary Peabody was summoned from her Salem exile to help as before, and the two sisters hired a room and a schoolroom for themselves at Mrs. Clarke's boardinghouse.

Mrs. Clarke's was a unique institution even in a city where every lady in reduced circumstances kept a boardinghouse — if she did not keep a school. Fortunately for the boardinghouse business, many married women enjoyed sufficiently delicate health to be "at board" instead of keeping house. And fortunately for such as Mrs. Clarke, these customers set more store by gentility than efficiency. Daughter of a minister and mother of one, Mrs. Clarke's reputation was unimpeachable — leaving her free to enliven her lot by incessant gossip. Woe be unto the evildoer whose sins she found out — but Mrs. Clarke reserved her worst condemnation for the "female" she suspected of "indelicacy" or "indiscretion," and she had a positive genius for thinking the worst and then spreading the news. Her boarders were of the best families, their gentility unquestioned — but she kept her eye on them just the same. It seemed to the perceptive Mary that Mrs. Clarke had her eye on Elizabeth in particular.

"Mrs. Clarke far out-talks all of us, even Elizabeth," Mary said. But Mrs. Clarke's artist daughter Sarah and her son, James Freeman, later a prominent Abolitionist, were good friends of the Peabody sisters.

A notable feature of the Clarke boardinghouse was the long dining room table where all the boarders ate together — or were supposed to. Conversation was the keynote, since conversation would help the boarders to overlook the inept table service, yet appreciate Mrs. Clarke's really fine cooking. Elizabeth felt it incumbent upon her to keep the conversation upon a high plane, while Mrs. Clarke liked to bring it down to earth and spice it with scandal. Intellectual conversation won out when Elizabeth saw that Jared Sparks, former head of Mrs. Cleveland's school and old friend of Lancaster days, was a fellow boarder. She took and held the floor at once as she talked along lines Jared Sparks would be likely to follow.

He was "crusty Jared Sparks" now, to quote Mary Peabody's opinion of him.[1] Over forty, he was but just married to the wealthy Miss Frances Anne Allen of Hyde Park, New York. After her first long conversational dinner at Mrs. Clarke's table, young Mrs. Sparks took the rest of her meals in her room, leaving the field to Miss Peabody. Sparks was engaged upon his *Writings of George Washington*, his desk littered with priceless manuscripts which he had appropriated wherever he found them — since his generation considered a Washington holograph fit for a bonfire. Elizabeth was engaged upon her textbook of Greek history but a similar interest in history as a subject brought only fierce arguments with Sparks. He had little use for the Greeks, Elizabeth still less for American history. It was Elizabeth's good fortune that Sparks won his case, leading her to little-known sources in private libraries.

Not that Elizabeth talked exclusively with Jared Sparks. There was George Hillard, admitted to the bar since the days when he frequented the Peabody parlor at Fayette Place. George Hillard was co-editor with George Ripley of the *Christian Register*, and he encouraged Elizabeth to write for his Unitarian weekly. Elizabeth was nothing loth; she chose "The Creation" for her subject, troubled not at all by its magnitude. Another title occurred to her — "Temptation and Sin." Mrs. Clarke would be certain to read that article — if only to find out how much Miss Peabody knew about the subject.

While Elizabeth was conducting her conversations, her sister Mary was listening and looking on. When Mary spoke, it was often just a mischievous word calculated to arouse Lizzie till her blue eyes sparkled and she vigorously defended a stand she might not have taken but for a little sisterly teasing. If Lizzie went too far, however, Mary's amusement would be tinged with remorse and she would try vainly to calm the storm she had raised. It was a little game Mary thought she played all by herself with no one even suspecting that she was having fun. Then one night she caught the laughing eyes of a man across the table from her. He knew exactly what she was up to. Mary reminded him of "The Boy Apprenticed to an Enchanter" — he told her — a long time later.

From now on, Mary could not help exchanging a glance with her fellow conspirator when something appealed to her own subtle sense of humor. She found she could depend upon the answering gleam. What was he really like, she wondered? He had white hair but his face was young, his eyes set in shadowy caverns under a formidable brow. He had a roughhewn nose and a mouth too large but wonderfully expressive, sometimes of sadness, sometimes of mirth. Was the man handsome? Mary decided not, yet he interested her more than anyone else at the table and she could not get him out of her mind. At first he had been a somewhat silent guest but Mary's friendly glances roused him out of his abstraction and he joined in the talk, not to argue but to lighten Elizabeth's argument with humor. Writing to Sophia in Salem, "Mr. Mann is intolerably witty . . . he well nigh destroys me," said Mary.

Hardly realizing it himself, Horace Mann had begun to look forward to Mrs. Clarke's dinner table. While at work upon his law practice during the day, he filed away in his mind amusing anecdotes to be told at night. And at night when he began his tale, he would look first at Mary Peabody for that delightful flash of appreciation which made him feel at his best. Mann had always been a gifted public speaker, charming in private conversation — a "radiant" man, his friends had called him. But recently he had been overwhelmed with grief. Laughter, he supposed, had gone from him forever — until he met Mary.

Born in 1796 in Franklin, Massachusetts, Horace Mann was a farmer's son — the brilliant member of a large family. His mother was widowed when he was thirteen. Of his childhood he remembered nothing except a terrifying Calvinist belief in the torments of hell, and unremitting labor on the farm which undermined his health. There was little hope of education until an eccentric itinerant teacher came along. In six months Mann had prepared himself for Brown University, his entrance examination placing him in the sophomore class. He wrote to his sister, "If the Children of Israel were pressed for 'gear' half so much as I have been, I do not wonder they were willing to worship a golden calf. It is a long, long time since my last ninepence said goodbye to its brethren."

At Brown, Mann's keen mind and quick repartee were long remembered, while as a law clerk and student under Judge Gould of Litchfield, Connecticut, Mann was considered "the best fellow and the best wit in the office." He was also the best whist player, but of that he was careful to say nothing while at Mrs. Clarke's boardinghouse.

Upon leaving Judge Gould, Horace Mann had started a law practice in Dedham, Massachusetts, and in 1827 he was elected State Representative. Three years later, well established at last, he had married Charlotte Messer. Charlotte's father had been President of Brown when Mann was an undergraduate but he was president no longer, having been asked to resign — the charge against him, heresy. He had become a Unitarian.

Horace Mann had been thirty-four at the time of his marriage, Charlotte barely eighteen. "There was a light upon earth brighter than any light of the sun," Mann said. "I did not think but that happiness which was boundless in present enjoyment would be perpetual in duration." But Charlotte was not strong. There were no children, a disappointment to them both. And then, after two years of marriage, it was discovered that Charlotte had tuberculosis. Hers was not the slow, wasting illness they called a "decline." She seemed more brilliant mentally, more beautiful than ever, her flaming cheeks the only indication of fever. Horace Mann was with her, unaware of any particular danger, when she suddenly became violently ill — out of her mind. He was alone with her the night when she died in his arms.

For many months Mann had lived alone with his grief. His health, never very good, was badly impaired and his hair had grown white. Problems arising in the legislature still interested him but he had put aside ambition. Of what use was it to rise in politics when Charlotte could no longer share his honors? He found a certain degree of comfort in espousing an unpopular cause — the care of the insane. He worked valiantly for funds to build a state sanitarium in Worcester and to educate the public in the idea that mental disease was no disgrace; no fault of the individual; that it might possibly be curable. There were those who believed that insanity was contagious, a point Horace Mann was ready to disprove at his own risk! But however valuable his work, it could not be called gay or cheering. To please his friends, he had agreed to try the genial atmosphere of Mrs. Clarke's boardinghouse — just to improve his health and spirits.

And now already, after only a few weeks, Mary Peabody found Mr. Mann "intolerably witty." Their friendship soon progressed beyond the matter of exchanged glances. To his surprise, Mann discovered that Mary Peabody knew what went on in government and that she was both interested and intelligent concerning his aims as Representative. Shrewd as he was, however, he never suspected that Mary deliberately led him to talk of the present and the future — never of the past. Mary knew little or nothing about his private life when they first met, but she could see that some sadness lay across his mind like a shadow and she made it her business to help him forget.

Elizabeth had missed the opening moments of Horace Mann's friendship for her sister Mary. When she finally noticed that Mary's cheeks were brighter, her eyes alight with that attentive look which made her the perfect listener — the delight of every brilliant talker — Lizzie looked about to see who was calling forth all Mary's charm. Almost at once, Elizabeth found herself just as attracted to Horace Mann as her sister was, although for different reasons. It was not his smile but the look of sadness in his eyes that drew Elizabeth to him. She had little interest in Mann's career in the State House but she longed to know the story concealed in his past.

With her genuine love of sharing another's burdens, Elizabeth laid siege to Horace Mann's confidence. It did not take her long to learn the tragic circumstances of Charlotte's early death. That, in itself, would have been enough to enlist Elizabeth's ever-ready sympathy. But Horace Mann told her something that still further melted her loving heart. He had no faith! He could not believe that he would see Charlotte in a better world and that she was even now waiting for him with outstretched arms. Elizabeth dusted off her philosophy books and felt that she had not studied in vain. She and Mary and Mr. Mann foregathered right after dinner and adjourned to Mrs. Clarke's parlor for a philosophical discussion. The other boarders soon tired of eternity as a subject for light conversation and left the field. Mary tried to change the subject. But it amused her to see that Mann was more than a match for Lizzie, competent lawyer that he was, well trained in debate.

From Channing's library Elizabeth brought fresh ammunition for her battle against Mann's gloomy Calvinist doctrines. These were the days when Channing was leading his contemporaries in the discovery of foreign philosophers, and Lizzie brought home Constant in the original French. It was a pity she could not have brought Constant's *journal intime*, if only to give Mrs. Clarke something to talk about. But it was the "Analysis of Locke," of course, which Mary and Elizabeth took turns reading aloud every evening to Horace Mann and which "occupies his mind," Lizzie said.

So successful was Elizabeth's school that she and Mary could afford not only a schoolroom and a bedroom at Mrs. Clarke's but a little private parlor as well. And it was only natural that the evening readings should soon take place there, since the other boarders were even less interested in Constant than they had been in eternity. In the Peabodys' little parlor, Mr. Mann would sometimes relapse "into one of those deep silences which cannot be broken." He would assume an attitude of grief which Elizabeth considered "Niobe-like."

It was like Elizabeth to imagine that she alone possessed the key to another's mind. She never dreamed that Mary was just as well aware of Horace Mann's moments of overwhelming sadness. But it was Mary, actually, who saw further and read Mann more accurately. She knew that it was his dramatic temperament, the very quality which made him a good lawyer, which now led him to dramatize sorrow in terms intentionally "Niobe-like" for the benefit of certain sympathetic young women. He could not resist an audience, and how well he played! Mary thought she was angry with him — she thought she almost hated Horace Mann. Yet the surge of emotion was not anger, although Mary was not ready to admit even to herself what it really was. When Mr. Mann became particularly Niobe-like, Mary would get up and leave the room, and she thought Lizzie ought to follow. But Elizabeth did no such thing.

Lying tense and miserable in her bed, Mary tried over and over again to imagine what was happening in the little private parlor after she had left her sister and Horace Mann alone together. How time dragged! She listened for the striking of a clock and then felt sure she had miscounted the strokes when only an hour had gone by. When Lizzie came to bed at last, she would tell everything, Mary knew from experience. Yet when Elizabeth came, Mary pretended to be asleep. It was to Sophia that Elizabeth confided the story, enjoying every detail of her experience, seeing herself and "dear Mr. Mann" as characters in a romance.

"I got up to go but could not leave him without making some sign of my sympathy and so took his hand to say goodnight — which I had never done before. He looked so mutely grateful — and yet so sadly — that it went to my very heart — and he still held my hand until Mary had gone out of the room — and then drew me nearer and throwing his arm around me — let the tears flow — which seem ever to wait this touch of sympathy. I held in my other hand that little book with Philosophy and Socrates upon it — and it was in line with his sight — so that after he had grown a little more calm — his eyes fell upon it and he said, 'He conversed with wisdom and so he suffered death — how mysterious — mysterious world!'

" 'We see but a part,' I said — 'the smallest part.'

"After another long pause — during which he lost his calmness again — he said, '*homeless*' and to this I had nothing to reply." [2]

Letters from Elizabeth and Mary reached Sophia at Salem in "the box" which traveled regularly back and forth by stage between the Peabody parents and their independent daughters in Boston. Although the box from Boston contained for the most part nothing but soiled laundry, there were often presents from Elizabeth, who could not resist being generous whether she could afford it or not. Once there was a book on chemistry for George and Nathaniel, who were keeping an apothecary shop and living on the premises. The book cost Elizabeth ten dollars which the brothers promised to pay at such time as they made any more than enough to pay their rent — a time which never came. The Salem-bound box almost always contained a little gift for Sophia, perhaps some coveted but expensive cobalt-blue paint, or a brush of a size she needed but could not find in Salem.

Sophia liked to be the first to open the box because occasionally there would be letters not intended to be shown to her mother. These she regarded with mixed feelings. Sometimes there were troubling reports of Wellington, who had not been expelled like George and Nat but suspended, and was now reinstated at Harvard. He was doing well in his studies but he had his "dandyish cut again" and his girls. Only when forced to admit it did Elizabeth mention that he also had his old persuasive way with him when he came to borrow money from his sisters.

Lydia Haven was visiting Sophia in Salem when the letter about Mr. Mann arrived. "Pray do not let anyone read what I say of Mr. Mann for sorrow is too sacred a subject of speculation," Elizabeth had said — "but I should like Lydia to know how much we care for him but take care not to go beyond sympathy." Sophia was nothing loth to share with Lydia such an interesting communication. Was Lizzie falling in love at last? It certainly looked like it and it was high time, for it was the spring of 1833 and Elizabeth was just turning twenty-nine. Lydia's reactions were unexpected, however. Her husband, Sam Haven, came from Dedham and he knew something about Horace Mann in his early days, Lydia hinted darkly. It was Sam's secret and Lydia would say no more, but Sophia was to write to Elizabeth in all haste and tell both Elizabeth and Mary to beware. They both ran the risk of a broken heart. Horace Mann was "irresistible to women!"

If there was anything in the world that Elizabeth Peabody loved better than other people's troubles it was other people's secrets, and now she would never rest till she got it out of Sam what he had against Horace Mann. Meanwhile she rose to the defense. "I assure you that all your impressions are a wretched lie," she told Sophia. "If Mr. Mann is not one of nature's noblemen, then there are no such persons. . . . He is too wretched or it would be pure delight to see and hear him every day. But I really should not wonder if he should not live. He is one of the few who might die of love." [3]

Mary said never a word. When she first heard the story of Mr. Mann's bereavement, she wept — but she wept secretly. Then, as she herself said later, "Every power of my soul was taxed to console and finally to cheer." She would win Mr. Mann away from thoughts of death. If he should ever remind her that he was "homeless" she might be able to lead him to the conclusion that there was something he could do about that, someone who would gladly make a home for him. "My interest in life was now more intense than I ever imagined it could be," Mary confessed — but she only told it in later years. In the spring of 1833, they went on picnics, taking the ubiquitous Elizabeth along of course. Mann climbed an apple tree to gather blossoms for Mary. Impudently, she told him he looked funny up a tree. He laughed and called her "Mary" as if she were but a child while Elizabeth, only two years older, was "Miss Peabody" still. So Mary went further and called him "Horace," forcing him to be young with her, to meet her on equal terms. Mary's first sensation of anger against Horace Mann for dramatizing his grief now turned against Elizabeth — for encouraging him, almost forcing him, to live in the past and to think of the dead Charlotte as with him still. There were words between the sisters who, until now, had lived together in reasonable harmony.

Sophia was relieved when there was little or no mention of Mr. Mann in Mary's letters. But there were passages in Elizabeth's which she found alarming and which she prudently hid from her mother. It rested "dear Mr. Mann," for example, to sit beside Elizabeth on the sofa and let her gently comb his hair. Mary would sing to him — but that seemed safe enough. Sophia hated an argument, however, so she hastily agreed with Lizzie that Mr. Mann was heartbroken, rather than a breaker of hearts. At Lizzie's request she tried to recall the lost Charlotte, whom she had met briefly in Dedham. Charlotte had been "exceedingly lovely," she had "very soft and very sweet dark eyes" and "children felt an uncommon affection for her" — that was the best Sophia could do.

These were days when Sophia had troubles of her own which she could not confide to anyone for she hardly understood them herself. She felt constantly under pressure and her violent headaches were accompanied by nausea; whereupon her mother urged upon her an almost nutrition-free diet of white bread and rice. Picture after picture arose in Sophia's mind, and she had no time to put them on canvas, since copying must go on. Although not allowed to live away from home and be self-supporting, it was still a point of pride with Sophia to pay for her own paint and supplies and to provide for herself as much as she could. Her sisters had invited her and could well have used her to teach art in their school — and how Sophia would have loved to come to live with them at Mrs. Clarke's! But with both Mary and Elizabeth away, Mrs. Peabody said she needed Sophia. The child's health was very delicate indeed, Mrs. Peabody said, the increasing violence and frequency of Sophia's headaches seeming to prove that she was right. Sophia felt helpless, as though caught in a trap.

Hardest of all to bear were Elizabeth's efforts to help her. Not a letter came without, to Sophia, certain painful paragraphs. "Theodore would be likely, I think, to buy 'Flight into Egypt.' When you have finished that, you might paint another for Mrs. Philbrick. . . .

As to the 'Salvator Rosa' and 'Flight into Egypt,' I hope to see them in the Athenæum exhibit . . .' I think Mrs. Rodman will like 'Salvator Rosa.'" Having no conception of how Sophia's artistic soul cringed before the thought of definite dates when work must be finished, Elizabeth would add the final touch of torture. "The Athenæum opens the 10th of May . . . the other exhibit the 4th of June." The desire of Sophia's heart was to exhibit, but she wanted to show something of her own, not potboilers. She wanted time to paint the best picture of which she was capable, but those terrifying dates would not have seemed so formidable if she could have faced them by herself without Elizabeth to force them upon her.

Sophia might have been able to deal with Elizabeth if Elizabeth's plans had not concerned the whole family. But in 1833, Elizabeth conceived a new idea which was to make all their fortunes, and in which Sophia was to share.

"In respect to my book," Elizabeth wrote. "The first part of it is to consist of questions on Grecian Theology and Mythology together with heroic legends and I wish to have everything illustrated by a drawing either of a statue or a gem or a cameo. I shall make tracings at the Athenæum of everything there is there which will suit my purpose (on thin paper). I enclose you Michel Angelo's Moses and would like to know if you think you could copy from such models."

On the question of art, Sophia always expressed herself with confidence. She told her sister just what she thought of the tracing. It was sloppy — careless. No one could work from it and she, personally, was not going to try.

Disregarding Sophia's remarks, Elizabeth referred to her new project in a casual postscript to a letter all about Mr. Mann. Hilliard, Gray were going to print her book, she said. She was to raise the capital and they would give her ten per cent on the retail price, which she considered a very favorable proposition. "The whole cost will be 4770 dollars for paper, stones, letter press and printing but besides that there will be baggage and wagoning for 100 stones, each weighing, I fancy, about an hundred pounds. This will be not short of fifty dollars more."

Naturally, Elizabeth had no such sum of money to invest. She was out getting subscriptions and Sophia's lithographs were part of her prospectus. "I must have whatever Sophia does, provided it does not break my neck or starve my children," Dr. Channing told her. And Allston's reactions were equally favorable because of Sophia's promised work.

Almost before the letter, a lithographer's stone arrived in Salem for Sophia. "Promised work, indeed!" Sophia had flatly refused but now she was trapped. If her work was essential to Elizabeth's success, she could not refuse to make the effort. She knew nothing whatever about lithography and there was no use in pointing out to Elizabeth that it was a special art requiring years of study. Sophia went to see a local lithographer who told her what he knew, which was very little, and who sold her some wax pencils. Feeling as though all of the one hundred stones had been heaped upon her shoulders, she set to work.

It was Mrs. Peabody who wrote the next letter to Boston. "I trust our dear one will feel better tomorrow. . . . Many causes have united to excite her, such as engagements, doubts about succeeding on the stone."

After numerous heartbreaking redrawings, Sophia sent her stone to Boston. The proofs were horrible. Elizabeth said that they were not bad at all and that after a little practice Sophia would do wonders. But Sophia knew that she could not become a lithographer in a thousand years. She began to have more violent headaches than she had ever before experienced. Sleep became a torture to her, for she endured an agony of recurrent dreams. Sometimes a bare bodkin appeared before her eyes and she awoke screaming that she was about to be blinded. She dreamed that she saw Elizabeth lying dead in a casket in the front parlor and she awoke sobbing and crying out that she loved Elizabeth.

The French philosophers which Elizabeth so much admired had nothing to offer in explanation of Sophia's troubled mind. But Elizabeth saw clearly that Sophia was now an invalid in good earnest and her loving heart overflowed with pity and anxiety. All the tremendous energy with which she had overwhelmed the artist Sophia she now devoted to Sophia, the invalid. A journey of health! That was the thing! To be sure, many young girls were taken from a darkened, tightly closed sickroom only to die on a long voyage. But a few, given sun and air, in time recovered even from "lung fever," and with death so tragically the rule, these few exceptions made the treatment popular.

Probably there was no one in Boston who did not very shortly know that Miss Peabody's invalid sister must go on a journey for health. All kinds of plans were discussed, at Dr. Channing's, at Mrs.

Clarke's — wherever Elizabeth went. Such journeys were only for the rich, Dr. Peabody reminded angrily, but Elizabeth was sure she could find a way. And finally Mrs. Cleveland of Lancaster and Salem conceded that something might be arranged for Sophia in Cuba. Her husband was now vice-consul at Havana.

Elizabeth wrote to Sophia the good news. But Sophia had begun to dread the sight of a letter from Elizabeth and to this one she replied, "Mrs. Cleveland is very kind to make such efforts for me but do not send me to Havana among strangers!"

Here was an obstacle which Elizabeth had not foreseen but she reassured Sophia. Her sisters would always take care of her. One of them would go with her to Cuba. She set about acquiring clothes, contributing most of her own wardrobe to Sophia and collecting, here "a muslin," there "a foulard," from friends. Sophia's spirits rose as she contemplated the thrill of foreign travel with someone to look after her, and she began to pack her trunks. Mrs. Cleveland sent a "Volante box" especially designed to fit the curious Cuban *volante* carriage.

And now Mary was the silent one. Her pale cheeks might have caused concern, had not everyone been watching over Sophia. She had been increasingly sharp-tongued with Elizabeth ever since those evenings when Horace Mann complained that his eyes hurt him. Elizabeth would turn down the lamp. More than once Mrs. Clarke came to the parlor unexpectedly and Mary felt her prying eyes upon them and saw skepticism in her face over the reason given for the dim, intimate light. While the two sisters were together, there was little Mrs. Clarke could say. But Elizabeth persisted in deliberately out-staying Mary and Mary spoke heatedly about it. Elizabeth was scornful of any harm Mrs. Clarke's formidable tongue could do.

It came to Mary that Elizabeth might not be so confident if there were not some sort of understanding between herself and "dear Mr. M." Mary lived over again a certain night. It had grown late and she took her lamp to go to bed. Horace rose, as always. This time he held the door for her, he looked down into her eyes and smiled. Love entered her unguarded heart.

Hoping in her heart of hearts that Horace loved her and might object, Mary offered to go to Cuba with Sophia. Elizabeth accepted the idea of it as if it had been understood all along. And Horace Mann hoped that Mary would have a pleasant journey.

CHAPTER SEVEN

Cuba Journals

NOW, although she had set out with a fair breeze, the brig *Newcastle* was becalmed before she could leave Boston Harbor for the open sea. Hours went by within sight of the tri-mountain city, its three hills not yet leveled to exist only in the name of Tremont Street. Mary and Sophia wrote letters to be taken back to Boston by the pilot but they could think of little to say which had not already been said during the parting moments on shore. It grew dark and after a meal made for the most part from their own provisions they went to bed in the scant privacy of the ladies' cabin. They were thankful that they had been advised to bring their own feather beds since their bunks proved to be nothing but grim-looking boxes made of bare wooden boards.

Sometime during the night a half-gale arose and the *Newcastle* heeled over and began to rip through the water. Her course lay straight into the worst storm the Atlantic Coast had seen for many years and she battled her way in a series of short tacks with the constant thudding of seamen's running feet heard on the decks, the bawling of orders, the shrieking of wind and running gear. Ships all along the New England coast were badly damaged and the schooner *Mechanic*, which had sailed with the *Newcastle*, was cast away near York, Maine. Reading in the *Salem Gazette* of the storm havoc, Mother Peabody was in an agony of suspense and commended her children's souls to God. She could not hope to get news, whether of their safety or of disaster, for many weeks.

While the heavy seas were running, Mary and Sophia kept to their bunks, too weak and miserable to know if the danger had passed. Sophia recovered first, thanks to her own good sense in getting herself into the fresh air on deck as soon as skies were blue overhead and the sun warm. She was too weak to stand, but she had her feather bed brought out and arranged in a sheltered spot and there she lay, pale and fragile and utterly charming to James Burroughs, who hovered beside her trying to think of something he could do for her. They had long intimate talks together with Sophia ever the sympathetic listener, her confiding gentleness going straight to his heart. She believed in the goodness of God, she told him earnestly; she believed that man was created in God's image — her friends in particular. James Burroughs had supposed that he knew about love but he found that something very beautiful had escaped him until now.

When Mary appeared on deck, James was kind, even attentive as though he particularly wanted her good opinion. But Mary did not like him. She was polite but distant, preferring to walk alone or gaze at the far, faintly circular horizon with no one at her side to interrupt her thoughts. When the *Newcastle* finally reached Havana, Mary felt as if she understood the meaning of eternity as a measure of time.

On the 30th of December, 1833, Mary and Sophia were at the Havana home of Mr. and Mrs. Richard Cleveland, their old friends from Salem and Lancaster. They were greeted with open arms by Mrs. Cleveland and Sophia wrote to her mother, "Here is your dear daughter, safe, quiet and enchanted in this great city." She spoke of James Burroughs as "devotedly attentive," taking her to ride in a hired *volante* along with Mary and Mrs. Cleveland.

The home of the American Consul to Havana proved anything but quiet, however, as Sophia soon learned. It was no wonder that Mrs. Cleveland looked ill, she said. As for herself — "The street cries of men and women with fruits upon their heads, the squalls of children, the continuous stream of talk from groups all about, uttered in the highest key, the monotonous hammering of coopers and tinkers, the screams of macaws and parrots and all the un-musical birds . . . almost put me beside myself." Noise always made Sophie's headaches worse. "O, I forgot the bells!" she added. "The bells! They are never still. Tinkle, tinkle, bang, bang, squeak, squeak, from morning till night and from night till morning, and at dawn a drum goes round to call the soldiers . . ."

The Morell hacienda was a day's journey from Havana and on January 8, 1834, it was Mary who took up the tale. "Here we are at Mrs. Morell's just one month after setting sail from Boston and when I tell you that Sophia rode 45 miles three days ago, over roads which pass all description for horrors, and that she slept soundly all that night, and was not wakened even by the great bell that hangs near the house, got up to breakfast, and has been better ever since, except being very tired and achy, you will allow that I was right in my expectations that she would be cured by this same trip to Cuba." The Morells had sent their confidential servant to arrange the journey for the new governess and her invalid sister but the ubiquitous James Burroughs had hired a horse and had ridden along to see that nothing happened to Miss Sophia.

Mrs. Morell received the young ladies from New England "very sweetly," Sophia said. Her more cautious sister Mary found Mrs. Morell "a very interesting, pleasing woman; much more so than I expected." But Mary also saw Mrs. Morell as "a sort of personification of the opinion of the world" and James Burroughs, presenting himself unannounced and uninvited at the Morell hacienda, was a person of whom Mrs. Morell could not approve. What sort of invalid was Miss Sophia — so young-looking, so pretty, and the object of so much attention! Although usually sensitive to a degree, Sophia noticed nothing wrong in Mrs. Morell's attitude and it was Mary who felt dismay.

"La Recompensa," the Morells' country home, had no touch of the fortress which characterized the Spanish type of house in Havana. It was only one story, with long verandas and with "all the rooms open to the lawn on each side." The "hall," where the whole family gathered every evening, was spacious and cool. There was a magnificent grand piano at which the family and every guest, young men in particular, seemed able to perform with concert perfection. Sophia brought paper and pencil with her of an evening, her intention being to make a sketch of everyone for her notebook — and not to provide parlor entertainment that rivaled the music, as it turned out. There was Dr. Morell, with his high, scholarly forehead, his handsome beard. He had been injured recently when his *volante* turned over, and he came to the hall in a long white dressing gown with a turban upon his head, looking picturesque and oriental. Mrs. Morell, black-haired, imperious, looked the French aristocrat that she was; while daughter Luisa, just approaching her sixteenth birthday, seemed at least six years older, Sophia said, so mature was her fine bosom, so sad her fathomless dark eyes. Two little boys, Eduardo and Carlito, completed the family circle and were Mary's especial charge. Guests every day, sometimes from midmorning till midnight, were Fernando and Manuel de Layas, young men from a neighboring estate.

Sophia decided to begin her portrait collection with the handsomest of the young men, the Marqués Don Fernando de Layas. At first the young Don was coquettish and covered his face with his pocket handkerchief when he discovered that the pretty American stranger was drawing his profile. Sophia promptly pretended to lose interest in him and to start on someone else. She could not have handled Fernando better had she been the most accomplished coquette herself for immediately she had the young *marqués* begging to be drawn, offering to sit to her for hours. Sophia's first quick sketch was an unusually good one. Even Madame Morell was impressed. As for Fernando, he was overjoyed, then utterly unable to believe his ears when Sophia told him that it was not for him but for her own notebook. He begged, he entreated her to draw him again and give him the picture. She yielded gracefully at last, just at the psychological moment before the young man, to whom nothing had ever been denied, got tired of exerting himself. Sophia's delicate pencil portraits, with their high degree of finish, were a tremendous amount of work and her objections to doing two were perfectly genuine and were in no way an intentional means of enslaving the young man — but again she proceeded directly to that end.

Now, when Don Fernando arrived at La Recompensa, it was for Miss Sophia that he inquired. Was she in the mood to exercise her art? Sophia's artistic gift impressed him far more than Luisa's music, carefully cultivated though it was. The sittings took place on the veranda with the whole family looking on and it was fortunate that Sophia had never minded having people look over her shoulder and comment freely on her progress. The picture went well. The high-arched nose was easy to draw, while its prominence assured a likeness from the start. The eyes were different, they were full of fire and spirit, Sophia thought; but at last, "I caught the look in his eyes so well I wanted to shout," she said. "I made the last touches and they all think it is the ideal of his face and Madame Morell says it is the best I have done yet."

Then poor Sophia added one touch too many, as plenty of artists have done before her — and the picture was ruined. "There are no words to express my vexation, for it was the most beautiful, soulbeaming face I ever had produced," she said. "But a touch of a pencil is omnipotent and a false one banished the living soul from the features and changed the high, noble look, into an expression of utter stupidity and ordinaryness!"

Sophia's reaction to this disappointment was the natural result of the years under her mother's too loving care. Mary added a post-script to the letter home. "Poor Sophy has spoilt Fernando's portrait and has gone to bed in an agony of vexation though it is not ten o'clock in the morning."

Sophia had a passion for horseback riding and the Morells put one of their many fine saddle horses at her disposal. "Guajamon" had been chosen for her because of his gentle gait but he was actually too lazy to suit her till Fernando lent her his whip and fastened one of his spurs to her heel. Then "Guajamon did nothing less than fly as smoothly as a bird on the wing," Sophia said. "It was perfectly glorious to go at that rate, through the delicious air. Luisa was before me and Fernando just behind and she going even faster than I. . . . At last down fell my ringlets, and then we all had to come to a full stop, while I gathered them up — but they still kept falling. . . ." She seemed to have forgotten that her mother would be terrified at the thought of such wild riding; she set Mrs. Peabody's fears at rest upon another score instead. Ladies, she explained, did not wear bonnets while horseback riding in Cuba!

"Mother, dear, can you realize it?" Sophia wrote. "I gallop off like any other person — ride six or seven miles without stopping, all the while my head is in a dewy moisture from the exquisite and genial heat — and the fresh pure air keeping it cool — so that it is like a cold bath without the shock. And when I come home, instead of lying down and being speechless I feel more animated than before I went and overflowing with real life. There is surely a change coming over the spirit of my dream."

Mary added to this her typically down-to-earth statement. "You need not trouble yourself about Sophie any more. She is getting well as fast as possible unless we should ask a miracle."

Mrs. Peabody, however, could be relied upon to trouble herself if possible, and Sophia all too promptly offered her just the excuse. "What think you, dearest Mother, I did this evening? You will never imagine in the world. I **waltzed** [Sophia underlined the word four times] and though I was very dizzy the first time, I whirled round without discomfort before I gave up."

Letters from home were long in coming and Sophia had time to waltz with Don Fernando and his brother Manuel while the moon-light shone bright and the nights were "like velvet." She had time to ensnare Manuel all unconsciously, till he sang at the piano of an evening — but sang only to her. Then came Mrs. Peabody's reply, in her best manner. "My dear One, do not let that Don tempt you to waltz. It may destroy all that has been done. I trembled to read of its effects for though they did pass off, repeated shocks might do you serious injury. Tell the young man your mother fears to let you and that ought to silence him."

Mrs. Peabody was deeply concerned lest Sophia might come to regard herself as a normal, healthy human being. "Perhaps no one better than myself can appreciate the benefit past years of pain have been to you," Sophia's mother wrote. "They have formed for you a character at once lovely and elevated, correcting, subduing, eradicating self-sufficiency, pride, obstinacy. . . . And now that your Father and mine sees fit to give you the enjoyment of tolerable health, you will devote all the energies of your enthusiastic and glowing mind to His Service and Glory."

Fortunately, Elizabeth's letters from Boston made more satisfactory reading for Sophia than did her mother's from Salem. "Cuba Journal," Sophia's letters were called when her mother had them bound in two slim volumes to be passed around among admiring friends and relatives. And "Cuba Journal" Elizabeth called her own letters, which she wrote daily in Boston and sent to her sisters in Cuba.[2] Elizabeth wrote the bits of gossip that she loved and told so well. Sophia would remember, for example, the beautiful Marian Marshall — who, dressed in her white robes, sat to George Flagg for her portrait. Well, the lovely Marian had been the cause of a duel in Boston. She had "flirted too much," said one young man and two others, who overheard him, called each other out over it! They fought but both pistols missed fire. Now, said Elizabeth, both were fugitives from Boston lest the law against dueling be invoked against them, but Marian "felt nothing" — she was "completely spoilt." Dr. Channing had preached about the affair. A little later, Elizabeth had more to add. Dr. Samuel Gridley Howe had become engaged to the beautiful Miss Marshall and Mr. Mann (who was his close friend) "wonders at his taste in women."

Mary realized that a similar series of letters was expected from her — doubtless to be known as still another "Cuba Journal." She would take up her pen and then she would find herself staring at an empty sheet of paper while an hour went by. She had heard of homesickness but had supposed that it was a childish feeling soon to pass. Hers was a real illness. Food lost all its flavor although Mary had always enjoyed new dishes, always tried to learn how they were prepared. The sunny skies which so delighted Sophia seemed to Mary unmercifully blue while the eternally obtrusive tropical flowers were not beautiful but cruel in their brilliance. Mary longed for the muted tones of a New England winter to match her mood. She collected flowers, tried to learn their names, and pressed them to take home to her mother, who shared her interest in botany. But when the flowers molded because of the dampness, Mary found she did not care very much. She had always been quiet but intense in her enjoyment of life. This apathy was new to her. Having given away her heart, this was how it was going to feel to live without it all her life long, she supposed.

Sophia noticed the change in Mary and Mrs. Peabody was made anxious by the lack of letters, so excuses had to be made. It was the climate that made her "languid," Mary said. A day of teaching two restive, somewhat spoiled little boys, followed by an evening reading aloud to Madame and Dr. Morell, left her feeling "used up." "I have no troubles to pour out, dear Mother," and this was true enough, she reflected, since her troubles were never to be told to any living soul.

Letters from home caused the heart which Mary had given away to pound painfully in her chest — which seemed a strange phenomenon. Try as she liked, she could not get over the hope that Horace Mann might write. She always contrived to be the one to open the packet and look quickly at the different sealed and folded sheets, but there was never one in handwriting larger, bolder — yet curiously like her own. She would next extract Elizabeth's letters so that she could be alone to read them. Surely news of Elizabeth's engagement to Horace Mann would come at any time. Mary tried to imagine the moment, not to torture herself but to practice the self-possession she was going to need.

Elizabeth's first letter was by no means good news. Lizzie was no longer at Mrs. Clarke's, she had gone to spend the winter with her friend Mrs. Rice, and she had been given the use of a little private parlor where a fire would be lighted for her whenever she wanted to see Mr. Mann alone. "We had a long and interesting conversation on the most interesting subjects," Elizabeth said, describing dear Mr. Mann's first call. "He left me for a fortnight's absence at Worcester and Dedham with the promise that I would write on the same subject as often as I could. I woke up about 3 o'clock and thought of quantities that I wanted to say on the topics he touched upon. Monday I wrote him a sheet full . . . after it was gone I continued on the same subject dating it Tuesday, and sent it next day. Tuesday night I wrote a third letter." Religion was the subject of the letters of course, and a more intimate one could not have been devised — or so it seemed to Mary. She herself had lain awake many a night thinking of Horace Mann but she had not written daily letters to him and she could not resist saying something sharp to her sister — a maiden lady who wrote daily to a widower!

But Mary was always anxious, after she had scolded Elizabeth, lest she had given away her own secret love for Horace. A letter came before long which set her fears at rest on this score although it filled her heart with pity for a man who suffered just as she did — and with even less reason to hope. "This morning, who should come in to see me but Mr. Lindsey," Elizabeth wrote. "When he came in he looked pale as a sheet and it was not long before he introduced *the subject* which has never left his mind. He asked me almost in so many words if you were engaged to anybody privately — and then if I thought it was any predilection for another person which decided your mind. Nothing but that seemed to him a permanent and enduring obstacle to interesting you. He is certainly most passionately in love and 'the mystery' of your unexplained refusal torments him. I never was more tempted to tell a lie than I was to tell him that your heart was given away." Mary could not help feeling a faint sense of triumph because she had kept her secret so well. But Elizabeth's letter went on. "He has a very clear idea of your character and a very just one although it is perhaps *idealized*." Mary smiled to herself. That was a sisterly reservation! But the next sentence was no smiling matter for she knew all too well how Mr. Lindsey felt. "He says not a waking hour since he first saw you but your image has been before his eyes. . . . Your letters have but fanned the flame. He has no confidant of his misery and despair — and hopes — for hopes he has. He related to me the whole course of his mind — how horrified he was to hear you were going to Havana — his sudden visit and the reason of his abrupt offer. He thought it was his precipitation that was the cause of his rejection." Mary realized now that she must write Mr. Lindsey, perhaps tell him the truth — that her heart was indeed given away — and then write no more. It was too bad. She had valued him as a friend and she hoped she had not been cruel for certainly she had no such intention. And then, whether she would or no, her mind drifted to thoughts of Horace Mann. If only she could write to him instead!

Mary could not resist writing to Elizabeth on subjects which would interest Horace. Lizzie would show him the letters, especially if she had been told to do no such thing! While the artist, Sophia, was enjoying Cuban sun and shadow, Mary had been appalled by Cuban contrasts in human destiny, and of this she would write. As in Spain, a few noble families lived in luxury, disregarding the misery of the masses just as they disregarded the mud and filth that collected in the city streets outside their palace doors. Mary Peabody was in slave country for the first time and the impact upon her was sharp. Madame Morell told her that the slaves were kindly treated and Mary could see for herself that, at La Recompensa, this was true. But on the Royal Road she had seen a long line of newly arrived Africans, chained together and marching under heavy guard. The shock of seeing such a concentration of human misery was something Mary would never forget.

"We talked of colonization and abolition, subjects naturally suggested by your letters," Elizabeth wrote and Mary was pleased. But the letter continued:

"All the while I was trying to think how to get around to subjects of deeper interest. At last, dear Mr. Mann got up to go.

" 'Well, now,' I said, 'I do not feel half done and I have not said what I wanted to say.'

"He took both my hands and drew me for one moment absolutely into his arms. 'Well, and can you say it now?'

" 'Not now, I believe,' I said. 'It wants time.'

" 'Well, you can write it.' "

On the shady veranda of the Morells' hacienda, Mary read her sister's words with mounting anger, for she had a temper as well as quick wit. What was Elizabeth thinking of to maneuver herself into Horace Mann's arms — for nothing! And what did Horace Mann mean by an attitude which Elizabeth described as "brotherly" but which Mary felt certain was not?

Below the veranda where Mary was sitting the orange trees were coming into bloom, sending wave after wave of perfume into the humid air. Somewhere a Negro voice was singing in Spanish, and from within the house came the faint padding of a slave's bare feet. Everywhere there was beauty and luxury — and Mary hated it all. With an angry heart she took up her pen and wrote to her sister that one of these days Mrs. Rice was going to walk unannounced into that little private parlor. Elizabeth's reputation would not last one week in Cuba, her sister told her — that it had proved thus far so durable in Boston was little short of a miracle.

Accusation and defense carried between the sisters by sailing vessel took endless time and was the worst possible way for them to quarrel, since anger which might have cooled went on record past retraction and the soft answer, if there was to be one, was long delayed. Having still no inkling of Mary's real feelings toward Horace Mann, Elizabeth was the more hurt and bewildered. "That you love me as well as you do Sophia, I do not doubt," Elizabeth said, trying hard to believe her own words. "But is it possible for me to believe I give you the moral satisfaction Sophia does? Yet nothing less will satisfy my heart or conscience and it is in vain to think of making me happy without it."

It was with horror, but with a secret sense of satisfaction, that Elizabeth learned just at this point that Sophia was not necessarily giving all the moral satisfaction she might. The discovery came as a result of living with Mrs. Rice, and it was confirmed all too abundantly by Mrs. Cleveland, who arrived from Havana aboard the *Hector* for a visit to Salem. James Burroughs, it seemed, had been boasting in a men's boardinghouse in Havana of his close friendship with Miss Sophia Peabody. He had read aloud "a very affectionate sentence from a letter beginning 'My dear James.'" He had many such letters, he said, and Sophia had accepted presents from him which he intimated were valuable.

Mrs. Rice proceeded to deal with the character of her brother James, and Elizabeth told it all to Mary. "Were he ever so much in love, he could not be influenced but for the transient era of passion even to the degree of virtue which good intentions involve. Mrs. Rice says that from her childhood he has been the most odd-tempered, disagreeable, unchildlike, unbrotherly person — 'a perfect Cain' was her very expression and that never did he seem even to try to do right."

Elizabeth did not ask for Sophia's side of the story. She was impulsive, excitable, but not as a rule unfair. The truth was that she considered Sophia's reputation ruined no matter what Sophia might or might not have done. There were times when Elizabeth was "modern" and times when her mind was a perfect echo of Boston. Art had been grudgingly accepted by Boston but artists were still under suspicion. They were "Bohemian," which was a polite way of saying that they were utterly untrustworthy where sex was concerned. Only a man like Washington Allston could be considered above reproach and he achieved that distinction by being married to a Dana, attending Dr. Channing's church — and painting Biblical subjects. The path of a woman artist was assumed to be primrose. Young Mrs. Jared Sparks was an exception because she went around to the houses of the best people copying pictures; she did nothing so drastic as to sketch in public or study from life. It was, however, considered fair enough to whisper that she was probably unhappily married, since she preferred painting to housework. Sarah Clarke, guarded by her mother's formidable tongue and her own excessively shy spinsterhood, could go West as Margaret Fuller's illustrator and return free from censure — since it was Margaret who wrote the "daring" book. But let even Sarah go to Rome and word would reach Boston that she was having a pretty good time.

Sophia Peabody's delicate health had always been her guarantee of propriety. The invalid artist struggling feebly to paint in spite of pain was a picture Boston accepted with sentiment, as Elizabeth should know for it was she who had presented Sophia in just that light. A healthy Sophia receiving gifts and sending letters to an unmarried man while living in luxury in Spanish Cuba — there was the perfect image of the artist of stage and improper French fiction. Behind closed parlor doors the legend of Sophia Peabody could start innocently enough with letters and trinkets and end up with an imaginary secret hacienda — all before teatime.

Mrs. Cleveland did her best in her "it hurts me to tell you but I think you ought to know" style, in Salem, just in case the whisperings had gotten no farther than Boston. She said that Sophia had kissed James Burroughs on the forehead right before the face and eyes of Mrs. Morell. Although she had not seen it, she enacted the scene. Elizabeth, although frantic with embarrassment, had the presence of mind to remark that the public nature of this chaste salute was proof of Sophia's innocence. But Mrs. Cleveland's mind worked along other lines and she made it clear that she considered Sophia's public gesture of affection as indicative of something warmer taking place in private.

Elizabeth turned angrily upon Mary in a long, fiery letter. In Lizzie's eyes Sophia was still an invalid, coddled and cared for like a child, and upon Mary she laid all the blame for James Burroughs's "improper advances." It never occurred to Elizabeth that Sophia, whether well or ill, was now twenty-five years old and capable of deciding upon her own course of action. When she assumed Sophia to be innocent of actual misbehavior through sheer helplessness, it was no great compliment.

"Certain revelations were made to me," said Sophia and she took to her bed. Her headaches returned in full force. Now a growing coolness in Madame Morell's attitude toward her was explained. For the first time, self-consciousness entered into Sophia's feeling for Fernando and Manuel de Layas, and all the bright gaiety of that friendship was spoiled. She became careful and correct and this seemed to please Madame Morell. It was possible that the sad-eyed Luisa, with her large dowry, was already the intended bride of one of the young noblemen — the family plans not as yet announced to the young people concerned.

Sophia directed Mary to deny for her the kiss upon James Burroughs's forehead. The whole thing had been pure fabrication. James Burroughs had proposed marriage to her during the voyage to Cuba. He had offered to leave his post as agent for sugar planters and settle in Cuba, building a hacienda for Sophia where she should have plenty of slaves and be waited upon hand and foot. He could afford to give her every luxury, he said, and he was probably right.

Sophia had refused James Burroughs. He was over forty and she did not love him. It was exciting, however, to have a man in love with her, and Burroughs was not one to give up easily. He had suggested that Sophia ought to continue to be a good influence in his life and she had promised him sisterly affection. She wrote him uplifting letters commending to him a life of virtue with its certainty of heavenly reward — and her letters, she frankly stated, were patterned upon her sister Elizabeth's letters to Horace Mann concerning immortality. Sophia stubbornly refused to ask James to return her letters, although commanded to do so by Elizabeth.

"She feels herself supported in this by her sister Elizabeth's precepts and example in respect to Horace Mann," wrote Mary with grim satisfaction.

It was true that Mary had been a little hurt to discover that Sophia had concealed her correspondence with Burroughs, but she would not have asked to see the letters in any case — as Elizabeth had said she should do. She did not particularly like Burroughs personally, but his sister's opinion of him cast a more unfavorable light on Mrs. Rice's character than on his. Burroughs, on one of his various trips to the United States, had gone to call on Dr. and Mrs. Peabody in Salem, and he had made a good impression. It seemed to Mary that he had been both honorable and sincere.

Sophia had been indiscreet. Mary granted that. But the story would die down in Cuba, where such things were regarded even more seriously than in Boston. The story would die down in Boston too — provided Elizabeth did not keep it alive by talking too much. Mary told Elizabeth that her habit of telling everything she knew made her the least trustworthy of confidantes and that as far as discretion went, Elizabeth had none at all.

Goaded beyond endurance, Mary now asked Elizabeth a question she should have asked her long ago. Did she, or did she not, love Horace Mann?

"It is a brother's and a sister's love on both sides," Elizabeth replied. "Not that it would not be possible for Mr. Mann to make me love him exclusively. But I could not do that unless he had or did try for it. And his situation, his grey hairs and his sorrow has ever precluded from my imagination that possibility. I know what the feeling of love is . . . and this knowledge has always given me assurance that, strong as my friendship is, deep as my interest is in Mr. M. it is a totally different feeling."

Mary felt as if Heaven had opened. It was true that Horace might "try for" Elizabeth's love at any time but if he planned to, he had already let slip many fine opportunities. Now Mary was full of contrition because of her sharp, unloving letters and the mental accusations she had made against Elizabeth. Her love for Horace must still be kept secret — all the more so because he had not "tried for it" and Elizabeth was so sure that accidents could not happen. But Mary wanted to explain herself to Elizabeth once and for all.

"I used to think that never to any human being would I show the inward workings of my soul and to wish that I had some power of disguising every emotion — it was this which gave me the habit of preserving a calm exterior," Mary confessed. "Since that time, I have often wished I had the power to manifest my feelings. . . . I have ever had in my mind an ideal image of one to whom I should open every avenue of my heart for the asking — and with that image have been connected all my visions of happiness. Time must prove whether that ideal ever takes human form."

Mary knew that Elizabeth would show this letter to Horace Mann. Had she said too much? She knew him to be subtle, capable of reading between the lines. It was January 1835 before she heard what happened. "He smiled like an angel all the time I was telling him," Elizabeth wrote, "and I know he loves us both all the better for knowing it all." Mary's heart must have skipped a beat when she read that but it soon developed that "all" meant merely the disagreement between the sisters.

"It is the supreme delight of my heart when one of us has a friend that the other may have the same," Elizabeth went on. . . . "I do not wish to be preferred, but I am rather better pleased that you should be preferred — as you are certainly preferable — All I want is to be *loved* and especially not blamed with regard to you. I never should have talked so freely with Mr. Mann about us and myself however, if *I* had felt it was impossible for him to be sincere and simple back again. . . .

"The first time, and it was soon, he laid his head upon my bosom and begged my pardon for taking such a liberty in his grief, I told him *I* needed a friend to my shattered mind and nerves — and would he be sincere with me always, and never flatter me, and never keep back a truth which an elder brother would tell me, I should be forever obliged — and should feel that my sympathy was infinitely overpaid. Again — again — and again he pressed me to his heart and with floods of tears *thanked me* and when I came upstairs I should have told you the whole — but you were sure that his was just the character that soon got over grief and I was just the character to be led too far in my feelings — and with all my passion for *telling* I could not tell to *doubt* what only *faith* could understand.

"I have got torrent feelings, I allow — but they are *feminine* and they are *sentiments* not *passions* and they should be treated therefore with delicacy. They do not come from the *blood* but from the intellectual soul and they are *pure*."

The letter was written with all the sisterly affection in the world, but it made Mary smile a trifle to observe how little Lizzie knew about love. There must have been another more satisfactory letter aboard the ship from the United States, however. Elizabeth soon made mention of a letter from Mary to Horace Mann; it must have been a reply, since Mary had made a promise to herself that she would not write first.

All the letters the sisters wrote from Cuba were placed together in a "packet" and addressed to Elizabeth. Sometimes a friend brought them, sometimes they came by post — and who but Elizabeth would have been expected to pay the charges, amounting on one occasion to as much as eight dollars? Lizzie would sort the mail, sending family letters home to Salem, handing around those addressed to Boston friends. She expected that all the letters would be sent unsealed so that she could read them first herself. Mary's letter to the Honorable Horace Mann came in the packet, to be sure — but it was sealed! Elizabeth protested. She sent the letter to Mr. Mann's law office with a note reminding him to bring it to her to read as soon as possible.

"Sunday Mr. M. came for part of the evening, being very busy," she told Mary. "He was very lovely indeed and looked brighter than before — forgot to bring your letter, he said."

CHAPTER EIGHT

Temple School

I CANNOT but rejoice that you and Sophia are so well provided for in these dreadful times," Elizabeth told her sisters soon after they left for Cuba. The nation-wide financial panic of 1837 was still to come, but in Boston the barometer was already falling. Mr. Rice, brother-in-law of James Burroughs, lost $60,000 in six months in the importing business. It was as well that Elizabeth had given up her school, for paying pupils were hard to come by. "If Mr. Emerson should offer me a place in his school," Elizabeth said, "I would take it for three hundred dollars." But Ralph Waldo's cousin George was having difficulties of his own and made no offer.

There remained Elizabeth's history books upon the sale of which she counted heavily. When the splendid scheme of having Sophia for illustrator fell through, Hilliard, Gray and Company lost interest. Although, in 1832, they had published *First Steps to the Study of History*, it was Marsh, Capen and Lyon who published *Key to History. Part II: The Hebrews* and *Key to History. Part III: The Greeks* in 1833. Elizabeth went around to see them in the hope of receiving something to tide her over a few months. She got nothing. Then she remembered a little book which she had edited and which Bowles and Dearborn had published in 1829. *The Casket: A Christmas and New Year's Present for Children and Young Persons* it was called. It had done fairly well, but Elizabeth had received little except promises. She saw Bowles and Dearborn now and they still had no cash for Miss Peabody, but they gave her "all of Miss Martineau's works in consideration of former matters they were sorry they could adjust no better."

Elizabeth had one more string to her bow. "Historical School" she called a series of lectures that she had begun in 1827 [1] and carried on at intervals ever since. The idea was her own, and stemmed from her own disappointment because higher education continued to be denied to women. Miss Peabody has been called the first woman lecturer in the United States. Certainly her "Historical School" was a forerunner of Margaret Fuller's "Conversations." Boston was soon to develop a passion for such lectures, an enthusiasm which would spread all over the nation by means of Josiah Holbrook's "Lyceum" series. The lyceum sponsored men speakers only, however. Only under the auspices of the first women's club would the woman lecturer finally receive sanction to speak on a public platform, to travel about the country for the purpose — and receive money for her pains. That time was still far off; so Elizabeth Peabody received little beyond later honor for having blazed the trail. Many people now called her "unfeminine," but her friends pointed out that she spoke only in private homes and when a course ended she traveled no farther afield than to Salem in search of the new audience so essential to a lecturer's success. In Salem, of course, she received only as much honor as a prophet might expect in his own country.

Evening lecturing was a field no woman had as yet dared invade. "Reading Parties" evening lectures were called, and some men such as William Russell of the coffee-colored coat would be invited to quicken the pulses of members of Dr. Channing's circle with renditions from Mrs. Hemans — and Shakespeare. But Russell was in Germantown with Alcott now, and when Elizabeth Peabody heard that her friends were "concocting a reading party" she wondered who the drawing card could be. Lizzie was almost overcome when Ellen Sturgis,[2] the young poetess, and Miss Russell of the Russell-Lowell clan called — and invited Miss E. P. Peabody to conduct their Reading Party! Miss Peabody was to read and discuss anything she pleased, the group would meet at the parlor of her choice, among her friends, and tickets would be put on sale at once. "Is this not being fed by ravens!" exclaimed Elizabeth. Like a true prophet, she was satisfied with little and when the sale of tickets brought in a hundred dollars she was perfectly content.

For material to present to her group, Elizabeth turned to Harriet Martineau, whose works had so recently come into her possession! Born in England in 1802, Miss Martineau was the daughter of wealthy parents whose fortune had dwindled. She began her career as a writer by contributing to a Unitarian publication, but soon became conscious of the serious social problems which beset England at the beginning of the manufacturing era. She originated a fiction-style method of discussing social evils which was something new to literature and sociology alike! Through sheer force of personality, she overcame the skepticism of a publisher and her phenomenal overnight success was something he could hardly credit even when both he and Miss Martineau began to profit enormously. To Miss Amory Lowell and her sister, Miss Anna, whose family had recently built the great Lowell textile mills — to their friends who represented banking, importing, exporting, railroads — Miss Peabody read of the cruelty and hardship in the Manchester mills of England, the bitter poverty, the excess privilege. And the women of Boston's privileged classes were not smug, no matter what outsiders might say of them. They listened, and they tried to learn. They believed in an industrial United States where Old World mistakes need not necessarily be repeated. (And within a few years they had Charles Dickens's word for it that the Lowell Mills were models of good labor relations.)

At first, Elizabeth read to her ladies from the books and said little. It pleased her when her adult class asked her to read less, to "converse" more and to lead a discussion where they could all express their views. Elizabeth loved nothing better, and her Reading Party was soon the talk of the town.

Elizabeth could not live on a hundred dollars a year, however, miraculously frugal though she was. Encouraged by Mr. Mann, she wrote innumerable articles for religious periodicals. It was a pity she could not have written fiction in the style of her friend Maria Sedgwick, pioneer American woman novelist. The "human interest" stories which flowed effortlessly from Elizabeth's pen when she wrote letters to her sisters would have supported her far better than contributions to publications so consistently insolvent as the *Christian Register* or the *Examiner*. But E. P. Peabody was a writer with a mission. "The Being of God" was a subject she felt she should tackle and she was almost apologetic when she chose anything so light as "Social Crime and Its Retribution." Horace Mann was disappointed in her. "If you could only write in the same vein as your letters," he reproached, criticizing "pretty severely" Elizabeth's "Character of Moses." But Lizzie was afraid to be human in print. Her articles were accepted — soon the *Christian Examiner* owed her $27.00.

Elizabeth arose at five in the morning at the Rices' house, in order to have time for her writing. At seven little Willie Rice presented himself for lessons and then, with time out for breakfast, came

"Lucia and the other girls" to be tutored till one in the afternoon. Miss Peabody charged nothing for these lessons because in this way she felt she could make a return to Mrs. Rice for her hospitality.

"I am delightfully situated," Elizabeth wrote, dwelling upon the occasional use of the Rice horse and chaise, Mr. Rice's enjoyment of her "society and conversation" at breakfast (his wife was a semi-invalid who never rose before noon), his satisfaction at seeing his children made to behave properly for the first time in their lives. Christmas at the Rices' was a lavish affair with many gifts for Miss Peabody; "an embroidered apron from Mrs. Rice, a tortoise-shell card case from Mr. Rice and a most beautiful seal cornelian fixed on a cross of gold having the motto of our family with coat of arms."

Perhaps it was the Rices' excessive gratitude which kept Elizabeth from being really happy with them. Not only did she believe that it was more blessed to give than to receive, but giving was necessary to her well-being. Her mother and her friends would have said that this was pure "disinterestedness." But it was partly pride. Old General Palmer himself loved to bestow largess whether he could afford it or not and his blood ran in Elizabeth's veins. She began to work on a new idea for a private school. During times of depression, boys must be educated as usual — girls could stay at home. Miss Peabody therefore would run a boys' school. A woman could not do such a thing, she was told, but men conducted girls' schools and turn-about was fair play. Elizabeth was wise enough, however, to count only on little boys, "to teach them Latin and first things."

"I wish Elizabeth could be at home," Mrs. Peabody said. "But I know she could not, for she is before her time in Salem at least. People cannot appreciate her mind or her mode of teaching. She will not manoeuvre, she will not flatter weak parents nor impose on ignorant ones." Elizabeth's plan was for a boys' school in Boston and "Willy Rice, the little Borlands, the little Blisses" were enrolled for a year; each to pay a hundred dollars. She began to visualize the schoolroom, and the room of her own where she would soon live, beholden to no one, but in a position to help others.

This was how matters stood in July 1834. Then Elizabeth renewed an old friendship and found herself able to do something for someone even sooner than she had supposed.

Mr. and Mrs. Bronson Alcott came to Boston to visit Mrs. Alcott's father, Colonel May. The school which Alcott had started in Germantown had come to an end, Russell was in Philadelphia, and Alcott had come to Boston with the idea of making some sort of fresh start. He called on Miss Peabody, armed with journals and letters written by his Germantown scholars, "all under ten years of age." He "stayed and talked like an embodiment of light and yet calm, solemn and simple as ever."

"I told him I wanted him to make an effort for a school," said Elizabeth, "and he said he wished to. . . . I told Mr. Alcott I would enquire about children in town and see whether there was a chance for him." Elizabeth started in that very evening, reading aloud to Mr. and Mrs. Rice the children's journals which Alcott had left with her. They promptly "engaged Willy." By the end of the next afternoon Elizabeth had transferred all the little boys previously promised for her school and was campaigning for more for Alcott.

Elizabeth stopped in at Colonel May's, found Alcott out but Mrs. Alcott at home and as articulate as always. "The school would never succeed without more book-learning" and Mr. Alcott "would never put his mind to that. He needed an assistant and yet it was out of the question to find an assistant who was competent and that he could afford to pay."

"I told her I would be his assistant," Elizabeth said. "That is, I would teach two hours and a half a day for a year in his school for such compensation as he could afford to pay. When Mrs. Alcott found I was really in earnest she was in a *rapture* — and Mr. A. too when he came in."

News of Sophia's health was extremely encouraging by midsummer of 1834. Mary's exile might last only another winter and Elizabeth explained matters to Alcott. "I told him I could only engage until your return," she wrote Mary. The "compensation" agreed upon was a hundred dollars a quarter (or two hundred dollars less than Elizabeth could have had if she had kept for a school of her own the six little boys promised to her). The Alcotts "both said the terms were altogether too small" and they were right. This was Elizabeth at her happiest, giving more than she could afford.

Lizzie was no saint, however, and Mrs. Alcott had but to bring up the subject of William Russell, her former partner, to prove it. "You have no idea what a sad account Mrs. Alcott gives of the Russells," Elizabeth said, almost licking her lips as she wrote to

Mary. "Mrs. Russell's sufferings from Mr. Russell's selfishness are all that we might imagine they would come to — an absolute destitution of every comfort at home, in order that *his* taste, *his* wardrobe, *his* whims might be satisfied. He has now gone into Philadelphia, taking a house of 600 dollars rent, furnished two parlors magnificently on borrowed money, made so many engagements as to be irregular in the discharge of them all and losing the little business that he got. The sooner he dies and his wife and children are in the almshouse the better for all, I should say." Elizabeth could go pretty far when aroused. "The very thought of them is enough to drive me raving distracted — and they think of coming here next spring!"

Mrs. Alcott was ever a copious source of gossip. Russell had told Alcott, she said, that if Elizabeth Peabody "were not shadowed a little by her personal objects (the necessity of the income from her school for her family), she would be ideal enough to answer the demands of her profession." Elizabeth punctuated that with four exclamation marks. "Mr. Russell's school has been reduced to one scholar," she added with understandable malice.

Unfortunately, it never occurred to Elizabeth that Alcott had been under the influence of Russell and that he too might be extravagant. Various locations for his new school were discussed and Miss Peabody made no protest when a room in the new Masonic Temple on Tremont Street was chosen. Winding staircases in the gaunt twin towers of this Neo-Gothic building led to an auditorium lighted by the upper section of an arched Gothic window. "And those two little holes" (as Elizabeth described the quatrefoils on the façade of the structure) also let in a little light. Elizabeth's description places the schoolroom three flights above the street, and when she said it was "about 60 feet solid" she came very close to the truth. It was an intimate little sixty-five by forty feet, with a nineteen-foot stud. A "stove apparatus" served to emphasize the chill of the outer walls, while "gas illumination" supplemented the Gothic-filtered daylight. Whatever else the room was, it was impressive. Alcott liked it. "Temple School" he named it, and on it he based his fondest hopes.

Again, Elizabeth should have been reminded of William Russell, but was not, when Alcott told her how he planned to furnish Temple School. "Mr. Alcott told me how elegantly he was going to furnish his school and we went into the Italians' where we selected some casts." A bust of Socrates and one of Plato were chosen to go on high pedestals at the front corners of the room.

"A head of Christ, in bas-relief larger than life," was selected to go over Mr. Alcott's chair behind his great pulpitlike desk. The Italians also supplied plaster casts of Psyche, a "child aspiring," a figure of "Silence with its finger raised," and busts of Shakespeare, Milton and Scott for good measure. What all this was costing no one asked. Elizabeth contributed a long table, a green sofa and her portrait of Channing. From Mrs. Rice she borrowed two large land-scapes in oil.

Alcott went back to Germantown to wind up his affairs while Elizabeth continued to labor in his behalf in Boston. Her friends George Ripley and George Hillard were starting a new periodical, contributions to be paid for — so they said. They asked Elizabeth to write an article for the sample copy they were preparing as a prospectus. "I gave George Hillard a piece I had written about Infant Education on the Alcott plan," Elizabeth told Mary. Elizabeth was to edit a page under the heading "Juvenile Instruction" and for this sample copy she included a "conversation" she had had with her Sunday School scholars.

Elizabeth urged her sisters in Cuba to teach the Morell children by the "conversation" method and to record everything that teacher and pupil said. Only Sophia must try to be accurate! "There is a great deal of difference between her accounts and yours," Elizabeth told Mary. It was Mary she believed, knowing full well that Sophia's artistic temperament would tempt her to paint a pretty picture in words as well as on canvas and that the simple truth would never strike her as quite pretty enough.

"Mr. Alcott can never remember so as to put down his conversations which is a great pity," Elizabeth observed. She had no doubt that she herself could be trusted as an accurate reporter.

In September 1834 Temple School opened, with "eighteen scholars, eight girls and ten boys." They were a "lovely set of children," but Elizabeth could see that "the three Tuckermans will be hardest to handle." Next day there were twenty students sitting at their little tables facing the wall. Some were there because Dr. Channing had endorsed the school but more than half of them were enrolled as the direct result of Elizabeth's calls, her letters enclosing Alcott's cards.

Although Elizabeth had agreed to spend only two and a half hours at Temple School, using the rest of her time to augment a slender living, she became fascinated with Alcott's methods and soon found herself arriving at nine and staying all day. When she was not teaching Latin, arithmetic and geography, she listened to Mr. Alcott's "conversations" with the children which seemed to her little short of Godlike — too beautiful, too precious, to lose. "Someone" should write down these immortal words, she had told Mary. Elizabeth was like everyone else when it came to seeing something that ought to be done. She differed from most people by invariably electing herself to difficult, arduous tasks instead of leaving them to "someone."

At first the notes that Elizabeth made, writing so fast that her hand hurt, were used "only for discipline." But on reading them over, both Alcott and Elizabeth began to feel that here was an idea for a book. *Record of a School Exemplifying the Principles and Methods of Moral Culture*, it would be called, and the "Recorder" was Alcott's name for Elizabeth. She was pleased when Alcott read in full to the children a poem she had written and suggested that she "record it" in the book. Five weeks of straight journal, culled here and expanded there, made up the first part of the book. The second section, under the heading "Self-analysis," dealt with Mr. Alcott's talks with the children on "aspiration," "insight" and so on. With perfection as their goal, these primary school children searched their hearts for secret sin and when they found it, earnestly promised to improve — or most of them did. "Is it aspiration to seek knowledge for our own good alone?" Mr. Alcott asked them. They knew that it was not. "Which of you have gone inward and viewed yourselves?" And Miss Peabody faithfully recorded, "None held up hands." Mr. Alcott strove to correct this deplorable condition.

While *Record of a School* was giving Elizabeth symptoms of writer's cramp by day, she nevertheless continued to write to Mary in Cuba each evening. The series of letters she wrote at this time might be called "Off the Record." The three little Tuckermans, although members of a family famous for "Christian philanthropy," "demurred" when asked if they ever should be punished. By December 29, "Off the Record" letters continued, that impressive room in the Masonic Temple was as cold as any tomb in Mt. Auburn Cemetery. The scholars arrived and took their seats at nine. Mr. Alcott asked them if there was anything they might want before eleven — since walking about or even wriggling and squirming in their chairs would be forbidden until that time. "A great many burst out that they would want to go to the fire." Elizabeth was in sympathy with this idea herself since the thermometer was below zero outside and the heat from the "stove aparatus" in the room could hardly be felt a few feet away. But Mr. Alcott discussed the advantages of self-denial.

"During the conversation, the three oldest boys, who have the coldest seats, maintained to the last that they did not think it worthwhile to attempt to bear the cold." One boy said "he did not think it a virtue to bear cold, not merely in this instance, but in general." Bronson Alcott assumed that this child was joking (although that was something he never did himself). "He passed over it, saying that he had no time except for serious conversation."

"I shall give my services for the first quarter," Elizabeth told her sisters when the end of the quarter came and she was not paid. According to Alcott's accounts his receipts for the year 1834–1835 were $1,784.00 [3] but as the end of each succeeding quarter rolled around, Elizabeth's services continued to be a gift. There was of course the rent of the room at the Temple to be paid; the great desk behind which Alcott sat had been especially designed and built for him and it must be paid for. Miss Peabody was a generous creditor.

Counting on her four hundred dollars from Alcott, Elizabeth had told Mrs. Rice that she would no longer need to be a guest at the Rices' house. And because of her ill-health, Mrs. Rice had decided that she could no longer keep house without Miss Peabody as unpaid governess. She had sent the children to boarding schools and she and Mr. Rice lived "at board" themselves. Elizabeth had found a home for herself at 21 Bedford Street, where the Alcotts were also boarding. Her parlor was about ten feet square, the bedroom opening out of it affording "barely room enough to stand." But Elizabeth was happy to have a little place to call her own. In front of the coal-burning grate she placed a bright brass fender of her own and over the mantel she hung George Flagg's painting "Contentment," which he had given her and which had recently been exhibited at the Athenæum. It showed a young boy leaning out of an open window and George's Uncle Allston had praised it highly. For the wall over her green sofa, Elizabeth wanted the picture Sophia had painted and which had been exhibited at the Athenæum after Sophia's departure for Cuba. It was not the original landscape Sophia had hoped to be able to show, but a copy of a Salvator Rosa, rich in light and shadow, vigorous in composition. The picture had been displayed as the work of Miss Peabody without credit to Rosa and Sophia had been greatly distressed over the mistake. When the exhibit was over, Elizabeth took the picture to her friends the Ripleys, having no place of her own for it. Now, when she went to get it, the Reverend George Ripley thanked her profusely, told her that Sophia's picture was worth at least three hundred dollars and that it gave him great joy, in his modest circumstances, to have received such a gift! Elizabeth could not bring herself to explain and take it away.

But the fashion for sculpture had now arrived and Lizzie made up for the loss of the painting. Her "little black bust of Locke" went on the mantel and her "Niobe" she placed on a pedestal in a corner of the room. Now all was in readiness for Mr. Mann to call. He came to ask if there were any letters from Mary. He threatened to steal the sketch of her that Sophia had sent and asked Elizabeth to have Sophia make one for him at once. For Elizabeth, he brought his latest work, "a Report of the Lunatic Hospital," with which she was delighted — as he knew she would be.

Eight articles in the *Journal of Education* and two in the *Annals of Education*, the Reading Parties and a few private tutoring lessons helped Elizabeth to pay for her modest quarters. She spent many a long evening copying out her notes and preparing *Record of a School*. Many of Alcott's ideas were not her own. As the daughter of a doctor, for example, she could not believe with Alcott that "illness of the body was the result of wrong-doing somewhere" — but she rightly judged that here was a theory to interest the public and she understood her duties as editor pretty well. Of course her anonymity as the Recorder did not last long, and it was a shock to Elizabeth to discover that her friends assumed that she endorsed all of Alcott's theories, just because she had written them down.

James Monroe printed *Record of a School* in 1835. It attracted a great deal of attention in educational circles both in the United States and abroad. Mr. Emerson wrote to Elizabeth to congratulate her on a delightful, readable book, and the friendship between Elizabeth and Waldo was renewed. It looked as if *Record of a School* would sell in a modest way, pay for itself, and even make a little money. Elizabeth's translation of an essay by the French philosopher de Gérando also sold a little — because of the interest the *Record* had aroused. Just as it seemed as though things were going to be easier for Elizabeth Peabody, a warehouse was burned and all remaining copies of these two books were lost. And now Elizabeth understood the sort of contract she had made with Monroe. It was no worse than customary in that day and age, but she found that she, personally, must bear the loss. *Record of a School* brought recognition to Alcott. To Elizabeth Peabody it brought both recognition and misfortune.

From the beginning, Elizabeth had made it clear to Alcott that she would assist him only until her sisters should return from Cuba. When that should happen, she and her sister Mary would once more attempt to establish a school of their own. And in 1835, "May the new year bring you safe to New England" wrote Mrs. Peabody to Mary and Sophia. While Sophia was not entirely cured of her headaches, she was definitely better and she now "dreamed of home" rather than of death or blindness. It was agreed that the two sisters would take the first available sailing vessel bound for Boston.

On April 28, Mary and Sophia left "La Recompensa" in the early dawn.[4] At noon they broke their journey at the hacienda of a friend of the Morells until the heat of the day should be over and before nightfall "frescoed houses heralded the city." This time, the sisters did not stay at the American Consulate but went to the luxurious home of Caroline Fernandez, married sister of Fernando and Manuel de Layas. As they climbed the ceremonial staircase from the inner courtyard, the two Peabody girls were met and kissed on each cheek by Caroline, then by her mother-in-law who stood a few steps higher, then by Caroline's grandmother at the top of the stairs. They were conducted to a high-studded room with curtained doors and marble floors where the rest of the family received them with all the courtesy of old Spain. Then Negro maid-servants led them away to a perfumed bath, refreshed them with scented powder the like of which they had never seen before — and arrayed them in loose, flowing white robes of fine linen. "Mary went back to the hall after these ceremonials" but the invalid Sophia "retired to a white linen tent-bed, more luxurious than eastern monarch ever possessed."

In the evening, Sophia arose to listen from the balcony to band music from the plaza — while Mary walked abroad and returned to report "that the ladies were dressed as if for a private ball and with heads uncovered except by transparent veils."

Next morning, Sophia was taken to the chamber of Madame Fernandez and shown a painting of the Magdalen. It was by the great Murillo, they told her — but age had so obscured the canvas that little was to be seen. Sophia dipped her finger "in some aromatic oil upon the toilette table and touched a corner of the picture. A gorgeous crimson tint was revealed." Sophia proceeded to clean the painting, while her friends looked on as though beholding a miracle. Not in their generation had they ever seen "the golden glory of the floating hair, the majesty of contrition in the upraised brow and lustrous eyes." In their gratitude, they promptly offered to let her take it home to the United States to copy, but Sophia was frightened to death at the very idea. She dissuaded them and they promised to bring the picture to her themselves on their next visit.

The sisters sailed next day but not before Sophia had made a portrait sketch of each member of the family. She had not quite finished Madame Fernandez when word came that it was time to go. Don Pepe, head of the household, sent word to the ship's captain. There would be no sailing of the *William Henry* till Miss Sophia had finished her picture and was ready to leave.

Before the sisters sailed from Cuba, while they were on the high seas, and after they were at home, Elizabeth made plans for them. At first it seemed simple enough to begin over again with a school in Boston. Eliza Lee Cabot, now Mrs. Charles Follen, had helped Elizabeth to "gather a school" and she could be relied upon again. But in 1835, Professor Follen was dismissed from his position as lecturer in German at Harvard because of his antislavery activities. Elizabeth learned that the Follens planned to start a school of their own. They would never succeed, Elizabeth's friends told her. Dr. Follen had become too unpopular. But Elizabeth scouted the idea, declaring that no two people better fitted to establish a school could be found anywhere. Only to Mary did she admit regret.

A new idea occurred to Elizabeth at once. A law had been passed in Spain forbidding the children of Cuban planters to be educated in the United States. The result was an immense popularity for an American education and the smuggling of children! Young Edward Morell was coming to the United States with Mary and Sophia but that fact was to be kept very quiet indeed and he would not so much as be seen with them till after the *William Henry* sailed. Elizabeth visualized a boarding school with Mary and Sophia as Spanish-speaking teachers, herself as head mistress. Mary must see about prospective pupils and Sophia must study Spanish much harder. But Cuban planters were interested only in well-established schools, one in Philadelphia being particularly popular.

Mr. Alcott's school was succeeding, Elizabeth decided. She would put in a word for either or both of her sisters, at the rate of a hundred dollars a quarter — which she was not getting but had never ceased to expect.

In the spring of 1836 Elizabeth, with that glowing faith in the future which made her at the same time so lovable and so exasperating, was beginning a new journal and "a new era of things." The journal was one of many begun and never finished. The "new era" dawned at the Alcott's house with, as Lizzie put it, "the plan of devoting my own time to a more regular prosecution of study than I have ever had opportunity for since I left Salem for Lancaster. I have a pleasant, well furnished room at Mr. Alcott's, 26 Front Street, for which with board [and here the sheet is accidentally torn] equivalent to two hours' time at the School, afternoons, teaching Latin and [again the tear, so that what else Elizabeth agreed to teach is lost] three hours on Wednesday morning in keeping Record in his school. . . .

"Today, when I first arrived, I played with the baby, my namesake, till dinnertime." This was "Beth," so lovingly portrayed in later years by her sister Louisa in *Little Women*. The naming of their child for Miss Peabody was an affectionate and grateful gesture, decided upon when Elizabeth had so generously helped in the establishing of Temple School. It was a pity that Miss Peabody's modest salary could not also have been paid in cash.

Elizabeth appreciated the offer of a home, however, and arrived feeling confident that as a member of the family group she would be able to give pleasure to everyone. Had not Mr. Rice enjoyed her conversation at dinner? She discovered the first night that, genius though he might be, Alcott was almost impossible to live with. Elizabeth brought up the subject of Mr. Graham who was lecturing in Salem and Boston concerning the merits of unbolted or "Graham flour." Mr. Graham had stated that the eating of "Graham bread" would prolong human life to two centuries, and Elizabeth humorously questioned both the plausibility of Mr. Graham and the desirability of living to be two hundred years old in any case.

Alcott sprang to the defense of Mr. Graham and accused the astonished Miss Peabody of having made "a suicidal statement." Elizabeth would have liked to laugh. But she merely defended herself by saying that she thought "that when we had lost a dear friend, it was perfectly pious to rejoice that we should probably not live an hundred and fifty years afterwards. Mr. Alcott said this was selfish and asked what claim a friend had on us? A question I did not understand in the connection and could not answer."

It was not that Elizabeth objected to "Grahamism," she reflected. She was willing to risk the night air and leave her bedroom window open, she liked fruits and vegetables and even wholewheat bread. But Graham began his lecture in Salem with pictures of bearded patriarchs and Elizabeth thought they were funny. He also made statements against doctors which were unfair. But Alcott now turned his Jovian thunders upon all professional men and upon doctors in particular as "a greater evil than good." Mr. Graham was right, Alcott said, when he insisted that doctors "fed like vampires on the community for the sake of money."

The stooped figure, the gentle, careworn face, of her father came into Elizabeth's mind and she ceased to have any desire to laugh. Perhaps Dr. Peabody was not the most brilliant physician in the world, perhaps not the best dentist although a good one — but his had been a life of service to mankind which he performed to the best of his ability. Returning to her room, Elizabeth confided to her diary that she saw difficulties ahead.

"I resolved in the future I would take more pains to be silent on a subject on which it is possible for Mr. Alcott to differ from me, or I from him. But I think I shall find it quite a trial to my patience to sit silent under this wholesale abuse of whatever has become the order of society or rather of whole classes of men. There seems to be a little envy at work where there is no more than gracious appreciation of what institutions and the Past have done for mankind.

"[Alcott] subjects everything to the test of his talismanic words, and as they answer to them in his predisposed ear, they take their places — nor does he do anything more, at the utmost of his liberality, than to endure the suggestion of a contrary view. It seems no part of his plan to search the thoughts and views of other minds in any faith that they will help his own. He only seems to look in books for what agrees with his own thoughts — and he rather avoids than seeks any communication with persons who differ from himself."

Within a few days, Alcott had ceased even to "endure" a point of view other than his own and Elizabeth had been warned not to talk about anything controversial. There were some young boys boarding with the Alcotts, among them Willy Rice, brought there through Miss Peabody's recommendation. Alcott felt that it would be bad for these young people to hear any opinions but his own.

Unquestionably, it was hard on Alcott to have to live with anyone as adept in debate as Miss Peabody. He was happier when arguing with seven-year-olds about enduring cold. Miss Peabody could be silenced temporarily but not for good, and within a few days she brought up the most controversial subject of all.

"Tuesday I had my Reading Class and we read about the Saxons . . . A good many hints might be taken from these old historians of the emancipation of the serfs — which would be valuable to show what should be avoided and what might be initiated by our states in the work of gradual emancipation. I merely said this much at dinner, avoiding the word 'gradual' and there was no explosion. But the subject was dropped." Poor Alcott! He might have said, with truth, that mankind never learns from history — but he was silent, perhaps for the first time in his life.

"I spent the evening again till one o'clock copying the Record and have completed the first seven conversations, which are all very fine," Elizabeth said. *Conversations with Children on the Gospels*, the new book would be called. It would bring not mere misfortune, but disaster, both to Alcott and Elizabeth Peabody. But, "I am very little of a conservative and exceedingly trustful of the future," she said — seeing herself with wonderful clarity.

CHAPTER NINE

The House in Charter Street

A SQUARE three-storied frame house crowded close to Charter Street as though determined to keep a sharp eye on all passers-by. Massive chimneys, small-paned windows and generous proportions proclaimed its pre-Revolutionary origin, while a portico with engaged pilasters, two fluted and two plain, indicated an effort to "modernize" its rather grim façade in the Salem Neo-Classic manner.[1] But in 1835 the house was not yet prized for its antiquity and the "modern" doorway was already merely out of date. The Peabodys were able to acquire the house — as a home for themselves and as an office for the doctor — at a reasonable figure.

To be sure, the Peabody parlor windows opened directly upon the old Charter Street burying ground, and prospective patients, waiting their turn, could count the leaning headstones and ponder upon their fate should the good doctor's remedies fail them. But patients were still few and far between and business was not likely to improve. Like his daughter Lizzie, Dr. Peabody was "before his time in Salem." At a period when the average Salemite demanded a good money's worth of vile-tasting medicine guaranteed to give violent emetic or purgative effects, Dr. Peabody was a homeopath and dispensed pink pills or sweet, colorless liquids which inflicted little, if any, additional suffering upon his patients. Even if they recovered from their illness, they felt cheated.

Dentistry was going rather better and Sophia reported more than once that the parlor was full of ladies waiting for Father to fix their teeth. But in spite of Dr. Peabody's radical ideas about the preservation of teeth, dentistry was still mostly a matter of extraction. And in this line, Dr. Peabody was preparing a bombshell for his fellow townspeople. In Boston, hypnotism, or "mesmerism" as they called it, was all the rage. Elizabeth had translated from the French an article about Mesmer, the German scientist, and she felt sure that she herself had "magnetism." Boston dentists were using hypnotism to perform painless extractions and while Dr. Peabody scoffed at Lizzie's personal pretensions, he nevertheless acquired a young hypnotist as a partner. Dr. Fiske assisted at perfectly painless extractions and most certainly the experiments were the talk of the town. But Dr. Peabody gained few if any new patients thereby. The whole thing savored too much of witchcraft to be popular in old Salem!

Dr. Peabody had time on his hands as always and he would have loved to spend it in his office, experimenting, theorizing — perhaps writing another book. But behind the house on Charter Street was a fertile but neglected garden which Mrs. Peabody intended should fill the doctor's idle hours. He found himself digging out dead currant bushes and planting a large vegetable garden, a project more likely to pay dividends than any he would have chosen of his own free will. There were seeds Mary had brought home to her mother from Cuba now growing in pots as house plants. The neighbors had exclaimed over them and now they must be set outdoors for the summer, brought in as house plants again in the fall. "Father was sure everything would die and Mother equally sure everything would live and when he found all the sweet company held up their heads he declared that Mother was a second Abel and that Heaven had regard unto her tillage."

It was Sophia who recorded the progress of the new garden and she who told of much cutting and turning and piecing of old carpets inside the house; the arranging of them so that bedrooms which had no stove would have at least a covered floor. She had returned from Cuba confident that her health was really improved. But here she was being "spared" an active part in the work of moving to a new home, ordered by her mother to "sit in her sweet room at her center table and look straight into Colonel Pickman's garden of flowers."

"I had an indefinite hope that such a great stir as a voyage to Cuba would alter the state of things but they are settling down again," Sophia wrote to Elizabeth. She was copying Allston's "Jessica and Lorenzo," promised long before her Cuba journey; and once more, when the work went well, she felt herself possessed by a force beyond her, mysteriously expressed through her brush upon canvas. All too often, this force left her and she sank exhausted into the hammock which had been slung across a corner of her room.

When Sophia's headaches returned, young Dr. Fiske was sure that he could cure them by mesmerism. He found himself with plenty of spare time due to the conspicuous lack of Salem patients willing to be "put to sleep." Sophia reported daily for treatments and said she felt "soothed." But when Dr. Fiske tried to induce hypnotic sleep in Sophia, he failed, much to his surprise and disappointment. She seemed so gentle and so pliable! He never suspected that Sophia had a strong will and that she prized the freedom of her spirit.

Elizabeth had often said that she could arrange a position either for Mary or for Sophia in Alcott's school, and the reasonably large enrollment at the school always beguiled Elizabeth into thinking that Alcott would keep his promise to pay. Soon after her return from Cuba, Mary went to see Alcott but was impressed only with the tremendous amount of work he would expect of her. "I am glad, dear Mary, you refused Mr. A's proposal," her mother said. "You can do better, I think." And Mary thought so too. She fitted up a room in the house on Charter Street as a school, in the all too familiar Peabody family pattern. Sophia would help by teaching drawing and also Spanish, if she could find any pupils. Elizabeth would continue with Alcott for, as her mother put it, "Energetic beings are raised up to carry on the great moral religious purposes of this world and I believe Elizabeth is one of them and that future generations will bless her." Mary was perfectly content to leave the regeneration of the world to Lizzie, but she renounced Boston with regret. She left Mr. Mann to Elizabeth with misgivings.

"Yesterday I received a letter from dear Mr. Mann," Elizabeth wrote. "He says he received 'a sweet but mournful' letter from you. He certainly praises your letters, which he does not mine. . . . I have urged him, in reply, to go to Salem and spend Sunday as you invite. Can you not ask him to stay all night when he comes? And Sophia could give him her room or put him in that front upper chamber. 'Twould be polite, I think."

Naturally Mrs. Peabody would not think for a moment of asking Sophia to give up her room but she was surprised to see the care with which Mary put to rights that "front upper chamber." Small square-paned windows were polished till they shone, the curtains freshly washed and ironed. From among Mary's few personal treasures, the choicest were brought to adorn the guest chamber and still Mary seemed dissatisfied. When Mrs. Peabody remarked that Mr. Mann was not, after all, more important than any other guest, she was startled to see a sudden flush on Mary's cheeks. Mary was usually so pale! Delicate hollows had appeared under her cheek bones and her gray-green eyes seemed more deeply set, more shadowy than ever. A touch of color was becoming, however, and Mary's eyes were smiling as she turned quickly away from her mother's too inquisitive glance.

Mr. Mann came, not once but often, and his presence changed the whole atmosphere of the house on Charter Street. He dared to joke with Mrs. Peabody, serious though she considered it her duty to be — and she liked it. Dr. Peabody had always enjoyed laughter, as Sophia once remarked, and now he looked forward to visits from Horace Mann for the sake of his anecdotes and his swift sallies. Dr. Peabody even went along with Mary when Mann was Lyceum Lecturer in Salem and admitted that Mann was better than George Hillard, who came next — but not as much better as Mary said.

During the winter of 1835 and 1836 an "unknown friend" gave Mary season tickets to lectures in Boston. It could have been Miss Guild or Miss Rawlins, or any one of several lonely and well-to-do ladies who liked to have Mary take tea with them or even spend the night in an elegant but almost empty home on Beacon Hill. Elizabeth assumed that it was Miss Guild. But by an odd coincidence, Mr. Mann was often at the lectures; and when he was not, he happened to meet Mary afterwards and take her to the train for Salem or wherever else she told him she was going. There was a pleased look in Mr. Mann's eyes that brought the quick, becoming flush to Mary's cheeks and she asked him to convey to the donor of her ticket her sincere appreciation. He would admit nothing, lawyer that he was, but his warm hand-clasp at parting was something for Mary to dream about in secret.

Elizabeth was seeing less of Mr. Mann these days and Mary was thankful. Consistent with her reiterated belief that Mr. Mann's first wife was in heaven yet close by, Elizabeth was solicitous and affectionate but almost as "sisterly" as even Mary could wish. Although making it clear that she did not consider her position permanent, Elizabeth was nevertheless absorbed in her work at Alcott's school and anxious to make a success of her association with that difficult man.[2]

On October 8, 1835, Elizabeth completed a letter to Alcott putting certain of her ideas into writing, since by now she knew that

Alcott never paid any attention to anything she said. Alcott carefully copied Elizabeth's letter.

> I rec'ed a note from Miss E. Peabody giving a plan of study for the quarter — made out much like mine. To this plan she adds:

> Having done with External matters I will now make a remark or two upon your views and practices of a more general character, which I *do not* agree with. And this I do merely that you may understand me, and not because I have the least expectation or intention of influencing you.

> One thing is that I think you are liable to injure the modesty and unconsciousness of good children, by making them reflect too much upon their actual superiority. . . . A collective disadvantage . . . is that of being talked about by the whole city, which is a great misfortune I think, though of an external character.

In Elizabeth's first *Record of a School*, the names of the children did not appear; but she was now preparing a second one for him and it was his intention to put in names. It was to this that she had reference.

Elizabeth's intention was to be patient with Alcott, to remember his many virtues. If she could have read his diary, she would have been surprised at her success. He was pleased to ride to Concord with her "to hear the Rev. Mr. Emerson." When Elizabeth took him to Emerson's house after church, it was his first visit to a home he was afterwards to frequent; the "Rev. Mr. Emerson" would become his stanch friend and benefactor.

On Sunday, May 22, Alcott's children were baptized at their home by his wife's brother, the Reverend Mr. May. The third little daughter was called Elizabeth Peabody Alcott on that day. It was not until later that Alcott crossed out the name Peabody and wrote in Sewell.

Miss Peabody took Alcott with her to tea at the Allstons' — where she was asked because of an article on Allston which she had just written for the *American Monthly Review*. Allston was so pleased with her article that Elizabeth said she felt as though she were receiving a proposal of marriage and she got so flustered that she started away without her bonnet. She was thirty-two, she reminded herself, and Allston twenty-five years older than she, his

interest purely "fatherly." Fortunately for the blushing Elizabeth, Alcott noticed nothing. Allston had said something about
Coleridge to which Alcott took exception and he spent a very
happy afternoon setting Allston right.

As always, Allston remembered to ask Miss Peabody for news
about her sister Sophia. He was delighted to hear that Sophia had
sold her copy of his "Jessica and Lorenzo" and that she was able
to get at least the promise of a hundred dollars a canvas these days
— twice what she used to charge. It showed she was building a reputation. Allston hoped of course that Sophia found time to do original
work as well as copying and he was disappointed when Elizabeth
said not. That happy middle ground, where an artist is flicked by
the whip of financial requirements but not terrified into failure
because of debts and stark necessity, was something Allston knew
it would be useless to explain although no one understood it better
than he.

Sophia came to visit the Alcotts on June 9, 1836. She was still
hopeful that the Cuba journey had restored her health although
headaches had begun to be more frequent. Elizabeth had urged her
to try her hand at teaching in Alcott's school, assuring her that
she had but to "teach without worrying" — though she did not say
how this was to be done. Sophia found herself much more interested when Alcott talked to her about illustrations for his forthcoming book, *Conversations with Children on the Gospels*. Mr.
Graeter, her former instructor, had done one illustration for Alcott
and Sophia felt as though she would be making progress in her
own chosen field if her pictures should appear with his. She was
dismayed, however, to find that Alcott wanted nothing original.
He wanted ten or twelve copies of "old masters" beginning with
a "head of Jesus from Leonardo da Vinci." How could she make
da Vinci look right in a woodcut! Meanwhile the students in the
school were reviewing the conversations which Elizabeth had already recorded and Sophia was put to work setting down any ideas
the children wished to add when the questions were asked them
again. She wrote as fast as she could, feeling important and efficient
— just like Lizzie. Doubts arose in Sophia's mind; what would
people think? Were some of Alcott's questions "indelicate"? They
were not meant to be, that was certain. Alcott was as pure-minded
as the children themselves, all of whom came from sheltered homes
where they had been brought up in the strict Victorian tradition.
In any case, there was no time to think while Sophia's pen raced

over the page. It had always been hard for her to hurry and some-times the conversations got ahead of her. She would be thankful when Elizabeth came back.

Elizabeth had gone to Lowell to take care of Lydia Haven. This was no happy vacation such as Sophia had often enjoyed with the Havens; that cough of Lydia's had finally been recognized as tuberculosis and a journey for health was proposed but Sam could not leave his law practice and Lydia was too weak to go alone. There had been a time when Sam Haven had complained that Miss Peabody still looked upon Lydia as a pupil of hers and tried to arrange her life for her even after she was married. All that was forgiven and forgotten now as Sam remembered how much Elizabeth loved his beautiful Lydia. He sent for her, knowing she would come. Passage was arranged on a steam packet bound for Mobile since surely "at the South" Lydia would recover. But it was too late and Lydia was not able to leave her bed when the steamer sailed. In the early summer of 1836, Lydia, who was "so timid about death," had faced it with Elizabeth Peabody at her side to assure her of life beyond the grave.

A box came to Salem from Sam Haven with all of Lydia's lovely clothes that she had wanted Sophia to have but it was years before Sophia could bring herself to enjoy them as Lydia wanted her to do. Lydia had been her first, almost her only intimate friend. Lydia's little boy was taken to Salem, where Mary loved and cared for him as if he were her own. Sam Haven claimed his son as soon as possible, however, for he said he felt "twice widowed without him."

Elizabeth returned to Alcott's school where the *Record* she had written and Sophia's additions were ready for the press. Gossiping tongues had been silent when she entered Boston drawing rooms but they were busy at the Havens' home where perhaps not every-one knew that Miss Peabody was connected with Alcott's school. Elizabeth read over *Conversations with Children on the Gospels* with a fresh viewpoint and better judgment as to how they would be received by the public. As the *Conversations* stood, they would never do!

Alcott might have received a qualified consent to his determination to instruct in religion (on Wednesdays only) had he been content to draw fire from that direction alone. In all probability, he had originally had no intention of discussing birth in connection with the Gospels, but he began with the vision of Zacharias. Ten of the children were under seven years old while eight were between the ages of seven and ten. Alcott's questions about the birth of John the Baptist brought out the fact that only two of the children knew that there was a "usual way" for babies to be born, while the others thought that angels might bring them as a great surprise to their mothers. "A mother suffers when she has a child," said Alcott. "When she is going to have a child, she gives up her body to God and he works upon it in a mysterious way, and with her aid, brings forth the child's spirit in a little body of its own." A more beautiful explanation could hardly be given, Elizabeth thought; but the questions Alcott asked, so that "no one should have wrong thoughts," would look as if he were forcing little children to talk about sex, whether they would or no. Boston would be up in arms about it, as Elizabeth could see now that she read over all the material. All the good that Alcott's school might do would be destroyed.

Elizabeth had a further reason for feeling positively panic-stricken lest the *Conversations* should be printed as they stood. Suppose it got out that the artist, Sophia Peabody, had recorded "improprieties" for Alcott! Mary had feared that Sophia's gay, carefree letters from Cuba would be called "wild" by those to whom Elizabeth had showed them. There was still the shipboard romance of which Burroughs might speak and Mrs. Cleveland, piqued perhaps because of Sophia's indifference to her young kinsman, Harry, might start new rumors. Elizabeth was fiercely maternal toward this youngest and dearest of sisters and she told Alcott that he must suppress his book. She wrote, since talking would be useless, and she withdrew her consent to have material used which she had recorded.

Apparently, Alcott made no reply. On the first day of August, he noted that Miss Peabody had left his school never to return. She had often told him that she planned to start a school for herself; his accounts showed no record of any money being paid for her services — but he was astounded. Where would he get another assistant? Margaret Fuller helped out but not for long, being too practical to work for nothing. Meanwhile, a letter came from Elizabeth Peabody from Worcester where she was visiting friends. It was dated August 7, Alcott said, and he copied it into one of his many notebooks.

DEAR SIR:

The very day after my letter to you I received a communication from a friend; by which I learn that much more extensively than either you or I were aware of is the discussion of such subjects as it is known were discussed in connection with the birth of Christ censured even by friends of your system and of yourself, and that something of an impression was gratuitously taken up that I left the School on that account — an impression for which I can in no ways account, except it was thought I ought to leave it . . . A great deal is repeated, I find, and many persons liking the school in every other respect, think it decisive against putting female children to it especially.

I have told you this in the spirit of friendship, and hope you will not despise it. I am conscious of the effect of a few weeks' freedom from the excitement of being a part of the School, or taking down that exaggerated feeling which made every detail of it seem so very important to the great cause of Spiritual Culture and I never was under half the illusion in this respect that you were.

But with respect to the Record: whatever may be said of the wisdom of pursuing your plans as you have hitherto done in the school-room, where you always command the spirits of those around you (only subject to the risk of having your mere words repeated or misinterpreted) I feel more and more that these questionable parts ought not to go into the printed book, at least that they must be entirely disconnected with *me*.

There are many places where this might be done, and thus the whole responsibility rest on you. . . . Besides this, I must desire you to put a preface of your own before mine, and express in it, in so many words, that on you rests all the responsibility of introducing the subjects, and that your Recorder did not entirely sympathize or agree with you in respect to the course taken, adding (for I have not the slightest objection) that this disagreement or want of sympathy often prevented your views from being done full justice to, as she herself freely acknowledges. In this matter yourself also is concerned.

Why did prophets and apostles veil this subject in fables and emblems if there were not a reason for avoiding physiological inquiries etc.? This is worth thinking of. However, you as a

man can say anything; but I am a woman, and have feelings
that I dare not distrust, however little I can understand them
or give an account of them.[3]

Alcott wrote a preface, clarifying nothing. He put the passages
Elizabeth had wanted deleted into footnotes and the review conversations at the end of the book — as she, in her despair, had suggested, when he refused to leave anything out. The result was utter confusion — the book hardly making sense even to those who
knew how and why it was so arranged. But Elizabeth, instead of
feeling triumphant, was deeply distressed when the role of Cassandra was forced upon her and she found that she had prophesied
correctly concerning Boston's reactions. The outcry against Alcott went far beyond her worst fears as he was castigated from
press and pulpit. Now was the time — if Elizabeth Peabody had
been a coward — for her to side publicly against Alcott and make
sure of a school for herself, built upon the ruins of his. She did
nothing of the sort, of course. She closed all doors against herself
by coming out in defense of Alcott in an article called "Mr. Alcott's Book and School" in the *Register and Observer*.

". . . Never were children more independent of an instructor,
notwithstanding the astonishing command he has of their attention. Mr. Alcott's method defends his pupils from submitting pas-
sively to himself. Were his the common mode of dogmatic instruction, I, for one, would not put my children under the guidance of
his mind. But being what it is, I should not fear to do it; — and
widely as I differ from him on many points of doctrine.

"It is said that Mr. Alcott's conversation has no logic. This is true
enough . . . Nothing can be further from the strong, clear, reason-
linked method of his favorite Socrates . . . than Mr. Alcott's way
of talking. He not only cannot lead his companions on the narrow
line of reasoning as Socrates did; but he cannot go upon it himself.
All this I admit, but I maintain that this is no defect with children.
Their young brains ought not to be exercised in chopping logic.
Their pure imaginations should wander free into the eternal reason . . ."

It was a long article and Elizabeth promised another if space
would be given her. It was not. "Is not anyone coming forward
to cast some oil on the waves of excitement that Mr. Alcott's book
has raised in this easily alarmed community; and to do him justice?"

she said. She was among the first to do so, and those who stood with her were few — but very distinguished: Miss Fuller, James Freeman Clarke and Ralph Waldo Emerson.

Elizabeth made no effort for a school, for she knew she hadn't a chance. As long as three years afterwards, when Mary was trying to start a school in Boston, the Alcott affair had power to injure. A letter to Sophia explains: "People ask me about my sympathy with Alcott. Sally G. said it had met her at every turn and Anna Hooper asked E about it saying she understood that I kept that part of the Record . . . which was put into the notes, you know. E told her that I did not, but she did not tell her that you did. . . . Anna Hooper said that if I did sympathize with Mr. Alcott she could not think of putting Willy under my charge."

The few hardy souls who dared to say that it was a pity that Alcott's school was ruined and the father of a family deprived of a livelihood, forgot about Miss Peabody, an unmarried lady with no one but herself to support — plus a family of brothers and sisters to help out at all times. Among the few friends really loyal to Elizabeth was Lydian Emerson, second wife of Ralph Waldo. After the death of his first wife, Mr. Emerson had caused many a feminine heart to flutter and his formidable Aunt Mary was said to have picked Miss Elizabeth Peabody as a suitable second wife for him and to have brought them together at her house for matchmaking purposes. If so, she was a less astute lady than she is usually considered. Both Miss Peabody and Mr. Emerson liked to talk and they could never have stood it to be married, much as they enjoyed a visit together. Miss Lydia Jackson, Emerson's fiancée, was freely criticized by other (perhaps disappointed) ladies but Lizzie liked her at sight. "She looks very refined," Elizabeth told her sisters, "but neither beautiful nor elegant — and very frail — as if her mind were out of her body. She is unaffected but peculiar. . . . She sat down by me and we had a beautiful talk about a variety of most intellectual and spiritual things. I should think she had the rare characteristic of genius — inexhaustible originality." When the storm broke over Alcott, Lydian Emerson (she changed not one but both her names upon her marriage) remembered Miss Peabody and invited her to visit in Concord.

Talks with Alcott had made Elizabeth "think less well of many persons, himself included — and myself also," Elizabeth had said. Now there were long talks with Emerson in the course of which he healed her mind as surely as a doctor might heal her body. "I have caught his faith — or rather he has kindled mine," she cried. "When each one feels that he is in the Father and the Father is in him — how can there be fear! My prayer is, may this vision last. This is my Mount of Transfiguration."

Elizabeth returned to Salem free of pity for herself and full of confidence in the future. She set about her favorite pastime, that of discovering genius; first there was Jones Very, a Salem poet. His fellow townsmen considered him insane but Elizabeth enlisted Emerson's interest and Emerson helped him publish certain of his poems. If Very was insane, said Emerson, then the world could do with more such madmen — and Elizabeth agreed.

Park Benjamin, one of the young men who used to call on the Peabody sisters at Fayette Place, was now married to Eliza Curtis, daughter of "Aunt Curtis" and their first cousin. Elizabeth had followed his career with interest as he edited, then bought, the *New England Magazine*, merged it with the *American Monthly Magazine* and proceeded, in a review in that magazine, to praise highly some stories by "a Mr. Hawthorne." No wonder Park Benjamin thought the stories worthy of being collected into book form. He published eight of them anonymously in his *New England Magazine* the year before. Elizabeth had been impressed with them, beginning with the anonymous "Gentle Boy" and going on through others signed "by the author of The Gentle Boy." People seemed to think "Mr. Hawthorne" a pseudonym but to Elizabeth it was a familiar Salem name — except for the spelling. She remembered a letter, full of wit and an elusive charm, written by Elizabeth Hathorne. If there was anything Elizabeth would have liked better than discovering a Salem genius, it would be to discover a woman of genius in her home town of Salem!

The Peabody family was startled to hear that Lizzie planned to call on the Hathornes in Herbert Street. Mrs. Hathorne was still just as much of a recluse as she had been twenty years before when Mrs. Peabody had invoked kinship to pay a call, and the habit of seclusion would seem to be contagious. Her three children had been normal enough while growing up, going to school and even to dancing school. Nathaniel had graduated from Bowdoin, having acquired several lifelong friends. But the habit of loneliness lay in wait for them in the old Hathorne house and as the children grew to maturity it claimed them, one by one. Like the Peabodys, the Hathornes were proud of a family whose fortunes had declined.

But the Hathornes refused to do battle with the world when it was so much easier to live in solitude than to make a social effort. All four members of that Hathorne household now lived in seclusion — even from each other!

Elizabeth Peabody now proposed to call on the most shy, the most sensitive, of the Hathorne family group — the oldest daughter. The sensitive Mary Peabody was aghast and protested Lizzie's proposed intrusion. But Lizzie put on her bonnet and shawl and made her way to number 12 Herbert Street, where a high, narrow house turned its gable end to the street as though reluctant to expose front windows to the public gaze. A path led to a door which seemed designed only to be shut and locked. Before her knock was answered, Elizabeth had plenty of time to consider her approach. She would not claim kinship as her mother had once done. She would remind Miss Ebe that they had been schoolmates — when Lizzie was four years old!

But it was Miss Louisa Hathorne who finally appeared at the door and the interview could not be said to go very well. Miss Peabody told Miss Hathorne what a genius her sister Elizabeth must be.

"My brother, you mean," said Louisa. And the secret was out, the mystery no mystery at all.

"If your brother can write like that, he has no right to be idle," said Miss Peabody, assuming that Nathaniel Hawthorne had written no more than the few stories that she had read.

Louisa thought of the novel *Fanshawe*, written, even favorably reviewed and then destroyed — or at least the oversensitive Hawthorne believed he had obtained every copy and destroyed them all. Other painfully produced pages had never been published but had found their way into the cast-iron stove in Hawthorne's lonely chamber. But Louisa was not going to give away family secrets. "My brother is never idle," she told Miss Peabody — and that was that.

If Nathaniel was at home, he was not summoned to meet his first literary admirer. Elizabeth returned home with nothing more than the full name and identity of "a Mr. Hawthorne," and the feeling that her friendly gesture had been very coldly received. Mary told her it was all she could expect.

But on March 6, 1837, *Twice-Told Tales* was published and Mr. Hawthorne sent a copy to Miss Elizabeth Peabody. Elizabeth was delighted. She had sent out many a complimentary copy of her own books — rarely if ever had she been given one. With an "I told you so" to Mary, she proceeded to encourage Hawthorne further by suggesting some writing he could do for the *Democratic Chronicle*. The idea was impossible because Hawthorne was not in the least interested in journalism, but he wrote to her courteously, of course. As yet, he did not realize the futility of telling Elizabeth not to be too helpful. They had still to meet.

It was Mary, writing to her brother George in New Orleans, who told of the first meeting between the Peabodys and Nathaniel Hawthorne.[4] "November 16, 1837" she dated her letter, and she began by affectionately warning George of the perils of the Mississippi. "It seems to me the most reckless risk of life to go upon that river." Then she took up the matter of books from home. "Elizabeth has been thinking of sending you Bacon but she cannot make up her mind to send so many sayings of which she cannot approve, and if Mr. Bancroft can take a book, we are going to send you Mr. Hawthorne's 'Twice-Told Tales' which will divert you."

Mary then told of Hawthorne's call, which took place November 11.

"He came to see us last Saturday evening and we were quite delighted with him. He has lived the life of a perfect recluse till very lately — so diffident that he suffered inexpressibly in the presence of his fellow mortals — but he has a temple of a head (not a tower) and an eye full of sparkle, glisten and intelligence. He has promised to come again and if he can get fairly acquainted I think we shall find much pleasure in him."

Elizabeth rushed upstairs to tell Sophia that Nathaniel Hawthorne and his sister Elizabeth had come to call. "He is as handsome as Lord Byron," Lizzie declared, knowing what might fetch the romantic Sophia. But Sophia had gone to bed with one of her headaches, she had learned to discount a certain amount of Elizabeth's enthusiastic statements, and she refused to move. On her center table was a beautiful edition of Flaxman's "Greek Poets," lent to her by Allston upon the promise that she would return it soon. It was Sophia's ambition to copy every one of these delicate Neo-Classic outline drawings and she had been exhausting herself over the exacting work. She suggested that Elizabeth take the book downstairs to show to the guests. As to Hawthorne — "If he has come once, he will come again," she said.

Elizabeth returned to the parlor with the Flaxman and as she sat on the sofa between the Hawthornes, holding the big book and slowly turning the pages, she talked of the absent Sophia. She created an image of an ethereal young artist — a prisoner to pain — as lovely and unearthly as Flaxman's Greeks. In due course Elizabeth got out Sophia's "Cuba Journal" and read some of the passages she liked best although she could see that Mary disapproved of this sharing of private letters with such newly acquired friends.

As the Hawthornes left, Nathaniel stole a glance at the house on Charter Street. The shadowy, moonlit burying ground contained the remains of some of his own ancestors, the witch-hanging Judge Hathorne among them. Peabodys were resting there too, whether he knew it or not. But Hawthorne was looking at a square of light from an upper window as it lay across Colonel Pickman's wintry garden. Would that be Sophia's room? His novelist's imagination was stirred by the unseen Sophia and he would indeed come again.

Just when the next call occurred no one seemed to remember, but it was soon. And this time Sophia came downstairs when summoned. She was wearing her white dressing gown and she looked as if she had floated out of Flaxman's imaginary world of classic innocence. Hawthorne leaped to his feet — then stood speechless and they exchanged a long look from which Sophia was the first to recover. She put out her hand and spoke with charming self-possession.

For once, Elizabeth had not exaggerated, Sophia was thinking: Nathaniel Hawthorne was extraordinarily handsome. Those eyes with their heavy brows and deep shadows would make the dominant characteristic of any portrait. Sophia looked again to see exactly what color the eyes were. They were a deep blue, so dark as to seem almost black.[5] Above them, Hawthorne's forehead with its already slightly retreating hairline seemed unusually high and white. It was well balanced by a prominent chin, however, while his nose and mouth were as perfect as the profiles Sophia had so often copied from Miss Burley's book of Greek gems. Sophia caught her breath and her heart seemed to skip a beat as she studied Hawthorne's mouth. It was full, sensitive, and so beautiful as to be almost womanish. At the same time, a slightly undershot lower lip suggested not only will power but a high temper. Here was a man who could be tender, passionate — but who was not to be trifled with. Sophia's cheeks grew faintly, becomingly pink as she told herself that she was thinking of Hawthorne only in terms of painting. His hair, for example, was a dark chestnut which would be very interesting in the high lights but difficult to attempt. Months spent indoors at his desk had given Hawthorne a pallor which Sophia found intriguing.

Elizabeth was aware of the first long look which Hawthorne and Sophia exchanged. She saw Hawthorne lose his shyness and become at ease. He seemed to put on charm like a garment, for there was more than a touch of the actor in him, as in most writers. And Elizabeth caught Sophia's eye upon Hawthorne again and again throughout the evening. "What if they should fall in love!" Elizabeth said to Mary later — as if this were the ultimate in disasters.

Whenever Elizabeth had anything on her mind she always sat down and wrote a letter about it. This time she wrote to Hawthorne explaining to him that the invalid Sophia would never marry. He replied and she quoted him as saying that "Sophia was a rose to be worn in no man's bosom." This pleased Elizabeth tremendously and set all her fears at rest.

Elizabeth had carried Hawthorne's *Twice-Told Tales* to Emerson on one of her visits to Concord. Much to her disappointment, Emerson had preferred the mad poet, Very, and found Hawthorne hopelessly wordy, impossible to read. (She did not tell him that Hawthorne felt the same way about Emerson's philosophy.) Longfellow's reaction to Hawthorne was much more favorable and Elizabeth set to work to arrange a social engagement where Hawthorne might meet Longfellow, Holmes, and others in a position to help him. Hawthorne refused all her efforts. He was intensely embarrassed to discover that, far from being discouraged, Miss Peabody was trying to get some highly paid position for him where he would have little work to do and could get on with his writing. Something in government should be just the thing, Lizzie thought.

Hawthorne's calls at Charter Street became very frequent and naturally there was talk. He was calling on Miss Elizabeth, people said. Mary was told by Aunt Pickman that an engagement could not be far off. But Elizabeth herself still declared that Platonic friendship was her ideal. Just as some men preferred to remain bachelors, so there are also some women who do not choose to marry, she pointed out. She could not help being a little flattered — Hawthorne was so handsome. But he seemed incapable of understanding that she could manage his affairs better than he could and he exasperated her by never doing as he was told!

CHAPTER TEN

Year of Years

ON Salem's fashionable Chestnut Street lived Miss Susan Burley, in one of the most beautiful, the most richly carved of the McIntire mansions. She was famous for her evening parties where her friends met visiting celebrities and where, under the handsome, black-haired Miss Burley's patronage, a Salem neighbor might become a celebrity himself in due course. Miss Burley had always welcomed the Peabody sisters, she was interested in Sophia's work as an artist and she was stanchly Elizabeth's friend throughout the Alcott controversy. When Elizabeth proposed bringing young Mr. Hawthorne to her next literary evening, Miss Burley was delighted.

Although he had refused all other invitations Elizabeth had arranged for him, Hawthorne put in an appearance at Charter Street to escort the Peabody sisters to Miss Burley's. Elizabeth should have been surprised, but she was not. It was Hawthorne who was surprised when he discovered, too late, that he was escorting Elizabeth and Mary but not Sophia. She never went out in the evening, Sophia told him. It was the night air which she must avoid, being an invalid.

Here was a fine situation! Recently Hawthorne had become so infected with his family's habit of seclusion that he never went out except by night — walking alone by moonlight beside the sea or upon Gallows Hill and telling himself sad tales he someday expected to be able to put on paper. It took him no time at all to change his custom. Sophia told him that she walked abroad by day, provided there were no east wind, and between them they agreed that she would need his strong arm to lean upon next time the sun shone and the wind was still.

Sophia had taken the surest means to please an author — she had been reading his works. And next she had drawn an illustration in the Flaxman manner for Hawthorne's "Gentle Boy." She brought it out to show him. "I want to know if this looks like your Ilbrahim," she said.

Hawthorne looked at the picture, and, with that exquisite tact that was his whenever he wished, he replied, "He will never look otherwise to me."

The invitation to Miss Burley's was but a nuisance since Sophia would not go, but Miss Burley's friendship proved useful just the same. She became interested in Sophia's illustrations and financed the engraving of one for a special printing of "The Gentle Boy."

Sophia went to Boston to see the proofs of her first printed illustration. She was full of happy anticipation and so her disappointment was almost too much to bear when the engraving resembled her original drawing hardly at all! The engraver "changed the position of the eyes of Ilbrahim, darkened the brows, turned the corners of the mouth down instead of the original curve." When charged with this and more, the engraver pleasantly remarked that he always changed drawings to suit himself. Were all the books of engravings of famous paintings which Sophia had studied no more reliable than this? Washington Allston assured Sophia that this was so. An artist was always at the mercy of ignorant engravers, he said, and Sophia was only a little comforted by Allston's praise of her original drawings.

Just by coincidence, of course, Hawthorne found himself in Boston while Sophia was there. She invited him to a party to meet her friends, Sarah Clarke, Margaret Fuller, the Reverend and Mrs. George Ripley and others. Where Elizabeth had failed, Sophia had no trouble succeeding, and in the course of the evening, there sat the shy Hawthorne conversing with that charm which always came to him once he found himself among friends. More remarkable still, at Sophia's request there sat Hawthorne reading aloud from his own works! She was "deeply impressed," said Sophia — and so she should have been for more reasons than one.

When "The Gentle Boy" appeared, it carried on the third page the following:

To
Miss Sophia A. Peabody
This Little Tale
To which her Kindred Art has given Value
is respectfully inscribed
By the Author

A preface made matters still more clear. "No testimony in regard to the effect of this story, has afforded the Author so much pleasure as that which brings out the present edition. However feeble the creative power which produced Ilbrahim, it has wrought an influence upon another mind, and has thus given to imaginative life a creation of deep and pure beauty. The original sketch of *The Puritan* and *The Gentle Boy*, an engraving from which now accompanies the *Tale*, has received what the artist may well deem her most attainable recompense — the warm recommendation of the first painter in America. If, after so high a meed, the Author might add his own humble praise, he would say that whatever of beauty and pathos he had conceived, but could not follow forth in language, has been caught and embodied in the few and simple lines of this sketch."

Almost exactly a year had passed since Hawthorne's first call upon the Peabody sisters. Instead of refusing to see him, Sophia sat down at her desk in a gay mood and wrote him a postscript to "Cuba Journal" — in return for his gift of "The Gentle Boy." With a hint of mischief, she began with a dedication.

> To Nath." Hawthorne Esqr.
> Whose commendation and regard
> Alone gives value to the previous
>   Journal, this closing record
>   is inscribed by his true
>   and affectionate friend
>   Sophie (as the bird said)

"Now does not that equal your dedication? And surpass it in being overshadowed by seclusion from the world — a private testimony of friendship and deference from me to you; for which the public is none the wiser?"

It was a different Sophia who gently teased Nathaniel Hawthorne, Esquire. Gone was the pale girl in the white dressing gown who took to her bed every time her sister Elizabeth planned her life overmuch or her mother urged her to rest instead of paint. Sophia had gained a little weight and there was color in her cheeks. Her new-found health came from long walks in the open air with Mr. Hawthorne, she frankly told her family.

Elizabeth attended a lecture in Boston on "Animal Magnetists" at about this time. Early electrical experimentation was going on and the "Animal Magnetists" believed that electrical impulses in human beings were capable of curing all sorts of ills. The lecturer said that "persons differed from each other as bodies do — in being positive or negative — and had attractions and repulsions thereby." He told Miss Peabody that she was "a highly magnetised body" when she went up to talk to him after the lecture. With but one purpose in mind, Elizabeth questioned him at length and wrote Mary all about it. "He said he thought I might magnetise if I could concentrate my power in a strong act of will — and I do not know but I shall try to cure Sophia. I asked him to tell me how to go about it and he did. So tell Sophia to be prepared!"

But it was Elizabeth who was unprepared in the end. Sophia was having nothing whatever to do with magnetism — or with mesmerism either for that matter. She had given up her treatments with Dr. Fiske and she was ashamed now that she had ever been so much as soothed by him. She hoped her sisters would not mention magnetism or mesmerism or Dr. Fiske to Mr. Hawthorne. Nathaniel Hawthorne had explained to Sophia that, to him, any form of hypnotism was intolerable; it was the surrendering of one immortal soul to the will of another — an evil thing in the sight of God and man. Sophia saw that something like this had been in her own mind when she resisted Dr. Fiske's efforts to put her to sleep.

That Sophia was under a different form of hypnotism was clear enough. But Hawthorne's influence was sane and wonderfully wise. Early in the spring of 1839, he put in writing some of the helpful things he had been saying to her on those long walks during the winter just past.

"Do grow better — physically, I mean, for I protest against any spiritual improvement, until I am better able to keep pace with you — but do be strong and full of life — earthly life — and let there be a glow in your cheeks. And sleep soundly the whole night long, and get up every morning with a feeling as if you were newly created; and I pray you to lay up a stock of fresh energy every day till we meet again; so that we may walk miles and miles without you once needing to lean upon my arm. Not but what you *shall* lean upon it as much as you choose — indeed whether you choose or not — but I would feel as if you did it to lighten my footsteps, not to support your own. Am I requiring you to work a miracle within yourself? Perhaps so — yet not a greater one than I do really believe might be wrought by inward faith and outward aids. Try it, my Dove, and be as lightsome on earth as your sister doves are in the air."

Hawthorne might have urged Sophia to cling to him and let him fight her battles for her — as so many people had urged her to cling, all her life long. She would have found it sweet to yield — at least for a while. Then the old conflict would have begun again as, inevitably, she longed for freedom. But instead of attempting to possess Sophia, Hawthorne gave her to herself. He could not have found a better way of winning her.

In after years, Hawthorne and Sophia liked to say that they fell in love at sight. Perhaps they did. Certainly, Hawthorne spoke soon of love. But old habits were strong and Sophia spoke of herself as an invalid and said that she had made up her mind not to be a burden on any man. The miracle that Hawthorne asked for was a necessary one. Sophia never said that she did not love Hawthorne. She was too honest for that. She sat in the Peabody parlor drawing a sketch of Hawthorne one winter evening. "I never beheld your face before I tried to represent it. Now I shall recognize it, I am certain, through all eternity," she said — willing enough that Hawthorne should know how much he meant to her.

The exact date of their engagement is a secret they kept to themselves alone; but Hawthorne came close to revealing it in his New Year's letter, written January 1, 1840:

". . . What a year this last has been! Dearest, you make the same exclamation; but my heart originates it too. It has been the year of years — the year in which the flower of our life has blossomed out — the flower of our life and of our love, which we are to wear in our hearts forever."

Three days later he wrote again of this year of years:

"Dearest, I hope you have not found it impracticable to walk although the atmosphere be so wintry. Did we walk together in any such weather last winter? How strange that such a flower as our affection should have blossomed amid snow and wintry winds — accompaniments which no poet or novelist that I know of, has ever introduced into a love-tale. Nothing like our story was ever written — or ever will be — for we shall not feel inclined to make the public our confidant; but if it could be told, methinks it would be such as the angels would delight to hear."

When Sophia promised to marry Hawthorne, she felt that she had fulfilled the conditions she had previously imposed upon herself. Her health was tremendously improved. She had occasional headaches to be sure, but she made light of them and they were no longer the kind that laid her low for days at a time. Her letters were full of rejoicing when friends had complimented her upon her remarkable improvement. With Hawthorne, however, there were conditions much harder to fulfill. He had no money and no job.

For years, the Hawthornes had been living upon dwindling capital. There were "lands in Maine" which had been sold off, a parcel at a time, to provide the wherewithal to live. But there were also litigations when people like the Tory Gardiner family laid pre-Revolutionary claims which cost money to defend — whatever the outcome. The land, therefore, was a doubtful asset and, in a subtle unsuspected way, it was a liability not only from a cash standpoint but from a spiritual standpoint as well. The Hawthornes felt like landed gentry and plain ordinary hard work hurt their pride.

Madame Hawthorne had passed her life in a sort of negative dream. Her brothers were good to her. They were Mannings, their forebears running a shop for the making and repairing of firearms — they themselves operating a Salem stagecoach service. Mrs. Hawthorne's brother Robert sent Nathaniel through Bowdoin — yet somehow Mrs. Hawthorne, because of her refusal to associate with anyone, seemed to be very delicately holding her nose at the whole dirty, smelly business of stagecoaching — lucrative though it was. The Manning brothers were always patient with her, building a house for their sister in Maine where she could have all the solitude anyone could wish. They even refrained from reproaches when Hawthorne showed no inclination to enter their business — no inclination either for medicine, the church or the law. And perhaps Hawthorne was using some of that tact of which he was so capable when he said nothing to his uncles about becoming a literary man.

As soon as Nathaniel Hawthorne put in an appearance on Charter Street, the Peabodys became eager, and perhaps too eager, to make friends with his sisters. They wrote little notes suggesting a country walk or proposing the Charter Street burying ground at their side door as the proper place from which to view an impending eclipse. Elizabeth Hawthorne proved at the same time the most difficult to know and the most intriguing. At first she insisted that, like her brother, she went out only at night; but she yielded to entreaty and found pleasure in Mary's quiet company upon a long walk by the sea. She sent home to Sophia a pretty pebble with seaweed clinging to it like a mermaid's hair. She had stepped into the water to get it, although the time was early spring and the water icy, but she would not go to Sophia's room even to receive thanks. At this time, Elizabeth Hawthorne was working on a life of Jefferson, with her brother's help and encouragement. But she would not for the world have confided as much to her new friends. Instinctively, Elizabeth Hawthorne knew that Sophia threatened Nathaniel's interest in his sister's work. Her book would never be finished. Elizabeth Hawthorne, surrounded by too many fading family portraits, would come to feel that life was best lived in eternal pale repose.

Already, all necessary contact with the world — the dealing with tradesmen, for example — was carried on by Louisa. Having little or no creative urge, no secret poetic world within herself, there was no reason why Louisa should become a recluse like the rest of her family. But Louisa was pathetically unsure of herself. She was not unattractive but a dress can be cut over and turned just so many times before a new one becomes imperative if a young woman is to feel at ease. For a guest at tea, one is tempted to buy just a few extra trifles that add up in the end. And in those days a servant cost so little that even the Peabodys had one. But Louisa kept family accounts. She knew she must answer the door herself — wear the frayed dress. It became a Hawthorne custom for each member of the family to eat alone and Louisa found it convenient not to let anyone see how little she kept for herself. Although making no recognizable gesture, Louisa was the Hawthorne sister most friendly toward Sophia.

From this family of three women, Nathaniel Hawthorne had gone periodically forth for brief sojourns in the world of men. He visited his college friend, Horatio Bridge, in Augusta, Maine, where he observed that the beautiful pillared white house belonging to the Gardiners had burned, that a new stone house in the new Neo-Gothic style had been begun and then abandoned as financial ruin descended upon the family. (Hawthorne was moved to moral reflections.) He journeyed to North Adams, living in country inns, observing, jotting down in his notebook every impression that might prove useful to him as a writer. Hawthorne enjoyed whatever cheer, liquid or otherwise, seemed most favored by the people whose splendidly earthy existence he tried to share — however briefly. Then he would return to his strange, silent home; to write if he could; to be seen by no one; to go out only after dark. All too soon, his mother and his sisters cast over him the dark enchantment of seclusion. Upon each return they hoped in their secret hearts that

Nathaniel would never go forth again — that their novice would finally take his vow and become a recluse at last.

Actually, the women spun their webs in vain. Hawthorne was more alive and aware of the world outside than they realized. He had plenty of practical common sense and he knew that sometime there would be no more land in Maine to sell; there would be an end to the proceeds of Manning energy — and that he, himself, must support his family. Louisa was right when she said, "My brother is never idle." He had edited the last six numbers of the second volume of the *American Magazine of Useful and Entertaining Knowledge*, writing all the material himself. Then the magazine had failed and he could not collect the money promised him. He had written stories, rewritten them, polished them — and then sold them for less money than a good bricklayer would have accepted for laying a sidewalk. For all of Park Benjamin's kind words and Longfellow's good review, *Twice-Told Tales* sold badly. When he met Sophia, Hawthorne's confidence in himself as a writer was at a low ebb. With his love for her, came strength and renewed courage.

Hawthorne was well aware that if Sophia had worked a miracle for him by regaining her health, he too was in the process of working miracles. In his New Year's letter he told her:

"It is such happiness to be conscious at last of something real. All my life hitherto, I have been walking in a dream, among shadows which could not be pressed to my bosom; but now, even in this dream of time, there is something which takes me out of it and causes me to be a dreamer no more."

Elizabeth was the first to be told of Sophia's engagement and, although she had been insistent that Sophia must never marry, she was also the first to accept the idea that Sophia was no longer an invalid but a perfectly normal and exceptionally happy young woman. Lizzie promptly redoubled her efforts in Hawthorne's behalf so that the financial difficulties which made a long engagement necessary could be solved as soon as possible. In spite of Hawthorne's objections that he knew not the first thing about the duties of a postmaster, Elizabeth decided that Cambridge Postmaster he must be — and she would arrange it. She failed (to Hawthorne's relief) but she did not give up.

One of the most faithful members of Elizabeth's Reading Parties and history study groups had been Mrs. Bliss, a wealthy widow. Recently, Mrs. Bliss had married George Bancroft, whose *History of the United States* had brought him fame if not entire popularity.

Bancroft was described by his political acquaintances as "a learned monkey" and Elizabeth Peabody thought very little better of him, but he was exactly what she thought Hawthorne should be – the literary man in politics. In 1837 Bancroft had become Collector of the Port of Boston. And Elizabeth, who was often at his home as a friend of his wife, urged that he do something for Hawthorne.

Hawthorne became "Weigher and Gauger" at the Boston Custom House in January, 1839. Writing to Longfellow, he said, "I have no reason to doubt of my capacity to fulfill the duties; for I don't know what they are."

Elizabeth's optimism had infected Hawthorne and he felt certain that he would be able to carry on his writing every evening after his work was over, using the rich material which life along the docks was bound to provide. But his duties, when he learned about them, were by no means nominal and he found himself not only exhausted every night, but covered with coal dust – from weighing the cargo of a collier. A steamer laden with salt was something to look forward to – the work would be just as hard but at least he would come home reasonably clean. Hawthorne found himself able to write only to Sophia – but his love letters were as beautiful as anything he would ever put on paper.[1]

Alone in his dreary hall bedroom, Hawthorne consoled himself by thinking of new and sweeter names with which to address his beloved. There was, for example, her middle name which perhaps Sophia herself preferred.

MOST BELOVED AMELIA:

I shall call you so sometimes in playfulness, and so may you; but it is not the name by which my soul recognizes you. It knows you as Sophia; but I doubt whether that is the inwardly and intensely dearest epithet either. I believe that "Dove" is the true word after all; and it never can be used amiss, whether in sunniest gaiety or shadiest seriousness. And yet it is a sacred word and I should not love to have anybody hear me use it, nor know that God has baptised you so – the baptism being for yourself and me alone. By that name, I think, I shall greet you when we meet in Heaven. Other dear ones may call you "daughter," "sister," "Sophia" but when, at your entrance into Heaven, or after you have been a little while there, you hear a voice say "Dove!" then you will know that your kindred spirit has been admitted (perhaps for your sake) to the mansions of rest. That word will express his yearning for you — then to be forever satisfied; for we will melt into one another, and be close, close together then. The name was inspired; it came without our being aware that you were henceforth to be my Dove, now and through eternity. I do not remember how or when it alighted on you; the first I knew, it was in my heart to call you so.

Goodnight now, my Dove. It is not yet nine o'clock; but I am somewhat aweary and prefer to muse about you till bedtime, rather than to write.

Yet Hawthorne could not long rest content without searching among words, which meant so much to him, for a name still dearer by which to call Sophia. Only a few weeks passed before he found it.

> BOSTON, *July 24 1839*
> *8 o'clock* P.M.

MINE OWN:

I am tired this evening, as usual, with my long day's toil; and my head wants its pillow and my soul yearns for the friend whom God hath given it — whose soul he has married to my soul. Oh my dearest, how that thought thrills me! We *are* married! I felt it long ago; and sometimes when I am seeking for the fondest word, it has been on my lips to call you "Wife." I hardly know what restrained me from speaking of it — unless a dread (for *that* would have been an infinite pang to me) of feeling you shrink back and thereby discovering that there was yet some deep place in your soul that did not know me. Mine own Dove, need I fear it now? Are we not married? God knows we are. Often have I silently given myself to you, and received you for my portion of human love and happiness and have prayed Him to consecrate and bless the union. Yes, we are married and as God has joined us, we may trust never to be separated, neither in Heaven nor on Earth. We will wait patiently and quietly and He will lead us onward hand in hand (as He has done all along) like little children and will guide us to our perfect happiness — and will teach us when our union is to be revealed to the world. My beloved, why should we be silent to one another — why should our lips be silent any longer on this subject? The world might, as yet, misjudge us; and therefore we will not speak to the world; but why should we not commune together about all our hopes of earthly and external as well (as) our faith of inward and eternal union? Farewell for tonight, my dearest — my soul's bride!

What Sophia replied to this beautiful and passionate letter can never be known. Long years later, Hawthorne burned "hundreds of Sophia's maiden letters — the world has no more such," he said; "and now they are all ashes. What a trustful guardian of secret matters fire is! What should we do without Fire and Death?" But that Sophia had replied to the letter above in sweet agreement, perhaps calling him her "husband" in return, is clear enough — since so many subsequent letters from Hawthorne were to "Mine own wife."

With a new-found physical strength and a great love to enrich her experience, Sophia worked better as an artist than ever before. She copied paintings industriously, now hoarding the money she earned toward clothes and household furnishings that she would need in the new life to come. In 1839, her sister Mary had started a small school for little children, in spite of difficulties resulting from Alcott's misfortunes. Sophia visited Mary in the spring, going to the Athenæum to see the latest Allstons, to an exhibition of miniatures, and to see some statuary. Of course there was a day set apart for ladies to view the statuary, since it was considered improper for men and women to go together to look at figures whose drapery might be shown as having slipped a little. Horatio Greenough's "Chanting Cherubs" were nude and there was "moral indignation" — ladies' days notwithstanding. Sophia felt daring to be at the exhibition at all. At the same time she began to wonder if she might not try her hand at modeling.

In Boston, just at this time, was a young man from Cincinnati, Shobal Vail Clevenger by name. Plaster casts of Plato and Socrates were all very well, he thought, but he had come to Boston to immortalize his own generation in marble. Since Boston considered itself easily the equal of ancient Athens, Clevenger's ideas were well received and he had a gratifying number of commissions. He was at work upon Allston when Sophia went to his studio. She found him about her own age, with frank, unassuming manners and a broad-shouldered, stalwart frame. He did not look like her idea of an artist but looked exactly what he was: the son of a farmer and a stonecutter by trade. Sent into the world by his father to learn to build a canal, Clevenger had seen the wooden statue of a goddess on the market house in Cincinnati and she had seemed to him the embodiment of beauty. The sixteen-year-old boy abandoned construction stonecutting and hired himself to a monument maker.

No one knew better than Clevenger what it meant to be an artist without the opportunity to study. He had once stolen into graveyards by moonlight and taken clay impressions of the carvings in order to study them. Clevenger's first encouragement had come from the editor of the *Cincinnati Evening Post*, and he promptly cut a portrait bust of E. S. Thomas direct from stone. Nicholas Longworth gave the young man the money for a series of lectures in anatomy at the Ohio Medical College and again Clevenger startled his contemporaries by cutting portrait busts direct from native stone — instead of using the traditional marble. Here was a young man who refused to copy European styles!

Sophia's disappointment in Clevenger's unromantic appearance quickly evaporated when she saw how eager he was to help her. He was delighted to have her watch him at work and to ask him questions, for he remembered the days when he would have given anything for a similar opportunity. There were wooden supports inside the clay, he told her, and he showed her how to make them. The clay must be kept moist until the work was finished and the casting done. Sophia bought some modeling clay and went home to Salem to see what she could do.

George Peabody had just returned to Salem from New Orleans, where he had made the beginnings of a successful business career. Soon all his debts would be paid and he would be in a position to help his family. But now he was stricken with a disease of the spine; he was suffering intensely and becoming increasingly paralyzed. The hopelessness of her brother's case was kept from Sophia, of course; but this was a different Sophia who now faced facts for herself, and she knew that George was going to die.

The Peabody's youngest son, Wellington, had just died in New Orleans. After Wellington left Harvard, word went around Boston that he had run away to sea — but such was not the case. Much against his will he had been shipped off aboard a New Bedford whaler, his mother and his sisters bidding him a tearful farewell. A contrite letter came from him in which he promised never to go into debt again and cause his family trouble and anxiety. The ship made a good voyage and Wellington's share would clear him (or rather his father) from debt. Then the ship put in at New York and, with calculating cruelty, crew members were beaten and starved. Wellington jumped ship, as was his captain's intention, and forfeited his wages and his share of the profit. He returned home in debt again, this time to his Aunt Putnam. When he went to New Orleans with his brother George, he at last began to fulfill his father's hopes for him by becoming a doctor's helper with a view to being a doctor himself in due course. Wellington courageously attended the sick during an epidemic in the desperately stricken city of New Orleans, until he too fell a victim to the dread Yellow Fever.

Wellington Peabody had been romantically, unbelievably handsome. A portrait of him remained but there was no likeness of George. Sophia went to work to model a portrait in low relief of George — knowing that she must work fast if she were going to finish it in time — praying that she might catch a likeness that would give pleasure and comfort to her mother in after days. While she worked, she talked and laughed with George — until no one but Hawthorne knew that she realized that these were the last hours she would spend with her brother. Hawthorne called on George whenever possible and Sophia found comfort and strength in Hawthorne's presence and in the knowledge of his great love for her.

In October the portrait was finished and Sophia and her father journeyed to Boston to have the clay model cast in plaster. Clevenger came eagerly to Mary's rooms to see Sophia's work. They placed the model upon a sofa and the romantic Sophia said that "the great man knelt before it." Mary laughed and said Clevenger didn't kneel, he "squatted." In any case, Sophia wrote to George that Clevenger "said he could find no fault with it — the style was good — the drawing perfectly correct. . . . He criticised the whiskers which he said were too fine to look well in plaster — that he had found by experience that hair only looked well in plaster when laid on in masses."

Sophia made a few changes and then Clevenger took her to the workshop where the casting was done. He laid it upon the soul of the Italian workmen to do their best and they promised with flashing smiles and expressive gestures. Sophia was almost beside herself with excitement as she watched the cast being completed. But she had hoped for too much. The cast was far from perfect, and she nearly cried with vexation while the sympathetic Clevenger tried to tell her that it was always so and that she might correct the plaster. Sophia took a penknife and altered the cast, sharpening the lines with a freedom and confidence that made Clevenger nod with approval. He was going to Rome very soon, the generous Mr. Longworth providing the money for foreign study, and he offered to take Sophia's cast with him and have it cut in marble by the wonderfully skillful Italian workmen. But a marble copy was more than the Peabodys could afford.

Inspired by the success of her portrait of her brother, Sophia modeled a similar bas-relief medallion of Charles Emerson, beloved brother of Ralph Waldo. She worked from pictures and from memory, since Charles Emerson had died in 1836. It was with trepidation that Sophia awaited Elizabeth Hoar's opinion of her work, for Miss Hoar had been Charles Emerson's fiancée and Sophia particularly wished to please her. Ralph Waldo Emerson wrote some pleasant news. "Elizabeth Hoar is very well content with the cast though she thinks it has lost some of its precision, as well as the agreeable tint of the clay. All our friends find the likeness — some of them slowly — but all at last. We all count it a beautiful possession; the gift of a Muse, and not the less valuable because it was so unexpected. You must now gratify us all by fixing a time when you will come to Concord and hear what we have to say of it."

In June 1840 Sophia visited the Emersons and entrusted to them the secret of her engagement to Hawthorne. Her letter telling Hawthorne about it was burned with the others but his reply suggests what she must have said. "It does my heart good," Hawthorne wrote her, "that thou meetest with sympathy there and that thy friends have faith that thy husband is worthy of thee because they see that thy wise heart could not have gone astray."

Sophia had fallen in love with Concord, with its wide streets that were hardly more than country roads, its elms and its placid river. She described to Hawthorne the dream house she would like to have there after they were married. And Hawthorne was perfectly willing that Sophia should choose the location of their future home. "Would that we could build our cottage this very now, this very summer amid the scenes which thou describest," he told her. But they would have to live on dreams for a long time to come.

It seems almost incredible that the year should be 1842 and the month February when Hawthorne wrote confessing that he had not yet told his mother and his sisters about his engagement to Sophia. He tried to explain to her how such a thing could be. It was "because of the strange reserve, in regard to matters of feeling, that has always existed among us. We are conscious of one another's feelings always; but there seems to be a tacit law, that our deepest heart-concernments are not to be spoken of. I cannot gush out in their presence — I cannot take my heart in my hand and show it to them. There is a feeling within me (although I know it is a foolish one) as if it would be as indecorous to do so, as to display to them the naked breast. . . .

"I tell thee these things in order that my Dove, into whose infinite depths the sunshine falls continually, may perceive what a cloudy veil stretches over the abyss of my nature. . . ."

Sophia loved Hawthorne and so she understood. She herself wrote to Hawthorne's mother and told her the news. The next letter was from a radiantly happy Hawthorne, who said that his mother had guessed the secret long ago and was pleased — that his sisters also accepted a new sister with affection. He exaggerated in the case of his sister Elizabeth, but it made no difference. Sophia was adept at winning hearts.

CHAPTER ELEVEN

The Shop in West Street

FROM leisurely, sunny Tremont Street, a narrow byway plunged toward the heart of Boston's business district. Cobblestone pavement amplified the deep-throated music of city traffic, the rumble of wagon wheels, the whir of carriage wheels, and the eternal click-clack of horses' hoofs. One traveled either north or south — on West Street, Boston. At the Tremont end, West Street opened opposite the Common, and borrowed from it an air of elegance and even a little sunlight, some tree shadows and the flicker of doves' wings. Elizabeth Peabody, in search of a place in which to begin a new life, found it at Number 13 West Street, which she acquired for a home for her family and a shop for herself.

The idea of going into business had been simmering in Elizabeth's mind ever since a teaching career had been closed to her. Had not old General Palmer been a merchant prince? Moreover, the real business world was securely closed to women and here was a challenge that Elizabeth Peabody could hardly resist. There were women shopkeepers of course, indigent widows as a rule, who kept a little stock of needles and thread in the front parlor of a home in some no longer fashionable district. Elizabeth had no such modest ideas when she selected West Street, a location somewhat residential, but one which would be famous for high quality merchandising for more than a hundred years. E. P. Peabody was going into business on an equal footing with men. Her stock in trade would be something she believed in, something she had loved all her life. She would open a bookshop.

Elizabeth's conception of her ideal bookshop was something new, different, and utterly delightful. Books are written by people, about people and for people. A bookshop, therefore, should be a place where people could meet, exchange ideas, talk about books — and of course buy them. The front parlor of the Peabody home would be the "bookroom," the shelves along the walls which Elizabeth was having built would look like bookcases in a rather large private library. Customers would be received as guests. With Elizabeth's enormous acquaintance in Boston she was bound to recognize at least by sight everyone who pushed open her door. And Peabody hospitality could be relied on to make the occasional stranger feel welcome.

As to choice of stock, Elizabeth would carry nothing she considered harmful or improper, and this was hardly a strictly business-like attitude. But, unlike many of her contemporaries, Elizabeth knew that everything printed in the French language was not necessarily immoral. She knew that German scientific books were not necessarily ungodly. Elizabeth would carry current foreign works and foreign classics for sale in her bookshop in West Street. So startling was this innovation, that some of her friends at first were to call her store "Miss Peabody's foreign bookshop."

Then there was the matter of foreign periodicals. Americans read *Blackwood's* and other English magazines and pirated from them without permission or payment — Elizabeth Peabody herself as much as all the rest. But these magazines were to be found exclusively at the Athenæum for members only, or in such homes as Dr. Channing's, whence they were borrowed and passed from hand to hand until they dropped apart. Elizabeth would carry English periodicals for sale, and (since the borrowing habit was too ingrained to break) lend them for a modest fee. Adding one innovation after another without stopping to take breath, Elizabeth decided to subscribe to foreign-language periodicals as well.

That critical English visitor, Miss Martineau, had been scornful of the education American women were receiving. They were all linguists, she complained — and she was right. But this was a point in favor of Miss Peabody, as her former pupils, now grown to woman's estate, leafed over the *Revue des Deux Mondes* and found that they could read it easily. Joyfully leaving the schoolbook world of syntax and exercise behind them, they stepped into the new world of a living language.

Before the shop in West Street was actually open perhaps, but long after her mind was made up, Elizabeth had asked Dr. Channing's approval of her project. She was thirty-six years old, yet she seemed to turn to him for permission like a child — perhaps in the hope of recapturing her youthful feeling for him. Whatever her sentimental reasons, however, she had one good practical one. She wanted Dr. Channing to advance money to his London bookseller for her account. This he did, though not without a touch of misgiving.

"I see nothing in the business inconsistent with your sex," wrote Dr. Channing, giving Elizabeth his accolade of approval, which she needed just as much as she needed his credit in London. "I have a great desire to see a variety of employments thrown open to women," he told her, "and if they may sell anything, why not books? The business seems to partake of the dignity of literature."

As to Elizabeth's business ability, Dr. Channing had his doubts; and he was right, as usual. She was too trustful, he warned, too unmethodical and given to putting too many irons in the fire. "Our country is a land of 'golden dreams,'" Channing said — and he feared that Elizabeth "might give in to these."

He might as well have told her to cease being herself as to stop dreaming, for Number 13 West Street was a shop built on dreams — all of them golden. It was advertised in August, and open to customers, or perhaps more properly speaking to guests, on the last day of July, 1840.

Dr. Peabody, either with or without his consent, was removed from Salem and was given a corner of the West Street premises. Nathaniel, the only surviving Peabody son, had a share in the project, for Elizabeth displayed for sale those homeopathic drugs which he prepared with much labor and little profit. The belladonna, the aconite, the sassafras, the horehound — whether they cured any ills or not — contributed a subtle fragrance to mingle with the smell of bindings, paper and printer's ink. Large bottles of amber liquid, little phials of pink pills, added a suggestion of necromancy to an already magic bookshop, and customers would never forget West Street as long as they lived.

By the front window in the bookroom was a comfortable rocker, the particular property of Mrs. Peabody. From it, she made sorties into the basement kitchen to impress upon the cook (whose name was Bridget) the importance of bread pudding as an economy measure. From her bookroom chair, Mrs. Peabody made excursions up the steep stairs to superintend the cleaning of spare rooms, sometimes occupied by paying guests — most of whom forgot to pay. But it was Mrs. Peabody's joy to tend shop, with her air of gentility which family pride imposed upon her — but with a fine ear for gossip all the same. She knew what everybody had read and what each customer ought to read next and it was not easy to get away from her without buying at least one more book.

It was according to the family pattern that Sophia should be "spared" the necessity of keeping shop. She had her painting room upstairs and her mother expected her to have her headaches as usual. But Sophia painted industriously, headaches or no, and her pictures were displayed for sale in the bookroom. Friends who hung Sophia's copies in their parlors were proud of her work but they did not necessarily tell outsiders how little they paid for pictures assumed to be "imported" and worth several hundred dollars. Sophia made no complaint. To be paid anything at all lifted her out of the dilettante class and made her a professional artist, something she had longed to be ever since girlhood.

Washington Allston was said to have suggested that Elizabeth sell art supplies, still another new departure in the book business. He wrote his favorite firm in London arranging for E. P. Peabody to become "sole agent in New England for Brown, of 163 High Holborn," as Elizabeth proudly advertised. Allston came often to West Street. He was nearly seventy now, his face haunted by dead hopes but capable of lighting still with undying ambition. When she heard he was in the shop, Sophia always left her "painting room" and ran down the stairs to see him. He was writing a novel now, he told her, and her sincere admiration gave him some of his happier moments. Allston bought his gamboge and ocher of Sophia, colors he had used too much and too long — but he carried away something more precious from the West Street shop. Renewed courage and self-confidence, rare as those commodities were, could always be found at Miss Peabody's by those in need of them. There would be no charge.

Always the rendezvous of intellectuals, on Wednesdays the bookshop soon took on a predominantly feminine air of suppressed excitement. It would become a "Babel of talkers," as Hawthorne put it, before Miss Margaret Fuller arrived there for her Conversations. Out came the battered chairs which had seen service in many a Peabody schoolroom. Ladies of all ages came from Cambridge, from country homes in Brookline, and from near-by Beacon Street. When everyone was seated, when the stage was set and the dramatic moment came, Miss Fuller swept into the room convoyed by a flushed and happy Miss Peabody. The chatter died down. There was a rustle of silks as Boston's most elegant, most devoted lecture audience prepared to be carried away by one who frankly considered herself a second Delphic oracle. Miss Fuller was right of course! Elizabeth had been among the first to confirm Margaret's high opinion of herself and to spread the news.

Out of loyalty to Elizabeth, Sophia occupied one of the shabby chairs at Miss Fuller's Conversations. What an artistic background the book-lined room made for Margaret! But the over-sensitive Sophia interpreted Miss Fuller's habitually superior air as disdain for her surroundings. Many of the younger women who listened with rapt attention to Miss Fuller had been pupils of Elizabeth's and had attended her Reading Parties in other years. Margaret was thirty and Elizabeth only six years older. Sophia knew it was foolish to be jealous for Elizabeth when Lizzie herself was not; but she could not help it. From the too close viewpoint of a sister, Sophia could not evaluate the charm which vitality and unfailing interest in others gave to Elizabeth, nor could she estimate how durable these assets would prove during the years to come.

Sophia felt the telltale color mount to her cheeks as she caught Miss Fuller's eye upon Elizabeth's hair. The "Grecian mode" might be appropriate to wear to a lecture on classic art but it did not go with short, plump Elizabeth, nor would the Psyche knot stay in place no matter how tightly Lizzie pinned it. Cheerful, forgetful of self, Elizabeth contrasted strikingly with the self-conscious, elegant if angular Miss Fuller — and Margaret knew instinctively how to make the best use of contrasts.

It never occurred to Elizabeth to charge Margaret Fuller for the use of the shop in West Street, nor did it cross Miss Fuller's mind to thank Elizabeth, whose unbusinesslike methods she despised. "Who would be a goody who could be a genius!" Margaret said, and she knew herself to be a genius of the first order. But for once Elizabeth's generosity paid off. Miss Fuller's "assistants," as she called her audience, were women who could afford books; and each week, as they lingered for a personal word with their adored lecturer, they glanced over Elizabeth's stock in trade. Elizabeth herself was all too apt to forget bookselling while enjoying delightful discussions brought on by the lecture — but Mrs. Peabody never lost a chance to make a sale. Mary would be there if she could possibly arrange it, unobtrusive as ever, but efficient as she circulated among the guests. She took satisfaction in selling every book Miss Fuller had mentioned in her lecture, and some that she had not.

Mary was seldom at West Street except for some special occasion such as Miss Fuller's lectures. Her school for very young children supplied her own modest needs and could be made to help out at home should Elizabeth's project go badly. Mary's feelings were divided between anxiety as to where Elizabeth's enthusiasms would carry her and relief because Elizabeth was too busy these days to see much of "dear Mr. Mann." Lizzie did not even inquire why Mary returned so often to her schoolroom to spend a long evening at work, and she never dreamed that Mr. Mann, now the first Massachusetts State Superintendent of Schools, would be there with notes for one of his interminable reports which Mary Peabody would write out for him and put in shape.

Sometimes Mary wondered why she worked so hard and so late — until she had to make an effort to hold up her heavy eyelids all next day. She wanted to be with Horace, that was all; to do everything he did and to become indispensable to his existence. She had accomplished this, she knew, but evening after evening he was too tired to so much as look at her or give her that warm pressure of the hand, that intimate smile from deep within his eyes, which meant so much to her. If proximity breeds love, then Mary had reason to hope; but it was hope deferred, and she felt sick at heart.

Meanwhile, Elizabeth found still another outlet for her energies now that Boston had accepted its first woman bookseller. She had a new shock in store for the community, as very shortly Boston had its first woman publisher — E. P. Peabody by name. This time competitors were less tolerant and the going was rough, but Elizabeth imagined that she was cautious, good at arithmetic, and sure to make money. She thought that honesty could be made to pay in a business which was unscrupulous to a degree at a time when business ethics were almost nonexistent in many quarters.

No presses rumbled in the back parlor at West Street, although Elizabeth would have loved the idea and would have wanted to operate them herself — further scandalizing her world. Publishing alone would suffice, she explained to Dr. Channing. She would act as agent, obtaining the work of others, having it printed by jobbers, then selling the result at a profit.

Again Elizabeth consulted Dr. Channing — after her mind was made up, as he could see. "I think of publishing a pamphlet," said the Doctor, "and should be glad to have you do it, if you can secure the profits to yourself — if there should be any profit." With this truly generous offer, Elizabeth's career as a publisher began, and nothing could have been more auspicious. Channing's pamphlet on Emancipation had long been awaited by his friends and foes alike.

It turned out to be a best seller, and Miss Peabody was on her way to make a modest success. The Channing pamphlet would keep her solvent while she became established, it would pay for a few mistakes, provided she did not publish failures too often.

Then the Antislavery Society asked for the pamphlet for distribution. They must pay Miss Peabody a fair profit to publish it, Dr. Channing told them, and he thought with satisfaction of the large order soon to be placed at West Street. But the abolitionists approached Miss Peabody in behalf of their cause, and she ran true to form. She said she would publish the pamphlet and let the society have it at cost, or release it and let them publish elsewhere. If Dr. Channing was exasperated, he had but to consider what must be waiting for Elizabeth in heaven — since it seemed unlikely that she would ever lay up any treasure on earth.

As a publisher and bookseller, Elizabeth was happier than she had ever been before. She had a sense of fulfilling her destiny, which stemmed directly from those days in 1836 when she used to visit in Emerson's home and he had shared with her his growing thought concerning a new philosophy: a line of reasoning that would burst the bonds of puritanism and replace the fear of God with a triumphant confidence in His infinite goodness.

It was in 1836 that Emerson had begun to meet a few choice friends to discuss the German philosophers, French philosophy as expressed by Cousin and Rousseau, English ideas according to Coleridge. Each member of the first small group in later years disclaimed the honor of being its originator, saying that it was Channing who suggested the idea that young Unitarian ministers should get together for discussions. They had met for the first time at George Ripley's house and five of them were there: Emerson, Hedge, Alcott, Convers Francis and James Freeman Clarke. "The Symposium" they were inclined to call themselves — or sometimes, "Hedge's Club" because Frederick Henry Hedge was the one among them who had been educated in Germany and who could interpret for them the German philosophers. After the first meeting, invitations had been extended to others, among them John S. Dwight and Theodore Parker. The truly radical nature of the club had been disclosed when two women were asked to join! They were Miss Margaret Fuller and Miss Elizabeth Peabody.

Both women were worthy of the honor for both believed in "inquiry" and in revolt against conventional thinking. Margaret Fuller was a "terrible antagonist" in philosophical discussion with her "man's logic" and her "woman's tongue." "Perfectibility" was a watchword with the group, and in it Margaret found authority for her supreme egotism as she saw herself approaching closer and closer to the goal. Elizabeth, whose influence over Margaret was "beneficent," Emerson said, found "perfectibility" in others rather than herself.

When Emerson's *Nature* appeared it became a textbook for this group, and when Bowen, Harvard teacher of philosophy, attacked the book, terming it "transcendental," the group welcomed the namecalling and turned it to their own uses. The philosophy they were forming for themselves seemed to spring high like a pure fountain of light and to overarch them all — so that "transcendentalists" they were, and they were proud of it.

It had seemed to these transcendentalists that their ideas should reach a larger audience than that of their own circle. Most of them wrote, but they were all too often writers without a publisher. Adopting the name which Alcott had given his private journal, they had begun the publication of the *Dial*, quarterly periodical of transcendentalism.

Transcendentalists were poets, almost every one of them, because the excitement of studying contemporary foreign thought and then of attempting to think for themselves was an exhilarating experience, producing moments of self-confidence and self-fulfillment which nothing but poetry could express. William Ellery Channing, nephew of the great doctor, was good when he described a mood evoked by wind and rain. Thoreau's "Sympathy" was good, if not as good as Emerson thought; and Emerson himself, in spite of pages of metrical prose, was a poet in frequent flashes. The Sturgis girls wrote well when, by means of transcendentalism, they dared to let themselves go a little. Now the transcendentalist poets were heard for the first time in the *Dial* — albeit anonymously, for the Sturgis family, for one, would never have allowed their women to appear in print. The whole group was blazing the trail toward a new freedom in poetry; but their ideas were too involved for verse, they let their heads get in the way of their hearts and they sometimes wrote like lexicographers. As essayists they were very much better.

There had been "a piece about Miss Peabody" in 1840 in the first number of the *Dial;* for she had opened her bookshop the day before. But it was not until 1841 that Elizabeth Peabody's first *Dial* contribution appeared; it was one of the best things she ever wrote.

"A Glimpse of Christ's Idea of Society" she called it, and she said, among other things, that the Apostolic Church is hard to study and that few realize that it might have been "below the mark." Here was a fine heresy and just the opening for the conservative clergy, who must have read their *Dial* from cover to cover, so fruitful was it in matter suitable for attack from the pulpit. But Lizzie went on. "There are men and women who have dared to say to one another; why not have our daily lives organized on Christ's own idea? Why not begin to move the mountain of custom and convention?" Elizabeth mentioned such Communities as the Shakers and the Moravians, but she said, "The great evil of Community however, has been a spiritual one. The sacredness of the family, and personal individuality have been sacrificed." A solution to social ills was being proposed by Elizabeth's friend and fellow transcendentalist, the Reverend George Ripley, and Elizabeth was presenting Ripley's ideas to the public for the first time. She granted that Ripley's plans for Brook Farm were still far from perfect, and she said so plainly. "To form such a society is a great problem whose perfect solution will take all the ages of time; but let the spirit of God move freely over the great deep of social existence, and a creative light will come at His word, and after that long evening in which we are living, the morning of the first day shall dawn on a Christian Society."

Elizabeth promised a sequel to this article, which appeared the following January. Meanwhile, she had her hands full because, in 1841, she herself became the publisher of the *Dial*. Margaret Fuller was editor, and Elizabeth's first move on becoming publisher was to promise that Miss Fuller's salary of a hundred dollars would be paid before any profits should accrue to the publisher. The former publisher, Weeks Jordan, had gobbled up all the subscription money for expenses, leaving nothing for salary. "That rascally firm," Elizabeth called them, but before long she was obliged to revise her opinion. Whatever their misdeeds, they had not misappropriated profits because there were none. There was still no money for Miss Fuller and she very wisely resigned. Emerson reluctantly took over the editorship, signed Elizabeth's notes for printing expenses, and between them they tried to figure out how to make ends meet. They had been printing 700 copies, only 300 of which were paid subscriptions. Elizabeth wrote Emerson that the *Dial* could not go on like this. Expenses might possibly be met if they printed only 300 copies but subscriptions must be increased. She thought perhaps James Freeman Clarke might sell some "at the

West." Emerson found the whole subject well outside his realm of thought.

Eventually Elizabeth turned the publishing of the *Dial* over to James Monroe and Emerson paid $120 to square her accounts. This was defeat, but considering the difficulties of maintaining a magazine without capital and without advertising, it was an honorable one. Monroe made fine promises and Elizabeth was to be genuinely sorry when he broke them, while Emerson discovered how very careful Elizabeth had been of his money and how close her defeat had been to victory.

Whatever the ledgers showed, Elizabeth's experience as publisher of the *Dial* brought her profit. There was her friendship with Emerson — which had now lasted almost twenty years. Business dealings on the *Dial*, instead of coming between them, were to bring a closer understanding as both tried to make a practical success out of a production too limited in appeal. Emerson brought his friends, the *Dial* contributors, to meet their publisher and if Concord was rapidly becoming the country home of philosophy, the shop in West Street became a city headquarters.

They were a young crowd, these transcendentalists. Emerson was not the hollow-cheeked old man of his more familiar portraits, but a young enthusiast still in his thirties, and only a year older than Elizabeth herself. George Ripley had been thirty-eight, two years older than Elizabeth, in 1840 when he first began to talk about Brook Farm; James Freeman Clarke and Theodore Parker just thirty. "The club of the like-minded," they sometimes called themselves — "I suppose," said James Freeman Clarke, "because no two of us thought alike." On West Street, it was George Ripley who most often assumed leadership.

Hawthorne, also, came often to West Street, of course. His engagement to Sophia was still a secret to the outside world, but not to Sophia's family, and the lovers were allowed discreet moments to be alone together, the ardor of their brief embrace giving Hawthorne something to dream about and to write to his "dearest Wife" about from "Castle Dismal," as he called his boyhood home in Salem. To the casual observer, it seemed merely as if Hawthorne called frequently at West Street to see his publisher. *Grandfather's Chair; A History for Youth*, by Nathaniel Hawthorne, came out under the imprint of E. P. Peabody. There followed *Famous Old People* and *Liberty Tree* in a series of children's books which Elizabeth was sure would make their author rich and famous — and enable him to marry his publisher's sister. Of course the books did nothing of the sort and Hawthorne, whose temperament was the opposite of Elizabeth's, had never really thought they would.

On days when Margaret Fuller was at West Street with her "Babel of talkers" Hawthorne was careful to stay away. But there was another group that he joined of an evening — settling himself down not to talk but to listen. Though George Ripley had begun by expounding his ideas of social reform only to his own transcendentalist friends, almost at once new disciples added themselves, and these were young indeed! The ardent, the observant Thomas Wentworth Higginson could not have been much over seventeen when he first felt Ripley's unforgettable influence. He, and most of the rest, were theological students at Harvard under Professor Norton and they became interested in Ripley, through Norton's castigation of him as a heretic. Meeting Ripley at the shop in West Street, some of these young students led him to state his side of the question and were impressed. Further meetings were arranged, and they brought their friends. They stayed in the bookroom to talk until the hour grew so late that the shop closed and the bookroom became the Peabody parlor — while they discussed the glowing vision which Ripley opened before them.[2]

The United States in the 1840's was just recovering from its second major depression. These serious young people had seen women begging in the streets of Boston, and they had been profoundly shocked. Such things must not happen again and they were sincerely in search of a solution to the problem, youthfully sure that they would find it. Ripley proposed a society free from the evils of wealth and poverty alike. He envisioned a world in which each individual contributed his best effort, each was rewarded with security and simple necessities, and all developed upon a higher, finer plane of personal achievement. There was no talk of compulsory labor. There was no hint of sacrificing the individual to the group and there was no suggestion of an all-powerful director, however beneficent his aims. Since God in his mercy had created men with different talents, so each member of the ideal community would find his own way in which to serve and all wants would be satisfied. Throughout all his talks, Ripley's sincere religious belief ran like a recurring theme of music.

As these conversations continued, the dream crystallized into Brook Farm. Elizabeth Peabody saw it as a school, for she was still the teacher at heart and to her a school was the most logical solution for the ills of society. "Brook Farm Institute of Agriculture and Education" was the name George Ripley gave to his project, so Elizabeth's understanding of it was not far wrong. Boys and girls were to live at the farm and be taught music and languages by the most brilliant young teachers of their time. They were not to give up Latin for the sake of modern languages, either. Brook Farm was not so radical a place as that.

But if teaching had been all, Hawthorne would never have sat in his corner listening to their plans. It was the farming idea that fascinated Hawthorne, as it did so many of Ripley's associates. Brook Farmers, almost to the man, had been raised on the proceeds of commerce. Their great-grandfathers might have been farmers but their own education had been purely intellectual, with emphasis on the classics. Just as they turned to Plato for their ideal of friendship, they envisioned Horace on his Sabine farm as their model for daily living; Horace singing sonorous praise of the pastoral and adding to the glory of the Augustan Age. Interpreting evolution to mean constant, rapid advancement for the human race, they confidently expected to surpass Horace in every way. George Ripley and his followers overlooked the fact that the Sabine farm was the gift of a wealthy benefactor and that slaves performed the labor which provided the peace and abundance upon which the spirit of Horace fed.

Ripley himself, with his wife, had spent several summers on a farm not their own. Food in abundance appeared upon the table through no effort of theirs and they never dreamed that the lovely meadows, the orderly stone walls, the pleasant woodland clear of underbrush, were the result of someone's back-breaking labor. When Brook Farm had been chosen as the site for the experiment but before the association was begun, the Ripleys spent some time looking over the property. Sophia Ripley found it exactly what she sought, namely, "entire separation from worldly care and rest to the spirit which I knew was waiting for me somewhere." And while dreaming of how easily the run-down farm could be brought to productivity, George Ripley found nothing more to do, physically, than to lie "for hours on green banks reading Burns and whistling to the birds who sing to him."

Never having so much as spaded a garden, Hawthorne saw nothing wrong with Ripley's picture of farm life. He desperately wanted to find a way to marry Sophia and support her without giving up his writing. This was it, Ripley assured him. A few hours a day of pleasant out-of-door work on the part of each member of the Community would guarantee food to all, while the sale of surplus crops and the tuition from the school would supply the cost of their shelter. If inspiration struck, Hawthorne would be free to throw down the hoe and take up the pen — his few hours of farm work being easily divided among the rest with no burden to anyone. A community without sacrifice of individual rights — George Ripley was certain that such a thing could be!

Sophia Peabody said that she would be happy to become a member of the Brook Farm Community. She would have consented to anything that Hawthorne proposed if it seemed to make their marriage possible. Although there were to be a men's dormitory and one for women, the Ripleys promised that married couples would have cottages built for them. Sophia liked to be with people, and many who planned to join Brook Farm were already her friends. She would teach drawing in the school and there would be time for her to go on with her modeling, time at last for her to paint those pictures which filled her mind — since she would be free of the necessity for copying.

It was entirely without misgivings that Sophia saw Hawthorne invest his savings from his work at the Custom House in shares in Brook Farm.

On April 13, 1841, Hawthorne wrote to Sophia from Brook Farm, her "future home." It had been snowing and the bleak farmhouse, the lonely, neglected fields, filled him with foreboding. Yet he wrote hopefully to Sophia and with the touch of humor which always broke through his dark moods when he knew instinctively that she, as well as he, had need of courage. Sophia must get herself a polar bear skin, he said — and make of it "a very suitable summer dress for this region."

The Brook Farmers themselves were equipped with smocks in the manner of French peasants but they went the peasantry one better and wore smocks of flowered chintz (made from their sisters' petticoats, it was whispered) and caps with tassels. In these costumes they paraded the streets of Boston to announce their emancipation from all things staid and stodgy such as the clothes their shocked elders told them were only decent. Calling at West Street, the Brook Farmers told Sophia that "Hawthorne has taken hold with great spirit and proves a fine workman." No one mentioned seeing Hawthorne on the street in a peasant blouse. Yet he too had one — of blue linen, made for him by his sister Louisa. If some of the others wore their smocks with an air of bravado, Hawthorne wore his with an air of elegance; the aristocrat playing the plowman. "Hawthorne is one to reverence, to admire with deep admiration so refreshing to the soul," wrote Mrs. Ripley in ecstasy over him. "He is our prince — prince in everything — yet despising no labour and very athletic and able-bodied in the barnyard and field."

At first Hawthorne rejoiced in the many people who surrounded him. He was a writer; people were the material with which he worked, and here was a laboratory made to order. He kept a notebook of his impressions. His letters to Sophia were full of humorous comment on such matters as the heifer which Margaret Fuller had presented to the community and which "hooks the other cows and has made herself ruler of the herd." But when it came to writing for publication, Hawthorne found he could accomplish nothing. It was all very well for Ripley to give him leave to lay aside the "four-pronged instrument" which Ripley "gave [him] to understand was called a pitchfork" and with which he had made many a "gallant attack upon a heap of manure." Hawthorne had discovered that farming is not done in a few hours but from sunup to sundown and, rather to his own surprise, he had also discovered that he could not let his friends break their backs over a heap of manure without him.

These very friends, however, with their eternal talk, their self-conscious culture and their organized uplift, had begun to be more than Hawthorne could bear. "Such a number of troublesome and intrusive people as there are in this thronged household of ours!" he exclaimed to Sophia. It was impossible for him to think consecutively.

"Thou and I must form other plans for ourselves," Hawthorne told Sophia in August, scarcely four months after he had joined Brook Farm with such high hopes. He had been promised upon joining that he might withdraw at any time and receive back the money invested in the project. But the Brook Farmers were loth to lose Hawthorne. They made him trustee of the Brook Farm estate and chairman of the Committee of Finance, on the theory that he might regain his enthusiasm by having a hand in management. The effect was just the opposite as Hawthorne learned of the precarious state of Brook Farm finances. It was autumn before he left the community, but he felt that he got away none too soon.

Monroe, the publisher, had proposed that Hawthorne write a series of stories. Elizabeth Peabody told Hawthorne that Monroe was "an abominable rascal" but when a man has only one slim hope of earning enough money to marry the woman he loves, he is unlikely to heed a warning. "I confess that I have strong hopes of good from this arrangement with Monroe," Hawthorne wrote Sophia; "but when I look upon the scanty avails of my past literary efforts, I do not feel authorized to expect much from the future. Well, we shall see. Other persons have bought large estates and built splendid mansions on such little books as I mean to write; so perhaps it is not unreasonable to hope that mine may enable me to build a little cottage — or, at least to buy or hire one."

During the summer, Sophia had been at work upon a bust of Laura Bridgman, that famous pupil of Dr. Samuel Gridley Howe who, though deaf, blind and unable to speak since early childhood, had been taught to read and to communicate with her fingers. Hawthorne regretted that "outward necessity" should force Sophia to work almost beyond her new-found strength, but she assured him that an occasional headache was a price she was willing to pay. She planned to buy the bedroom furniture for their future home.

Sophia herself forgot that the furniture was secondhand by the time she had finished decorating it with outline drawings. "Upon the bedstead is an outline drawing of Guido's Aurora," she said. Phoebus drove his chariot of horses, Dawn floated before them and "the little genius with the torch" was the morning star. On the foot of the bed was a similar allegorical drawing of "night," and Sophia felt that no one had more lovely furniture than she.

After an engagement of what had seemed a long three years to Hawthorne and to Sophia, the wedding date was set.

CHAPTER TWELVE
Wedding at West Street

THE shop in West Street was as great a satisfaction to Mrs. Peabody as it was to Elizabeth. Gradually Mrs. Peabody had abandoned her earlier attempts to force a great career upon her husband and he was now allowed to putter around with his herbs and his medicines without interference. (Dr. Peabody had long ceased to hope for interest or approval.) Mrs. Peabody had business of her own to mind at last for Lizzie really needed her in the shop and how she loved the books and the people! Her own book was on sale at the shop, *The Legend of St. George, paraphrased from Spenser's Faerie Queene.* It was a great source of pride to her if not of revenue.

Also on sale in the shop and advertised in the *Dial* was *Flower People: Being an Account of the Flowers by Themselves; Illustrated with Plates.* This was Mary's book, adapted from a series of Sunday School lessons given by Elizabeth while Mary was in Cuba. Elizabeth had always meant to put them in book form but it was Mary, much to Lizzie's relief, who found time between school teaching and working on school reports for Mr. Mann. Mary had left out some of Elizabeth's moralizing and had added interesting facts about botany which she had gleaned with difficulty from German works since so little was as yet published in English, so little known about natural history in the English-speaking world. Mrs. Peabody had no difficulty in selling Mary's book to parents in search of something educational as well as moral for their children.

In her new-found satisfactions, Mrs. Peabody almost forgot the invalid Sophia. She did not believe that Sophia would really ever marry. A long engagement contingent upon perfect health which never came seemed to her a romantic arrangement and she wanted it to go on forever. Sophia ought to be content to be worshiped from afar and not risk the hazards, the inevitable suffering which must come with marriage. When it became clear that Sophia was eager to marry, and wanted a June wedding, her mother was shocked.

Well, there were warnings only a mother could give which ought to make Sophia change her mind. Mrs. Peabody forgot that her children were now adults; that her oldest daughter, Elizabeth, was thirty-eight, her second daughter Mary thirty-six and Sophia by no means a child-bride at thirty-three! Men were domineering and inconsiderate, Mrs. Peabody told Sophia, they hurt you, and woman's only alternative to submission was ill-health.

Smilingly Sophia assured her mother that Hawthorne was different. There would never be any question of submission between them for she had given him her whole heart. Let the wedding be the last day of June perhaps — if that would make Mother any happier.

"Dearest, the last day of June is Thursday of next week," wrote Hawthorne and he begged for a morning wedding so that they might not waste half a day before beginning their new life together. This suited Sophia perfectly because she had been afraid that Elizabeth would invite the whole bookshop circle — Margaret Fuller and her followers, the Brook Farmers, Emerson and half of Concord — if time were allowed for them to arrive at West Street.

Loving peace and privacy as she did, Mary took Sophia's part. The back parlor must be closed off from the bookroom, Mary said, so that West Street could become homelike for a while. And Sophia asked that only two friends be invited, Cornelia Parks — at whose house Sophia often visited and who had bought several of her paintings — and Sarah Clarke, Sophia's companion in art ever since the days of Mrs. Clarke's boardinghouse. The immediate family would be there of course — and Bridget, the cook, who loved Miss Sophia and would not be forgotten.

It seemed as if it would be a lovely wedding. Mrs. Peabody agreed, while continuing to do her duty as she saw it. The warnings went on. Sophia must never have a child; if she did, it would kill her. Sophia must have a servant and Mrs. Peabody set about getting one of Bridget's friends for her — a young girl of perfect morals who promised never to have a "follower." Of course Sophia would never paint again, once she was married — she would be too worn out, too ill. Sophia only laughed and continued packing her paints, canvases and brushes. And then, suddenly, Sophia lost all her new self-confidence! She became ill and took to her bed, while Mary was commissioned to tell Hawthorne that the wedding was postponed. "Indefinitely postponed," Mrs. Peabody intended that the message should be.

But Sophia sent for Dr. Wesselhoeft, a homeopath who was attaining the success denied her own father. The young German physician, with possibly a shade of a twinkle in his eye, assured Sophia that she was not the first bride to run a temperature; and Mary told Hawthorne, not that the wedding was indefinitely postponed, but that Sophia had set a new date — the ninth of July.

Sophia had asked that Sarah Clarke's brother, James Freeman Clarke, should be the minister to perform the wedding ceremony, and Hawthorne wrote to this close friend of the Peabody sisters:

54 PINCKNEY STREET, *Friday*
July 8, 1842

MY DEAR SIR:

Though personally a stranger to you, I am about to request of you the greatest favor which I can receive from any man. I am to be married to Miss Sophia Peabody and it is our mutual desire that you should perform the ceremony. Unless it should be a decidedly rainy day, a carriage will call for you at half past eleven oclock in the forenoon.

Very respectfully yours,
NATH. HAWTHORNE

Rev. James F. Clarke, Chestnut Street

It did not rain. On the morning of her wedding day, Sophia woke early and ran to the window to see a misty dawn with clear blue sky overhead after days of clouds and showers. Then she went back to bed to wait for the doctor as she had promised her mother she would do. But this time, when her mother brought him in, the doctor could find nothing wrong save a rapid pulse which he assured Mrs. Peabody was no more than right and proper under the circumstances. Sarah Clarke and Cornelia Parks had arrived. Now they were allowed to come to Sophia's room and "arrange the bridal robe." Cornelia braided Sophia's hair and Sarah "dressed" it with pond lilies.

Sophia would not have liked to admit that she was superstitious but she could have cried with vexation when the clouds gathered and a spattering of rain tapped upon the parlor windows as she came down the stairs. Then she saw Hawthorne and he looked to her like "sun shining through a cloud." He was a "seraph" such as she had once tried to paint and he had come down from Heaven just to find her. At the moment when Mr. Clarke pronounced Sophia and Nathaniel man and wife the sun broke through the clouds and "shone directly into the parlor in West Street."

The wedding journey was the trip from Boston to Concord by carriage. "Dear, dear Mother," Sophia wrote, "every step the horses took, I felt better and not in the least tired. I was not tired at the tavern and not tired when I arrived. My husband looked upon me as upon a mirage which would suddenly disappear. It seemed miraculous that I was so well." This miracle, however, was one that Mrs. Peabody would have to accept. As time went by, Sophia would feel tired or fall ill like other people but she would also recover, like everyone else. The invalid Sophia Peabody had ceased to exist. It was Sophia Hawthorne, a supremely happy young woman, who had stepped into a carriage and driven away.

They drove along the old road through Lexington, through the dusty, tree-lined Concord streets, and on almost to North Bridge where a gaunt old house stood far back from the road behind an avenue of trees. Hawthorne was the first to call it the "Old Manse," but the Emerson house had been there in the days when General Palmer, with his son at his side, rode into the Concord fight.[1] Intrepid Mrs. Emerson had been watching the "embattled farmers" (as her grandson Ralph Waldo would one day call them) from her dining room window. And now those shining windows, fifteen tiny panes to the sash, twinkled a welcome to Sophia and Nathaniel. If the old house was the drab color of tree trunks, the meadows around it were summer-green, sun-filled, knee-deep in grass. The Concord River, just below the back garden, shone a placid blue between lily pads; and white pond lilies, the bride's own flower, grew almost at her door.

It is probable that neither Sophia nor Hawthorne had seen the Manse before. On one of her visits to the Emersons Elizabeth heard that the place was for rent and arranged everything. The Emersons sent over Thoreau, who was working in their garden that year — an experiment in the simple life — to make a garden for the bride and groom. Mrs. Alcott, who had recently moved to Concord, had gone with Elizabeth Hoar on the morning of the wedding to decorate the old house. A van had also gone to Concord before the wedding, and trunks and boxes lay scattered helter-skelter along the hall. But Hawthorne "smiled light," Sophia said, as they went from room to room and found flowers everywhere.

Sent ahead likewise was Sara the cook, a friend of Bridget's, who proved famous for her "peach pan pies." But Sophia's first domestic conference with Sara revealed that nothing in the kitchen had been altered or improved since the Concord fight. Sara was in despair and dinner, which should have been ready by two, was not on the table till after six. A new cookstove, "for $16.00," would be the first household purchase made by Mr. and Mrs. Hawthorne.

Fortunately for the Hawthorne's slender resources, the Manse had been rented to them furnished. They were at liberty to use everything or to store away in the attic such pieces as they wished to replace with their own. While waiting for the first meal in their own home, the Hawthornes explored their domain to see what they had fallen heir to and where to put their own belongings.

A little room to the left of the front entrance would be their private sitting room, Sophia decided. It was small, intimate — and the fireplace looked adequate to heat it. On the mantel was a stuffed owl. Sophia thought it was hideous but it amused Hawthorne so they agreed to let it stay. The wallpaper was old-fashioned, Sophia thought, and she tried to imagine the splashing patterns in red or gold she would have had if she were rich. Then she looked again. An almost black background seemed curious but the colors of the tiny nosegay pattern sparkled against it with refreshing charm. The artless-seeming flowers had been good French design of an earlier day and Sophia saw that they were painted very well indeed. On the table by the window was the place where she would put her little music box, a wedding gift. Its tinkling tunes would somehow set to music the happy feeling of this little room.

Opposite, across the hall, was the old family "parlor," smelling faintly of forgotten funerals. The young Hawthornes would have little use for such a room; but past generations of Emersons, ministers one after the other, and the late Mr. Ripley, a minister of course, had found this a parlor to be proud of. Was it the dark mahogany that made the room so gloomy, Sophia wondered? The plaster cast of Apollo, another wedding gift, would go well in here — if anywhere! Sophia had her husband move the dining room table into the parlor and the Hawthornes, flying in the face of New England tradition, sometimes took their meals in this sacred room. Perhaps this was why Sophia, half asleep on the sofa one evening, thought she heard the rustle of a ghostly gown and felt the passing of an unseen form.

The regular dining room opened directly behind the parlor and it was like passing over the threshold into a happier world to leave the parlor and enter it. One glance and Sophia knew it for her own — her studio. She worked best during the morning hours and at that time the room would be flooded with cold north light from the window overlooking Concord Bridge. By afternoon, two beautiful western windows filled with slanting sun. Glimpses of the Concord River almost persuaded Sophia to paint a landscape not of Italy but of America. To paint the beauty at her doorstep would be to defy the taste of her generation, and yet perhaps if Sophia had lived long enough in the house by the Concord bridge she might have become Rebel enough to do it. Upstairs in his study, Hawthorne could write of his native land — unpaid and unappreciated as his work must be. If his wife could not believe in herself enough to pioneer a Concord school of art at the same time, at least she never failed to believe in him and in his genius.

Sophia loved her studio the more because Nathaniel's study was just above it. Upstairs, two western windows framed the sunset and the river, as in the room below, but in Hawthorne's study the windows were half width, the lower sash just three panes high by three panes wide; the upper only three by two. These windows set the scale for the room — charming, intimate and odd! Engravings of clergymen long dead hung on the walls but Hawthorne banished them all to the upper regions, the attic. They looked "strangely like bad angels," he said, "or at least like men who had wrestled so continuously with the devil that somewhat of his sooty fierceness had been imparted to their own visages." In their place, Hawthorne hung the views of Lake Como which Sophia had copied for him from pictures brought home by the Channings from Italy long ago. She had given them to him during their engagement, adding to one of them a shadowy figure in white which she said was herself, waiting for him. Hawthorne had never owned a painting before, he told her. He knew nothing of art, he said, but he could see that they were very beautiful. Would it do harm, he had asked, if he should kiss the dainty figure in the picture? He supposed it would. Now with Sophia his own at last, there was no need even to consider kissing the unfeeling canvas but Hawthorne would have his little pictures always in whatever room he chose for his work. To the study in the Old Manse Sophia added the "astral lamp," her pride and joy, with its Argand burner, its cylindrical wick. Although Dr. Peabody had packed it, the shade was broken and Sophia was justifiably distressed for no such shade would be found in Concord.

The Hawthornes completed the tour of inspection of their new home, they finished their first meal together, and they had just seated themselves for the first time beside their own hearth when they heard voices in the kitchen. Sophia hurried out to find Elizabeth Hoar, daughter of Judge Hoar and a near neighbor. Miss Hoar had not meant to call upon the bride and groom but intended merely to slip into the kitchen with a gift of four pounds of butter!

Since she was caught, Miss Hoar came into the little sitting room and consented to take off her bonnet, indicating that she would sit awhile. Perhaps it was the intuitive Hawthorne who made her admit that it was she who had filled the house with flowers — although she tried to give Mrs. Alcott the credit.

Sophia had become acquainted with Elizabeth Hoar at the time when the portrait medallion of Charles Emerson had been made. It was delightful that Miss Hoar should be the first Concord friend but at the same time Sophia felt a constraint that was almost shyness. How similar Miss Hoar's life had been to her own, yet how different! Miss Hoar's engagement to Charles Emerson had been a perfect love affair between two brilliant, gifted people. Miss Hoar's father had offered Charles Emerson a law partnership, and a home in Concord had been waiting for them. Fate might just as easily have placed them in the Emerson house, where, instead, Sophia and Nathaniel had come as bride and groom!

Sophia remembered the lines her sister Elizabeth had copied off and sent to her at the time of Charles Emerson's death. Although written long ago and expressing the grief of another, they seemed to speak for Elizabeth Hoar.

> Sleep on, my love, in thy cold bed
> Never be disquieted!
> My last good night! Thou shalt not wake
> Till I thy fate shall overtake:
> Till Age or grief or sickness must
> Marry my body to thy dust.[2]

Almost ten years had gone by and Elizabeth Hoar had found no other love. She would always remain married to dust. It was not until she got up to go and Sophia went with her to the door that anything was said about Sophia's wedding. Then, "Is this your bridal gown?" Miss Hoar asked. It was. She lifted the tunic to examine what was to her a new style. "I am perfectly satisfied. I approve entirely," she said with mock solemnity. All Sophia's feeling of constraint slipped away as she saw that Miss Hoar could share in her happiness and could even increase it by means of her generous, affectionate friendship.

And now it was time to carry candles to the beautiful chamber over the parlor. A solid wall of paneling, broken only by a small fireplace, reflected the flickering yellow light. There had been time during the afternoon to banish the carved mahogany four-post bed to the attic and to set up in its place the bedstead painted by Sophia. Upon it there was no feather bed, which Sophia preferred, but a mattress because Nathaniel had said that a mattress was what he liked. Other pieces of furniture painted by Sophia took the place of Emerson mahogany, and Sophia looked about her with great satisfaction. "Our golden bedroom" she called it, and now it seemed right and very beautiful.

There was no fear in Sophia's heart such as her mother had foretold. She felt nothing but joy and confidence in the man she loved. Had not Hawthorne also foretold, in his letters to her, what this hour would be like? He was the prophet she knew she could believe, now that the hour had come.

Sophia awoke early next morning. She would always be the first to awake and would slip out of bed to some warm room, usually Nathaniel's study, where she could sew or write in the journal she and Nathaniel kept together. On the morning after her wedding she lay still and listened to the birds singing just outside her bedroom window. Sophia had never before lived where birds came so close and she felt as if they sang just for her. They must know about us and our happiness, she thought.

During the days that followed, Sophia felt a gaiety, a release from tension, such as she had never experienced before. She took long walks with Nathaniel and in the early morning she rose to open the journal and add her account of their joyous adventures to his own. Even their first quarrel was memorable for the sweetness of reconciliation. It happened because the city-bred Sophia knew no better than to walk across an uncut hayfield. The equally city-bred Hawthorne had just learned at Brook Farm that ripe grass must not be trampled. When she would not turn back he climbed the hill another way, meeting her in the woods beyond.

"This I did not like very well and I climbed the hill alone," Sophia wrote in the journal which they shared. "We penetrated the pleasant gloom and sat down upon a carpet of dried pine leaves. Then I clasped him in my arms in the lovely shade, and we laid down a few moments on the bosom of dear Mother Earth. Oh, how sweet it was! And I told him I would not be so naughty again, and there was a very slight diamond shower without any thunder or lightning and we were happiest. We walked through the forest and came forth into an open space whence a fair, broad landscape could be seen, our old Manse holding a respectful place in the plain, the river opening its blue eyes here and there, and waving mountainous ridges closing in the horizon. There we plucked whortle berries and then sat down. There was no wind and the stillness was profound. There seemed no movement in the world but that of our pulses. The earth was still before us. It was very lovely but the rapture of my spirit was caused more by knowing that my own husband was at my side than by all the rich variety of the plain, river, forest and mountain around and at my feet."

After a day spent in happy wanderings out of doors, Sophia returned home, not to her bed as her mother would have supposed, but to dance in the evening to the tune of the little music box. "I once danced very well," she confided and she showed Hawthorne the "Cach a cha." She danced as she had seen Cuban girls dancing but as she had never dared dance before. "You deserve John the Baptist's head," said Hawthorne, teasing her a little.

Sophia's "love letters" were burned, but her letters to her mother after marriage were certainly all about love — and they remain.

"Say what you will, there never was such a husband to enrich the world since it sprang out of chaos," she began. "I feel precisely like an Eve in Paradise. We have not done much but enjoy each other yet — we wander to the doors and sit under the balm of Gilead tree . . . We converse silently a great deal and wonder if the earth does indeed contain such unmingled happiness and charm as we have found . . .

"A limited number of hours as I have always formerly seen him, has constrained us. It seemed as if we met only to part. But now! All our life is before us. There is no hurry so he blooms into more consummate perfection every day and I find that even I did not quite know him."

Even in the midst of her new-found happiness, however, Sophia was troubled about her mother. By August, she wrote: "While I was at home, I never dared once to refer to our separation for I knew that it was too tender and overcoming a subject for both you and me to talk about. I knew I could not bear your emotion without being nearly beside myself. . . . Nothing should have brought it about but this alone . . . If my husband had not found me till I had gone to heaven . . . I would never have left you. I bequeath my vocation now to Elizabeth and Mary. Elizabeth understands you best of the two; but Mary is a lovely angel though she does not comprehend you very well. . . . She is generous as light and does not mean to reproach."

Mrs. Peabody, however, could not as yet relinquish Sophia and she strove to hold her as before — by means of Sophia's invalid condition. With infinite patience, Sophia continued to free herself. "My precious Mother, it sounds strangely to have you speak of being 'summoned to my sick bed.' . . . I seem to be translated out of the former Sophia Peabody . . . nothing can be further from my purposes than to be upon a sick bed . . .

"Do not fear that I shall be too subject to my Adam, my crown of Perfection. He loves power as little as any mortal I ever knew. . . . Our love is so wide and deep and equal that there could not be much difference of opinion between us upon any moral point. . . . He is completely under the dominion of his intellect and sentiments. Oh who ever saw such a union of power and gentleness, softness and spirit, passion and divine reason! The heavenly hosts may come and pitch their tents round about us as in the first Eden and easily mistake my husband for one of their hierarchy. I think it must be partly smiles of angels that makes the air so pleasant here. I think seraphs love as he loves me — ardent, rapt, tender, devout and holy. . . . Ah, dear mother, I ask daily and hourly 'Oh why should heavenly God to me have so much regard as to place me here with such a husband.' I am grateful with my whole heart, mind and strength. We do not forget God, my mother. We constantly together thank him."

Mrs. Peabody continued her forebodings of disaster but she kept Sophia's letters. In spite of herself, she began to enjoy reading over the details of her daughter's married life. There was the matter of the "urn-shaped teacups" and the wineglasses. One of each had been broken, although Dr. Peabody had packed them with care. Mrs. Peabody had told him they would break. Then there were Sophia's new friends. Doubtless they tired Sophia but it was gratifying to have her well received.

Within five days after the wedding the calls had begun, Mr. and Mrs. Emerson arriving on Sunday afternoon. Sophia was enchanted to be addressed as "Mrs. Hawthorne" for almost the first time but when they left she was even more pleased to hear the Emersons call her "Sophia." She served tea in the urn-shaped cups, feeling experienced and competent and at the same time like a child pretending to keep house. The Emersons told her that she looked "fair and rosy," and "very pretty indeed" was the description of the bride that went the rounds of Concord tea parties.

Toward nine that same Sunday night a "rousing knock" at the door announced George Hillard and Harry Cleveland — friends of old days at Fayette Place. George Hillard was now Hawthorne's friend as well, Hawthorne having rented a room in his house during the days when he worked at the Custom House. This time, not the teacups but the wineglasses were brought out.

There were callers in a steady stream now — the Alcotts, Mr. Thoreau. Sophia was struck with the ugliness of Mr. Thoreau's roughhewn countenance. She was so fond of beauty that it was hard for her to like a man with such a big nose. Hawthorne had been working in the garden, wearing his blue linen smock of Brook Farm days,[3] and he was most grateful to Thoreau for the valuable gift of a garden planted early, so that the bride and groom could have fresh vegetables almost as soon as they arrived at the Manse. The two men took to each other at sight. Hawthorne had found an Indian arrowhead one day as he hoed his corn and he could see that Thoreau, when he heard about it, shared the peculiar pleasure that such a discovery brought.

Sophia really began to feel friendly toward Thoreau only after he called one afternoon, feeling sick and miserable. She lent him her little music box to cheer him up. He was like a child in his pleasure and she told him to keep it as long as he liked. She and Mr. Hawthorne were so happy they did not need it, she said.

On a Sunday toward the end of August, Sophia and Nathaniel were sitting in the parlor when they heard a step in the hall. Sophia "sprang from her husband's embrace" wondering if her hair were completely disheveled and whether her face were as pink as it felt. There stood Margaret Fuller — "Queen Margaret," Sophia called her. "She came in so beautifully . . . and he (Hawthorne) looked full of gleaming welcome." Out came the urn-shaped teacups. Margaret was divested of her bonnet and shawl, she discoursed brilliantly and then was shown the whole house, praising Sophia's painted furniture and noting with personal satisfaction that her wedding gift, a bronze vase, stood in Hawthorne's study filled with ferns. She stayed until moonrise, before returning to the Emersons' where she was visiting.

Friends drove out from Boston, by chaise if they were wealthy, by coach if they were not. Some were friends of Hawthorne's but more were Sophia's friends or people Elizabeth had talked with at the bookshop and sent out to call. All returned with the same story. Nathaniel Hawthorne was not a recluse. He was not even shy but a most gracious host — and the women inevitably added that he was the handsomest of men. A few, who had known Hawthorne before his marriage, congratulated Sophia upon the change she had wrought in him but she always denied that she had done anything at all. They just had not understood Mr. Hawthorne. He was and always had been friendly, she said.

Another triumph for Sophia's contagious friendliness however (whether she admitted it or not) was the visit from her sister-in-law, Louisa Hawthorne. Louisa arrived about August 22 as a result of numerous letters begging her to come and explaining to her just how to take the train to Boston and the coach to Concord. One would suppose that she was being told how to cross a continent; and indeed, to such a recluse as Louisa, the journey seemed fully as formidable. Once arrived, however, Louisa found that she had become another person. Mr. Thoreau had sold to Hawthorne a little boat ideal for voyaging upon the placid river. With Hawthorne at the oars, Sophia and Louisa took long, leisurely excursions, gathering the lovely white pond lilies and the cardinal flowers that were just beginning to bloom in such abundance that Hawthorne referred to them as "whole colleges of Cardinals." There were long walks in the woods and Louisa gathered berries, eating them as she went along — as she had not done since she was a child. When callers came, Sophia so sweetly expected that Louisa would want to meet her friends that Louisa forgot her shyness and passed around the urn-shaped cups as though she had been doing that sort of thing always. The change in Louisa continued even after her return home and in due course she delighted Sophia with the news that "Aunt Dike," a sister of her mother's, had offered to take her traveling and that she had accepted with joy. Mr. and Mrs. Dike were well off and childless, and Sophia shared Louisa's pleasure in the pretty gifts they gave her and the pleasant, normal life they insisted that she share with them.

When summer was over, the bride and groom left the Manse, Sophia to make a visit at home, then to join Hawthorne for her visit to his family. Sophia had been looking forward to this. She had always been loved in her own home and she assumed that her welcome in her husband's home would be affectionate. It was not. Madame Hawthorne could not change the tragic unsocial habit which had fastened upon her, even to welcome a new daughter. Elizabeth Hawthorne, always difficult of approach, was now positively hostile, and Sophia could not understand the reasons. She knew nothing of the writing Elizabeth had hoped to do in collaboration with her brother, she could not realize that Elizabeth saw clearly the changes in Hawthorne and knew that she could never again draw him into the dark shadow of seclusion. And Elizabeth Hawthorne saw that Louisa also was escaping into the sunlight, with Sophia to help her.

Not that Sophia was blameless in her approach to her new family! It was a pity that, secure in her new wifehood, she should see fit to make suggestions in a letter concerning the housekeeping at Castle Dismal. As a doctor's daughter, as a recovered invalid, she was sure that she knew what was good for the health, and Castle Dismal could stand a good airing. The pillows on her bed had been musty. It was a comment to annoy even a sister, and it was one a sister-in-law could not be expected to take — especially since it was true. Louisa forgave Sophia in due course. Elizabeth forgave her never!

Back home at the Manse, the Hawthornes faced the coming winter with happy expectation — and with two new airtight stoves. The capable cook Sara had left; had been replaced by an equally capable Margaret who had also now departed; and in the dim and ancient kitchen of the Old Manse reigned Mary Brian, a pink-cheeked girl from the Old Country and hardly out of her teens. She could make Irish stew and that was all. Nor would it avail Sophia to get her a cook book. Mary Brian could not read or write. Sophia had never been the born teacher that her sister Elizabeth was, but here was a challenge she could not resist. Mary Brian reported at the dining room table every morning for lessons. She made good progress, soon learning to write her name, but she did so hate to sit still! Half a page of reading exhausted her as all the cleaning, washing and cooking never did.

Sophia turned to her painting once more, for the first time since her marriage. She borrowed from Mr. Emerson the monochrome painting, "Endymion," copied from a bas-relief. Sophia had become enamored of sculpture and this picture combined both sculpture and painting in the problems it presented. It was subtle, difficult to draw, but Sophia was happy in her work as never before. The sleeping Endymion became the symbol of her own love, herself the moon goddess. She intended the picture for display and sale in the West Street bookshop, and the money would be welcome — but perhaps she could afford to keep it after all and give it to Hawthorne. He had an agreement to supply three magazines with a monthly contribution apiece, he worked hard at them, sent his stories out on time — and surely enough money would come in to provide everything they needed for the quiet kind of life they liked to live.

It was as well for Sophia that she had her own work. She would have been tormented by the temptation "just to look in" upon Hawthorne and it would have driven him crazy. Or, being naturally sociable, she would have become lonely and filled the house with guests they could ill afford and who would have infuriated Hawthorne by interrupting his work. It was still more fortunate for Sophia, however, that she was an artist and not a writer. Hawthorne made it exceedingly clear how he would have felt about that. "I cannot enough thank God, that, with a higher and deeper intellect than other women, thou hast never — forgive me the base idea! — never prostituted thyself to the public, as that woman [Grace Greenwood] has, and as a thousand others do. It does seem to deprive women of all delicacy. It has pretty much the same effect on them as it would to walk abroad through the streets, physically stark naked."

How fortunate for Sophia that Hawthorne did not consider painting a self-revealing form of expression! He had hardly looked at a picture in his life until Sophia taught him to notice them. Never would he see in paintings the things she saw, but he was willing to accept as true whatever she said she found. Hawthorne was intensely proud of Sophia's work and when "Endymion" was done, he too wanted to keep it.

When spring came, it seemed to Sophia that one particular bird, the one which had sung to her the most beautifully on the morning after her wedding, came back to her to sing again. She had never been in the country in the spring before and she was in an ecstasy of joy. She put seeds into the ground for the first time in her life — seeds given her by Lydian Emerson and Elizabeth Hoar.

She smelled the fresh earth released from frost and she watched the Concord River at flood. In the diary she still wrote with Nathaniel, she said, "My soul is a mighty river also, free from frost and ice — no not frost and ice neither, for I have been free and unshackled all through the cold weather in the heavenly summer of my husband's heart — but still it breaks forth. I have a new hope — partly from the sun of joy in my dear love's eyes, for he has sighed much for the warm days and flowers and green grass and now he is very glad — and partly, I suppose from the involuntary response to the budding trees and rushing waters and birds' songs and voices. But I could not be satisfied in feeling this mighty springing upwards and forwards unless I were in love. I am thankful that I first knew spring after I was married."

Sophia stood at the first of the two western windows in her husband's study, thinking long thoughts about the will of God. She took her diamond ring and wrote upon the tiny pane:

> Man's accidents are God's purposes.
> Sophia A. Hawthorne
> 1843

And her husband, coming to stand at her side, took the ring and wrote:

> Nath Hawthorne
> This is his study
> 1843
> the smallest twig
> Leans clear against the sky.
> composed by my wife
> and written with her dia
> mond

Sophia finished:

> Inscribed by my
> husband at sunset
> April 3rd 1843
> In the golden light
> Sun d S.A.H.

During the winter just past, Sophia had had an early miscarriage.[4] She had gone out upon the frozen Concord River, not to skate for she could not, but to slide upon the ice while her husband swooped and circled about her on flashing blades. He stopped to play with her but could not keep her from falling. The fall was not necessarily the cause of her illness, but her mother was summoned and poured dire predictions into her ears which Sophia scoffed at. Yet her mother might be right and Sophia secretly feared lest she be too frail to bear living children. When she so soon lost her hope of having a child, her husband had comforted her by telling her that God would someday give them back the soul He had first sent them. Was this true? With all the intensity of her ardent spirit, Sophia longed for a child as this second year of her marriage approached; this first springtime of love. By early June she dared to hope that her prayers were answered, and in August of that first happy year of 1843 she wrote to her sister-in-law, Louisa Hawthorne, "I am not quite sure, but I think it is more than two months now that we have been made happy by this promise of new life." The only proper way for Sophia to refer to her condition was to say that she was "*enceinte.*" And "a saint" she was, indeed, Hawthorne told her, teasing her for using a word her mother favored along with "interesting condition."

On the third of March, 1844, Una Hawthorne was born. The baby "lingered ten dreadful hours on the threshold of life," Hawthorne said. But at last both Sophia and the child were doing well.

On the northern window in Sophia's studio, Hawthorne wrote:

> Una Hawthorne
> stood on this window
> sill January 22d 1845
> While the trees were all
> glass chandeliers a goodly
> show which she liked much
> tho' only 10
> months old.

CHAPTER THIRTEEN

Again a West Street Wedding

IT WAS March 28, 1843. Sophia and Nathaniel had just returned to Concord after their first round of visits since their marriage. They rejoiced greatly at being home again and wondered how they could ever have left the Old Manse. Then a letter arrived from West Street. Mary Peabody was engaged to be married! Sophia could hardly believe her eyes when she read the words. She had seen Mary just a few short weeks ago and nothing had been said about romance. Sophia tried to think back to see if there had been any hints she should have caught.

Immediately after her return from Cuba, Mary, who had been so unutterably homesick abroad, seemed to bloom again with the charm of her earlier youth. No one noticed when she passed her thirtieth birthday. There are always women who grow more attractive as they grow older and, for a while at least, Mary had been one of them. She would return home from a jaunt to Boston with a translucent look that betrayed an inner, secret happiness. She bought a new bonnet and arranged her hair a new way. It was wonderful, her family said, what Mary could do with so little money — but it was love that was so becoming to her, and the hope that she might be loved in return that made her so beautiful. No one could remember exactly when the brightness began to fade. During the years at West Street, Mary had begun to look thin and weary. Always careful in her dress, she became too precise. She was thirty-six now and she looked it.

Mary had by no means lost her sense of humor, however. There was no question but what she enjoyed startling Sophia and exploding a bombshell in her family's midst when she announced her engagement to Horace Mann. Elizabeth was speechless for almost the first time in her life. Certainly she did not want to marry Horace herself but he was somehow hers, at least in her own mind, and Mary had snatched him right out from under her nose. She had never suspected anything. That was the hardest to bear because Elizabeth loved to believe that she knew everything about everybody. The glint in Mary's eyes indicated that her own love of secrecy was in direct ratio to Lizzie's love of prying into private lives.

In all probability, Horace Mann did not consider it necessary to ask Dr. Peabody formally for the hand of his daughter in marriage. Mary could be presumed old enough to know her own mind. But Mary loved and understood her father. She looked for his quiet, approving smile and was happy when she saw it.

Mrs. Peabody enjoyed her usual mental conflict. She hoped Mary would be happy but she supposed it was too much to expect. There never was a man living quite good enough for one of her daughters, but Horace Mann came as close as any. It was about time he declared himself, Mrs. Peabody thought — looking back over the long friendship, the frequent calls, the Salem visits. But she assumed this would be a long engagement.

Then Mary exploded her second bombshell. She was to be married at once and was to go to Europe on her honeymoon.

In spite of her joy at being home again, Sophia went back to Boston on April 11 to hear all about it. As to the romance, Sophia learned precious little. Mary's habit of secrecy had been practiced too long. There might have been a sort of "understanding" the previous summer when, with Horace, Mary had gone to Lexington to see his nieces graduate from Normal School, their uncle having educated them. Horace Mann had done enough now for his brothers and sisters and his sister's children.[1] He could afford to think of himself. It was something of a shock and a surprise to him to find that he could not think about himself without thinking of Mary Peabody. She had quietly walked into his life and without her he had no life at all. During visits to Mann's married sister, Rebecca Pennell in Wrentham, and his maiden sister Lydia, the teacher who lived near Providence, Mary had felt herself approved. An "understanding," however, was nothing that Mary would ever tell about to anyone. She was not happy enough at the time of Sophia's marriage to interrupt Sophia's paeons of joy with news of her own.

It would be years before Mary could confide to anyone the secret of her long hopeless-seeming love for Horace Mann. She had returned from Cuba with certain hopes, it was true. But in 1837 Horace Mann had given up his political career to become the first Massachusetts Secretary of Education. Fifteen hundred dollars was grudgingly voted to him for his salary and the position was distinctly without honor. But it was Horace Mann who had created the Board of Education, and it was his choice to administer it no matter how difficult the task. Mary loved and admired him for it while at the same time her heart was filled with despair. On that salary, it would not be likely to occur to him that he could support a wife. About the only thing Mary could do was to show him what a thrifty person she was and how little she expected out of life in the matter of worldly goods.

Mary understood, however, just why Horace Mann took a step which, to his political associates, seemed so disastrous. He had lost his appetite for political power through the death of his first wife. Because of Elizabeth and Mary Peabody, he had become interested in education, and through Elizabeth he had met Dr. Channing. If Dr. Channing was right, and God dwelt in man, ever ready to inspire and lead the individual to finer, higher living — then nothing could be more important than education. The educated man, expressing the will of God in his own being, could create a world where oppressions would cease; where murder under the guise of war would be outlawed; and where a peoples' government could function with justice to all without corruption. Horace Mann was no Brook Farmer. He knew too much about the toil which the soil demands. He cared nothing for community living, because he so loved the hearth and home of a private family. Writing in a mood of exaltation and prophecy he said — and Mary carefully copied it down:

> Whence comes the wealth of Massachusetts? I do not mean the gorgeous wealth which is displayed in the voluptuous and too often enervating residences of the affluent, but the *golden mean* of property . . . which carries blessings in its train to thousands of householders; which spreads solid comfort and competence through the dwellings of the land. . . . The families scattered over her hills and along her valleys have not merely a shelter from the inclemencies of the seasons, but the sanctuary of a home. Not only food but books are spread upon their tables. Her commonest houses have the means of hospitality; they have appliances for sickness, and resources laid

up against accident and the infirmities of age. Whether in her rural districts or her populous towns, a wandering native-born beggar is a prodigy. . . .

One copious, exhaustless fountain supplies all this abundance. It is education — the intellectual, moral and religious education of the people.

Although at work in Massachusetts, Horace Mann did not think in terms of his own state alone but of the nation. "In a government like ours," he said, "each individual must think of the welfare of all as well as the welfare of his own family, and therefore of the children of others as well as his own. Are they so educated that when they grow up they will . . . be guided by a sense of justice, a love of mankind and a devotion to duty?"

If America was to be a true democracy, then in the public schools the finest education must be made available to all. When he looked into the matter, Horace Mann found that the public schools were mere places of detention for children whose parents had no money. They were taught by men, most of whom were unfit for any other employment and therefore totally unfit to guide and direct the development of a child. Worst of all was the public apathy toward the situation.

Mann began by holding what he humorously called "revival meetings" all over the state to discuss public schools and ways and means to improve them. At first the meetings were attended by only a handful of people, most of whom were women. But Mann was a brilliant speaker and now he was inspired by a great cause. His small audiences went away to spread the new gospel, and when Mr. Mann returned a month or two later he would find a larger group, a school properly heated perhaps, with less opportunity "for the study of astronomy through the holes in the roof." Teachers would be doing a better job through consciousness of public support.

It occurred to Horace Mann that women would make the best public school teachers — and it must be admitted that this was partly because he knew a woman would take less money than a good man would accept. Strangely enough, there were almost no women teachers and in some communities there was an ordinance against "females" teaching in the schools. But here was a new field for women which would not be frowned upon by society as soon as public schools rose in quality and in favor. That teachers should be trained was just as novel an idea as that females should teach — but to Horace Mann the idea came. His "beloved Normal Schools" his friends called them, as he went up and down the state crusading for funds, buildings and staff. Young ministers, of whom there were more than enough at the time, appealed to Mr. Mann as the most likely timber to head up his training program.

When Horace Mann first went to Salem and visited Mary in her home it was as a Lyceum lecturer, his purpose to entertain. Then he came again, hired a hall this time and spoke to his usual pathetically small group of people. As a man with a fiery purpose, he was a better speaker than he had been before. He was staying at the Peabodys' again, and right down in front of the lecture hall sat Mary Peabody, her deep eyes alight. It was an inspiration to look down into her vivid little face with its sensitive color that seemed to come merely at a well-turned phrase. By 1838, Horace Mann was coming regularly to Salem to hold the "Common School Convention." The handful of people had grown to a large audience, female teachers predominating. But Mr. Mann had no trouble locating Mary Peabody, right down in front as always. He did not realize how much he depended upon her answering radiance each time he made one of his fine effects. He looked forward, however, to sitting late in the Peabody parlor with her, telling her all his fine dreams for "common schools."

In 1839, Mary went to Boston to open a school for very little children and to live by herself "at board." The Alcott affair was over but not forgotten and it was at this time that Mary was severely catechized as to whether she intended to give religious instruction or to discuss any of the miraculous prophecies of birth with her five-year-olds. Mary said emphatically no, but it was strange how Elizabeth's connection with Alcott had power to harm her. Only a handful of children were enrolled and if she had not wanted so very much to be in Boston, Mary might have given up her project.

Always honest with herself, Mary admitted freely in her own mind that she had come to Boston in order to be nearer Horace Mann. It seemed a wonderful idea at first, especially when she offered her services in helping him prepare the school reports which were important beyond measure. It was not the facts and figures which Mary copied so diligently — it was the use Horace Mann put them to, when he appeared before the legislature to ask for more money for new school buildings, new Normal Schools, better salaries. He never asked for money for himself although even his traveling expenses came out of his painfully inadequate salary. There was no money for a secretary and this, as far as Mary was concerned, was the only bright spot on her horizon. She could make him accept her services as a contribution to the great cause and so find an excuse to be with him constantly. But she would have given anything if Horace had not seemed to have renounced all thought of a home and family along with every other sacrifice he was prepared to make.

Absorbed though he was in education, Horace Mann was not a person of one cause alone. Temperance, treatment of the insane, prison conditions and antislavery all received his ardent attention. He made speeches, enlisted friends. His was that rare combination of keen legal ability and personal charm, so that he was made moderator of many a meeting where tempers were likely to flare. He had a way with people and he could prevent the literal hurling of mud as well as insults. He was moderator at the turbulent meeting when a crowd of Boston's leading citizens tried to find a means of rescuing runaway slaves who had been caught, imprisoned, and were about to be returned to their masters. Outside the building and battering at the doors were other leading citizens waiting in happy expectation of tarring and feathering every antislavery man they could lay their hands on. Mr. Mann was perfectly calm, his friends said.

Proud as she was of him, Mary would have been just as well pleased if Horace Mann had given up a cause or two provided it left him time to think of her a little. She never knew exactly what happened to bring about at last the change she longed for. Was it his freedom from responsibility for his relatives? It was partly that. Or was it because there was romance in the air as Dr. Samuel Gridley Howe fell desperately, romantically in love with the beautiful Julia Ward of New York? Howe had long since escaped the wiles of the flirtatious Marian Marshall but he had an eye for beautiful women, a tendency Horace Mann deplored. Mann and Howe were the most intimate friends, their letters to each other delightful documents full of frankness and humor. It would not have been unlike Howe to tell Horace Mann straight out that what he needed was to remarry. Mann was ill; and Dr. Howe's diagnosis might well have been that he suffered from overwork to be sure — but from loneliness most of all. Dr. Howe had captured his Julia after a whirlwind courtship. Perhaps Horace now decided to see if he could sweep Mary off her feet with a swift declaration!

The Howes were going to Europe, where the doctor would study education of the blind, prison conditions, the care of the insane — and his bride would tell him whether or not these were suitable occupations for a honeymoon. He urged Horace Mann to come along on the same boat, make it a double honeymoon — and study common schools. Perhaps Mary had not forgotten Elizabeth's letters and how they once hurt her. But she was too happy to care when at last she herself was the one that Horace "took entirely into his arms." He asked her if she could possibly be ready to be married by the first day of May — the day the Cunarder sailed.

There must have been a twinkle in Mary's eyes. It was all very sudden, she said. But she thought she could manage.

Mary made an overnight visit to Wrentham, where Horace Mann's sister, Mrs. Pennell, lived and where he had made his home from time to time. She was received with open arms, and all the neighbors were called in to help the family rejoice in Horace Mann's good fortune. Mary was not surprised exactly but she was made happy almost to the point of tears. Because of ill-health, Mrs. Pennell would not be at the wedding at West Street but she would be there in spirit, Mary well understood. Mary wrote to Eliza and Rebecca not only to come to the wedding but to visit at West Street, beforehand.

And now, almost before she had time to catch her breath, it was May Day and Mary was to be married. No sunshine slanted through the West Street parlor windows as it had upon Sophia's wedding day, no light shower tapped upon the glass. It poured! The rain made a solid sheet of water moving across the pane. Mary hardly noticed. She put on her wedding dress of white "grassecloth," its only ornament a lovely lace collar made and embroidered by a former pupil. In her dark hair she wound a heavy gold chain, the wedding gift of the groom. Her mirror told her that she looked pretty — that Horace would be pleased.

A note came from Sophia. She had planned to come from Concord — but of course the rain! Although no longer an invalid, old habits clung to her and she never went out in bad weather. Brother Nathaniel Peabody arrived with his wife and children. But Mr.

Mann's sister, Miss Lydia Mann, though expected, did not come. It was eleven o'clock now, time for the wedding, but Rebecca and Eliza had not appeared. Half an hour passed. At last, the all too patient bridegroom lost patience and told the minister to proceed. "Mr. Mann looked delightfully during the ceremony," Elizabeth said — "so sweet and bright and happy."

Mary told in her own words what she felt. "When I was being married I realized I could not grasp the felicity that was mine — it seemed to elude my grasp but soon after it seemed all natural like the stars and the ocean and the course of the sun. . . . I suspect it is the music in the heart of the universe, the eternal harmony of things, which now I hear."

Elizabeth went with the bride and groom to the wharf, the aging Dr. and Mrs. Peabody fearing the storm. Mary looked anxiously at Elizabeth to see if she seemed happy. She looked "perfectly satisfied," and it was a joy to Mary to remember her sister's unclouded face at parting.

For the second time in her life, Mary watched her beloved Boston recede into the distance. To the great relief of the sentimental Sophia, the sun broke out in the afternoon and at least half of Mary's wedding day was beautiful. Mary saw the statehouse dome vanish in the rain and then emerge in sudden sunlight against a clearing sky. She had not realized how different two sailings could be. There was still the moment, like death, when the ship left shore. Her throat hurt as she realized that her father and mother were growing old and might not be alive upon her return. But this was a different feeling from the pain of leaving for Cuba, believing that she would never see Horace Mann again. She stole a glance at him. And it was good to find that he was looking at her with as much love and pride and happiness as her heart could desire.

Mary arranged everything in their stateroom aboard the *Britannia* — "with reference to Mr. Mann's being seasick," Elizabeth reported. And Mary, being an excellent sailor, was the only "live lady" at dinner that night, she said herself. But Mr. Mann provided a happy surprise. By next morning he had found his sea legs, thanks to a certain prescription given him by Dr. Howe. He wrote his mother-in-law about it the day after the wedding. "You must tell the Tee-to-tallers that we have all drunk brandy all around this morning but we considered ourselves out of the jurisdiction of the American Temperance Society and under the law of Neptune and Nations. So much of my crooked hand as you cannot attribute to my writing in my lap, in a rolling, pitching ship, you may attribute to what you please!"

On May 3 they reached Halifax and began the kind of sight-seeing they would continue throughout their journey. They spent three hours visiting schools! "The children looked dirty and squalid," Mary thought, "and not as if their intellects were enlisted in the cause of learning." For the first time she saw soldiers walking about the streets in considerable numbers and she remembered that it had been so in Cuba. It "ever gives me the impression that law does not prevail but only soldiers," she said.

They reached London on May 15, and now both Horace and Mary Mann saw Europe as though through a window in West Street. The Marquis of Westminster, commented Mr. Mann, had a private garden of "over fifty-two acres or about the size of Boston Common." And Mary, looking at the mansion of that same gentleman, said that it "appeared to me as long as West Street." Certain corridors in Windsor Castle were "about as long as Park Street."

The Manns were impressed but not favorably impressed. "The differences of conditions here strike me constantly and most painfully," said Mary — "such splendid mansions and equipages and such squalid misery side by side." She had been to London's "Jews Quarter" the previous day and she could not get the picture out of her mind and heart. People lived "in pent-up lanes, holes, and caverns. What a place to lie in immediate proximity with so much luxury, voluptuousness and superfluous wealth!" They had been to the Tower of London and had been shown the royal regalia but Mary did not even like the Queen's crown. It looked like a little boy's cap without any visor, she thought. And Mr. Mann had been shocked when he was told that the regalia was valued at three million pounds. "With almost three million of destitute, almost starving subjects!" he exclaimed.

"Mr. Mann boils with indignation and rejoices that he is not an Englishman," Mary said. "I am very much afraid he would bite the Queen's fingers instead of kissing her hand if he should get so near — so much more does he detest royalty and its collaterals than he did at a distance."

Most of the Manns' time was spent in visiting schools, of course. Since Mr. Mann had been sick and discouraged over conditions in the common schools at home, he could not help taking a little comfort from the fact that some of the schools in England seemed even worse. Schools for children of the lower classes were under the control of Established Church and the Manns learned that, in order to obtain employment, a child of needy parents must present a certificate, not from any good school, but from a Church of England school. "How does this differ from the persecutions of noncomformists which drove the Puritans from England!" Mary Mann demanded in righteous wrath. To teach in "poor schools," a schoolmaster need only be orthodox, it seemed. One schoolmaster could not write his name, Mr. Mann was told; while another, upon being asked if he could read, replied, "Summat; at any rate I keeps ahead of the children."

Where he found schools of which he approved, Mr. Mann took copious notes for his report which he intended to make to the Massachusetts legislature. He endeavored to be fair but he never failed to point out that these good schools were undenominational and that they received all children of whatever creed.

Leaving London, the Manns traveled northward by coach to Scotland. Mary saw the roofs and towers of Abbotsford above the trees and she nearly cried when she learned that there would not be time to stop to see the home of Sir Walter Scott — for she and her sisters had read every Waverley novel as soon as it was received in the United States. But there were insane asylums, prisons, and above all schools, that Mr. Mann must visit, and there would not be time for everything. On the whole, Scottish schools fared better in Mr. Mann's estimation. While he deplored their rigorous discipline, he thought that a poor boy had a better chance of obtaining an education in Scotland than in England — and Horace Mann never forgot his own hard struggle and never ceased to battle for a better chance for young people in narrow circumstances.

But all this time Mary was deeply concerned to see that her husband was overworking on this journey supposedly for health. He was sleeping badly and a muscle in his cheek jumped uncontrollably, making him more nervous every day. He became convinced that he had not long to live and that he must finish his study of foreign schools and complete the system that he was devising for the common schools of his own country as quickly as possible. When Mary found that she could not influence him to take more rest she began to work as hard as he in the hope of lightening his load as he gathered material for the *Seventh Report of the Secretary of the Massachusetts Board of Education.*

By July 3, the Manns had arrived in Hamburg, Germany. At that time, Germany was the acknowledged leader in the world of education; and now Horace Mann began to mend in health, not through rest — for he worked harder than ever — but through the satisfaction of finding what he had come to Europe to seek. It was not that the German schools were ideal. Mr. Mann objected to the memorizing of verses from Scripture with no comprehension on the part of the pupil of the meaning of the words and for no better reason than to obtain a certificate. He objected to their principle of having different schools for children from different walks of life — "poor schools" and then "very poor schools"! But of far greater importance than any of the faults of the German school system was one great virtue. The teachers "were the finest collection of men I have ever seen," Horace Mann said. They were "full of intelligence, dignity, benevolence, kindness." They bore "in their countenance and demeanor the impress of conscientiousness and fidelity to their trust."

Horace Mann knew almost no German at all but wherever he went he thought of a thousand questions he must ask the teachers, about theories of education, methods, their attitude toward the students. But, as a young girl teaching in Brookline, Mary had taken German lessons and had kept up her study of German ever since. She acted as interpreter — a very imperfect one, she said she was, but she had a quick ear plus an intuitive mind, and languages were easy for her. She enjoyed her experience in Germany just as much as her husband did. "The White-haired Gentleman," German teachers called Mr. Mann, not knowing who he was or whence he came — but recognizing a courteous friend.

Through Saxony, Bavaria and Holland went the Manns, visiting museums and palaces occasionally — to please Mary — prisons, insane asylums and schools always. In Dresden, Mr. Mann almost permitted himself to admire a picture gallery — save that "the arts have flourished amid an immeasurable extent of misery." In Paris, he was impressed not by the Louvre, but by the size of the foundling hospital. The number of illegitimate children deposited there, he said, was many times greater than the whole number of births in the city of Boston. This confirmed exactly Mr. Mann's preconceived ideas about the morals of Paris versus Boston!

The Horace Manns were homesick and ready to return to Boston by the autumn of 1843. Their passage was the worst since the shipwreck of the Apostle Paul, Mr. Mann declared. But Mary said she was "very well indeed" and she assured him that he would live. His health was better than it had been when he left home, she told him, and — once on land again — he admitted that she was right.

He felt full of vigor, eager to write the result of his European school survey.

Mary wanted to set up housekeeping in the country but she found there was no hope of this until the report should be finished. They engaged three rooms at the old Coolidge House on Bowdoin Square where she could give all her time to translating German pamphlets and documents into the English for the report.

No single creed, to the exclusion of other creeds, should be forced upon students in the public schools, Horace Mann was going to say. Public schools should be open to all, should give equal advantages to all, whatever their social status or religious preference. The Seventh Report was going to cause a controversy in Boston and Mr. Mann looked forward to the battle. "My heart is in the work or fifteen hours a day would kill me," he said. He did not say anything about where Mary's heart was but he knew that the report would surely be done on time.

In February 1844, however, Horace Mann discovered that there was one thing that could bring about a pause even in work such as his and in Mary's unfailing aid. On February 25 their son, Horace Mann junior, was born!

It was Sophia who made the most apt comment. "I suppose his first words will be a school report," she said.

CHAPTER FOURTEEN

Paradise Lost

THE brilliant artist, beautiful, wealthy Sophia Peabody," was the way a Concord neighbor described the bride of Nathaniel Hawthorne.[1] Sophia would have laughed to hear it but the word "wealthy" would have pleased her a little. While never for a moment pretending to be rich, Sophia nevertheless loyally concealed as best she could their increasingly desperate financial situation lest anyone dare accuse her husband of failing to provide properly for his wife and child. Letters to Mrs. Peabody spoke of Hawthorne's incessant labors lasting into the small hours of the morning; of how he turned out two stories in one month — "Earth's Holocaust" and "The Christmas Banquet." When it became necessary to admit, to her mother alone, that Hawthorne was paid only in promises, Sophia put it as a woman would who had unfaltering faith in her husband. "Oh for the $1,300 justly due my husband!" she exclaimed, having arrived at the figure after going over her carefully kept accounts. "It is rather depressing [to Hawthorne, Sophia meant — not to herself] that people do not pay their debts to him. Mr. Lowell, notwithstanding his voluntary promise a fortnight ago to pay his part — has not yet fulfilled it — and an awful pause seems to have swallowed up Epes Sargent, and the Langleys delay."

The rent of the Old Manse was a hundred dollars a year. Hawthorne marveled constantly at the productivity of the garden which he kept immaculately free from weeds with two hours' work each morning. There were apple trees, pear trees and even a peach tree on the place, which bore in such abundance that it was impossible to eat, preserve, or give away quite all the crop. What a contrast this Concord land was to barren, worn-out Brook Farm! The services of little Mary Brian, for cleaning, washing and ironing, cooking in the antediluvian kitchen, and "preserving" the surplus food from the garden, never came to more than three dollars a week. Hawthorne's daily exercise was cutting and splitting wood (his for the trouble) to feed to the eternally hungry airtight stoves. A thousand dollars a year, Sophia figured, would make them comfortably well off and it was no wonder that she thought longingly of the thirteen hundred her husband had earned and could not collect. "The magazine people do not pay their debts," Hawthorne said.

A hundred dollars arrived from New York one day, however. It would help out; among other things, Hawthorne could buy the paper and ink with which a writer must pursue his trade. He walked to Concord village "to change the bill at the bank." But it was "New York money" and the Concord bank would not touch it. Hawthorne had to locate a private individual willing to take a chance!

Sophia wrote rarely of her husband's anxiety, instead she usually told of his gaiety, his wonderful puns about their poverty. Watching her at her mending one evening, "We are a holy family," Hawthorne had said, "and you are the holiest." As to the tear in his dressing gown, "He said he was a man of the largest rents in the country and it was strange he had no money."

Mrs. Peabody shared Sophia's letters with Elizabeth — who could not read them without wanting to rush into the breach for her sister. When she read, "James Lowell owes us seventy dollars, I believe," she doubtless called in person and caused still further delay resulting from exasperation because of her well-meant efforts. To Hawthorne, Elizabeth proposed the obvious. He should seek a government position and she made a series of calls suggesting Hawthorne for all sorts of posts, whether already held by other people or not. "It is so much better not to interfere," Sophia told Elizabeth, gently but firmly. "Our hopes center now on King Polk. Mr. Bancroft is at court and in favor."

Hawthorne had never been active in politics but he had already come to the conclusion that he must have a public office and he had already marshaled his friends to his aid, not like a writer and a dreamer, but like a man of the world such as he could always be when he chose. Franklin Pierce was a senator and promised to speak to President Polk. Bancroft, under whom Hawthorne had worked at the Boston Custom House, was now Secretary of the Navy and in a position to be useful. Then there was O'Sullivan, editor of the *Democratic Review*, who had promised Hawthorne regular pay for regular contributions, who had failed often in the matter of pay but who promised to do better in political influence. Most genuinely helpful was Bridge, now a naval officer, who invited the New England senators, Pierce, Atherton and Fairfield, with their wives, to visit him at the Portsmouth Navy Yard to meet Mr. and Mrs. Hawthorne. Here was Sophia's opportunity to use her natural charm, to help her husband appear to his best advantage. Together, they almost managed the "Naval Officership of Boston which is $3,000 a year." Almost, but not quite. What a fortune it would have seemed!

Meanwhile the old home and lovely garden that Sophia often called "Eden" were lost to her "Adam" and herself — not through the eating of those apples from their orchard, whether baked or in pies, but simply because the owners of the Old Manse wanted it for themselves. From the little study window where Sophia and Nathaniel had written their names, they watched the mosses being knocked from the roof of the kitchen ell beneath them, sacrilegious new shingles taking the place of old ones in a prudent, Emerson-Ripley manner. There was even a threat that the Manse might be painted — an idea which Sophia would once have applauded but which now the old house itself had taught her to shudder at. The Ripleys told the young Hawthornes just when the angel with the flaming sword would appear at the gate of their paradise — in the form of a moving van.

Where does a young family go when they have no home and no money? The question was not a new one but it was new to Sophia. She tackled it with courage. She thought of the house in West Street first of all, where she would have been more than welcome and where all Elizabeth's "ladies and young girls wanted to see" the baby, Una. But, as Hawthorne put it, there was "an immense multitude" at Mrs. Peabody's "caravanserai." Rooms vacated by the two married daughters and all other available rooms had been rented. Elizabeth was having difficulties with her book business and it would never do to take away this source of revenue, precarious though it might be. One other cogent reason against West Street remained. Hawthorne could not and would not be able to live in the same house with Mrs. Peabody and Elizabeth!

Sophia wrote to her sister-in-law, Louisa Hawthorne. It was August 24, 1845, and they must be out of the Old Manse by November. She explained about her mother's house being "filled with boarders," and she proposed that Louisa "should hire of Mr. Manning for Una and me the room beneath your parlor for our sleeping apartments and pay you the price of board at table." Sophia made it clear that she wanted to pay her way but at the same time the Peabodys knew the Mannings. Gunsmiths, blacksmiths, owners of a stagecoach line; they were hardheaded Yankee businessmen and Sophia prepared to strike a bargain. A house in Boston, she said (doubtless meaning Number 13 West Street), rents for four hundred and fifty dollars, and a single room in such a house brings a dollar a week without board. The old Manning house could not be considered in any such rental category and therefore a room in it should cost very little. Moreover, the room Sophia had in mind was an old kitchen in an unoccupied portion of the house. "If Mr. Manning should sometime rent the other half of the house to which my kitchen belongs, we can leave," said Sophia, making it clear that her proposal intruded upon the Hawthorne private domains hardly at all. "Nathaniel says that room is nothing but an old kitchen; but I do not care how old or ugly it is if it will only shelter our heads."

Sophia mailed her letter feeling full of confidence that she had solved a serious problem but she might as well have dropped the letter into the Concord River instead of into the postoffice. There was no reply.

By the first of September, there was still no answer. "I should tell my friends that they must not disturb your seclusion by coming to see me but must be content with my visiting them when I had time and inclination and in this way your parlor would be just as unintruded upon as it is now," Sophia wrote. She had put her finger upon a difficulty, of course. But nothing in her own experience prepared her to understand the effect of her communications upon that household of recluse women now her relatives by marriage. She could not picture the compressed lips, the pale faces as each took her letter to read in solitude and to shudder over while contemplating the horror of having a friendly young woman and her baby *almost* in the same house! It was not Sophia's friends that the Hawthorne women dreaded — it was herself. They knew they could not let her in without letting in the light upon their lives.

On September 1, Sophia wrote with a note of panic because events outside her control were forcing her hand. "But it is absolutely necessary that some decision should be made at once, for the Rev. Ripley has written today to tell us he will be very happy to have us out of his house this week!"

The Hawthorne women knew all along that they could not refuse Sophia's request. They just delayed long enough to hurt her and deprive themselves of the pleasure they should have had in extending a cordial welcome. Now Louisa wrote that arrangements had been made with the Mannings for her to have a parlor, not the kitchen. Nathaniel would have his old boyhood room again.

"I think Mr. Manning is rather exorbitant but it cannot be helped," Sophia said. "I am very happy to have a better room if it do not cost a cent more; but as I am strongly for economy just now, I would rejoice in the kitchen if it be cheaper." Sophia's naturally buoyant spirits rose, however, as she thought about this room which was to be her new home and she wrote to Louisa a sheetful of questions which doubtless Louisa found it irksome to answer.

"I wish you would tell me how many feet long and broad the front parlor is and whether there be any recesses or jogs so that I may judge about my carpet. I think I shall put down my chamber Brussels carpet. . . . I shall take some cane-bottomed chairs, large and small, a washstand, a looking glass, a table to stand under it, a light-stand, the black haircloth easy chair, my bureau and some bookshelves for my chamber — and all the crockery ware it needs. . . ." They would bring all the airtight stoves that were so much the pride of their hearts. "And you shall have in your parlor, that one with the beautiful vase," Sophia promised. The Hawthorne ladies were also to have Sophia's astral lamp for their parlor and it would give Sophia pleasure to have them use it.

The Hawthornes had been supremely happy in Concord, so much at home among the group of philosophers and writers, people of great thoughts and simple tastes like themselves. But Sophia felt little actual regret at leaving because no paradise is happy where the shadow of financial anxiety falls. Perhaps they would return to Concord someday, she told herself — someday after the world had found out what she already knew, that her husband was a great writer. Meanwhile she faced the immediate future, certain that it was bright.

The future, whatever else it held for Sophia, would bring little opportunity for her development as an artist. She had attempted a portrait bust of Hawthorne soon after their marriage. She began with joy and confidence, but she soon discovered that an artist should not be in love with the subject if accurate objective work is to be accomplished. Her mental image of Hawthorne could not be rendered in clay or in any other medium.

"Eden in Miniature" Painted by George Harvey

*Water-color view of Boston Common in 1830, gift of
George Harvey Chickering to the Bostonian Society,
reproduced with their permission*

Sophia Amelia Peabody

Portrait probably painted by Harding in 1830 and here repro-
duced in full for the first time by permission of Hildegarde Haw-
thorne, granddaughter of Sophia and Nathaniel Hawthorne. Pho-
tographed especially for The Peabody Sisters of Salem *by Julian*
C. Smyth, great-grandson of Sophia and Nathaniel Hawthorne

Nathaniel Hawthorne in 1840

From a painting by Charles Osgood reproduced
by permission of the Essex Institute, Salem, Massachusetts

The House in Charter Street

Photograph of this home of the Peabody sisters reproduced by permission of the Essex Institute, Salem, Massachusetts

The Old Manse

From an early photograph by A. W. Hosmer, Concord, Massachusetts. Reproduced for The Peabody Sisters of Salem *by Keith Martin, Concord*

Mary Peabody Mann, Soon after Her Marriage

*From a daguerreotype reproduced by permission
of the Massachusetts Historical Society*

Horace Mann, President of Antioch

*From an engraving reproduced by permission
of the Massachusetts Historical Society*

ANTIOCH COLLEGE

Antioch College on a Letterhead

*Reproduced by permission of Horace Mann,
grandson of Antioch's founder and first president*

The House in Mall Street, Salem, Where Hawthorne Wrote
The Scarlet Letter

*Photograph reproduced by permission of
the Essex Institute, Salem, Massachusetts*

"Wayside," Concord

Photograph by Keith Martin, Concord, Massachusetts

Elizabeth Palmer Peabody in 1887

*From a photograph reproduced by permission
of her grandnephew, Horace Mann*

Scarcely two months before her child was born, Sophia finished the painting "Endymion." "I always go through the valley of the shadow of death in painting every picture and the more worth the picture has, the more dismal my journey. But at last I stand on the delectable mountains and now I seem to be there with Endymion," she said. The words were prophetic. With the coming of her children, the artist Sophia now sank into sleep like the mystic shepherd of Mount Latmos.

Since she had not really been the wealthy Sophia Peabody, she could not afford to hire nurses while she went on with her work. But this was not the reason that "Endymion" was her last painting. Sophia was too happy — she had too complete a sense of fulfillment in motherhood. She would always be an artist in the way she used her eyes and the beauty of her children would give her constant delight. Mentally, she painted Una's red-gold hair, and in imagination she modeled the baby's hands a dozen times a day. But the Sophia who once prayed to be possessed by the power to create now held in her arms all of creation in the form of her child. She did not even think to ask Louisa Hawthorne if the Manning parlor had a north light.

It gave Sophia satisfaction to be able to write to her mother: "We have authentic intelligence that my husband is nominated by the President himself for Surveyor of the Custom House [in Salem]." But when she said that the salary would be twelve hundred dollars she was mistaken. It was only one thousand, and Salem prices were higher, and there was no prolific Concord garden or orchard to rely upon. Hawthorne, once more tied down to uncongenial work and once more within the shadow of Castle Dismal — as he still called his old home — was not the same happy Adam of Concord days. Sophia made no complaint, however. She was, in fact, so happy and so sunny that "Phoebe" was the name Hawthorne now called her. Sophia herself said that she was happy, not only for Hawthorne but "for the sake of the future child."

By May 1846 the Hawthornes had found a house in Boston, and were settled there, Hawthorne himself commuting to Salem to carry on his work at the Custom House. The expected child was not to be born in Castle Dismal. Their joy in getting into a home of their own was so great that Sophia said "It seemed as if we were never so happy before." In addition, it was wonderful to be "easy in mind about bread and butter." Sophia could even afford one modest luxury — instead of making all the baby clothes herself as she had done for Una, she could afford to have what few additional ones the new baby would need made to order at Brook Farm.

And now a collection of Hawthorne's stories written in Concord and called *Mosses from an Old Manse* appeared, published by Wiley and Putnam. Sophia's cousin, George Putnam, had gone to New York with his widowed mother ("Aunt Putnam," Mrs. Peabody's sister Catherine was always called in the family). Aunt Putnam had started a successful girls' school, and George had gone into the book business, also with success. It was Elizabeth, of course, who had brought pressure upon Cousin George to publish Hawthorne's book. But Hawthorne's contemporaries at this time either disliked his work, as Emerson did, or made his moral lessons the theme of sermons as at King's Chapel — where Elizabeth heard young Mr. Frothingham conclude with "three pages quoted from . . . 'Fancy's Showbox.' " The book did not sell, and George Putnam said he never thought it would.[2]

Sophia, however, had a capacity for getting the utmost pleasure out of every event of her life. She dressed little Una in her best, tucked a presentation copy of *Mosses from an Old Manse* under her arm and (because it was raining) took a carriage and called upon Miss Burley, that old friend and Salem patroness of the arts, now in her town house in Boston. Una presented Miss Burley with a copy of "Papa's book" — enacting a little scene contrived by Sophia in loving pride. Sophia had always stood a little in awe of Miss Burley. It was fun to be an author's wife and feel that now the tables were turned.

The months spent in Salem had not been entirely happy. Sophia never said so, but sometimes it was between the lines in letters she wrote later to Louisa Hawthorne. "I regret very much that I had so little intercourse with Elizabeth," she said. "I think we could have enjoyed each other very much. . . . But now the time is past and I do not see as we can ever have another chance to become acquainted as my husband will never go back to Herbert Street, he says, under any circumstances. . . ." Certainly it had never been Sophia's intention to be at sword's points with her husband's family. She won Louisa's friendship and had kept it in spite of a few misunderstandings and under difficult living conditions. Sophia now appealed to Louisa in a way that should have been hard to resist.

"I write especially now, to ask if you will come after my confinement to have an eye upon Una. I should much prefer your coming to having Anna Alcott, and if you can come I will not write

for her. Otherwise, I suppose I must. Anna will be tender and trustworthy but I fear would not induce her to obey and could not
manage her about going to bed and bathing. Una, besides, is extremely fond of you and likes to be with you. I think your mother
cannot object, for the sake of her new little grandchild as well as
for Una's sake. Aunties are always in requisition in such emergen-
cies."

Sophia knew now that certain Hawthorne peculiarities, although
shared by Louisa, were not necessarily Louisa's. "Tell your mother,
with my love, that old Miss Saunders can go to the front door and
send everybody away and that those who go to the back door can
go away when they are tired of knocking."

There was, characteristically, no answer from Louisa and Hawthorne wrote a postscript to Sophia's next letter of Monday, June 22.

"P.S. A small troglodyte made his appearance here at ten minutes to six this morning who claims to be your nephew and the heir
to all our wealth and honors. He has dark hair and is no great
beauty at present but is said to be a particularly fine little creature
by everybody who has seen him."

Hawthorne then added his plea to his sister to come, but if she
ever did, it was not till after Sophia was able to write and say, "We
have finally named the baby. He is henceforth Julian Hawthorne.
We hope you will like it." The Hawthorne ladies had not liked
the name of Una and, although their brother told them to say
nothing, Sophia had certainly found out that they were hard to
please.

September 1847 saw the Hawthornes back in Salem, where neither
of them had ever expected to be again. Boston had proved to be an
inconvenient commuting suburb to Salem. More important still,
Madame Hawthorne was aging fast, and suddenly she needed her
son and his wife to make a home for her. Sophia found a house on
Mall Street, a bargain at two hundred dollars a year rent. Tall and
narrow though the house was, its gable end faced the street while all
its row of front windows were flooded with sunshine and opened
upon a small garden. The street itself, although nearly as narrow
as Herbert Street, had a more cheerful air borrowed perhaps from
the bright grass and tall trees of Salem Common at one end and
from the fine brick mansions that faced the Common — turning
their backs on Mall Street to be sure, but built upon its northern
corners none the less. Deep formal gardens were shielded from
Mall Street by high wooden fences but the flowers presented their

perfume to Mall Street residents free of charge and without regard to social standing.

Sophia looked forward to a second experience of living close to the Hawthorne ladies with determined optimism. "It is no small satisfaction to know that Mrs. Hawthorne's remainder of life will be glorified by the presence of these children and of her son," she said. "I am so glad to win her out of that Castle Dismal and from the mysterious chamber, into which no mortal ever peeped till Una was born and Julian — for they alone entered the penetralia. Into that chamber the sun never shines. Into these rooms in Mall Street it blazes without ceremony or stint."

Sometimes nothing is harder to bear than a person whose attitude is so correct as Sophia's! Madame Hawthorne was a pitiful figure as they took her from her darkened chamber and carried her (doubtless in a carriage with curtains drawn) toward the relentless sunlight that awaited her; up Herbert Street, along Essex Street and around a corner of the Common. The distance was about five blocks. Did she look out at the streets that she had forsworn upon the death of her husband? She probably leaned back and closed her eyes, because a woman who had passed thirty-nine years in a stubborn revolt against a single stroke of fate would hardly give way to human curiosity now.

The scene had changed little, in any case, since Madame Hawthorne walked abroad as a young woman. Less than a hundred years would pass and then the cobblestone street leading to the Common would be broadened, boulevarded — and named for the son to whose home she was being taken. His statue in massive bronze would brood over the city that he hated, yet could not cease to love. In the autumn of 1847, if Hawthorne sat beside his mother in the closed carriage, he was acutely conscious, as he always was, of the silent protest within her mind. Bound by stern New England convention, he could not take her hand, tell her that he loved her and that he knew she did not want to come to the home he was giving her; to Sophia, the children and the sunshine. He could only hope with all his heart that the two women, as opposite from each other as day and night, would somehow learn to live side by side — since he cared so much for both of them.

Almost two years went by while Madame Hawthorne lived in the "suite of rooms" which Sophia described as "wholly distant from ours so that we shall only meet when we choose to do so." She found the sunshine not entirely distasteful after all. The children played in the garden beneath her windows and at first their voices startled her and interrupted the tired flow of her thoughts like the song of birds after a long winter. Then their voices grew familiar. She was less conscious of them but depended upon hearing them more than she knew. She encouraged their frequent little visits to her room. Hardly realizing why, Madame Hawthorne began to remember the childhood of her own children, and she cooked for Hawthorne some of the things he had loved as a boy — gingerbread which Sophia said was "red-hot with ginger," baked Indian pudding. She carried great bowls of coffee to him in his study which delighted him and of which Sophia disapproved. But Sophia had learned to keep still. She continued to believe rice, milk and breast of chicken the best diet because all the food was white in color! But now she asked her mother-in-law for her recipe for Indian pudding — since Hawthorne enjoyed it so much.

In July 1849 Mrs. Hawthorne was stricken with a sudden illness. Her suffering was intense and Sophia cared for her night and day. Her two daughters were not so much unwilling as unable to do anything for her and when, on July 31, the shadows of the grave of which she had been a part for so long claimed her at last, she died in Sophia's arms.

After this, Hawthorne was taken ill. They called it "brain fever," as they did almost everything where there was high temperature. Elizabeth Peabody was summoned to Salem to look after the Hawthorne children and, no matter how pressing her affairs at West Street were, she came at once. The children proceeded also to have some sort of fever. But Sophia, the former invalid, nursed them all — and remained in perfect health.

CHAPTER FIFTEEN
Famous Husband

FOR three years — between April 1846 and June 1849 — Sophia and her husband would have the experience of living on a regular salary. Her husband, her mother and her sisters therefore urged her to "buy a handsome gown or a new pelisse." But an early life of financial insecurity had made Sophia a cautious, thrifty woman. "I should as soon think of purchasing of the Persian King his largest pearl," she told her family. She ripped apart her old "Thibet," had the "Thibet" cloth cleaned, and it came back from the "mantua-makers" "transformed into a very graceful and elegant garment." Her sister Mary had given her a silk dress, and there was still a box of lovely garments given her after the death of her dear Lydia Haven, the use of which brought affectionate memories. "Then the silk of Lydia's petticoat has made me a very handsome bonnet," Sophia told her mother, "so that I have now an exceedingly comely walking and calling costume — as good and as tasteful as that of any millionaire lady."

Then there was the matter of the children's clothes. For Julian, "those little blue caps embroidered with gold lace are such unbecoming and vulgar devices that I will not buy one," Sophia said. The milliner agreed to make a wire frame for "a round, flat hat with a low crown" and Sophia would cover it herself in black velvet.

Sophia's first despair over the fact that Una's hair was the unpopular, despised color of red had evaporated before the undeniable evidence of her artist's eyes — that red hair was beautiful. Una must wear a "dove-colored cloak, a blue cashmere dress, a blue hat" to match her eyes. But it still seemed important to Sophia that Una's hair be called "auburn."

In the new house on Mall Street there were no furnishings conveniently left behind by former occupants, as at the Manse. It

would seem as if there should have been certain age-blackened Hawthorne pieces to bring from Castle Dismal and expose to the sun —
but perhaps there were only enough for Madame Hawthorne, for
her daughter Elizabeth — the "invisible entity" Sophia saw "but
once in two years" — and for Louisa, who was often with Sophia
but who (Sophia said) "never intrudes." Writing to Lizzie in Boston, Sophia asked for help. "I wish we could chance to get some
furniture as cheaply as Mary did at some auction — yet so pretty
and new."

Elizabeth answered promptly. She had seen a "sophy" for dear
"Sophie" — a used pun, evidently, but still usable, like the furniture
Lizzie had her eye on. The sofa was "exactly like the one I gave to
Mary," she said. It "will probably sell for less than nine dollars."
A "windlass bedstead made of hard wood" was ten dollars, but
one made of varnished pine could be had for seven. Elizabeth had
been given plenty of shopping to do and she did it with her usual
gusto. A rake, a hoe and a spade for the garden, "well made," she
acquired for fifty cents.

One luxury Sophia could not resist. "At Daniel's are large Russian shawls imported to make gentlemen's gowns for five dollars;
then you must provide lining, wadding and making." Hawthorne
must have one to wear in his study which was "high from all noise."
Sophia would buy the Russian shawl if she possibly could and she
told Elizabeth with pride and satisfaction of the arrangements she
had made to provide a place where Hawthorne could go on with
his writing during the hours when he was free from work in the
Custom House. There had been no workroom for him since the
days at the Old Manse with its loved little upper chamber with
western windows. "He has now lived in the nursery a year without a chance for an hour's uninterrupted musing and without his
desk being once opened," Sophia said.

In November 1847 Sophia wrote, "My husband began retiring to
his study on the 1st November and writes every afternoon." But
Sophia could not know what torment Hawthorne was suffering in
that study which she had provided with such loving care. He could
not write. He thought that the spirit had gone from him and that
he was never to write again. A story was taking shape in his mind,
to be sure, but not a word of it would go down on paper. Sophia
was always early to bed and then early up and about as the birds
began to sing at dawn. Hawthorne's mind awoke late, it was increasingly on fire with creative energy as the night wore on — till

at last he dropped into bed, burned out with fatigue yet sleepless till later still. These nights on Mall Street he sat late in his silent study, his mind like a wild animal in a trap. He must write. He ought to write. There would be no trouble about placing a story for which someone might accidentally pay. Then there was reputation. Hawthorne had begun to be known — as living in the Old Manse in Concord and writing *Mosses*. Where was he now? So frail a beginning would never survive a long silence. Anxieties haunted the moonlit study, and when Hawthorne focused his attention on the story which stirred in his mind he found that for the present it was an affair of ghosts and half-remembered dreams.

At Elizabeth Peabody's insistence, Hawthorne sent her a manuscript, "The Unpardonable Sin." It was full of genius, Elizabeth said — but too gloomy. She would like to have Hawthorne send her another, "something as great as well as more cheerful." Hawthorne did not reply. He only hoped fervently that his sister-in-law would not come back to visit Salem for a long time.

During these days of nervous tension for Hawthorne, Sophia seemed to him the same happy, busy person that she had always been. As always, she reminded him of a small bird, hopping cheerfully from branch to branch, capable of short flights for pure joy; given to brief domestic song. Her simplicity rested him. He saw her absorbed in her children and he believed that she forgot to ask him how his work was going. But with all his "dreadful insight" Hawthorne underestimated Sophia, who, though no angel, knew where she should fear to tread. She knew very well that the work was going badly. She enjoined Elizabeth and her mother to say not a word; to ask no questions; to let her handle the letter-writing between the families.

Sophia took out her paints and brushes. But Elizabeth was not allowed to borrow for her some popular painting, a copy of which would sell for a hundred dollars or more. This was no time for Sophia to enter her valley of the shadow — while Hawthorne was lost in his own. Moreover, children's walks, their meals, their baths, left no time during daylight hours for concentrated work; while the children's misplaced zeal with tubes of paint made the possession of a borrowed picture dangerous. Sophia was painting lamp shades. Elizabeth got the orders for her in Boston at five dollars apiece and Sophia, by dint of much contriving, could finish one in about a week. Then, of course, the customer felt free to say that the size or the color wasn't quite right after all — and Mrs. Hawthorne would have to make another for the same five dollars!

Fire shades or screens were popular too, such as were held in the hand to keep the heat of a log fire from a lady's face while she endeavored to sit close enough to the hearth to keep warm. The handles and frames of hand fire screens were made of ivory and Sophia learned to inlay them with designs in ebony or mother-of-pearl. On the parchment shade, she painted such suitable scenes as the Temple at Paestum or the ruins of the Forum at Rome — copied from engravings lent by the ever helpful Miss Burley. These screens sold for ten dollars and the best market was in Salem where even airtight stoves were regarded with suspicion. Whenever Sophia sold a lamp shade or a fire screen, she hid the money away. "I cannot bear to spend a cent till it must be spent," she said, when Elizabeth or her mother suggested that she buy something pretty for herself. Because Salem commerce was decreasing, the surveyor's salary, never the originally promised twelve hundred a year, had been further reduced below the actual one thousand dollar level.

In the autumn of 1848 there was a Whig victory and Horace Mann went to Washington as a Whig member of Congress — pledged to stop the spread of slavery; to see that whenever a new territory became a state it should not become a slave state but free. Sophia wrote to congratulate Mary upon her husband's success and to give her some of the advice Mary had previously been so free with. Now it was Mary who must have clothes — and a "nursery woman." And Mary replied much as Sophia had done. The salary of a Congressman was eight dollars a day. There was no telling how long Congress would remain in session and Mary was not going to spend her money before she got it. But since she could not go to Washington with Horace, she would hope for a short session no matter what the effect was on the family exchequer.

Although a Democrat appointed by Polk, Hawthorne had never been involved in partisan politics and at first the Whig victory meant nothing to him except as a source of satisfaction because of Mary. But it soon became evident that the autumn elections would bring to the Hawthornes a different story. Another man wanted the surveyorship, poorly paid as that office might be. Charges were made against Hawthorne; that he had used his office for the benefit of his party against the public good; that he had endeavored to oust Whig officeholders; that his writings were political. Hawthorne promptly wrote to Hillard, who was politically prominent. And

Horace Mann just as promptly forgot political differences to help Hawthorne present evidence that the charges were false. Mann would have enjoyed instituting a libel suit against those who accused Hawthorne of "loafing around with hard drinkers," for the story was ridiculous. But in June the blow fell, Hawthorne was removed from office, and he refused to carry the fight further. He wrote to Hillard on the day of his dismissal. Sophia had not heard the news but he said, "She will take it like a woman — that is to say, better than a man."

Sophia surprised her husband, sure of her though he was. It was good news, she told him. Now he could go on with his writing. It would go much better now, she said, and he saw that she had known all along that he had been having difficulties. Then she unlocked a drawer in her desk and showed him a hundred and fifty dollars in bills, in silver, even in coppers. The money represented lamp shades and fire screens. As to how long the money would last — well, the savings resulting from made-over garments and furniture bought at auction were nothing compared to the economies Sophia could practice if she set her mind to it.

Hawthorne went to his study to experience a miracle. The spirit was upon him and he could write again. "He writes immensely. I am almost frightened about it," Sophia said. But she made no protest because she saw that what she called his "shining look" was back again. She had not needed to ask how the work went when it went badly and she had no need to ask about it now. She knew.

The Scarlet Letter was conceived as a short story. Hawthorne had never done anything but short stories (with the exception of *Fanshawe*) and the market which he thought was open to him was in the short-story field. Although he talked little about his work, *The Scarlet Letter* seems to have been no secret, apocryphal accounts to the contrary. Elizabeth Peabody, in the course of one of her cyclonic descents upon the Hawthorne family, found out all about it and if Sophia told her she betrayed no confidence. Sophia spoke of her husband's work freely in letters to her mother — but not in detail, for Mother cared more for details about the children.

Elizabeth certainly did not return to West Street and remain silent about Hawthorne's new spurt of writing. In spite of his marked avoidance of her society, he remained her discovery, the greatest genius she had ever proclaimed to Boston. To be sure, she daily encountered others, and now most of them were men younger than she, in whom she saw the seeds of greatness. But Hawthorne was her proof that she could prophesy.

It is a trifle hard to believe Mr. James T. Fields of the Boston firm of Ticknor and Fields when he states that he called on Mr. Hawthorne in Salem merely to ask after the health of a still obscure young author. Fields was rarely if ever what Elizabeth called "disinterested." His success in life had never been the result of mere kindly impulse, nor was it accidental. But the story of his call on Hawthorne, as he told it, made excellent publicity. He found Hawthorne "hovering near a stove" in a depressed mood, he said. They talked of his work and Hawthorne expressed bitterness at his unpopularity.

"I remember I pressed him to reveal to me what he was writing," Fields said. "He shook his head and gave me to understand he had produced nothing. At that moment I caught sight of a bureau or set of drawers near where we were sitting; and immediately it occurred to me that hidden away somewhere in that article of furniture was a story or stories by the author of 'Twice-Told Tales' and I became so positive of it that I charged him vehemently with the fact. He seemed surprised, I thought, but shook his head; and I rose to take my leave, begging him not to come into the cold entry, saying that I would come back and see him again in a few days. I was hurrying down the stairs when he called after me from the chamber, asking me to stop a moment. Then quickly stepping into the entry with a roll of manuscript in his hands, he said, 'How in Heaven's name did you know it was there?'"

Fields remembered that he recognized instantly the greatness of *The Scarlet Letter;* that he instantly communicated his jubilation to Hawthorne. But when it came to publication, he moderated his joy to the extent of printing only five thousand copies and then dispersing the type. Within ten days after publication, he was in need of a second edition.

But if Fields enjoyed writing himself into a drama, he also had an inspirational quality. It struck him at once that *The Scarlet Letter* was a book-length novel, not a short story, and for this one thing he deserved Hawthorne's affectionate gratitude. For years, Hawthorne had been struggling with the short story when it was not his medium. It held his spirit in a strait jacket and in his efforts to conform he suffered torment. Now he was free and now indeed he "wrote immensely," the words pouring out upon the page like a spring torrent through a broken dam. Moods of melancholy he would have again, as a matter of course, but Sophia when she looked upon her love would see again her "Hyperion" of Concord days, with his dear "shining look."

The Salem gossips were doing their worst against Hawthorne while he wrote and his revenge was pitiless. "The Customs House," a biographical introduction to *The Scarlet Letter*, stripped them all of their pretensions. He was accused of cruelty and his was actually the cruelty of the vivisectionist. All the rest of their lives those men, described by Hawthorne, would walk the streets of Salem with their secret sins exposed and their self-esteem cut and laid bare to the public gaze. They deserved it. They should never have crossed swords with such a master.

The Scarlet Letter was in the press before it was completed. When Elizabeth Peabody, during one of her descents upon the Hawthornes, asked him how the story would end, Hawthorne said he did not know. Lizzie could not understand it! Always more than willing to arrange other peoples' lives for them, she could not see that Hawthorne was under obligation to let his characters work out their own destiny consistently and logically. Each act brought its consequence, and the story ended in tragedy. Elizabeth was indignant for she had wanted a happy ending. But when Hawthorne read aloud the last chapters, in the living room on Mall Street, Sophia cried into her sewing basket and enjoyed her tears and so would countless other women after her. Hawthorne himself could hardly control his voice. He had not meant to make his book so somber, he said. But he could not help it any more than he could help making it immortal.

By August 1849 the Hawthorne sisters had decided to leave Salem. After the death of Madame Hawthorne, nothing held them there. Louisa went to live for a time with Manning relatives and Elizabeth took lodgings with a farmer's family by the name of Cole in Montserrat, a part of Beverly. Here, she had but to cross the road to be in the woods, the sea was only a mile away, so that the adventurous scent of it stole into her chamber as she read every book she could beg or borrow. There was a cat, and Elizabeth was passionately fond of cats. She spent all the rest of her days at Montserrat, therefore, but one thing she brought with her from Mall Street and that was the affection of her nephew and nieces, Una in particular. They visited her often.

His sea-captain ancestors had bequeathed to Hawthorne a love of the sea also, and he first considered Manchester, Massachusetts as a possible new home — or Kittery, Maine, where his good friend Bridge was stationed "at the Navy Yard."

But suddenly, in September, the Nathaniel Hawthornes decided to "go West"! They would place their worldly goods in a boxcar. A little red cottage had been found, for which "the owner will take $75.00 for four years," as Sophia reported, feeling that she had captured the first prize in bargains.[2] And the location — "at the West" — was Lenox, Massachusetts.

Before embarking upon this journey to the frontier, Sophia took her children to Boston to visit her mother. Everywhere she went she was met by news of *The Scarlet Letter*. Fifteen hundred copies of the second edition had been sold in three days, she was told. Mrs. Gardiner, from Gardiner, Maine, said that "as a tragic poem it had never been surpassed and hardly equalled." Mr. Emerson said that the introduction "was perfect in *wit*, in *life* . . ." that there was "nothing equal to it in the language." Sophia underlined all of Mr. Emerson's superlatives because she knew that he was, as she put it, "never satisfied," and she wanted her husband to savor the full extent of this praise. Sophia's sensitive face would light with joy again and again as she met friends and even strangers who spoke to her of her husband's work. She was unconscious that she, herself, was undergoing a new scrutiny as the wife of a famous man and that she was undergoing it very well. Sophia was still an artist and, in her one silk dress, her made-over cloak and bonnet, she was a pretty picture. That touch of the exiled princess in her manner, due to Palmer pride, became her well as the wife of a famous man. And since her pride was now all for her husband, not herself, people smiled a little but liked her for it.

By the end of November 1850 Sophia's letters to her mother were coming from Lenox. Born in Salem and living either in Salem or Boston for most of her life, Sophia found Lenox a lonesome place. The hills frightened her, yet she knew that the view from her western windows out over the famous "Stockbridge Bowl" was the finest she had ever seen. Once, soon after her marriage, Hawthorne had tried to limit Sophia's adjectives. "It takes a great deal of strength to say, 'See that flower' instead of 'See that lovely, beautiful flower!'" she said plaintively. Standing before her western windows at sunset in the Berkshires, strength failed Sophia and she said it was all "very superb." But the paints and brushes remained packed away in boxes. Even if her husband, her children and her home had not absorbed all of Sophia's energies she would still have painted only the Italian type of landscape — with hills not awesome but merely pretty; lakes reliably blue, never savage with storm.

Sophia devoted her attention to making her family comfortable in the story-and-a-half cottage by the side of the road. "Four good sleeping rooms upstairs" had no heat, but the airtight stoves had made the journey "West" and Sophia's first task was to turn one of the bedrooms into a study for Hawthorne. Mother Peabody had given to Hawthorne her son George's desk and Sophia polished the brass handles, put new black velvet on the writing surface and cleaned the ink spots off the mahogany. By December, Hawthorne was going to his study every morning right after breakfast to work until four in the afternoon and the desk was destined to be a famous one, for *The House of the Seven Gables* was being written upon it.

Elizabeth arrived for a visit bringing the gift of a rug for the parlor — red leaves on a brown ground. Red curtains at the parlor windows and a red cloth on the center table made it a cheerful place. Sophia bought very little that was new, but she would not have been to blame if she had become confident that financial difficulties were now over. A letter from Mr. Fields to her husband, dated October 5, 1850, gave her every encouragement.

DEAR HAWTHORNE:

I forgot to say to you in my last that when ever you want any money call upon us. There is always to your credit a supply ready to your order. Don't fight shy of our money box when the lid is always open at yr call.

Very truly
JAS T. FIELDS

Unfortunately, it did not occur to Hawthorne or to Sophia, who kept the family books, to ask Mr. Fields just how much money *The Scarlet Letter* had earned, how much was due the author and when the money would be paid. Instead, they made Ticknor and Fields their bank, but a bank which never issued a statement. They wished to allow royalties to accrue as a balance and Sophia, at least, was perfectly content to imagine that the balance must be large, while living as though it were small. She rejoiced over the price of three dollars a cord for firewood and worried over the number of cords the airtight stoves consumed.

On December 11, 1850, it began to snow. The airtight stoves had to be kept red-hot to counteract the searching winds which seeped through the walls of the red cottage. Her landlord, the wealthy Mr.

Tappan, took Sophia to the village store in his sleigh, warning her to lay in plenty of supplies for soon the roads would be drifted over, opportunities to drive to town but few. While Sophia was in the store doing her errands Mr. Tappan's horses ran away, breaking up his sleigh! Sophia never felt so lost, so far from civilization before.

But there was an intimacy in being snowbound with her husband and children, a sense of being safe from the world that Sophia loved. Before the middle of January, Hawthorne began to read his manuscript aloud. "Oh Joy unspeakable!" exclaimed Sophia as she trimmed the lamp, took out her sewing, and pulled her chair close to the red-covered table. The children were safe in bed. Let the wind howl, the snow pile in great drifts against the door outside and even in tiny drifts within, around a leaky window sash — there was happiness inside the room. They agreed to read till ten o'clock, but could not stop until the tale was done. Phoebe was the name of the heroine, one of Sophia's own names that Hawthorne had given her, one which she had heard oftenest during the dark days in Salem when she was his light.

Later, Sophia took *The House of the Seven Gables* and read it for herself. Much as she loved the "sweet thunder" of his voice, she was eye-minded and she saw even more in the manuscript than she had heard. She could not fail to recognize a sort of composite portrait of the Hawthorne womenfolk in Hephzibah. Once Elizabeth Peabody had frankly asked the Misses Hawthorne why they did not teach school and try to support themselves. But they did not like children, they said — and Lizzie had been impatient. Hawthorne had understood, and explained, through Hephzibah, how some women could be utterly incapable of earning a living — while at the same time anxious to try. Sophia's patience with her sisters-in-law had been endless — but it did her heart good to know that her husband had seen his family's failings.

Sophia was startled when she read her husband's opinion of mesmerism. How much had she confided to him about her father's partner, Dr. Fiske, and his soothing of her headaches? Hawthorne had a faculty of knowing more than he was told and she was glad that he knew she had never been hypnotized and had given up the treatments as soon as he expressed disapproval. Hawthorne's character, young Holgrave, the daguerreotypist, made Sophia smile. Already, several portraits had been painted of Hawthorne, doing ample justice to his brow, his mouth, and his romantic eyes. Recently a daguerreotype had been made, probably at Fields's request, and Sophia could almost hear Hawthorne's comments about it as she read in *The House of the Seven Gables* that the sun revealed the man in this early form of photography. "Look at that eye! Would you like to be at its mercy? At that mouth! Could it ever smile?" So Hawthorne made Holgrave speak and so he, himself, had spoken of his own picture. His eyes, in the daguerreotype, were not romantic but haunted, as though they saw evil both within and without — and forgave nothing. The mouth, with its lower lip thrust out, seemed the product of a long line of sea-captain ancestors with their will to command and their yardarm justice. Sophia had only laughed at the daguerreotype and had said that the portraits were the true likeness. But she would not let the daguerreotype be used for publicity and she rarely showed it to anyone. The truth was somewhere in between. There was a ruthless streak in Hawthorne which the camera had caught and which drove him to force fate and clear all obstacles from his path. It was a tribute to Sophia that he never thought of her and the children as being in his path.

On January 27, 1851, "to Ticknor and Fields goes *The House of the Seven Gables* which was finished yesterday," Sophia said. She watched Hawthorne stride along the country road, the manuscript under his arm, on his way to the express office. She felt as if something had gone out of her life with the finishing of the book, yet at the same time she felt a sense of release.

Sophia went into the kitchen to interview the gaunt Mrs. Peters, her household assistant. Mrs. Peters was a Negro woman of considerable temperament, always feeling put upon, always threatening to leave. She had promised to help out the Hawthornes for a little while, just as a favor. Now Sophia asked Mrs. Peters to promise to stay at least until the end of May.

"Till after my confinement," Sophia begged. As an inducement she offered to teach Mrs. Peters to read. Mrs. Peters agreed and lessons began next day.

There were snowstorms in the Berkshires as late as April. The Hawthornes were much alone, which was a pleasure to them rather than a trial. Almost their only visitor was Herman Melville from near-by Pittsfield. Melville was at work again upon his *Moby Dick*, and he felt that his walks and talks with Hawthorne during the previous summer had given him the needed lift to finish a difficult task. In Melville, Hawthorne found the first friend of his own trade who was really congenial. Emerson had been too remote, William Ellery Channing too erratic and Thoreau, who came the closest in the Concord group, had really seemed to prefer the society of woodchucks. The Hawthornes greeted Melville with enthusiasm, entertained him with a drink "manufactured of beaten eggs, loaf sugar and champagne." It was guaranteed to send thoughts sky-riding and to loosen the tongues of two usually rather silent men. Sophia made it — and sipped a little herself.

Spring came too slowly for Sophia. She missed the flooding Concord River and the birds that came so soon and sang so close to the Old Manse. Hawthorne felt much the same way. "I find I do not feel at home among these hills," he wrote to an old friend, William B. Pike. Mr. Pike was to look for a permanent home that the Hawthornes felt they might now be able to buy. "Very little land would suit my purpose," Hawthorne said, "but I want a good house with space enough inside, and which will not need any considerable repairs." Such a place should be available, he thought, for fifteen hundred or two thousand dollars, and Concord would be a good place to go to look for such a property. The Hawthornes would need to stay in Lenox only a little while longer now.

On May 20, 1851, Rose Hawthorne was born. Her parents had named her Rose long before she came into the world, her mother said. Their joy was just as great as it had been over the birth of Una and Julian — with perhaps this difference. Hawthorne felt securely confident, now, that he could support his family by writing.

CHAPTER SIXTEEN
Congressman's Wife

SINCE her marriage with Horace Mann, Mary had come into her own at last. Elizabeth had always assumed leadership; life had been made easy for Sophia, the youngest, the prettiest — the gifted daughter. Mary had been the forgotten middle sister to whom everyone turned for help or sympathy and then promptly forgot. But once Horace Mann's eyes were opened to her delicate charm, Mary found herself the center of his private universe.

Horace was constantly afraid that some disaster might befall his beloved. He was away a great deal, traveling about the state in behalf of public schools and Mary must write to him every day and he to her. She delighted in the letters; but once, when someone else addressed the envelope for her, "my heart took several large jumps," Horace told her — in fear lest she might be ill. Once, when he was at home and Mary lingered overlong at tea with friends, she returned to find him pacing the floor in torment lest she might have been killed by some runaway carriage horse. It was, of course, the death of Charlotte, Mann's first wife, that made him so fearful that this second happiness could not long endure. Mary understood and reassured him, but it was sweet to be so loved. She could not help but enjoy his anxiety a trifle when her heart had been starved for him so long.

Mary was writing poetry these days, since so much happiness needed to be expressed. She rarely showed her verse to anyone; but she confided in Sophia, offered to exchange poems if Sophia would send something she had written. Their roles were reversed, however. Now it was Sophia who was so much at the service of others that she had no time for self-expression. "I am as strong as a lion, as elastic as India rubber, light as a bird, as happy as a queen might be," Sophia replied — "but my dear child what leisure do you find I have, to sit down and write poetry or draw pictures. I wanted to shout when I read your request for poetry. Could I be paid a dollar a word, it would be impossible. . . . I often pass a day without having a thought to myself — not one. . . ."

Mary's husband, the subject of most of her verse, wrote her no lines in return but he knew how to please her just the same. When, at an education meeting, Horace Mann was presented with a rose and a bud, representing the normal schools "brought from bud to flowering," he passed on the tribute but with a new meaning attached. The flowers were now "a compliment to you and the baby," he said as he gave them to Mary.

Rooms in the hotel on Bowdoin Square were no longer adequate. In 1845 the Manns found a house at Number 77 Carver Street on the edge of Back Bay, and by December of that year Mrs. Peabody was writing to Sophia, "Mary looks as well as can be hoped. . . . She appears to look forward to her event with cheerfulness." Sophia replied with much sisterly advice about strange, practically nutrition-free diets which she considered just the thing for Mary's "condition." Mary paid no attention but her mother's word "cheerfulness" did not at all describe her state of mind. She was supremely happy. Horace had said that he wanted not one child but a whole family.

And at the closing of the year 1845 Horace Mann wrote to George Combe, an Englishman whose writing on phrenology he admired and whose personal friendship he treasured. "We have another little son, born the 27th of December. He is a fine, healthy little fellow, fat enough to be an alderman." Mr. Mann wanted to know if it would be all right to name the baby George Combe Mann. And Mr. Combe, who was childless, agreed with surprised delight.[1]

The two babies were not as strong and healthy as Mary could wish, however — fat though the younger might be. Horace, the first-born, was high-strung and sensitive. He was tortured by an itching rash — which would now be considered an allergy, perhaps, but for which no cure was suggested except country air. Mary took her children to Wrentham, to the home of her husband's widowed sister, Mrs. Pennell. There was never any question of their being welcome, but Mrs. Pennell was the mother of four children, now grown to be sure, but often at home. Then there was the aging Mrs. Pennell, not entirely easy to live with. Mrs. Peabody, serenely certain that none of her remarks could be applied to herself and her "caravanserai" at West Street, described the situation to Sophia.

"How glad I shall be when she [Mary] leaves Wrentham. It is a most confused family. Seems to me, if I lived with a married daughter, I should not frighten peace and quiet from the home. It makes sad work in the family when each one does not know her place and business and infringes on the rights of others." [2]

Mrs. Peabody need not have troubled herself about it. The Manns were already looking for a place of their own, and in West Newton, close to the railroad station, they found the home they both considered perfect. They called it a farm in the country and so it was — with woods and fields all around it and a cow pasture down the road. In fact West Newton was almost too rural. "We need a gate, for cows walk in and eat our produce sadly," Mary said.

The description of the house by Sophia was tinged with just a shade of envy. Mary had a furnace, a wonderfully modern contrivance which heated the entry, the downstairs rooms and the nursery. The bedrooms upstairs still depended upon airtight stoves, since obviously one could not expect too much of furnaces, remarkable though they might be. The real innovation, however, was next to the nursery — "a bathing room with a pump, as hot as Tophet, and a water closet annexed, hotter still." With such luxury as this, Mary could afford to overlook Sophia's remarks about the heat. Only one thing troubled Mary a little. "As I sit in this bedroom writing, I hear the rats scampering in every direction," she told her husband. "What shall we do with them!"

As usual, Horace Mann was away from home a great deal and it was Mary who laid out the drive, hoping that she had it just the way he wanted it. When his friend, Mr. Downer, sent over two hundred fruit trees and berry bushes, Mary had them set out where they would do best; she had a vegetable garden plowed and spaded over because she took particular delight in planting and tending the fruits and vegetables that Horace preferred. She taught her little boys to help her in the garden, being very patient with them when they pulled up seedlings instead of weeds once in a while.

But the new home cost a good deal of money in spite of Mary's careful management, and the salary of the Secretary of the Massachusetts Board of Education, although a little better than at first, was not adequate. There was the *Common School Journal*, from which Mr. Mann was supposed to receive six hundred dollars a year — but he never collected that much. He just enjoyed himself writing such articles as "English Colliery Serfs in the Land of the English

Aristocracy." His articles always brought letters of protest, which he enjoyed even more. But protests and replies, while they made the name of Horace Mann a byword in educational circles, buttered no bread. Some better means of support must be found.

Early in 1848 a new opportunity presented itself. John Quincy Adams, United States Representative from Massachusetts, died leaving an unfinished term in Congress. The name of Horace Mann was proposed to the governor and Mr. Mann's Free-Soil sentiments as well as his reputation in education made him an excellent choice to fill the vacancy. Mary rejoiced over the honor done her husband.

The only unhappy angle to being the wife of a Congressman was that it involved even longer separation than Mary was accustomed to already. She would gladly have moved to Washington — but she was once more expecting a child. This time, she would surely have a little girl, Mary promised her husband. He was not to worry. The ordeal would never be as bad as it had been before because now the doctors were using chloroform to ease the pains of childbirth!

Mary wrote about a friend of Elizabeth's who had a child "under the influence of chloroform." "Dr. Bigelow was her physician and he let her have it in her own hands, and she managed it better than he could have done. She said she knew everything, but it was like a summer afternoon's nap, undisturbed by a sensation of pain." It was a triumph, certainly — for the capacity of human beings to survive.

Dr. Peabody came to West Newton to look after Mary. There was no indication that he was missed at West Street, but he was more than welcome in his daughter's house and he found himself of importance to someone at last, after so many years of being merely tolerated. It was a happy old man who pottered about the garden with his two little grandsons trotting at his heels. If he planted a rose bush in just a little the wrong place, no one scolded him very much while he cheerfully moved it, and when he mended the lock on the cellar door he was thanked and even praised for his skill. Mary told him all about the chloroform and, with his passion for new things, he promised to get some for her and help her use it. But he insisted that Mary's regular doctor should also be called in case this chloroform might not be just the thing after all.

In Washington, Horace Mann experienced more anxiety on Mary's account than he had ever done before. "I cannot conceal from myself the chances there may be that the event which has proved fatal to many others, may not spare your dear, most dear life," he wrote. And in another letter, "I never thought, if I were alive, I could be absent from you under such circumstances."

The baby would be a girl, of course, and would be born on the day her father expected her — so thought Horace Mann with the assurance of a person who makes a habit of being right. When the expected telegram did not come, he found he could not work, nor rest. He walked about the streets only to pass by chance a cemetery where a funeral was in progress. It was a child's casket he saw them carrying toward a grave and he hurried back to his boarding-house full of foreboding. Not until three days later did he receive the news. "Oh, dearest . . . it is like a gleam from Heaven!" he wrote. But the child, born on April 30th, 1848, was not a daughter; it was Benjamin Pickman Mann, their third son.

As soon as she was able, Mary began again her daily letters to her husband. His unmarried sister, Lydia, of whom Mary was fond, had come to be with her. When it came time to use the chloroform, Mary had tried a little and had felt afraid. Suppose it should injure her child! She pushed the cylinder aside and told her father to take it away. Lydia took her hand and "Lydia's hand seemed to be the same shape as yours," Mary told her husband. It had "something of the same magnetic power."

It was not surprising that Mary had a difficult time, for she was forty-two years old when her third child was born. She was not lacking in courage, however, for she wrote, "I must give you one daughter to comb your hair and kiss you dearly. . . ." Meanwhile she hoped that Horace was not too disappointed, because this new baby was wonderfully dear to her heart "when he wakes and nestles after me to nurse once or twice in the night."

Benjy was just a month old when Sophia and her children arrived for a visit. Julian proved to be "an incalculable power" and they had to shut him up in another room every time he engaged in fist fights with his little cousins. And then it was Una whose disposition seemed suddenly unbearable. Then a rash appeared, and the Hawthorne children had scarlet fever! A little belladonna would "disperse the fever," Sophia had heard, although cold baths and fresh air were surely the best cure. She proceeded along those lines, although the children showed little enthusiasm for playing out of doors with their cousins and the neighbors' children. Hawthorne came, when he heard the news, and took the children to Boston where Dr. Wesselhoeft could attend them. "Cold baths and fresh air preserved them," in both Mary's and Sophia's opinions. At any rate, something did, for they lived.

"I told Mr. Hawthorne," Mary said, "that we had a fine time with the children and no jealousies, the only symptom of our preferring our own being that Sophia thought mine screamed louder and oftener than hers did, and I thought hers screamed louder and oftener than mine. He seemed rather impressed with the idea that his were good screamers, I thought."

Dr. Peabody had supposed that soon after the birth of Mary's child he would no longer be needed. He would return to West Street to wait for dental patients who never came and to be forgotten by everyone unless he happened to get in the way. But he found himself needed more than ever in West Newton, when, even before Sophia left, Mary's children came down with scarlet fever. They were very ill, much more so than the Hawthorne children had been, and while their hot little bodies could not be plunged in cold water as Sophia would have liked, their grandfather bathed them patiently, somewhat reducing their fever. The fresh air treatment was almost out of the question. "Horace has a terrific fever but he goes out for an hour, sitting on the rocks with Sophia," Mary said. And in the same letter — "George was violently seized with fever."

By a miracle, the baby seemed to escape illness. When he cried, "Father sang to him," Mary told her husband. She and her father sang together sometimes — and the baby smiled. And now the shadow which threatened Mary's happiness grew less until at last the little boys were well and she could breathe a sigh of relief. If only she could see her husband again! But Horace Mann was delayed past the date of his expected return and he was engaged upon a matter so important that Mary would have felt shame had she uttered a word of complaint.

It was Dr. Samuel Gridley Howe who had asked Mann to take the Drayton case in Washington.[3] There was danger in it. Men had been assaulted in Boston for their abolitionist activities and in Washington a lawyer for the defense of Drayton could have been shot. Horace Mann was angry with Howe for talking to Mary and frightening her with this possibility, but he was proud of her for telling him to go ahead just the same. Captain Daniel Drayton was master of a small schooner detected carrying fugitive slaves into free territory. "There are a hundred and forty slave cases," Mann told Mary. "Three or four will probably be tried and they will settle the fate of all." He had undertaken one of the test cases and to win it meant more than personal achievement.

All through his preparation of the case, Mann was haunted by fears for his family. The death of Emerson's beloved little son — of scarlet fever — shocked Mann dreadfully for did not his own sons have the same dread disease? He worked with added intensity in order to dull his anxiety and although he was exhausted each night, he never failed to write a word to Mary, for he knew that she suffered even more because he was so far away. On August 10, 1848 — "Ah, dearest," he wrote, "the verdict was against us again yesterday. It seems impossible at the present time here to have an impartial trial. No jury in a free state would have convicted Drayton." The case was appealed — it would go on and on. From Horace Mann's personal point of view, each delay meant further separation from Mary, from his two boys, and from the child he had never seen. One comforting thought sustained him. "I feel in this case as tho' I were not working for Drayton . . . only, but for the whole colored race."

"We look for you on every Western train and long for the day and the hour," Mary told him. "But we know you are working for a holy cause and we can wait."

Inadvertently, Mary had said to five-year-old Horace one day that his father would be home "soon." Late in the afternoon, she found Horace sitting on the stairs, watching the front door. It was nearly bedtime, she told him; he must come. But he was waiting for his father, Horace said, and he would not move.

Mary sat down on the stairs beside the child to explain. At first he would not listen and then suddenly it was borne in upon him that, in the adult world, "soon" might be weeks or even months away. He burst into tears. His mother comforted him as best she could. She told him that in faraway Washington there was a man in prison who also had a little boy — and who might never see his boy again unless "Papa" stayed to help him. The child's sobs quieted gradually. He had been asking a great many questions lately and his mother had been telling him about his "Father in heaven." Was "Father in heaven" the same thing as "Papa in Washington"? It would seem so. Horace allowed himself to be led off to bed.

When Horace Mann returned at last it was only for a few weeks of late summer and early autumn. He went back to Washington before Congress convened, because of the Drayton case. Christmas came and Grandfather Peabody appeared bringing a turkey and "a huge squash." The little boys were busy making presents for everyone and had forgotten themselves, Mary told their father. But Dr. Peabody had made little wooden snow shovels for them and on Christmas Day he went out to help them build a snow house.

It was spring, almost strawberry time, before Horace Mann came home. Drayton had been again convicted but the case was carried to the Circuit Court. Drayton was "liable to twenty years' imprisonment for each of forty-one indictments" but in the end he was sentenced to four years only. Mann had made himself as much a prisoner in Washington as the captain, but now he too was free.

Four years later, a stranger came to call on Mrs. Horace Mann. He wanted to thank her, he said, for giving up her husband's company for so long. He told how Mr. Mann used to visit him in jail to keep up his spirits and how they would both talk about the families they longed to see. His name was Captain Daniel Drayton.

CHAPTER SEVENTEEN
The End of the Shop in West Street

T HE Peabodys were not given to putting down roots in any
one locality but when Sophia had returned "home," after her
marriage, it was to West Street. Mary had been pleased when she
and her husband found rooms in Bowdoin Square – near home.
From 1839 through 1854, Dr. Peabody had stubbornly advertised
himself as a Salem dentist; but even he added that he was also
from Boston, and eventually he too considered West Street his
home.

With the marriage of her two sisters, each from the West Street
parlor, Elizabeth had been left in sole command of the shop. She
could not be said to mind it. Now she could plunge into ardent
"disinterested friendships," and neither sister was on hand to warn
her to be discreet. She could plunge headlong into a new enterprise
without having Mary remind her to be practical.

The often sentimental Elizabeth liked to believe that she had not
lost sisters but gained brothers. When Mary and her husband returned from Europe, Elizabeth expected "dear Mr. Mann" to spend
a good deal of time with her, telling her all about foreign education.
She took his part in the fierce controversy which arose over his
stand concerning religion in the schools. Now, since German education had seemed to him so valuable, she longed to go to Germany
to see for herself. Mr. Mann delighted in nothing so much as to
talk education, so he gave her all the time he could. She must go
to Dresden, he said, and he gave her the names of the many friends
he had made there. His news of a struggle in Hungary for independence so kindled Elizabeth's imagination that she promptly
wrote a book about it.

But when Elizabeth tried to establish herself exactly on her old
footing and talked to Horace Mann about his dead wife, Mary

stepped in. She had brought Horace back to life, and there would be no return. She was the present Mrs. Mann; the first one must be allowed to rest in her grave. Mary was never good at talking over matters which troubled her but she could write her innermost thoughts. "There is such a thing as being sympathized with too much. It is the last touch of delicacy which sees this," Mary wrote to her sister. She understood all too well that Elizabeth probed deep into another's secret heart never for a moment realizing that she was motivated by curiosity fully as much as by sympathy. Mary would have to put a stop to this, at least where her husband was concerned. "There is a plane where human communications had better stop — as when it interferes with married life, particularly," she said.

Mary tried to tell her sister what it was like to be married. "The nearness of two souls knit into one is fearful to think of," she said. Elizabeth was not to come between "what God has joined."

Elizabeth tried to learn her lesson — and failed as usual. It might have helped her if she could have realized that Mary was and always would be jealous of the lovely and long-dead Charlotte Messer. This was a secret, however, which Mary herself unwittingly revealed only in her private diary.

Elizabeth's possessiveness toward Hawthorne was of a different nature. She had never so much as held his hand and it was unthinkable that he should ever have laid his head upon her shoulder. But she had been secretly thrilled and flattered when Salem gossips had coupled their names. He was hers, by right of discovery, as a gold nugget might have been or a literary rarity found in some dim shop of an antiquarian and brought to light. She constantly attempted to commend him to the notice of prominent people who might help him, unaware that nothing infuriated him more and forgetting that, with Sophia at his side, he was perfectly capable of helping himself. It was hard for Elizabeth to see that it was Sophia who had brought Hawthorne to maturity and self-confidence. Sophie was supposed to be the little sister, herself in need of help.

Sophia's habit of dependence was something Elizabeth thought she could count on. Once more, she was faced with a change and a new lesson. Sophia was depending on Hawthorne now, for her happiness, while in matters concerning her house and her children, she depended upon herself. Characteristically, however, it was not Sophia who wrote Elizabeth some unvarnished truths such as Mary had written. It was Hawthorne, often the most tactful of men, who was goaded into cruel frankness. God had not intended Elizabeth to be married, he told her. She was utterly unfit for matrimony but there was one thing she could do and that was to mind her own business. Lizzie felt that she had been cut adrift and it was fortunate for her that she had the bookshop to occupy her mind.

In 1843 when Sophia and Mary had both married, Elizabeth was approaching forty. Her formidable vitality had continued undiminished. She was generous to a fault, tender-hearted and affectionate and she had almost no one upon whom to lavish these gifts.

In 1841, there had still been Dr. Channing, whose friendship had weathered various storms. When gossips had said of Elizabeth that she was a sort of hanger-on of Channing's, while she was his unpaid secretary — that Channing had wanted to be rid of her — Elizabeth's pride had stood her in good stead. She had ceased her daily calls and awaited invitations that often seemed long in coming. And when the bookshop was opened, she had had her reward. Dr. Channing soon came every morning to the shop to read the papers. He stayed for the sake of the people he would meet, Orestes Brownson, George Ripley, and above all Theodore Parker. When summer came and Channing went to Newport, Elizabeth wrote him long letters, which she called his "newspapers." These contained, besides news of Ripley's Brook Farm "Institute" and Brownson's socialism — which she hated because it threatened family life — the latest in theology according to Theodore Parker, of which she approved. Channing replied in his almost illegible writing, asking for more news and taking pains to defend the Biblical miracles attacked by Parker, and to assure Elizabeth that to believe in them was the simplest act of faith.

Mrs. Peabody was heard to remark that Dr. Channing had not put in much of an order for books. But Elizabeth was perfectly content. When she had found Emerson's philosophy more to her liking than Channing's, Dr. Channing had not bothered to argue. That he should now refute Parker was pleasing proof that Dr. Channing once more cared about the state of Miss Peabody's soul.

Dr. Channing's daily calls at the shop ceased because of his failing health, but he would come if urgently summoned to meet a new personality. Elizabeth had one for him toward the close of the year 1841. A young man had come into the shop, asking for Kant. Elizabeth was instantly on the alert — not to sell him some volumes — but to find out why he wanted to read the German philosopher.

They fell immediately into a discussion of the Trinity versus "Tritheism." The young man said that Theodore Parker's sermons lacked unity, and that Emerson could not preach to the poor. These distinctly uncalled-for blows against two of her most admired friends left Elizabeth reeling — but she rallied quickly. The young man must meet Dr. Channing, she said.

Leaving metaphysics aside for the moment, the newcomer told Elizabeth that he was Lieutenant William Batchelder Greene.[1] Elizabeth got the idea that he had graduated from West Point with high honors. He did not. He attended about two and a half years. He did become a lieutenant, however, and served in Florida under Captain Bonneville. He had read nothing but military biographies and the poems of Byron and Shelley, he said. Then, one night alone in his tent, a religious revelation had come to him. He had thrown his volume of *Queen Mab* out of the tent door, "then rushed to his valise and took out the Bible that his mother had put into it." Elizabeth was enchanted. While her mother waited upon customers, her lips tight with exasperation, Elizabeth talked to her new enthusiasm, a young man of twenty-two, excessively handsome.

Dr. Channing arrived "a few days after" and sat down in pleasant anticipation. Elizabeth had told him that Lieutenant Greene believed in "irresistible Grace." This belief was untenable, Dr. Channing said genially, because of a human being's God-given right to choose between good and evil — and take the consequences. Fellow students of Greene's at Harvard Divinity School spoke of him as "mercilessly opinionated" but even those who disliked him admitted that he was "very entertaining in conversation." Next morning Dr. Channing was again at the bookshop, resuming his habit of daily calls. He referred to Lieutenant Greene as Elizabeth's "young friend," and asked her why she had seemed so overwrought concerning the question of "free will and the pardoning Grace of God."

Elizabeth could not exactly explain what she so little understood. The handsome young man had reminded her of her own early approach to love with its tragic ending. Once more she felt a conviction of sin because of "poor L.B," and now it was Lieutenant Greene, with his "Grace of God," who must give her absolution. Once Dr. Channing had been "the sudden bursting of the Tropical morning," and Elizabeth had felt free from sin. Truth to tell, Elizabeth's feeling of guilt had provided her with the means of intimate friendships with kindred spirits, a subject for heart-to-heart talks, an approach to love-making with retreat left open. She could hardly live without these synthetic courtships, but it was a pity that the object of her present attentions should be so young and handsome a man. People would laugh at her behind her back and the friends who loved her would try in vain to save her from making a fool of herself.

Dr. Channing's visits to the shop to talk to Greene were partly for his own pleasure, partly in the hope that he could bring Elizabeth to see that the young man was after all something a little less than a reincarnation of the prophet Isaiah. They had long discussions — about Channing's articles on Napoleon, Greene saying that Channing was wrong; about transcendentalism, Greene announcing that all of them except Emerson had missed the point. It developed that Greene's grandfather had been, as Elizabeth put it, "the great Baptist saint and preacher Batchelder — the odor of whose sanctity still lingers in the air of New Hampshire and Maine." The grandson had begun to study Baptist theology, had found it wanting, and was now having a good time for himself in Boston telling Boston Unitarians how to improve.

During the spring of 1842, Elizabeth had gone to see Dr. Channing at his home. He was packing his books and papers preparatory to going to Newport for the summer and he asked her to sit and talk to him while he worked. At last she got up to leave. He came and took both her hands, a thing she dearly loved. "Well, will you write to me this summer, and make me a partner in your new thoughts?" he asked.

In other years, Elizabeth would have promised joyfully. But now, "I do not know, sir," she said. "I have hardly learned how to clothe them with words."

There was much of the loneliness of age in Channing's persistence. "If you learn anything from this young friend of yours, or from any other source, don't you think *I* have the first right to it?"

With her capacity for telling the worst about herself, Elizabeth later confessed that she did not write. But it was not until early autumn 1842 that she realized that she had received Channing's last letters and heard his last words to her.

She was sitting in the bookroom crying over the letter which brought the news of Channing's death when Washington Allston entered the shop. He sat down, "overpowered by the news," then returned to his studio, soon to work upon the design for a monument to his friend. And Elizabeth Peabody, realizing suddenly that she had been losing sight of Allston, came to his house to call.

The old master rallied at the sight of a former admirer. He took out an old portfolio filled with India ink sketches made long ago, in Italy, in England, in the days when hope was new and he had been sure that he was born to do great things. "I have enough sketches, enough work planned out in my studio for a hundred years to come," he told Elizabeth grandly. He should have been the head of a school as Michelangelo had been. Talented young apprentices ought to be at work upon canvases sketched in by the master and finished by the master hand.

"Let me tell that in Boston," cried Elizabeth. She could have students clamoring at his door and the money raised for a great studio within a month and Boston would become the art center of the world. For a moment, Elizabeth's tremendous vitality fed his dreams and rejuvenated the old man. His cheeks flushed and he saw himself indeed the great master. But at the same time, he was appalled. The indomitable Miss Peabody was capable of anything and unless he stopped her, the students might actually arrive. Their young eyes would see him for what he was — an empty husk.

Allston selected a small sketch from the portfolio and gave it to Elizabeth. It showed a man with a hat on, sitting upon the bank of a stream, and Allston turned it over, signed the back and added the date when it was done — 1797. He sat for a second staring at the date, his mind forty-five years away. "Moore's drawing school in New York is quite good," he told Miss Peabody. He began to quote from one of his own poems which he had memorized for just such occasions as these — when it was necessary to cover from his own eyes his inadequacy.

Elizabeth was so easily led aside from the subject of art that Allston was almost sorry that he had discouraged her so soon. But her admiration of his poetry was all he could desire. Properly urged, he was able to recall nine long stanzas from another poem of his, recently published. He recited it with "an expression of reverence which was sublime," Elizabeth said.

"I felt as if I were in the holy of holies of his mind." That was a spot Miss Peabody loved to believe she reached with everyone — or at least with all she considered to be possessed of such a place. Allston went to his desk and took out a copy of the poem, kept there in readiness for just such a listener. "We had risen into the electric sphere which needs no words," said Elizabeth — for she had just been about to ask for it. And at this point Miss Peabody delighted Allston by memorizing his poem! What other admirer had gone so far!

Three weeks later, Allston was dead. All one evening he had climbed the scaffolding to reach his still unfinished "Belshazzar's Feast," had painted a few strokes and descended to cross the studio to get the effect. The effect was always wrong. He climbed again to try again — over and over. At last he left the studio, a tragic, broken figure. But his wife's relatives were gathered round the dining table and he straightened up, entered and greeted them with fine effect. He talked well on art — better than ever before, it seemed. They left him in his great armchair, before him a glass of wine. But when the last guest was gone and his wife sought him out, she found him, not sleeping in his chair — but dead.

Elizabeth would not have missed the funeral for the world. The family did not ask her but she was sure they had only forgotten and she went anyway. Allston was buried at night. The clouds gathered over the moon, broke and gathered again. Then came "students from the University" to stand by the open grave with lighted torches. Even while she wept, Elizabeth thought how Allston would have enjoyed the scene. She thought how she, herself, would like to write about it and really do it justice.

In 1844, Margaret Fuller went to New York as literary critic for Horace Greeley's *New York Tribune*. For several winters she had given her famous Conversations at West Street. Emerson said that Margaret had benefited by knowing Miss Peabody, "who, by her hospitality to excellence, has made her modest abode for so many years the inevitable resort of studious feet." Margaret herself probably denied receiving anything at all. She would have said that the shop in West Street was much indebted to her, and so it was. The women and girls who had flocked to West Street to hear Miss Fuller came rarely now. They stopped to buy their books at the Old Corner shop as it happened to be more convenient. By 1845 Mrs. Peabody was forced to admit, whether Elizabeth did or not, that "business is at a perfect standstill."

"Let us all pray for Peace," advised Mrs. Peabody, "for even the humblest suffer in consequence of the expenses incurred by our rulers." It was a war of boundaries to which Mrs. Peabody referred. The United States had recently invaded a disputed area in the vicinity of the Rio Grande, would soon annex the Republic of Texas and send a fleet to California. "Expansion," President Polk and his Democratic party called it, but it was "aggression" to the

Boston Whigs. Of course, when it came to Northern boundaries, where slavery would never be a question, there was a matter of six hundred thousand square miles of Pacific slope to be added to United States territory; and "aggression" suddenly became "expansion" again, with cries of "Fifty-four forty or fight!" Call war by any name, it still hurt business, Mrs. Peabody found. In 1846, "We jog along in the usual routine," she said, "doing all we can, and hoping every day to see the faces of our old friends in the Bookstore. They are returning gradually . . . but business is horribly dull."

While it hurt her pride to admit it, Number 13 West Street was now more of a boardinghouse than a bookstore. Elizabeth was obliged to feel grateful to the boarders, however. They helped her to keep her beloved bookroom open a little longer. They might even have helped her to weather the storm — or rather the calm — that had overtaken her, if she had been able to withstand the claims of those who had more "moral value" than cash in their pockets. Lieutenant Greene, for example, was sometimes a resident of West Street with a faulty memory when it came time to pay his bill. Elizabeth, almost at her wits' end, began to teach school again.

Mrs. Peabody kept shop. There was less money in their coffers in 1848, she said, than ever before. "We have not received a dollar these two days, not half of one." It was particularly hard on her only surviving son, Nathaniel, Mrs. Peabody thought. Elizabeth could not give him any more money and he had such a large family. Quite reasonably, Sophia wanted to know why her brother could not come and work in the shop? For it was beyond her mother's strength to tend shop and keep boarders as well. But to this, Mrs. Peabody made no reply.

Elizabeth's teaching position was in a new school for boys just opened in Boston by Dr. Kraitsir, a Hungarian. Discipline at the school was of the Medes and Persians variety of which Elizabeth disapproved. But Dr. Kraitsir had a theory of language which he said would unlock all foreign tongues and make language study easy. This intrigued Elizabeth and she easily persuaded Dr. Kraitsir to give lectures, tickets for sale at West Street. A pamphlet — *The Significance of the Alphabet*, by Charles Kraitsir, M.D. — soon appeared; then two more, published by E. P. Peabody and also for sale at the shop in West Street. Dr. Kraitsir's theories enjoyed a brief popularity while Harvard students flocked to his lectures in the hope of finding an easy way to read German — a study in high favor. German poetry seemed simpler when touched by this philosopher's stone; but when they plunged deeper into German, hard study proved still the only alchemy. Dr. Kraitsir's popularity flickered out long before all his pamphlets were sold.

It was not to be expected that Elizabeth could teach in Kraitsir's school, publish his pamphlets and promote his lectures without becoming interested in him personally and without mixing in his private affairs. She knew that he was married and had left a wife and child in Philadelphia. In due course, she received a strange letter from Mrs. Kraitsir threatening to come to Boston and make trouble. Elizabeth "thought it proper," as Mrs. Peabody put it, to show the letter to Kraitsir, whose "lips for the first time were unclosed on the heart-rending subject, and he went on rapidly detailing things that convinced Elizabeth that Mrs. K. was insane." Mrs. Kraitsir "would rant and rave at him in front of his scholars," Dr. Kraitsir said, and Elizabeth went to Philadelphia to persuade the poor woman not to come to Boston to break up her husband's school.

Of course Miss Peabody got herself talked about — although her mother declared that "all she has had to do in the affair does honor to her head and heart and has been full of her self-sacrificing spirit." Mrs. Kraitsir was judged insane, placed in an institution, and a home found for her little girl. Kraitsir set out for Hungary to take part in revolutionary activities and the gossiping parents in his school rather shamefacedly gave him six hundred dollars — at Elizabeth's solicitation. He promised to write political letters to Elizabeth which she would edit and try to get published in the *New York Tribune*. Lieutenant Greene would carry on the school until Kraitsir returned.

Kraitsir proved unsatisfactory as a revolutionist, however, his followers almost preferring Austrian tyranny to his high-handed leadership. He came into conflict with Kossuth, who was already established as a champion of Hungarian liberty. No political letters were forthcoming and Kraitsir sank from sight. Meanwhile Lieutenant Greene found schoolteaching little to his liking. It interfered with his researches in Oriental literature — whether it would have paid his board bill or not — and he withdrew. The school was no more.

As for Elizabeth, she was heart and soul in a new project. She had ceased to publish the *Dial* in 1843. The profits which James Monroe and Company had promised failed to materialize and Emerson found himself paying a larger deficit than Elizabeth, as publisher, had ever incurred. Elizabeth was grieved, as was every transcendentalist, when the *Dial* was given up; but she was only human when she felt satisfaction because Monroe was even less successful than she had been. There ought to be a magazine of the intellectual type in Boston, however, as everyone agreed. Elizabeth thought she had learned how to publish one.

Now letters between the sisters were full of "Elizabeth's book." The magazine was called *Aesthetic Papers* when it finally appeared in 1849. In the introduction, E. P. Peabody said, "Whoever is so far pleased with the current number as to desire another is requested to send an order to that effect to the Editor, who is also Publisher, No. 13 West Street, Boston." There were people who were pleased, but almost none of them was sufficiently pleased to subscribe — so the first number of *Aesthetic Papers* was also the last. Appreciation increased throughout the years, for the contents of *Aesthetic Papers* was really good, the copies so rare as to make it a collector's item. This was a form of success, however, which could do the Editor and Publisher no good whatever.

Elizabeth had pestered Hawthorne till he gave her "Main Street," one of his best efforts. She thought it was gloomy with "Joshua Buffum standing in the pillory, Cassandra Southwick led to prison" — couldn't Hawthorne think of something more cheerful? He could not and Elizabeth had to admit that, whether gloomy or otherwise, it was "masterly" and she should be thankful to get it.

Her own contribution was the most readable essay Elizabeth Peabody ever wrote. "The Dorian Measure," she called it, and there were those who laughed and said that she was advocating that Bostonians should go about draped in sheets and spend their time dancing barefoot on Boston Common. As a matter of fact, Miss Peabody was describing the Feast of Apollo and doing it very well. Then she went on to say, "The importance of this great act of worship is apt to be overlooked, especially by England, Old and New, who, on account of their Puritan preoccupations, are not accustomed to look for important results from a form of worship whose festive and entertaining character give it, in their eyes, a trifling tone of amusement." Elizabeth suggests that it might not be a bad idea to "see God" as the Dorians, "in the sunshine and the flowers rather than in the storm and wilderness."

This was heresy, of course, but there was worse to come. Miss Peabody advocated the teaching of music and dancing and art in the public schools! She went further, and suggested that really large sums of money be spent on schools. "It is plain, that if we can spend a hundred millions of dollars a year for so questionable a purpose as the late war with Mexico, we have resources on which we might draw for public education."

The year was 1849, but let a century go by and Elizabeth would still be in advance of her time.

Elizabeth looked upon all war as wrong but certain wars bore a deeper stain of evil than others. What was the Florida War, for example, but a glorified national slave hunt! Escaped slaves had been given sanctuary with the Florida Indians and the United States Army had been ordered to go in and take the slaves and punish the Indians for the benefit, not of the nation as a whole, but for slaveowners. The Mexican War was aggression, she felt, but it was worse than that — for again there was the black stain of slavery since Elizabeth, the like-minded Mary, Mrs. Peabody and all their friends and associates feared that new land to the south and west must certainly become slave territory.

It was one of Elizabeth's charms that she could be so right one moment and wrong the next. At the end of *Aesthetic Papers* she championed Dr. Kraitsir, whose theories pointed toward a universal language which Elizabeth hoped might be very soon developed. Some critics had described *The Significance of the Alphabet* as "a dark hint rather than an elucidation of the subject." Elizabeth sprang to the defense. It was an "enlargement by Dr. Kraitsir of some notes by a hearer of one or two of his lectures." As Miss Peabody was quite a hearer and a taker of notes at lectures, who this person might be was an easy guess.

The failure of *Aesthetic Papers* depressed Elizabeth more than most disappointments. She had put her heart into the magazine. But she was soon riding high again on the crest of another new idea. A Polish general by the name of Josef Bem had contrived a system for learning historical dates which seemed to her miraculous. Elizabeth set to work making charts with a series of colored squares running in utterly baffling patterns. Anyone with sufficient patience to work out the meaning of the colored squares must have found the memorizing of dates mere recreation. Elizabeth could not afford to have the charts printed in color, so she colored them herself, working late into the night. She permanently injured her eyesight, but she felt that it made no difference since the Boston School Committee would surely see how wonderful the charts were and would place a large order. She would receive similar orders from other cities. Elizabeth would at last make the Peabody family's fortune just as she had always expected to do ever since she could remember. Then the Boston schools turned down the idea.

Never one to accept defeat, Elizabeth took her charts and traveled widely, demonstrating them in private schools. Horace Mann had helped her to meet the right people connected with the Boston schools. He was as disappointed as she, if not equally surprised, when she failed to make her sale. Normal schools were springing up, not only in Massachusetts but all over the country, all of them looking to Horace Mann as their inspiration. To these he sent Elizabeth to lecture on history — and if she could also sell some charts, so much the better. Elizabeth did make sales to normal schools as well as to public schools. She also made friends — something always easier for her and infinitely more satisfying than making money. Reporting on her progress, Horace Mann said, "She always finds enjoyment in her path, for she always makes herself so agreeable that she is in the greatest demand everywhere and the object of the most devoted attention."

In November 1850 Sophia wrote to her mother from Lenox. Elizabeth had come for a visit, having been at Great Barrington lecturing and selling charts. "She seems to have great success and is led from place to place by some good spirit who wishes well to her. Father will feel encouraged by the solid dollars she takes home with her." Lizzie also brought gifts from New York to the Hawthornes for whenever she had a little money she could not resist spending it on someone dear to her. She attempted to teach dates in history to Una and Julian Hawthorne but found them most unwilling students. The little Mann cousins, she told them, could recite dates by the chartful.

For nearly a year, Elizabeth traveled, lectured and sold charts. She made money enough to support her parents, but she could see that their strength was failing. The time had come to give up the shop.

As a home, Number 13 West Street had become less desirable. Although the glimpse of Boston Common at the top of the street still brought delight, the din of traffic from Washington Street was increasing every year. After all, ten years bring changes in every city, and West Street was no longer a residence street with a few discreet shops; it was a business street with scarcely a boarding-house, however discreet. Elizabeth took her aging parents to West

Newton, not to live with Mary, but to live at a farm near by. Here her mother could have a garden again. She was never so happy, she said, as when gardening or wandering in the woods "botanizing." In her daughters' attitude there was a touch of reproach toward their father because he had not provided many gardens. With a patient sigh, Dr. Peabody went out to spade up this last one, glad of the help of a neighbor's boy.

And now the shop in West Street had come to an end. It had been Elizabeth's brightest dream and it had lasted a long time — as dreams go! She went back for a last look, her footsteps echoing on bare boards. Surplus stock, old copies of the *Dial*, had been sent to her brother Nathaniel's apothecary shop. The empty bookshelves stared at Elizabeth like old friends suddenly become strangers by some sad mischance. She glanced at the end of the room where Margaret Fuller used to stand, entrancing her women and girls with subtle scorn and skillful flattery. Margaret was dead. Whether she had been truly the Marchioness Ossoli or, as Hawthorne believed, the mistress of a fake nobleman, she had snatched at life with both hands before the sea claimed her. The tragedy was scarcely a year old and Elizabeth could hardly believe that Margaret would never return.

It was growing dark and Elizabeth instinctively turned toward the place where an empty lamp bracket still remained. The shop had been at its best after dark. George Ripley would come and those earnest young theological students would be serenely unconscious that a bookshop might have a closing time. Brook Farm was gone now, the land sold at auction, and there had not been enough money to pay off the shareholders, Hawthorne among them.

To West Street, as a home, belonged the weddings of two sisters. Elizabeth gave the old parlor an affectionate farewell for their sake — not for her own. It was the shop she had come to take leave of; the shop that was so much a part of herself. She thought of the individuals who had come there in search of books but who had returned again and again to see Miss Peabody. Lieutenant Greene, coming into her life too late, had troubled her heart too much. It was one more Platonic friendship and if this was the ideal relationship between the sexes, as she had tried to believe, why had it not brought more happiness? He was abroad now, in search of further knowledge — or merely in search — an occupation which suited him. Elizabeth would always think of him as the young Lieutenant Greene, no matter how old he might become, for, with his handsome self-assurance, he was the young man she had hoped to meet twenty-five years earlier. He was also like the son she knew now she would never have.

Elizabeth turned quickly from the empty room. She had never lived in the past and now she stepped outside, shut the door of the West Street shop and turned the key. Certain, as always, that a new and better day was dawning, she was glad to go.

CHAPTER EIGHTEEN
Parting of the Ways

LEAVING her parents in West Newton, Elizabeth set out in search of fresh fields for lecturing and for selling Bem's Historical Charts. "It is refreshing to see her elasticity and perennial faith and trust in her fellow mortals," said Mary. "The world is always a new world to her."

Mrs. Peabody, uprooted from West Street and deprived of her occupation of keeping store, seemed suddenly old and feeble. Very shortly, however, Mary noted that Mother was feeling better "because the garden was being dug up." Since she could not possibly be expected to dig or to plant anything personally, Mrs. Peabody found that garden a challenge to her executive abilities. She rose to the occasion while Dr. Peabody protested as usual but did as he was told. He gave only moderate satisfaction of course — as had been the case for about fifty years.

The political activities of her favorite son-in-law, Horace Mann, did Mrs. Peabody almost as much good as her garden. She dearly loved a cause which she could promote with zeal and next to a cause she loved a bit of gossip with an opportunity for righteous indignation. Mr. Mann provided her with everything and her letters became even more pungent as old age took toll of her body but never of her mind. Her point of view was unashamedly personal. "Mr. Webster has made a virulent attack on Mr. Mann," wrote Mother Peabody with relish. "I know absolutely nothing about the merits of the points in dispute; but two things I do know. Mr. Mann is an honest, high-minded, moral, religious, independent Citizen of the Country — unselfish, unambitious — devoted to the best good of the people. Mr. Webster is, in spite of his fine sentences and sophisticated reasoning, dishonest, low-minded, immoral, irreligious, devoted to his own aggrandisement. He is grossly intemperate – he is unchaste, keeping not one only, but many colored mistresses, this is a known fact as notorious as his intemperance." However "virulent" Mr. Webster had been against Mr. Mann, he had met his match in Mrs. Peabody!

The two Peabody sons-in-law were in different camps politically and Mrs. Peabody's method of sending each the written works of the other did nothing to diminish the rift. They left their wives to carry on the correspondence. "I read Mr. Mann's speech," said Sophia, upon returning it to her mother, "and think it admirable except that I am sorry he stooped from the dignity of parliamentary debate to fling innuendos at General Pierce and trample on Mr. Webster . . . why not let God take care of Mr. Webster and punish him in his own way? As for General Pierce, he cannot be hurt by innuendos. . . ." [1]

General Pierce was beginning to be mentioned as the democratic candidate for the presidency, and in Mann's opinion Pierce would be the "merest tool of slavery." There was a rumor that Hawthorne might write a campaign biography of Pierce and to this Mann said, "If he makes out Pierce to be a great man or a brave man, it will be the greatest work of fiction he ever wrote."

(In 1852 "God took care of Mr. Webster," and Mrs. Peabody made it clear that she did not mourn her country's loss of a statesman. "The survivors of this wicked Husband and Father are objects of deepest sympathy," she said.)

When Horace Mann left for Washington, "He will not like Congress nor Congress him," Mrs. Peabody prophesied, and she was right. She went on to air her views with her accustomed vigor. "He [Mr. Mann] will act up to his own convictions, independent of party – and unless a man consents to be the tool of a party, he stands no chance in our degraded community. The most august Body in the civilized world – drinking, gambling, fighting duels – swearing etc. etc. to the end of the chapter of disgusting crimes. What a comment on Republican freedom!"

So vigorous was Mrs. Peabody's mind that only Mary knew how feeble she was in body. In January 1852 Mrs. Peabody was taken so ill that Mary, at Dr. Wesselhoeft's request, wrote to Elizabeth urging her to hasten home. Sophia was summoned for a last farewell. But Mrs. Peabody rallied; and by February, Mary was able to carry out a cherished project. She took her three little boys and went to Washington to be with her husband.

Political differences had in no way lessened the real sympathy between the sisters, and Mary lent the West Newton house to Sophia and her family until such time as the Hawthornes should find that home of their own they could now afford. *A Wonder-Book*, begun in Lenox the first of June, 1851, as a direct result of Hawthorne's pleasure in telling stories to his children, was a success in spite of Fields's rather gloomy forecast. But Sophia would see to it that a home would not be bought hastily or at too high a price. Mary loved West Newton and Sophia thought she would look around at some of the available property.

Unfortunately, all of Mary's friends began to call. Mary had been holding a little dancing school at her house for her children and their neighbors. The mothers were determined to make Mrs. Hawthorne feel at home. Then there was the group of friends from the Normal School who had been keeping up their French by meeting once a week at Mary's house to read and converse in what they sincerely hoped was a Parisian accent. They wanted to meet Mrs. Hawthorne, but they wanted still more to make the acquaintance of her celebrated husband. Sophia was adept at guarding Hawthorne's privacy but she could not help it if he heard a gabbling of women's voices in Mary's parlor every day.

In West Newton, Hawthorne wrote *The Blithedale Romance* with Sophia to guard his study door. But he could hardly indulge in his favorite recreation — long, solitary walks in the country — in a locality where so many friendly Peabodys had made solitude an impossibility. Although the plot was pure fiction, there were scenes in *The Blithedale Romance* which really took place at Brook Farm. Hawthorne's disillusionment lent edge to his satire, and there were characters who sufficiently resembled certain well-known Bostonians to cause laughter in Boston parlors. Speculation arose as to whether "Zenobia" was really Miss Fuller, for example — and all the talk was good for sales.

Before *The Blithedale Romance* was published, the Hawthornes had found the home they wanted. By this time, Hawthorne hated West Newton; he even disliked Mary's house with its wonderful furnace which gave him ideas of writing a story about a house built over hell with evil spirits rising out of the hot-air radiators! Concord, with all its happy memories of honeymoon days, would be the place to live, and it was simple to find a house there without central heating. The Alcotts owned Hillside, a house with forty-two acres of land on the Lexington Road. It was for sale and Nathaniel Hawthorne bought it for fifteen hundred dollars.

The Hawthornes called it Wayside. Mr. Fields had proposed selling the copyright for *The Blithedale Romance* in London and Hawthorne thought that perhaps he might get fifty pounds for it. But Chapman and Brown of London paid two hundred pounds, and Sophia wrote, "This windfall enables him to pay up for this place which is a great contentment to him."

Mrs. Peabody would never be able to visit Wayside, but Sophia wrote her mother faithfully. First of all Sophia's concerns had been Hawthorne's study and she "proposed to have it the best adorned room in the house." Her painting of "Endymion," handsomely framed, had hung in the West Street shop, for sale at a hundred dollars. There had been times when Sophia was sorely tempted to lower the price and take whatever it would bring. Now she was thankful that she had never yielded to quite that degree of despair, for "Endymion" had not been sold and now it was hers to hang in her husband's study. He had always wanted that picture and it seemed a good omen that "Endymion," painted in Concord, should return to Concord to their new home. Perhaps paradise had been regained. Sophia's paintings of Lake Como were also in Hawthorne's study, but Sophia was not so egotistical as to decorate the room with nothing but her own works. A fine engraving of Raphael's "Transfiguration" hung on one wall, while Sophia's prized wedding present, that plaster cast of Apollo, stood in a corner. If art could stimulate Hawthorne's genius, Sophia had done her best.

Wayside's pre-Revolutionary origin was no asset in Sophia's eyes. The "horrible old house," she called it, and she was not satisfied until she had all the woodwork downstairs "painted in oak." A new Brussels carpet of "lapis lazuli blue" with a "figure of fine wood color" with here and there "a lovely rose and rosebud" covered the old floor in Hawthorne's study. In the dining room the disgracefully old and wide boards were modestly hidden beneath another Brussels carpet of brown and green.

Now all was fairly satisfactory. In summer, Wayside proved stiflingly hot but Sophia made little complaint. She merely lay down to rest on the parlor sofa and put a newspaper over her face "to keep off the terrible flies." The water in the well suddenly "proved too bad to drink or cook with. It has the most offensive odor and looks thick and discolored" — but the Hawthornes went to a neighboring farmer for their water for a while. "Mr. Hawthorne has sold his grass for thirty dollars," Sophia told her mother. "He has cut bean poles in his own woods." Paradise, with just a few drawbacks, was surely theirs.

It was July 17, 1852, when Sophia wrote to her sister-in-law, Louisa Hawthorne, for the last time. She had been urging Louisa to visit Wayside and this last letter, like all the rest, was full of affection. "Last night I received your note from Saratoga Springs and I can hardly express to you the delight I felt that you were there, notwithstanding our disappointment that you are not here," Sophia said. "But your visit to us can keep, while this enchanting freak of the excellent Mr. Dike can occur but once perhaps, in a thousand years. If Mr. Dike gets tired of Saratoga you can easily excurse round about; and pray do not fail to go down the Hudson and see the great Gotham."

On the twenty-seventh of July, the Hudson River steamer, *Henry Clay*, bound for New York, was approaching her pier. Hudson River boats were still a novelty and the order was "full steam ahead" for a final burst of speed to impress the crowd. There came a roar. A boiler had burst and in a moment the steamer, its decks lined with sight-seers, was a sheet of flame. The Hawthornes read of the disaster in the local papers.

Three days later, a friend from earliest Salem days came to Wayside with terrible news. Louisa Hawthorne had been aboard the *Henry Clay*. No one ever knew just how Louisa died. She was last seen sitting in her cabin reading a book and her body, horribly burned, was identifiable only by a brooch she wore. The dreadful unknown interval was filled by Hawthorne with frightful imaginings. Had his sister been suffocated there in her cabin, or trampled by the panic-stricken crowd, or had she flung herself into the river, her clothes ablaze? Hawthorne could not escape the pictures in his mind and this time he did not turn to Sophia for comfort. He wandered alone on the hill.

Sophia tried to comfort her children, who were fond of their Aunt Louisa and who were frightened. Within herself, she was facing a hard test for her creed of optimism. For years she had been urging Louisa to go out into the world, certain that the normal sort of life was the right one. She had suggested to Louisa to take this very trip which had ended in disaster. How could God let such a dreadful thing happen to someone who was only doing right! For once it seemed as if an accident of man could not possibly be one of God's purposes.

She must write to her mother. "Tell my sister Elizabeth not to stop here as she intended," she had to say. It was no time for Hawthorne to have to listen to Elizabeth's unbearably voluble sympathy.

Elizabeth might blunder through misguided affection, but she was sensitive, and from now on she came frequently to Concord, rarely to Wayside. Sophia would hear that she had been at the Emersons', would feel hurt and neglected, but would fail to give the invitation Elizabeth awaited. By August, Hawthorne was actually at work upon his biography of General Pierce; and now Elizabeth, with her increasingly strong antislavery convictions, could not have been invited and would not have come if asked. Mary was even more out of accord with the Hawthornes, for she had become the most politically minded of the sisters.

Mary's visit to Washington had been fully as stimulating as her trip abroad. She had met a group of people entirely unlike any she had known before, and at first she was inclined to be cautious. Grace Greenwood, one of the first American women to become a newspaper correspondent, struck Mary as a "natural, somewhat uncivilized person." [2] Then, within a very short time, Mary had discovered "riches in mind and heart" in Grace Greenwood and they became fast friends. Mary began to wonder if being "civilized" in the New England sense were entirely desirable.

Then there was Lucretia Mott. Mary was not prepared to like a woman who was a preacher in the Hicksite Quaker Church and the founder, with Mrs. Elizabeth Cady Stanton in 1848, of the movement for women's rights. Surely Mrs. Mott must be a horribly aggressive woman who neglected her five children. Mrs. Mott invited the Manns to dinner as soon as Mary reached Washington and Mary's preconceived notions took flight. Mrs. Mott was sprightly, impulsive, full of charm. Antislavery was her preoccupation these days, but her husband and her children were partners in all her projects, first in her affections. Mrs. Mott considered her eloquence as a preacher as a direct gift from God; her husband, also a Quaker, thrust her into prominence and encouraged her to use her gift of leadership. What Mrs. Mott herself really liked to do was to cook, and so did Mary Mann. They were exchanging recipes before the evening was over.

At first Mary was shocked when she heard her husband called "Horace" by everyone at the Motts'. Her own mother and her sisters were not supposed to do that and she referred to her husband as "Mr. Mann" in all her letters. When the strangeness wore off, Mary found herself liking the Motts' informality. It made the white-haired Horace seem younger. A large group of friends of all ages had gathered at the Motts' during the course of the evening, and Horace seemed the contemporary of all of them. Before the evening was over Mrs. Mann, fresh from West Newton, was due for another surprise. They were calling her "Mary." She was startled and the name "Lucretia" stuck in her throat for a while longer. But she was also pleased; they liked her; she was accepted. Mary had supposed that it took half a lifetime to form a real friendship but this was a theory she could now dispense with.

The Manns were invited out a great deal, and Mary had always liked a good time although she had had but little opportunity to enjoy society. Some of her old sparkle returned, with the added charm of a well-informed mind. Men liked to talk to her. It was a little disappointing to them to find that her husband was her best subject — but Mary enjoyed herself thoroughly one evening, convincing a young reporter that "Mr. Mann had no personal malice against Webster." She thought she won her case but whether she did or not, her gray-green eyes sparkled, her cheeks grew pink and she looked pretty in debate. She had a light touch, a trick of making people laugh just when they might have become angry.

All the provincialism by no means dropped away from Mary. She detested "Southern cooking," for example. Because of her husband's well-known antislavery activities, she was not invited to any homes where she might have tasted real Southern cooking; and she failed to realize that the "Southern cooking" at the boardinghouse was merely atrocious — not regional!

Although life in Washington was fun, the three little boys presented problems, as they always would. Shortly after they arrived, Benjy developed whooping cough! Coffee was the proper cure for it, Mary was told. But coffee seemed to do no good at all, either to Benjy or to Horace or Georgie, who came down with whooping cough in turn. Whether because of the coffee or in spite of it, there was little sleep for any of the Manns.

And then, after Mary had had only a few weeks of really living with her husband — a pleasure she had known all too little during her married life — Horace Mann decided to go on one of his trips. Mary had followed him to Washington only to have him leave her as usual. Her one comfort was the absolute certainty that he did not want to be away from her, and that it was only the need of "several hundred dollars" to meet a mortgage payment on the house in West Newton that forced him to go. The way to "raise the wind" was by "selling some of my own wind," Horace said, and he arranged a four-week lecture tour through upper New York State. Congress was in session but they were doing nothing but wrangle over who would be the next President and Mr. Mann said he would never be missed. Such casual absences were the common thing among legislators who became too disgusted with Congress to stay around for sessions!

Mary was lonely but not unhappy as she had often been in West Newton. Her sister Elizabeth visited her — and sold some date charts to a boys' school. And Rebecca Pennell, her husband's niece, was with her, helping Miss Peabody. Mary wrote her husband every day as always — but she paused to do a little prophesying, when letters seemed slow and unsatisfactory. "One of these days friends will not think of communicating in any other way than by lightning and then space will be all but annihilated. . . ."

On March 9, 1852, Mary received a letter from her husband which was of more importance than either of them realized. Horace Mann was in Lima, New York, visiting a Dr. Tefft, president of "a small Methodist college."

"A man came to see me this morning," Horace Mann said, "who is one of a company engaged in getting up a similar college, tho' perhaps of a somewhat less sectarian stamp, at Yellow Springs, Ohio. It is to be for both sexes, is well endowed, and will pay their president from 2500 to 3000 a year.

"How should you like to be the wife of its president?"

Mary thought she would like it very much, provided college presidents did not have to be away from home. The subject, however, was much discussed both pro and con before a decision was made. Henry Ward Beecher had just had a heartbreaking experience trying to start a college in the West. And Samuel Gridley Howe was against the idea because he thought that Horace Mann could become Governor of Massachusetts.

Before the hot weather set in, Mary returned to West Newton, arriving there the fifteenth of May. Full of energy after her visit to Washington, she started a school for children in her home because she was convinced that no one could teach her own children as well as she could do it herself. Then along came Sarah Clarke and her mother, looking for a place in the country for the summer. Mary took them to board. Elizabeth came, tired out from lecturing and selling charts and with her clothes in rags — or so Mary said.

Friends gathered to "quilt Elizabeth a petticoat" and — with Mrs. Clarke to give them all the gossip — it was like old times at Somerset Court.

Her husband reproached Mary mildly, reminding her that she did not really have to teach school or take in boarders. But she explained that she was lonely now that he was away again — this time stumping the state for governor — a "Free-Soil independent Whig." Mann was doing this first of all because of his sincere conviction that the way to abolish slavery was to establish "free soil" everywhere except in a few Southern states. New states, even in the South, should no longer be allowed to choose slavery by plebiscite; they must have freedom chosen for them — and so the evil of slavery would be localized, then cured, like a disease in the human body. This campaign for governor gave Mann a chance to air his views, which he enjoyed. It pleased his friends, Howe in particular; but he had no illusions as to his chances of becoming governor. The best he could hope to do would be to split the opposition and weaken the pro-slavery forces. Horace Mann continued his consideration of a college in the West — as yet unborn.

Mann was a formidable opponent at law, his wit was razor-sharp and he used it ruthlessly, dangerous weapon though it was. He had many enemies whose attacks he invited and enjoyed. One outstanding characteristic he had which seemed at variance with all the rest. This was his unfailing faith in human nature. As talks about the new college proceeded, Mann believed that "Antioch" would be all the name implied — the place where "Christ's followers were first called 'Christians!'" He believed that founders of Antioch wanted him because he was capable of leading young men and women toward the Christlike life. He even believed that Antioch had the endowment he was told they had. Here, then, was a chance to prove that the salvation of mankind lay through a Christian education. Mary was consulted again and, although she repeated certain warnings she had heard, she too saw the vision.

The truth about Antioch at that time contained the seeds of bitter disillusionment. The college was being promoted by a man who had made money in railroads and who now intended to cash in on a real estate boom as Yellow Springs became a university town. He interested friends in the scheme and together they designed some buildings to look like the hotels at Saratoga with just a dash of a castle on the Rhine plus a touch of railroad-station architecture.

This monstrosity they had engraved on stationery — which was as far as it suited them to go, at least for a while. They approached the foremost educator in the United States, Mr. Horace Mann of Boston, expecting nothing more of him than that he would be a symbol of culture like their Neo-Gothic wooden arches — and no more functional than the twin towers of their school.

On September 15 Horace Mann was nominated for Governor of Massachusetts. On the same day, he was chosen President of Antioch, and he accepted the latter honor. He called together a tentative faculty to meet at his home and discuss the policies of the new college. It was to be nonsectarian. Women were to be educated at Antioch as well as men, and they should be as equal as was humanly possible.

Horace Mann glanced at Mary now and then. There was an off chance that she might have become a governor's wife and she would have graced the governor's mansion. Mary had never felt as personally affronted as Elizabeth had, or even Sophia, when faced with the fact that only her brothers had a right to a college education. She was more willing than her sisters to take life as she found it. But she was a Peabody just the same, and her husband could see that her joy was hardly less than his — because it would be Horace Mann who might open the door to education to the women of a younger generation. She did not care for being a governor's wife. Mary preferred to be the wife of a college president.

There was one serious flaw in her happiness. Yellow Springs was as far away as the sunset when it came to the separation from her mother. Several illnesses, probably heart attacks, had weakened Mrs. Peabody during the past year and Mary knew that she could not attempt to return from Yellow Springs should her mother be ill again. When the subject of Antioch was broached, however, Mrs. Peabody ran true to form. She would worry about Mary, since steam packets might blow up, "rail-tracks" were so dangerous and barge canal boats still worse. But what would Mrs. Peabody have given, as a girl, to go to a college like Antioch! What would it have meant to her to teach there as Rebecca Pennell was going to do! Mary must say good-by without regret — and write often.

It was Mrs. Peabody, however, who took the longer journey from which there is no return. She was ill again in January 1853. Elizabeth was with her and Dr. Peabody took care of her at night, glad to be able to ease her labored breathing with the medicine Dr. Wesselhoeft had left. During the afternoon of January 11

Dr. Peabody went to Mary's house to stay with his three little grandsons so that Mary could be with her mother.

"Do you want Sophia?" Elizabeth had asked. Mrs. Peabody said no, Sophia must not leave "the poor baby" — meaning Rose. And then, although Elizabeth and Mary were watching, death came so quietly that at first they thought their mother had fallen asleep.

When he moved from West Street, Dr. Peabody had been distressed because his lathe and his toolbox failed to arrive in West Newton. They had come safely at last, and now, in his little workshop, he had been making a trellis for his wife's roses. Well, there was no use in finishing it now, he thought. Mary's house was for sale so he could not give it to her for her garden. Dr. Peabody picked up a plane, then put it down again, the pleasant feeling of it in his hand failing for once to give him solace. He tried to think what he would do now that his wife was gone — but he knew there was no use in making plans, for Elizabeth would settle everything the way she always did.

He would have liked to go to Yellow Springs with Mary. Not only Rebecca Pennell but her brother Calvin were going with the Manns. But they were young and they were going out to build a new college for young people. There would be no room and no use for an old man.

There was Sophia, of course. But while she lived in Lenox her father had made her a visit and Sophia had written that Father must not make so long a visit again. Mr. Hawthorne could not be disturbed. It was too bad because Mr. Peabody had supposed he was being useful — that cottage of theirs had been sorely in need of repair. The hammering, he supposed — he took up the plane again and put it down. It made no difference because the Hawthornes were going to Europe very shortly anyway. The Pierce biography was finished and Franklin Pierce was President — although not entirely as the result of Hawthorne's misguided efforts, as some of his antislavery friends reproachfully told him. A grateful President was sending Hawthorne to Liverpool as United States Consul. Sophia's brother Nathaniel would borrow Wayside. Dr. Peabody could go there but no one had invited him with any particular enthusiasm.

It was Elizabeth who furnished the solution, just as her father had feared she would. She abandoned her lecturing for the time being and took a teaching position at the Theodore Weld school at Perth Amboy, New Jersey. The independent life she had been leading suited her and she felt that she was making a sacrifice so that her father could live with her and have nothing to do but to sit at his ease in an armchair. Dr. Peabody understood all this. There had been times when he thought he wanted nothing so much as to stop gardening and sit down in the shade. But now he found it impossible to be happy with Elizabeth or properly grateful to her. He hated the armchair — and the feeling that went with it, of being of no use to anyone.

CHAPTER NINETEEN
College President's Wife

THE shop in West Street had formed a link between the Peabody sisters for many years. It was more than a common home to which married daughters might return: it was a common enterprise, the success or failure of which affected them all whether each had an active part in it or not. With the passing of the shop, Mrs. Peabody's indefatigable letter-writing, her retailing of news, had kept the sisters within a family circle. Upon her death, it became suddenly apparent that each sister had been carried far upon the separate current of her own life and that their closeness to each other had been for some time but a sentimental delusion of their mother's. Sophia would now go to Europe, where she had longed to be ever since her earliest days as a young artist, and she need not spare a backward glance. Perhaps she might never even wish to return. Elizabeth, although she felt that her wings were clipped when she gave up her lecturing, was certainly accountable to no one now and she could take up whatever new project chanced to kindle her enthusiasm. Her father would continue to speak forcefully in favor of practical common sense, but Elizabeth would heed him even less than before. And Mary, always the dependable one, could go West feeling that she had a right to go and that she left no unfulfilled promises to her family — no duty to her parents which she had not done.

Sophia had gone West as far as the Berkshires, taking leave of family and friends as though she were bound for the Rockies. Elizabeth would lay plans to carry Bem's Historical Charts to the West Coast — and end up in West Newton with an adventure tale to tell. Mary, however, set out on about a thousand-mile journey to Yellow Springs, Ohio, as calmly as though she were going from West Newton to Boston for the day. She had with her three small boys just the right age to be enchanted with the brightly painted canal boats, then to become bored by their slow progress — and finally to jump ashore while the boat waited for a lock to open — to become the object of frantic search before a fresh relay of horses should drag their boat out of sight. Rebecca and Calvin Pennell, Horace's niece and nephew, might have been expected to help keep an eye on the children and they tried to help. They preferred, however, to sit with their uncle and talk Antioch till the college yet to be founded seemed more real than the lively, noisy crowd aboard the Erie Canal boat; more actual than the fertile fields of upper New York State through which they crept upon their road of glassy water.

As the Manns journeyed westward, more and more was to be heard about "Indian trouble." The little boys listened avidly and strangers were loud enough in their talk of settlements left in ashes, dead bodies found beside a lonely homestead. By daylight, it was all very exciting and the boys practiced war whoops and ambushed each other on the narrow decks of the barge. By night it was different. They heard war whoops in their dreams and awoke needing to be comforted and reassured. Their mother's steady hands, her gentle voice in the dark, were things to be remembered always. This was adventure and it was heartening to little boys to know that their mother loved it.

When the journey grew too long, even for Mary, she would look over some of the letters from Yellow Springs — for her imagination was just as much aflame as her husband's over this college yet unborn. It would be the first in which men and women would be admitted upon an absolutely equal footing. Requirements would be as stiff as at Yale or Harvard. Girls would take part in graduation ceremonies — they would sit upon the platform with the men — and they too would receive a degree! It was unheard of! Mary looked at the printed letterheads showing a neo-Gothic Antioch, surrounded by gardens — with a fine puffing locomotive and a train of cars in the foreground. There was a sight worth traveling all these weary miles to see!

And at last even this longest of journeys had an end. There had been the train — the Mad River and Lake Erie Railroad; and beyond Springfield, Ohio, they had come at last to Yellow Springs. But where were the twin Gothic buildings, one for women, one for men? A single structure was in process of completion. Everyone was too tired to care very much just then, but the president's house was finished only as far as the first story. The Manns had no roof over their head — only a second floor. Crates of furniture, also, seemed to have gotten lost on the canal, and Mary hoped that the delay was not due to "Indian trouble."

On the fifth of September, 1853, the inauguration of her husband as the first president of Antioch took place. All the day before, Mary had watched with amazement as people poured into Yellow Springs, apparently from nowhere! There were the "million-dollar farmers" as the men who had made successful land deals along canals and railroads were called — with their fine horses and carriages. Then there were the buckboards of the less prosperous, loaded down with children. Mary's heart went out to the women she saw, with their careworn faces full of joy at the thought of education for their sons and daughters. Then, last of all, there were the old people, those who had made this land their own, with the marks of their struggle still upon them but also a look of having proved themselves; of being the equal of any man. Mary Mann had always cared more for people than places, for things of the mind rather than worldly goods. Now Yellow Springs seemed suddenly like home to her, whether she had a house to live in or not. It no longer mattered whether she had so much as a bed to sleep on or whether the Indians had taken her bed and all her china dishes. She was glad she had come.

Long before night every available room in Yellow Springs was occupied and latecomers slept in their carriages or on the ground. Three thousand people assembled before the outdoor platform next morning to see the new president and hear him speak. Mary sat on the platform where she could look down into the faces of those people who had come with such a longing, to receive the gift her husband had brought them — that thing called "college education" that was to do so much for their children, and for the West of which they were so proud. The people had a "drinking-in expression," Mary said. Her husband's words "reached deep into their hearts."

Also upon the platform with the new president of Antioch and his wife were the handful of teachers Horace Mann had been able to persuade to come with him. Mary looked upon two of them with peculiar pride. They were "lady professors." The trustees, local Yellow Springs men, had accepted their applications with enthusiasm. But right at that point had occurred the first Antioch conflict. The trustees had assumed that a lady professor would be paid about half as much as a man — and the ladies had assumed the contrary. Rebecca Pennell wrote a firm letter in the most elegant handwriting. She was a Normal School graduate, which, up to that time, for a woman was highly educated. She had had several years of teaching experience and she was worth as much as any man, she said. A thousand dollars a year was what she was asking and she was going back East at once if she didn't get it. Miss Pennell won her point. (In due course her salary would be in arrears like everyone else's; her principles never!)

One hundred and fifty students passed the entrance examinations. Then forty of them were told they would have to go home because there was no place for them to live. The rest went shivering into their dormitory because the man who "set stoves" had gone to the inauguration of President Mann. " 'I been lottin' on hearin' that 'ere speech today,' he said, 'and I aren't goin' to set stoves for nobody.' "

But before the inauguration crowd dispersed, Mr. Mann announced the results of the examinations and the forty students who could not be accommodated at the college were taken in by townspeople. In all, a hundred places in private homes were offered and the departing farmers assured Mr. Mann that sixty more students would be coming right along. It had been understood that the backers of the college were giving Antioch thousands of dollars, but now this proved to be a matter of paper promises. The men and women from the farms dug deep into their small savings and donated six hundred dollars in cash to complete the college buildings.

One old homesteader, about to take his leave, paused to ask Horace Mann his age. It was fifty-seven. The homesteader approved, yet something baffled him. Here was a man with white hair — with the frail physique that became the scholar — but when he stood upon the platform and spoke of the future of Antioch, Horace Mann looked young. He seemed like a strong man about to run a race.

"And how old is your woman?" the homesteader wanted to know. She was forty-seven, Mary told him, and she smiled as she imagined such a question being asked back in Boston. Again the old fellow was surprised. Mary's forehead was unlined, her figure, if a little spare, was trim and neat, and she wore her black silk gown with an air of elegance. There was no gray in her hair. A pioneer woman of forty-seven would have thought shame to look so young! How many children had she, the old man asked sharply.

He approved of three sons but would have thought still better of six. Turning to the new college president, "Well, good-by, Horace," he said.

Mary and Horace exchanged a quick glance of amusement. So this was the West. Well — they liked it. Before the year was out, they would be calling themselves "Buckeyes" and feeling that Ohio was their home.

The president's house was finished before winter set in and Mary took great pains in furnishing it. "They have put cast iron marbled fireplaces in all the rooms," she wrote with pride and she thought them "much handsomer than our marble ones in West Newton." The straying crates of furniture arrived safely at last and on her marble-topped parlor table Mary put her brass lamp with pendants and on the mantel the "two gilt candelabras to match." To be sure, window shades ordered from Cleveland months before had not come and the sun was fading her carpets and Mary was worried. But she had lace curtains and damask ones besides to shut out the light.

The president's study came in for just as much careful decorating as the parlor and was just as much a source of pride to Mary when she finished it. Here were black walnut bookcases lining the walls, with Dr. Channing's portrait in the place of honor over them. Here President Mann received the student who must be reminded that if he drank, smoked or swore, he could not graduate. Here he forgave many a young man, however, for these sins and possibly others — provided the student promised to sin no more. Here he also received young lady students and here, before long, he was obliged to remind some of them that, while they were allowed to learn "gymnastics," they were not to perform where the young men could see them.

Less formidable interviews took place in Mary's "sitting room" where young people were encouraged to gather around the piano and sing, the president's wife often singing with them in her still sweet contralto. In the sitting room was the haircloth sofa and the little black walnut tea table, items of great elegance, both of them, in the eyes of the boys and girls. In this favorite room of Mary's bloomed her mother's calla lily, brought all the way from Boston and flowering now for young people who had never seen the like.

But if her sitting room were her favorite, the guest room was Mary's greatest source of pride. Horace had bought the furniture for her in Cleveland, all ten pieces, enameled in white and trimmed with gold bands and bunches of flowers. The bed was "French" — like Sophia's, Mary said — and on the mantel was "Mother's gold vase." Lace curtains, and muslin ones as well, hung at the windows. Now let distinguished visitors come from the east to stay with the college president and his wife. They would be shocked by the "unfinished look" of Ohio, Mary knew — but she planned to show them that there was elegance "among the Buckeyes."

The first year went smoothly enough. President Mann and his faculty were paid their salaries. If promises could be relied upon, the college was solvent — at least on paper. But the number of students was disappointing. Some left when for months there was no water either from wells or from cisterns and water obtained from private wells in town proved brackish and evil-tasting. Mary tried to take a hand in the management of the college kitchen, and insisted that drinking glasses ought to be washed after every meal and not just occasionally when they got to looking brown around the rim. It was not a good idea to cook cockroaches in the dried applesauce, she told the staff. If the students left, who could blame them, she said!

By the second year, living conditions had improved. Four hundred students enrolled; although, to Mary's disappointment there were only a few young women. The reason was not far to seek. While there was little opposition to equal education in progressive Ohio, it was easier for men students to earn money for their own tuition. Where there were several children on a farm, the boys must have the first chance and their sisters must stay at home and help them with the butter and egg money or by teaching school. In the town of Yellow Springs there was little or no opportunity for men students to earn money, and for girls there were not even enough domestic jobs to go around. In the town also there was dissatisfaction because the college was growing so slowly. Real estate values had not jumped as had been expected. Business was not appreciably improved, for so many of the students were too poor to spend any money.

The storm did not really break until 1857, however — the year of the first graduating class. It should have been a glorious year but it was bitter with anxiety. Probably Horace Mann was unaware of a downward business trend which was making his wealthy patrons repent of their generous promises. These promises were now to be broken and Mann was too impatient, too fiery-tempered and too

much the lawyer to remain friends with trustees who, in his opinion, were cheating the college. Mann was not a person to be taken
in a neutral manner; he would always be loved with blind devotion
or hated with fervor. He had always enjoyed his personal enemies,
for he dearly loved a verbal battle — but now he made enemies for
the college that had come to mean everything to him. The knowledge that he had only himself to blame destroyed Horace Mann's
happiness at its very source, and he became even more short-
tempered than before. Mary needed all her gentleness and tact to
smooth down the ruffled feelings of trustees and to calm her excitable husband, who was suffering from dyspepsia and sleeplessness.

The trustees knew better than to oust Horace Mann without
reason. He could be depended upon to blazon their perfidy nation-
wide, and his many friends would rally to his standard — perhaps
carry Antioch elsewhere. The thing to do would be to alienate his
following first. Mann knew exactly where the attack would come.
He had invited such prominent Bostonians as Theodore Parker and
Ezra Stiles Gannett to lecture at Antioch and, out of personal friendship for him, they had come. The prestige of these men was tremendous in the West and Antioch had shone in reflected glory.
But President Mann had invited his guests to speak to the students
at chapel, and here was the opening his enemies wanted. These
eminent men were Unitarians and to a large proportion of Ohio
settlers this meant that they were little less than anti-Christ. Let
them lecture only on Plato or the Persian poets. If they spoke in
chapel, they would corrupt the youth of Ohio.

It was so much pleasanter to repudiate a pledge and withdraw
support from Antioch for religious reasons than because business
was bad! The opponents of Horace Mann leaned back in their
swivel chairs in their various small offices about town and waited
for the Easterner to pack up and start for home — leaving his salary
unpaid. They would then select a minister of the Christian Church
as president, who would be the figurehead they had expected Mann
to be. The college would become denominational, very poor perhaps, but entitled to denominational funds.

The plot had just one flaw in it. If it made his opponents feel
better to let the college go to the Christian Church by default, it
cheered Horace Mann immensely to fight for a college free of religious intolerance. His enemies underestimated his stubborn courage and they forgot one other thing — that he was a lawyer.

The time of Antioch's first Commencement arrived and once

more the whole of Greene County and people from every county in
the state arrived at Yellow Springs as they had done for Mann's
inauguration. They had come to see a show and they got one. Before the earnest young seniors filed on to the platform, Horace
Mann had Antioch sold for its debts! The college was assigned to a
Mr. Palmer, a trustee. The faculty disbanded but a new board of
trustees met immediately to re-elect Horace Mann as president with
power to nominate his own faculty, subject to ratification by a
committee.

It was no accident that Horace Mann executed this flanking movement just at Commencement; that the governor of the state was
there now to say that Antioch was the most liberal institution in
the world — the pride of the West. "Three thousand dollars was
subscribed on the spot" to buy up the college. As Mary Mann put
it, "All the evil-minded and unrighteous plotters against Mr. Mann
and the college were dumbfounded and aghast." Mary thought it
wise, however, not to tell her sister Elizabeth quite the whole story.

Mr. Downer, a close friend who took care of the Manns' business affairs back East, knew more about that dramatic three-thou-
sand-dollar subscription. "I suppose you will think me a fool . . ."
Mann wrote, "but it really was a question whether this one liberal
Institution in the midst of a world of intolerance . . . should be
sacrificed or I should be. I chose the latter: in consequence of
which, it is necessary for me to raise five thousand dollars by
the first of August next." Mr. Mann instructed his friend to sell the
"Orono Bonds," and the "Capen securities" and to get at once the
thousand dollars owed to Mann by a private individual. Mr. Downer
would not like to carry out these directions — Mann's letter fore-
stalled objections.

This sacrifice was Mary's fully as much as Horace Mann's. She
had taken in boarders and kept school when it was not urgently
necessary and she had watched the family savings increase little by
little until the modest investments could be made. Horace Mann
did not preach equality without practicing it, however, and everything he did was with Mary's full consent. As the college president's wife sat on the "tastefully decorated" platform at Commencement, happiness welled up within her, for Antioch was hers
as well as her husband's. The "Lady Seniors," of whom there were
but three, were particularly dear to Mary's heart.

Each Lady Senior read an essay full of noble sentiments and Mary
felt her own knees grow a little weak as each arose — she breathed

a sigh of relief as each reached a rhetorical climax in a slightly quavering voice and sat down. They were all beautiful in Mary's eyes but Ada Shepard was a trifle her favorite. Ada was engaged to a very serious young man by the name of Badger who aspired to a teaching position at Antioch, a thousand dollars a year and "a chance to grow." But he was not to have his Ada immediately. She would be off on the adventure of her life — to Italy as governess to the three children of Nathaniel Hawthorne. She would carry not only Mary Mann's affectionate greetings to Sophia Hawthorne but also an unbounded admiration for the Mann family that the Hawthornes might find a little hard to bear.

After the first Commencement, and with the future of Antioch assured, as she believed, Mary had perhaps the happiest summer of her life. She and her husband took the children to Mackinaw Island, where the air was "like that of Eden," Horace Mann said, where the children played in the woods and made friends with Indians, and where Mary enjoyed the luxury of "a really good cook" all summer long. Horace Mann found a place in the woods among the roots of a great tree where he could hide with his tablet of paper and his pencil and write the endless letters that Mary so carefully copied in ink for him afterwards. He dared his boys to find him and they searched day after day but could not come upon his "hidey-hole." When at last they caught him he was as glad as they and played with them as they had never known him to have time to do before. Mary had to warn the boys not to disturb their father too often but she could not be very severe when it gave her such pleasure to watch her husband with his children.

The summer passed like a happy dream, and then the Manns returned to Antioch to find the old anxieties waiting for them. There were the usual unpaid pledges, the mounting liabilities — and the old criticism. Partly in the hope of raising some money, partly to divert her mind from worry, Mary began to write a book. It was not the romance about Cuba which had always been simmering in the back of her mind — it was a cook book! Surprisingly modern in many ways, Mary's book was really on the subject of nutrition — and, because she believed that to guard one's health was a Christian duty, her book was called *Christianity in the Kitchen*. There were plenty of recipes but any woman buying Mary's book for those alone was due for a shock. Almost on the first page was the story of Alexis St. Martin, the young man who "had a orifice in his side" enabling Dr. Beaumont to discover that "fatigue and annoyance retard digestion." Nervous indigestion was a condition Mary had observed in her husband many a time and she was delighted to come across the account of this famous experiment and to pass it on to other women whose husbands might be similarly afflicted. It would cheer them to know that all attacks of indigestion were not necessarily the result of their cooking. Cod-liver oil was earnestly recommended in Mary's book, as were fresh vegetables. And Mary further startled her generation by suggesting that flies be kept off meat, "especially in summer." Mary was the doctor's daughter as she quoted "Liebeg's Letters on Chemistry" and "Dr. Beaumont's Table of Digestion" to prove her points.

But it was Mary Mann, the wife of a severely moral college president, who spoke harshly of the social customs of her time. "Compounds like wedding cake, sweet plum puddings and rich turtle soup, are masses of indigestible material which should never find their way to any Christian table," she preached. And just in case her readers' mouths were watering: "It looks ominous," she declared, "to see a bridal party celebrating by taking poison." She was almost as severe in the matter of late supper parties, which had been so fashionable in Boston when last she was there. Stifling the faint stirrings of homesickness, Mary wrote, "The habit of eating oysters in the evening and ice creams afterwards, as is frequently done at large parties, is very pernicious."

Mary brought a long introduction to a close with a few well-chosen words about alcohol. She had forgotten an evening in Boston at the Cabots' in 1827 when Mr. Harding, the artist, had brought along a bottle of what he said was "mountain dew" and "Burns's inspiration." Harding had "made a beverage," afterwards admitting that his mountain dew had been whisky; but Mary, at the age of twenty-one, had found the drink "really very nice." She was the wife of a stanch temperance man now, who, as college president, had become a total abstainer. Mary now felt it her duty to pass on some dreadful warnings she had heard lately. A living human being was reasonably "incombustible," she said. "But some instances have occurred in which spirit drinkers have taken fire and been consumed. This fire has been kindled by inflammable vapors in the breath."

When Mary turned her attention to recipes, it was a relief to learn that it was not Christianity alone of which she approved but that she also favored plenty of fine hearty food in the kitchen. Here were no directions for starving on a lettuce leaf or for preparing a full meal on a shelf in the living room in ten minutes. A twelve-pound haunch of venison would take four hours to roast,

Mary said, and she did not anticipate that anyone would have any trouble getting such a piece of meat at the store. It would also be good baked in cream.

One must be careful about macaroni. There might be "insects inside it." But having attended to this, cooked it and "dressed it with cheese," the way to brown it was with a shovel "heated red hot and held closely over it."

Calf's-foot jelly, starting with "four large feet," required a page to describe, two days to make, with a "four-legged stool" as part of the equipment. It included a pint and a half of Madeira wine and a teacupful of brandy. But it was a required item as a gift to those who were ill, and apparently the spirits, once properly mixed with the calf's large feet, would not cause spontaneous combustion on the part of an invalid friend.

Ordinary jelly could be "corked" with beeswax and even the Christian housewife need not feel guilty if she gratified her desire for the beautiful by placing her currant jelly in the window to flame gloriously in the sun. She could leave it there "a few days" to set — before her conscience told her that she was getting too much pleasure out of the sight of it and also showing it off to the neighbors.

Mary approved of French cookery, thereby causing an occasional raised eyebrow among her readers. She said that in France "many articles are made into savory dishes which, in our American haste and carelessness are thrown away as useless." In spite of her solemn warnings, Mary Mann enjoyed good food and liked to cook it, so that *Christianity in the Kitchen*, when it was published in 1858, was very well received.

Mary's cookbook was no gold mine, but any money she made she needed to keep her family going while they waited for a salary eternally in arrears. During 1858, Antioch's desperate need of funds increased while written appeals for money failed. An agent, the best that they could find but not a very good one, was sent around the country to ask for money for Antioch the following winter. But the year was 1859, and while only a few clear-sighted people like Theodore Parker knew that the nation was on the eve of civil war, there was tension everywhere. Horace Mann's wealthy or influential friends to whom the Antioch agent was sent paid about as much attention to him as they would have to a boy begging for pennies.

*   *   *

The Manns were getting no salary and it was costing them two thousand dollars a year to keep open house for the college. Mary worked miracles of economy with vegetables from the garden, fresh in summer, dried or preserved for winter use. She took up and turned faded breadths of carpet with a skill acquired in Peabody homes long since. While it was hard to see savings dwindle, Mary had lived in straitened circumstances before and she had never been afraid of hard work. It was when she saw her husband's health breaking, when her sweet contralto singing of an evening failed to give him rest, that she became anxious — almost to the point of desperation.

The first member of the faculty at Antioch to be chosen by Horace Mann had been Austin Craig, a young minister of singular sweetness and purity. Inspired by Mann's passion for education, Craig had abandoned the ministry, convinced that to serve youth and future generations at Antioch was the more worthy cause. Craig had seemed a sort of young Sir Galahad to Horace Mann, who idolized him. But in 1859 Craig told Horace Mann that the crusade for education in the West was hopeless. The young minister would return to preaching, not a remunerative occupation exactly, but preferable to starvation at Antioch. Mann, if he knew what was good for him, would also give up and go.

"Judas!" Horace Mann called this dearly loved friend, in a heart-broken yet passionately angry letter.

Mary Mann, her face white with the fear of what she did, told her husband that Craig was right. It was their first disagreement, and it was a serious one. Mary was capable of limitless self-sacrifice, and she was willing to risk losing her husband's love in order to save him from a lost cause and from people who (as she believed) were mercilessly exploiting him. Horace did not call her names, but it would have been easier to bear if he had. The silences, the feeling that confidence between them, once so complete, was now at an end — all this was misery for the sensitive, the gentle-hearted, Mary.

Mary was never good at expressing her innermost feelings. If only she could make it clear to Horace that her only reason for opposing him was fear for his health! She liked Yellow Springs and now Horace seemed to think that she did not. Why, any place on earth would be home to her so long as her husband was with her — but she could not seem to say so. The rapidly dwindling savings might be a cause for alarm to the careful Mary, but surely Horace must know that she cared nothing for money — only for him! Suppose he died!

Then indeed Mary would not care where or how she lived or whether she lived at all — except for the children. But all these things lay locked in her heart while her eyes were bright with un-shed tears.

The fact that her husband's niece Rebecca sided with Uncle Horace was no help to Mary. Rebecca had lived with the Manns until lately, when she had become Mrs. Dean with a home of her own in Yellow Springs. As a girl she had been her uncle's favorite, and she had always resented his marriage a trifle; and now it was gratifying, when she called by to see him every day, to have him tell her that she alone understood him. Of course he must not leave Antioch, Rebecca said, in her young confidence unable to see that his health was in danger. Mary could almost have found it in her heart to hate Rebecca.

In the summer of 1859 Horace Junior was invited to visit the home of Dr. Samuel Gridley Howe. It was the boy's first long trip alone away from home and his father wrote to Dr. Howe, men-tioning young Horace's changing voice with affectionate humor, concealing not at all successfully his pride in the boy. His parents were glad that young Horace was away when there came a long drought with excessive heat at Yellow Springs. The garden soil seemed to turn to burning sand, the college well ran dry — as did most of the wells in town. What water there was tasted warm and brackish. A fever was going the rounds, and Mary had it.

Afterwards they realized that Mary must have had typhoid, but it was an idea which did not occur to the local doctor and everyone thought it odd that Mary should be so ill — so slow to regain her strength. Word came that young Horace had been taken desper-ately ill almost as soon as he reached Massachusetts, having prob-ably carried the typhoid infection with him. Dr. Howe was a fine physician but Mary was frightened. She should go East, her husband suggested, see young Horace and perhaps visit her brother Na-thaniel in Concord. In Yellow Springs she would only make herself ill again with worry, while a change of climate might restore her own good health. Niece Rebecca would be willing to come and keep house and take care of George and Benjamin.

Mary made one last appeal. The previous summer, Horace Mann had been elected "President of the Faculty and Professor of Ethics in the North Western University of Indianapolis." He had de-clined the honor, unwilling to give up his unfinished task at Anti-och. But if the climate at Yellow Springs was bad for her it was bad for her husband, Mary argued. If he would only leave, plenty of opportunities like the one at North Western would be offered, and he could first rest and regain strength, then serve the cause of nonsectarian co-education elsewhere — and live longer to do his great work.

Horace Mann refused to listen. He thought that Mary did not understand his feeling about having set his hand to the plow; about loyalty to principle and ideal. Danger to his health he discounted entirely, and he urged Mary to go without giving her even the assurance that he would try to take care of himself. He promised to join her later — perhaps. And it was understood that she would return and work with him for Antioch as she had always done. Each had hurt the other, nevertheless — but only because they loved each other.

Antioch had failed financially again. Again Horace Mann bought the college at the appraisal price, there being no other bidder when it came on the auction block. Money came in from the East, particularly from the aged Josiah Quincy. Western support, however, was still lacking — with Mr. Mann's liberal religious views again under fire. He could not help remembering that Mary had said he was casting pearls before swine. Several faculty members left early to take jobs so that they could afford to teach another year since there was no money in salaries anywhere in sight. Horace Mann himself planned a lecture tour. Meanwhile he took the place of the absent professors and of others who were ill with the still prevalent fever.

Commencement Day came, and Mr. Mann was so pressed with work that he began to prepare his Baccalaureate only on the morning of the affair. He read it just as it was hastily jotted down, having no time for revisions. It was probably his finest speech. "Be ashamed to die until you have won some victory for mankind," he told the graduates.

The festivities of Commencement Day began at seven in the morning and lasted twelve hours. After everything on the program had taken place, crowds of people adjourned to the president's house, where they held an impromptu reception till the small hours. Next day Horace Mann was aware of fever but continued committee meetings and college business. His two younger sons had fever also and were sent to bed. Mary postponed her trip east indefinitely, writing to Elizabeth that she could not possibly leave little Benjy.

Horace Mann wandered about the house, unable to rest. He could not eat but he found some fruit juice Mary had preserved the summer before and it seemed to quench his thirst a little. He thought about how rain would sound on the tin roof of the piazza and remembered that it had been a month since rain had fallen. There would be no fruit from the garden this year. He was anxious about his children, but for the first time during their married life it seemed impossible to write to Mary. He knew what she wanted to hear — that he would leave and come East to her, at least for a rest. And that was the one thing he could not do. He wondered if a three-day rest would make him feel well and like himself again.

Days and nights seemed to merge into each other after that, and he lost track of time. "At last a flash of lightning pain passed over him, which, he was sure, disorganized his very substance." Horace Mann could speak, his mind was clear, but he could not move. "Loving and devoted students watched over him and his sick children for many weeks" — Mary said, omitting mention of herself. Mann refused to see a doctor; but finally the local doctor came, and then a doctor from Cleveland.

During the years just preceding his marriage to Mary, Mann had been morbidly certain that his life was to be a short one. Now he was equally confident that he would soon recover. He laughed and joked with the Cleveland doctor — and composed himself for sleep. Then they told him that the Cleveland doctor had "little hope of recovery," and that the local doctor had given him just three hours to live.

Horace Mann roused himself with a tremendous effort of will. He sent for a student whose conduct had given him anxiety, and asked the boy to promise "to make something of his life, henceforth." The boy gave his word and, whether he was able to keep it or not, the scene was one that he would never forget. Now other Antioch students who lived near by heard the dreadful news and came crowding into Horace Mann's room. In a strong, clear voice he bade them farewell, reminding them of their responsibilities as educated members of society. They must be leaders against intolerance in all its forms. When in doubt concerning a course of action, they should ask themselves what Jesus Christ would have them do. The faithful few, those members of Horace Mann's faculty still with him, came to his room and he talked to them of his vision of the future of Antioch. The college must be "a light in the darkness," he said.

Almost exactly three hours went by and Horace Mann's strength suddenly failed. "Will not friends fall back?" he said. But students, faculty, townspeople and even strangers still lingered. Mann fought for breath and was given stimulants. When death came it was not a peaceful going to sleep, but a struggle to the end. He did not mean to die. It was as if he did not realize that he had already won his own victory for mankind.

Antioch friends spoke to Mary of the beautiful deathbed scene. She listened with tight lips and angry eyes. She had been deliberately kept from the man she loved, she felt, and Rebecca's tearful reiterations that they had not known how sick Mr. Mann really was served only to increase the bitterness in Mary's heart. All these people had been with her husband and had kept her from giving him the care she would have given. Mary kept faith in "rest and homeopathic remedies," believing that Horace would be alive — but for these people. They had killed him. She hated Antioch and everyone connected with it.

Rebecca gave Mary a sheet of "last words" spoken by Horace Mann and told her it was Mr. Mann's request that she address the women students.[1] There were other verbal requests. Mr. Mann wished to be buried in Providence beside his first wife, Charlotte. Mary promised. She spoke in chapel, outwardly calm and gracious. She reminded the girls that Horace Mann had laid down his life for Antioch but when the girls asked to see her personally, she refused. They would only cry and perhaps break down her own icy self-control. It would be years before she would feel any affection for anyone at Antioch.

Elizabeth Peabody, coming from Boston "as quickly as steam could carry us" arrived with young Horace. Not understanding all the underlying bitterness, Elizabeth marveled at Mary's calm manner as she "arranged to leave" Antioch.

It would be wise to sell some of the furniture rather than to take it back to New England — a long, expensive freight trip. Mary decided that the dining room table must be the first to go. Then she looked at it and recalled the gatherings around it, her husband at its head, his brilliant eyes, his generous mouth — the loving pride with which he regarded his wife and family. She could not part with the table, nor with anything that had been his and hers together. Still outwardly calm, Mary packed all her household goods and took her leave. But to the trite phrase, "Do come back," she invariably replied with candor. She never would return.

CHAPTER TWENTY

Sophia at the Court of Kings

THE news of Mary's loss came to Sophia while she was still abroad. It was shocking news for she knew how much Mary loved her husband and Sophia had but to picture for a moment what her own grief would be like were Hawthorne to die. She wrote offering Mary the use of Wayside for herself and her boys as long as they should need a home.

The Hawthornes had been happy at Wayside. They had done a dangerous thing in returning to the scene of their honeymoon for no spot on earth could be as beautiful as their memories. Yet Concord was idyllic and could stand the test. For Hawthorne, however, there remained the specter of poverty which had haunted his first years of marriage. He was a success but he could not get over the fear that he might sink back into obscurity with his next book — or that another theme for a novel might not come into his mind. Anxiously, like a squirrel hoarding acorns, Hawthorne stored away ideas in his notebooks, but he knew he could never use one of them until it should possess him, body and soul. He dared not ask Ticknor and Fields exactly how much his three most popular novels had earned — lest the answer discourage him past the possibility of future success. And it suited Ticknor and Fields very well just to send a check once in a while, large enough to surprise and please the pessimistic Hawthorne — telling him that there was more money for him if he needed it. Hawthorne always replied approving the idea that his publishers keep a balance in case of necessity. He cast about for a way to earn some money in the form of a salary which might put his fears at rest.

General Pierce was grateful to Hawthorne for making a hero of him in his biography and he loved Hawthorne sincerely as a friend. He was also good at making promises. When Pierce visited the Hawthornes and they gave a reception at Wayside in his honor, he dazzled Sophia's eyes with pictures of her husband as Ambassador to the courts of kings. How about Portugal or Spain? It was Hawthorne who brought both Sophia and Pierce down to earth by reminding them that he knew no modern languages — not even French, the language of diplomacy. In that case, a high post in England would be the thing, Pierce thought. It should be easy for the future President of the United States to get an old and valued friend a place worth thirty-five thousand dollars a year. That was the figure Sophia remembered Pierce's mentioning. When the appointment for the Liverpool consulship came it was a disappointment even to Hawthorne, who had expected little. But it carried social prestige, Pierce told him. And it was Hawthorne's understanding that it was worth twenty-five thousand.

Living expenses would be higher. The Hawthornes had never spent any more than two thousand dollars a year, however, so it seemed to them generous to allow five thousand to cover the expenses of a socially prominent consul. In four years, Hawthorne figured that he would have saved enough money to make him independent. Then back to Wayside and to writing! If a theme had to be abandoned, he could say to Ticknor and Fields that there would be no book and they could protest in vain. If a theme possessed his soul and must be written, it would make no difference whether Ticknor and Fields thought the book would sell or not.

The Hawthornes made plans to stay abroad four years exactly. It seemed unlikely that Franklin Pierce would hold the presidency for more than one term, and with a shift in chief executive there would be changes all along the line, as Hawthorne well knew from his Salem experience. This, to Hawthorne, was a point in favor of accepting the post, not a liability. At first, freedom from writing would be a release, for since 1850 he had written *The Scarlet Letter, The House of the Seven Gables, The Blithedale Romance, The Life of Franklin Pierce, A Wonder-Book* and *Tanglewood Tales* — a tremendous output. But before the four years of consulship were over he would be longing for freedom again — freedom to write once more.

There would be friends who would shake their heads and say that Hawthorne should have known better than to leave peaceful Concord and the work for which he was intended. Theirs was the wisdom of hindsight. Hawthorne's foresight was as wise as he, being only human, could make it. And he had one delightful recompense which, in his careful calculations, he almost overlooked. Sophia was supremely happy.

All Sophia's fashionable friends and all her intellectual ones had been abroad and talked about it incessantly. She had never forgotten, also, how Washington Allston had talked of the necessity of foreign study for every artist and how this dictum had plunged her into despair. Well, she would visit the great galleries at last, perhaps even take up her brushes again and bring to realization some of those old dreams which she had put away as childish things. The exuberance of Sophia's letters revealed her secret sense of triumph although she would have denied that she had any feeling of rivalry with regard to her sisters. "It was a very noble act of General Pierce . . ." she wrote to her father on March 27, 1853, when confirmation of Hawthorne's appointment to the consulship at Liverpool came through, "the office is second in dignity only to the Embassy in London and is more sought for than any other and is *nearly* the most lucrative." They were taking two servants with them, Sophia said. Mary and Ellen Hearne were so eager to go that they would take English wages when they got there. They had been promised a chance to see their parents in old Ireland.

The Hawthornes would also need a cook and Sophia wrote to Mary Mann, feeling somewhat under compulsion to prove that she could keep three servants busy. "I wanted Ellen for the baby. Ellen sews a little and takes care of Rose and washes and irons muslins and baby's wardrobe. . . . Mary is housemaid." She "sweeps, dusts, tends and lays the table, is also chamber maid and presides in the butler's pantry (as we have no butler) and whenever she sits down in the day, she does some plain, coarse sewing for me. . . . Mary has to lay and clear away the table four times. . . . Emily is cook and cooks very well and she also hems towels. . . ."

The Hawthornes sailed on the steamer *Niagara* which Sophia assured her father was one of "Ericsson's caloric ships" and "as safe as a parlor." Mr. Fields came to see the Hawthornes off, and Sophia's last glimpse of her father was as he stood talking with Fields. Dr. Peabody was smiling, and it occurred to Sophia that she had not seen him smile very often.

Sophia was almost disappointed to reach Liverpool in only ten days after leaving Halifax. "If we had had more difficulty, storm and danger, I would have realized it better," she said. "But it seemed like a pleasure excursion on a lake." Sophia was always a good sailor. They steamed (caloricly) up the Mersey on a Sunday, and church bells were ringing, which Sophia considered a good omen. But the rest of the family, looking at the dismal gray city of Liverpool and the muddy river, were homesick and they thought "of dear Wayside with despair."

Entertainments for the new American consul began at once and Sophia was gratified but did not admit to being surprised when she found that everyone she met considered her husband a great author. *The Scarlet Letter* was the work most people had read and the one they praised most often. Sophia found copies of it in all the bookshops, a copy even on the Isle of Man. It was fortunate that she so much enjoyed the praise of her husband, for no royalties had ever been paid him on thirty-five thousand copies sold in England.

Again it was no surprise to Sophia to observe how well her husband played the part of consul. In America his air of the exiled nobleman had been noted but not with approval. In England it went well. To be sure, Sophia had trouble with Hawthorne over a white starched cravat, he preferring his black silk one. He suffered horribly from stage fright, knowing he would have to make after-dinner speeches. But when the moment came for him to be called upon, his sense of the dramatic stood him in good stead. He was brief, witty — and handsome! "After sitting down," he said, "I am conscious of an enjoyment. . . . It is something like being under fire, a sort of excitement, not exactly pleasure, but more piquant than pleasure." This was not the Hawthorne either Concord or Salem knew. Only Sophia knew that he had genius in more than one direction. When he used one gift he put aside all others and there was no writing now, save jottings in a notebook. At home again in Concord, there would be no social life beyond an absent-minded nod to passers-by.

Notably social all the time, Sophia was in her element as consul's wife. It was proof of her adaptability and her capacity for sharing her husband's happiness that she could be equally content as the wife of an author — when it also came time for her to change roles. At the present moment, she reveled in the elaborate homes where she was entertained, and no gilded paper on the wall was too bright for her, no golden damask hangings too opulent. Mary had written home of such magnificence, but while Mary had been haunted by the idea that every luxury had been purchased at the expense of the underprivileged, Sophia was troubled by no such thoughts. Why worry about something you could not change?

In early life, unpleasant things had been kept from Sophia; and, since her marriage, she had dwelled in Hawthorne's dream world of romance.

Scarcely a fashion note had appeared in Mary's letters. But Sophia could have contributed a page to *Godey's Lady's Book*, and it was a pity she did not. In Liverpool, during the summer of 1853, the ladies were wearing "white muslin dresses over rose colored silks, and black jackets, basque-shaped, with a dozen bracelets on their arms which were bare with flowing sleeves." Back in 1843, Mary Mann had worn her "grassecloth" wedding dress, for formal occasions, sometimes with a black satin pelisse over it, sometimes without. Mary would not have been human if she had not felt a twinge of envy over Julia Ward Howe's beautiful New York trousseau but she was taken to visit public institutions more often than she attended balls. At common schools, insane asylumns and prisons, her "grey habit" would do. Sophia found, when at last it was her turn to visit Europe, that the dresses she had brought from home would not do at all, because the parties at which she was expected to appear were grander even than her fondest dreams.

For years, Sophia had turned and remade her old clothes, had accepted with gratitude a silk dress or a foulard from a more prosperous friend. She was entitled to every bit of pleasure she got out of a French "head dress" of blackberry vines, blossoms and red, black and green fruit. There were "little gold balls to imitate a plant that grows in Ireland — fretted gold. Small flowers [were] woven closely in, over the top of the head, and behind the ears the long streaming vines hung in a cluster." Now in her forty-fourth year, Sophia Hawthorne was still a pretty woman, made more so by happiness and pride in her husband — irresistible, no doubt, in her blackberry vines! This was but an afternoon head-dress, however. For evening, Sophia wore an affair of pearls, with a dress of "superb, pale-tinted brocade, low-necked and short-sleeved." Mary, who had to hear all about these pieces of finery, was as pleased as Sophia was — albeit a little disappointed when Sophia made no report on the state of public education or the condition of the working classes in Great Britain.

Elizabeth had been figuring out her sister Sophia's income. She saw by the papers, she said, that ten thousand ships arrived in Liverpool from the United States each year. From each ship, Hawthorne would receive four dollars, Elizabeth figured, and there was Sophia with an income of forty thousand a year! Elizabeth wrote for help in supporting her father, and she also asked for money for her brother Nathaniel and his family, now living rent free at Wayside. Then of course there were various public causes which could use a generous donation. Summer, with its gay but expensive social season, had passed, and winter's dismal chill hung over Liverpool when Sophia received the letter. But for the fact that she really wanted to help her father, Sophia would have laughed. As it was, she cried and then sat down to try to explain matters to her sister.

"Instead of 10,000 ships, not quite 700 arrive yearly from the United States," she said. Not all ships paid the same fee. "Most of the income comes from the invoices of the great steamers. Ten and twelve thousand dollars has been hitherto the whole yearly income from whatever source." It looked to the Hawthornes as if the coming year would be a lean one, as if trade might fall off and they would be lucky if they received as much as ten thousand dollars. Even if they were very careful it was going to cost them six thousand dollars to live. For a man who expected to continue for an indefinite number of years in a reasonably secure position, this would have been more than satisfactory. But Hawthorne hoped, in four years, to save enough money to provide for his family for life — and it would never do. Hawthorne sent money to Sophia's father at once, but he left it to Sophia to continue to explain to Elizabeth why he would not contribute to any of her other projects.

She could get no meat for less than fourteen cents a pound, Sophia said. Potatoes were thirty cents a peck and peas twenty. Rice cost twice as much as at home and there was no tea for less than a dollar a pound — with the dollar variety not good. They were doing without fruit. Grapes were a penny apiece.

"We gain one thing here and that is an open fireplace," Sophia said. "Coal is cheap, comparatively, and it blazes delightfully and we can really sit round a glowing hearth. Mr. Hawthorne truly enjoys it. It is what he had always wanted." The Hawthornes' enthusiasm for airtight stoves had vanished so completely that they had forgotten they had ever had it. "It is certainly a gloomy custom to bury the fire in tombstones and then set up the graves on our very hearth," said Sophia.

There was one added expense to Liverpool living which Sophia did not mention. Hawthorne could never resist the hard-luck stories with which American seamen stranded in Liverpool came to him. Some of the tales were false, he knew. Some situations were covered by regulations and paid for by the government. But Hawthorne dug down into his own pocket for many, concealing the fact, however, and made angry if anyone mentioned it. Sophia dared not tell her sister Elizabeth because Hawthorne had an aversion to being praised for his good works and Elizabeth's praise he avoided most of all.

"The drafts Mr. Hawthorne sent" were acknowledged with gratitude by Dr. Peabody. Sophia wrote her father of her pleasure in being able to give him a comfortable easy chair, which was what Elizabeth said he wanted, and other comforts as well. Then came a letter from Elizabeth to Hawthorne, asking him to tell Sophia that her father was dead.

Sophia had supposed that she knew her husband well. She had always feared lest Hawthorne's work be interrupted by her father and she had contrived to keep them apart a good deal during her father's infrequent visits and to cut his visits short. Now she found that Hawthorne really thought a lot of old Dr. Peabody. "I really do not believe anyone else ever listened to his stories and his conversation with as much love and interest. Whatever is real and simple and true attracts my husband," she said. Always confident that she knew what heaven would be like, Sophia thought of her father as standing "meekly in the presence of God." But perhaps at this point she was confusing her image of God with that of Mrs. Peabody! Perhaps her father needed to be meek no longer.

The Hawthornes' second summer in Liverpool was not as enjoyable as their first because the children all had whooping cough and so did their parents. This is not to say that there was any thought of quarantine. Such an idea had yet to be heard of and in September they blithely carried their whooping cough into Wales. Sophia said, "We had some charming excursions in Wales to beautiful old castles but I whooped in them all like an Indian warrior!"

Sophia was a long time getting well and the doctor suggested a winter in Madeira. Hawthorne said that Sophia must go and take the two girls, leaving Julian in Liverpool. The O'Sullivans had arrived, the "Count," as Hawthorne affectionately called him, on his way to Lisbon as American Ambassador to Portugal. Sophia could go with the O'Sullivans and spend some time at the court of the Portuguese king.

"The mosquitoes are bad but the fleas are worse," reported Sophia from Lisbon. But she had promised to keep a journal of her travels, so into it went descriptions of the king, his court, and their strange formalities. She enjoyed herself mightily, talking to the king, counting the diamonds on his uniform as she did so — and mentally comparing him to her kingly husband, to Portuguese royalty's disparagement. No thoughts of the superiority of a republic over a monarchy disturbed Sophia as such thoughts would have distracted Mary. On the other hand, she considered a king as no more than her equal.

The climate of Madeira proved enervating for Sophia. She was always better off in crisp, dry air. The novelty of court scenes wore off and Sophia was lonely and homesick. She began to picture future winters spent away from her husband because she could not live in Liverpool unless she recovered her health — and of this she despaired. It would be good to have this consular experience over with, and to return to quiet Wayside to be the wife of an author once more.

In 1856 the expected happened, and Franklin Pierce was not renominated by his own party. His supporters in the North had believed that he might bring about peace on the slavery question. The repeal of the Missouri Compromise had infuriated the North and lost him all support. Pierce had appointed Jefferson Davis Secretary of War as an act of conciliation to the South, but Davis had sent men into Kansas to enforce a pro-slavery majority under the guise of enforcing law. And John Brown had come back North, telling of lynch law and murder.

But Pierce was still Hawthorne's personal friend. "I feel a sorrowful sympathy for the poor fellow (for God's sake don't show him this)," he wrote O'Sullivan, "and hate to have him left without one true friend, or one man who will speak a single honest word to him." On July 1, 1857, Hawthorne resigned his office at Liverpool.

Hawthorne's last act as consul was to write a memorandum to Washington urging that a bill be passed to help American seamen stranded abroad — and to help British seamen working their way home in American sailing vessels, some of them destitute after unsuccessful ventures in the California gold fields. Washington paid not the slightest attention to Hawthorne. But it is to be feared that Sophia, in her pride in her husband, talked out of turn, for Elizabeth wrote praising Hawthorne to the skies for his efforts in behalf of seamen. Hawthorne replied angrily to say that he never involved himself in a cause, however good. He was not to be accused of altruism when all he had done was to ask for justice. Hawthorne was acutely embarrassed and feared lest his tender heart be discovered under the protecting shell he had tried to build for it — his good works shown before men. As far as Elizabeth was concerned, he need not have worried, for she was not in the least likely to understand him.

With the ending of his consular duties, Hawthorne was glad to close the door upon the social side of his nature. He began to live in the world of his mind, exploring for the theme of his next novel, while he looked at the world without, much as a traveler watches the landscape through a car window. He observed quickly and accurately, but nothing he saw concerned him personally. Wayside, where everything contributed to the daily discipline of writing, would be the place to go, now that leisure to write had been earned at least in part. But Hawthorne had not forgotten how much it would mean to Sophia to go to Rome.

In 1858, the Hawthornes set out for the Continent. Disapproving of everything to do with Louis Napoleon, they paused in Paris only long enough to look askance at it. They went by rail to Marseilles and by boat to Civitàvecchia, the port of Rome. The blue Mediterranean could be treacherous when it chose but both Sophia and her husband were excellent sailors. Tiny Italian fishing villages close to the water, each guarded by its castle on the nearest hill, filled Sophia's romantic heart to overflowing. These were the Salvator Rosa landscapes of her girlhood come to life — and she longed to stop and paint; yet she was still more eager to reach Rome.

But the weather was cold and rainy when the Hawthornes, in Rome at last, established themselves at the Palazzo Sarazini on the Via Porta Pinciana. Hawthorne hugged the fire while the stone floors in the old palace gave off a chill more powerful than any blaze and he felt his feet grow numb, then he felt the cold mount till it congealed his bones. Sophia, however, bought sketchbooks for all the children and for Miss Ada Shepard, who had joined them in England and would be their governess for two years. They sat among the ruins of the Roman Forum, avoiding a kind of filth Sophia had never before seen in a public place, concentrating their attention upon a broken column — and telling each other that the watery sun was really very warm. They climbed the broken staircases of the Colosseum, they sketched the flower venders on the Piazza di Spagna. Julian lost his sketchbook but it was of no use — his mother bought him another.

Every day, along with sketching, went visits to the palaces where the great paintings were to be seen. Sophia's diary became a series of exclamations over the familiarity of the pictures, engravings of which she had studied so earnestly in Salem and Boston. Those engravings had been but grotesque misrepresentations in many cases, however. Sophia wondered now why she had ever loved them and thought them beautiful. The beauty of the originals was something she was unprepared for and it overwhelmed her like a rising tide. After a few weeks, she put away her sketchbook and when Julian lost his again she did not buy him a new one.

Sophia had always been inclined to accept the judgments of others and to distrust her own except in the matter of art. As she sat in the Sistine Chapel and in the Vatican Picture Gallery she made up her own mind. Allston had said that Titian was the greatest of the old masters, but Sophia did not think so. Raphael overwhelmed her but Perugino made her happy — so she liked him best and said so, regardless. A small portrait at the Barberini Palace fascinated Sophia. It was "Beatrice Cenci" by Guido Reni. The technique was smooth and meticulous like Sophia's own. Brush strokes were not used to produce an effect of strength; they were concealed to produce softness. Sophia loved the picture so much that she decided to bring Hawthorne to see it. She took him to look at pictures as often as she could pry him loose from the fireplace and he would seat himself resignedly before a canvas and ask her what he was supposed to see. When she took him to the Barberini Palace, it was not the brush-stroke technique that he saw, although she called his attention to it — it was the person behind the portrait. Beatrice Cenci had murdered her own father, he remembered.

But Beatrice Cenci was innocent, she had been driven to crime by cruelty and had suffered remorse, Sophia said — thinking of what she had read, as well as what she saw on canvas. Those eyes in the portrait were faintly red from weeping, Sophia told her husband as he sat there, smiling absently. He always loved Sophia's flights of fancy; they touched off something in his mind. What a challenge it would be, for example, to attempt a written portrait of a girl goaded beyond endurance into complicity with murder!

Such a character would create her own story. They left the gallery of paintings and Hawthorne smiled happily to himself as they walked through the streets. He heard only so much of Sophia's cheerful chatter as he would need for future use; he saw everything, yet was aware only of what would contribute to the story stirring in his mind.

Sophia was facing a private disappointment. The examples of great art which she now saw for the first time were teaching her that, although she was gifted in art, she herself would never have been a great artist. She looked at her husband and her children and realized that the possession of genius could not possibly have made her any happier. "If I had only been able to come to Rome to study when I was young!" Sophia said — still feeling the need to soften the blow to her pride a little. And Hawthorne, seeing her perennially young as he always did, began to picture her as a young artist in Italy.

"I was *not* Mr. Hawthorne's 'Hilda,'" Sophia would declare again and again after *The Marble Faun* was finished. She would not have needed to deny it so often if those who knew her had not found her in the book.

CHAPTER TWENTY-ONE
Pattern from the Past

ROME had been cold and cheerless, an almost incessant drizzle dampening even Sophia's spirits at last.[1] And then, during the third week in April, the skies miraculously cleared. Cascades of purple wistaria burst into bloom against gray garden walls and the Villa Malta, near by, became "a precipice of roses." The Hawthornes had hardly time to grasp the metamorphosis. They set out for Florence, arriving on the twenty-fourth of May. Once more they established themselves in the inevitable palace, decaying, tarnished, with peeling murals and arched ceilings which dropped chunks of painted plaster on the marble floors leaving, overhead, some frescoed nymph or cupid minus head or hand. But at the Casa Bella there was a garden which Sophia remembered as always sunny and full of birds and flowers.

From the first, Florence had a dreamlike quality which captured the hearts of both Hawthornes. It was as though they had come home, as though Florence had been the place of origin of that urge to create something beautiful which each of them had felt from time to time. Hawthorne was awakened from his mood of abstraction by the discovery of rare manuscripts in Florentine libraries. He astonished Sophia by asking to be taken sight-seeing — but only to the church of Santa Maria Novella, because it was there that Boccaccio's young lords and ladies met at the time of the great plague and agreed to go to Fiesole to pass the time in telling tales. Hawthorne obediently looked at a Cimabue madonna, while there, to please Sophia. It was ugly, he told her. But she stoutly insisted that it was beautiful and they both agreed that they preferred the simplicity of Florentine churches to the Roman churches with their "tornadoes of saints," as Sophia said.

Sophia reminded Hawthorne that in Mr. Emerson's study in

Concord there was a copy of Michelangelo's "Three Fates" and Hawthorne agreed to have a look at the original. "The weird sister who stands in the middle seems to me to have a slight compunction in her mouth and eyes," said Sophia. How like Sophie! Hawthorne loved her the more for not understanding when he told her that a Fate with sympathy becomes "not a Fate but a Providence."

The Brownings were in Florence and if Sophia had a little difficulty in converting her husband to art, Hawthorne had no trouble at all in turning her attention to poetry in the form of two living poets, both of them rising rapidly upon the literary horizon. Hawthorne had first met Browning in London. On the eighth of June, 1858, Browning "made this day memorable by calling at Casa Bella." Sophia found him astonishing yet charming. His handclasp had tremendous vitality and he seemed to her "like a rushing river." She was delighted to be swept along. Browning had come to invite the Hawthornes to spend the evening at Casa Guidi, and by eight o'clock they were on their way.

Casa Guidi was in a newer part of town and the Brownings' apartment was comfortable in the direct proportion to its lack of Old World charm. Sophia found it romantic, none the less, from the moment when she encountered the Brownings' little son in an upper hallway with a servant. "In the dim light, he looked like a little waif of poetry dusted up into a dark corner, with long curling hair and buff silk tunic embroidered with white." Robert Wiedemann Browning, or, as he so much more melodiously called himself, Penini, took the Hawthornes through an anteroom into a drawing room and out onto a balcony. Here, in the better light, Sophia saw that the boy looked "lovelier still with brown eyes, fair skin, and a tender, graceful figure." Mentally, she contrasted him with her own equally handsome but much more sturdy Julian.

"In a moment Mr. Browning bounded upon us with emphatic welcome," Sophia said. From a church across the street came the sound of bells, then a choir chanting. Overhead a deep blue sky was studded with stars and Sophia became aware of perfume and saw that she was surrounded by white flowers, not cut, but "growing and blooming on the balcony." Again, as so often, Sophia felt the dreamlike quality of Florence as she tried in vain to make it seem true that she really stood at Casa Guidi windows.

The author of *Casa Guidi Windows* now made her appearance, by no means unaware that she was the star of the drama entering upon a stage all her own. It was a perfect climax but Sophia was unprepared for Mrs. Browning's appearance and she was shocked. Mrs. Browning was "weird"-looking. Sophia could think of no other word. Black hair fell "in large curls" on either side of Mrs. Browning's face "so as to nearly conceal her features." Her eyes were "sweet." But Sophia observed faces with the accuracy of a portrait painter, and saw mirth also in Mrs. Browning's eyes — perhaps at the sensation she was causing. Mrs. Browning's eyes were "arched," Sophia said, and she drew in her diary an eye having the lower lid following the curve of the upper instead of opposing it. Those eyes were "musing and far-seeing" but Sophia was forced to add — still unable to find another word — that they were "weird." They were set in a narrow, colorless face which was "deeply ploughed" with lines of pain, and Sophia imagined that "water torrents" of tears had "worn channels" in Mrs. Browning's white cheeks. A black and white dress completed the "peculiar effect of her appearance."

A strong, vital handclasp from Mrs. Browning's seemingly frail hand further startled Sophia but gave her pleasure. She recovered sufficiently from her first shock of surprise to present to Mrs. Browning "a branch of pink roses and buds, twelve on one stem in various stages of bloom." Mrs. Browning "put the flowers in her bosom with lovely effect to her whole aspect." They went into the candlelighted drawing room with its tapestries, paintings and carved Italian furniture, and now the scene was beautiful to Sophia once more. She had managed to adjust her ideas of what a woman poet ought to look like to the strange but increasingly fascinating appearance of Elizabeth Barrett Browning.

It was a disappointment to Sophia when other guests were announced. They were Americans: the poet Bryant and a Mr. and Mrs. Eckley. Sophia had yet to learn that Mrs. Eckley, wealthy, dull but devoted, would be Mrs. Browning's shadow on all occasions. Mrs. Browning found her the perfect companion, refreshingly free from strange fancies or mental torments, delightfully incapable of writing poetry!

The "three poets" talked of literature, Sophia said, placing Hawthorne in a category to which he always denied he belonged. Ada Shepard had been invited to the party, to her great delight, and Mr. Eckley found her pretty in her white muslin dress with blue ribbons and devoted himself to her. But for the ubiquitous Mrs. Eckley, Sophia had Mrs. Browning to herself. It was Mrs. Browning who brought up the subject of spiritualism. She found Mrs. Hawthorne eager to listen, ready to believe — but without experience at table-tipping or other manifestations. Mrs. Browning regretted that she was going to the seaside at once and could not personally help to correct this state of ignorance. She would see to it that some of her friends arranged a séance for Mrs. Hawthorne to attend immediately.

A word or two caught Robert Browning's attention and he jumped vigorously into the conversation, speaking against spiritualism in all its forms. Sophia surmised that the argument which ensued between the Brownings was by no means their first one on the subject. Hawthorne joined forces with Browning while Mrs. Browning upheld her contrary view with considerable fire. One of Sophia's greatest social assets was her ability to listen — but she agreed with Mrs. Browning and privately determined to attend a séance as soon as possible.

On the twenty-fourth of August Sophia wrote again of a day made memorable, not because of seeing the Brownings this time, since they had left Florence, but because Mrs. Browning had kept her word. Her friend Miss Blagden had arranged to have a group of people meet at her house, to sit around a table in a darkened room and wait for messages from another world. Although protesting that the whole thing was nonsense, Hawthorne agreed to go with Sophia and Ada Shepard went along, all agog with curiosity.

The affair must have been unutterably dull at first as six people sat around a table "and tried to make it skip." The table was unobliging and "there were no raps." This went on for two hours! Then Ada suddenly assumed a strange role. She picked up a pencil and asked if there were any spirits in the room. She found herself writing, "Mary Runnel" and then the name "Robert Walden" and "Marie Notres." Neither she nor anyone in the room had ever heard those names before, they said.

Finally Ada wrote the word "Mother," asked whose mother and found herself writing "Mrs. Hawthorne's." Ada's "hand was seized to write, 'My dear child I am *near* you — I wish to speak to you. My dearest child I am oftener with you than with any one." Sophia believed implicitly that her mother was in the room in an invisible, spirit form. She was much excited — and yet her New England ideal of good manners never deserted her for one moment. It would never do to talk intimately with her mother before all these strangers. "I wanted immediately to be alone with Ada so that the blessed spirit could say more to me," Sophia wrote in her journal when she returned to her room that night. But Miss Blagden and her guests stayed right where they were and Mrs. Peabody's spirit, motivated by the same ideal of good breeding doubtless, said no more. "It is very curious and wonderful," said Sophia. It was unhealthy and could be dangerous, was Hawthorne's opinion, and he much preferred to see Sophia absorbed in art and letting spiritualism alone.[2]

The Hawthornes were living at the Villa Montaudo at Bellosguardo now, having moved there the first of August in search of cooler air among the hills close to Florence. Here was the enchanted palace of every fairy tale, the scene of every cloak-and-dagger romance! Hawthorne and his children climbed the ruinous tower at an appalling risk to their necks. While the children played in the gardens, Hawthorne sat on the terrace, trying out the story of *The Marble Faun* in his mind, twisting it this way and that — and finding that it had a way of telling itself. He had broken the news to Sophia that he had "no more power left to look at a fresco vanishing into the past." The Giottos which "made her glad" were making him "desperate," he said; and she laughed, understood — and left him to his thoughts.

Sophia might have been lonely, but now she began to discover not only ancient Florentine art but modern sculptors, Englishmen and Americans mostly, who had hired studios in and around Florence. Hiram Powers, the Vermont farm boy, had arrived in Italy via Ohio and Sophia found him cordial and friendly while he enjoyed her intelligent questions about his work and her appreciative comments, which were the result of knowledge gained by her own efforts at portrait sculpture. Sophia had little use for Powers's giddy young daughters, whose chatter made her head ache, but she could always leave his drawing room and go down below stairs to his studio, where, one day, she found "workmen chiseling upon Washington's coat."

Another even more satisfactory artist friend was William Wetmore Story. Story was born in Salem but he was ten years younger than Sophia and the Peabodys had never been able to afford to move in the same social circle as Judge Story and his family. The Storys had moved to Cambridge in the same year that saw the Peabody family in Boston for the first time. Their paths had not crossed until young William Story became a law partner of Sophia's good friend George Hillard. When Nathaniel Hawthorne,

just before his marriage, took a room at Hillard's, he had encountered Story. The young man wrote poetry, modeled, painted
a bit and studied music, Hawthorne had been told, and these interests should have made the two congenial. It was doubtless Hawthorne who had been too little inclined for adventures in friendship. In 1847, Story had brain fever — because of "his incessant
law labors," his family said. (It could have been because his family
would not hear of his leaving the law and told him he was "mad"
when he proposed becoming a sculptor.) In any case, the young
man's life was despaired of, and he set out for Italy convinced
that it would be but a stopover on his journey into another world.
It proved to be paradise itself, for Story gained not only health
but a tremendous reputation as a sculptor. Just a year after the
Hawthornes were married, Story had married Miss Emelyn El-
dridge; she had gone to Italy with him expecting to console him
in his last hours on earth. She stayed to become the hostess in his
lavish home and to make it famous for brilliant gatherings.

It is not always that an opportunity can be neglected once, only
to return. This happened with Hawthorne and William Story,
however. They met again in Florence, recognized this time how
similar were their tastes, and became intimates almost at once.
Sophia liked Mrs. Story and the friendship of the two families had
all the reassuring quality of long acquaintance (since they had
come from the same environment) plus the added charm of new
discovery. There were Story children the age of the Hawthorne
children, and it was soon agreed that Edith Story should have
lessons with Una under Ada Shepard.

William Story, as a poet, spoke Hawthorne's language, and when
he talked of his joy in sculpture, Hawthorne made mental notes.
Hawthorne could use an insight into the thoughts of a sculptor,
if he was to write about one. Story, as a poet, could understand
perfectly when Hawthorne had seen all the frescoes by Sodoma
that he could possibly stand and when even the famous floor of
the *Duomo* gave him no sensation save that of cold feet. Hawthorne would be left to sit in the sun in the garden while Sophia
could be relied on never to have seen enough Sodomas and to become properly excited over them all.

Story had become a wealthy man upon the death of his father;
in Italy he lived like a prince — and better than most of them. He
had seven horses for his coach and enough liveried servants to form
a small army. Nothing would do but the Hawthornes must travel

to Rome with the Storys in a coach of their own — with six horses. It was a journey that seemed like a prolonged version of Cinderella's trip to the ball.

This time the Storys saw to it that the Hawthornes lived, not in some romantic though moldy palace — but in a modern apartment, at Number 68 Piazza Poli. It was in the Quirinal section of Rome, at that time a place of vineyards and small villas with here and there an ancient palace, such as the one occupied by the Storys, not far away. It was said of the Storys that the carved stone lions on the ballustrade leading to their apartments were the only lions in Rome never to climb those stairs to attend one of Emelyn Story's soirées.[3] Hawthorne was lionized with the best of them, and submitted with such grace and good humor that he surprised Sophia. It looked as though he might further delight Sophia's heart by taking her to the Storys' next ball.

Sophia loved the parties but she was happiest in the studio. Here she was welcome to come as often as she liked and here she would sit in silence to watch William Story at work upon his huge figure of "Cleopatra." It was a disillusioned, unhappy Cleopatra, in whose face Sophia saw all that Story meant to put there and perhaps more than he was actually able to express. Sophia explained it, not only in her diary but also to the somewhat baffled Hawthorne; and Hawthorne's subsequent description in *The Marble Faun* of "Cleopatra" as seen through Sophia's eyes made this statue the most famous, the most popular of Story's works.

The modern observer, coming upon "Cleopatra" by William Wetmore Story in a museum, will wonder why she is so big and how Story could possibly have known that she would cut her nails off short and square. But Sophia asked no such questions, because she was lost in wonder over the fact that Story could model a fingernail with such precision. Story belonged to the school of realism soon to be carried to deplorable perfection. No detail would he omit, and no object would he find unsuitable for rendering into marble. With fur or curling whiskers, with rose point lace or with velvet, he could be painfully successful. It was part of his popularity as a portrait sculptor that he could model a full beard in marble and make it look soft enough to shave!

Through the Storys, Sophia was introduced to other British and American sculptors living in Rome. "I went with my husband to visit Miss Hosmer's studio," she said. But they did not see Harriet Hosmer, the girl from Watertown, Massachusetts — who had gone

West, where she had had a mountain named for her, who had studied medicine in order to perfect her knowledge of anatomy and who was now, at twenty-eight, a well-known sculptress. Miss Hosmer was "modelling Lady Mordaunt's nose," the Hawthornes were told, and she could not be disturbed. She invited them to come to tea later; and at that time, while Hawthorne wandered about the studio, taking note of everything and at the same time wishing he were elsewhere, Sophia and Harriet Hosmer became good friends over a statue, "Zenobia," just completed. Miss Hosmer had had experiences with spiritualism, she confided. And Sophia replied that she also had had a strange experience. Looking about the studio, Sophia could so easily imagine that it might have been hers — had she too been able to study in Rome for seven years!

But all through these days of happiness there runs the thread of coming misfortune as Sophia wrote in her diary of "Roman fever" — now called malaria. As early as January, 1859, Ada Shepard was taken dangerously ill. There was no going to the Storys' ball, after all, while Sophia watched over Ada like a mother. Then, on January 16, "Una had a dreadful chill this morning, worse than any she ever had before." The child already had malaria, then, and had had it for some time. They told her it was the night air. But Una would ride out at night. She was sixteen, unusually lovely to look at, with red-gold hair, a full sensitive mouth like her father's and her father's deep violet-blue eyes. With Edith Story or Annie Crawford — Julia Ward Howe's little niece — she loved to ride upon the Corso in the Storys' luxurious carriage; when a French prince tossed a bouquet into her lap, he was showing good judgment. Every time a bout of malaria came, Una would struggle hard to get well, and usually the attacks lasted only three days. They increased in intensity, however, to destroy the first happy experience of Una's young girlhood.

On March 22, Una's real illness began, and by the sixth of April the whole Anglo-American colony in Rome believed that the lovely Una Hawthorne was dying. Mrs. Browning came in person to see Mrs. Hawthorne, an unheard-of thing, for Mrs. Browning never called on anyone. Mrs. Story came every day — one day bringing the first lilies of the valley. Elizabeth Hoar of Concord was spending the winter in Rome and she was constantly with Sophia, renewing the friendship begun on Sophia's wedding day and now strengthening Sophia in her own quiet way. Sophia watched by her child's bedside all night, snatching occasional rests during the day. She, the former invalid, was now immune to fever it would seem, ill with fatigue sometimes, but able to go on, night after night giving Una the medicine which did no good, soothing her when the child's mind wandered in delirium.

Friends somehow had the impression that Hawthorne did nothing during the long siege of anxiety, save to grow older, to become slow of step. This was not true. He had been working upon *The Marble Faun*, and had written Ticknor and Fields that he had completed a first draft. But when Una became ill, he found he could do no more work whatever upon the new novel. He took his little daughter Rose to the Pincian Gardens every day, played games with her, kept her happy. It was a time she was never to forget. Somehow, he managed to tell stories to Rose and Julian as he had done in Lenox days; stories, however, never destined to become a further *Tanglewood Tales* — for afterwards he could not bear to recall them.

There were no entries in Sophia's diary between the eleventh of April and the twenty-ninth. It was during this time that she was said to have lost hope and to have given her child back to God. This seems unlikely for, in the diary record for April 10, Una was "brighter" and, on April 30, "Una continues to improve." Certainly Sophia gave her child to God and she gave herself, also, in constant prayer. But she would not have been Sophia Hawthorne if she had ever given up hope!

Once Una was on the road to recovery, the Hawthornes could not leave Rome soon enough. They hated the place which had once seemed so delightful and they hastened to England, a long and unbelievably tedious journey. After a short stay in London they went to Redcar, a seaside town not far from Whitby Abbey. Hawthorne fell to work upon *The Marble Faun* — which at that time he called *The Romance of Monte Beni*. Whitby had been originally a priory established in the seventh century by Saint Hilda. "Hilda" — here was a name for a heroine, should anyone be looking for such a thing.

Sophia sat upon the sands and read or walked along the water's edge with her children. She was considerably "out of health," and wrote to a doctor who replied suggesting that she take Gallic acid, be magnetized and drink beer. Of course Hawthorne would allow her to have nothing to do with hypnotism and she detested beer. The tonic, however, tasted bitter enough to make her hope it would surely be a cure. The sun and the sea were better; best of all the sight of Una growing strong again. It was good to know that Nathaniel wrote mightily each day and was reasonably satisfied with his work.

Longed-for letters from home arrived — but among them was the news of the death of Horace Mann. Sophia could hardly believe that such a tragedy could strike her loved sister Mary. Where was God's Providence — that Mary's long-deferred happiness should last so short a time?

On the eighth of November, 1859, Sophia noted in her diary, "My husband finished his book, 'Romance of Monte Beni.'" The next day was the Prince of Wales's birthday, with bells ringing and flags flying. The Hawthornes, smiling among themselves, pretended that the bells rang for joy because the book was done. The family went to London because Mr. Fields and his bride (the beautiful Annie) were there, and Mr. Fields had arranged to have the new book published first in England. It appeared, at the end of February 1860, under the title of *Transformation* and it was Fields who suggested *The Marble Faun* for the name of the American edition, and kept Hawthorne's own title, *The Romance of Monte Beni*, for a subtitle. With his usual good business acumen, Fields arranged a series of dinners and soirées, so that Londoners might meet the author of *The Scarlet Letter*, the former American Consul at Liverpool, Nathaniel Hawthorne, whose new book was just coming out. Again the grace and good humor with which Hawthorne allowed himself to be lionized astonished Sophia.

Mrs. Hawthorne was included in all the invitations; but now it was she who suddenly seemed the recluse as she wrote to Fields of her "irrevocable resolution to make no visits." Those who knew what she went through during Una's illness could not have been surprised to hear her say, "My fatigue is something infinite." It was more as though the former Sophia Peabody had said the words, however, than as though the valiant Sophia Hawthorne were speaking.

By the end of June 1860 the Peabody sisters were again in New England for the first time in seven years. For the first time since Sophia was married, the sisters found themselves living in the same town. There were joyful reunions at Mary Mann's attractive white house near the center of Concord, where Elizabeth also lived, if she could be said to have a home anywhere. Wherever she went, at the Emersons' or at the Alcotts', Sophia was apt to encounter one or both of her sisters, and at first it was an enchanting new experience. But as soon as the excitement wore off, Sophia found herself spiritually further away from her sisters than ever before, just down the dusty road though they might live. Mary, in her quiet unobtrusive way, was nevertheless an ardent abolition-ist, while Elizabeth must be watched lest she talk to Una about the horrors of slavery. Una was too young to hear the least hint of unhappy reality, Sophia told Elizabeth. As for slavery, it was a subject not for action but for prayer, and preferably for silent prayer.

Disappointed and hurt by the widening rift between her sisters and herself, Sophia was glad to be busy remodeling Wayside. Whether the poor old New England farmhouse could ever look like an Italian villa or a Gothic manor house was doubtful, but Sophia was going to see what she could do! Low ceilings were un-healthy, Sophia felt; straight lines over doors and windows un-lovely. A new high-studded room was added, to be known as "Mrs. Hawthorne's parlor." Above was a guest room, and over Hawthorne's old study a room was built for Una, as high and nar-row as possible. Over every door and window, in the new addi-tions, half-round molding left outer corners at a sharp angle, to meet above the middle in a high peak — the "Gothic" effect. The old house seemed to be looking at itself with raised eyebrows — and no wonder!

But worse was to come. Rising from the back, a wooden tower peered over the roof at the road and the Concord meadows. It was Hawthorne's new study, where Sophia pictured her husband alone and above the world, at work upon those future great novels they were both so sure could now be written. If such a silly thing as that tower were entirely the idea of the incurably romantic Sophia, at least her husband approved — until he tried to use the place. Then it was cold in winter, every icy wind penetrating its walls, and hot in summer beyond bearing. Recalling as it did the tower in *The Marble Faun*, it was not bad publicity — but the Hawthornes never thought of that. They were as disappointed as children when the new study proved a failure.

Of course the cost of rebuilding Wayside rose far beyond esti-mate. It was when Hawthorne saw the bill for a genuine Italian marble mantel that he became anxious. He went to Ticknor and Fields to see how his finances stood. During his years as consul, the publishing firm had been receiving drafts from him, representing savings. Investments had been made, in bank stocks and in mortgages. The Hawthorne account was in wonderful shape, Hawthorne was assured. There was plenty of money to remodel and refurnish Wayside, and *The Marble Faun* was doing better than expected. Mr. Fields asked Hawthorne about another book.

Whether Hawthorne actually saw any figures or not, he did not say, nor did Sophia. In any case, he returned to Wayside reassured and confident, ready to set to work upon the story of his English experiences. Sophia must visit Mrs. Fields in Boston and select wallpaper and draperies for her new parlor. The Fields and the Hawthornes had returned from Europe on the same ship and Sophia had enjoyed long shipboard talks with Mrs. Fields, but had not seen her now in six months or more. Word of Mrs. Fields's success as a hostess had reached Concord, however.

Sophia had presented herself at the court of the King of Portugal with perfect confidence, but she was right when she felt trepidation upon appearing in the drawing room of Mr. and Mrs. James T. Fields, at 37 Charles Street. This was the Court of the Intelligent. The wealthy, the socially prominent, were not barred — but they had to be bright. Those without money in the bank must be endowed mentally, and beyond that they must have a subtle touch of ruthlessness which would force open the door of success sooner or later. In the Fields's parlor, wits were sharpened and reputations for brilliance were made and kept bright.

King of the court was James T. Fields himself. At this time he was junior partner in the firm of Ticknor and Fields, but he could never have tolerated the word "junior," nor could it have fitted him. Mr. Fields was formidable, with his long hair swept back from his forehead in a manner he undoubtedly considered leonine. His enormous, curling beard was apparently modeled after some antique head of Homer or even Moses by Michelangelo.

Overwhelmed by all this proof of masculine virility, convinced that a heroic pose expressed the man, observers were not supposed to notice a pair of small but very shrewd eyes with which Mr. Fields watched his world as a fencer watches an opponent. Sophia, with her portrait painter's instinct, saw those eyes and felt afraid. She tried to propitiate Fields with excessive flattery, and she tried to convince herself that his genial reaction to this proved him as great and good as she kept telling him he was.

Mr. Fields was forty-four when Sophia first knew him, but he seemed to have been born sixty. He wore handsome black broadcloth, affected the cape, the high silk hat, the gold-headed cane — walked with heavy step and sat majestically in the best chair. The drawing room at Charles Street was equipped with many chairs almost as comfortable, however, for the use of the writers whom Fields considered "his," and whom Fields wished to cultivate in the same purely unselfish manner in which a farmer raises corn, fattens pigs and curries horses. Fields's efforts were not only in behalf of his publishing house. At exactly this time, 1861, Fields had become editor of what his wife called "The Magazine." It was the *Atlantic Monthly*, and as editor, Fields combined all the talents of a brilliant general, a circus barker, and a kind but firm parent. Subscriptions were "increasing daily," Mrs. Fields said; Bostonians would read no other publication, and although it was "almost impossible to extort a manuscript" from the aging Emerson, Mr. Fields could do it.

After his return from Europe, Hawthorne was more and more often bidden to Charles Street, to see and be seen by literary society. Sophia was always asked with him, since, at least at first, he would not come alone. Being a law unto himself, Hawthorne sometimes refused a royal summons to Charles Street and sent Sophia as proxy! This could have annoyed Mrs. Fields, who liked to find herself admired by authors and who invited women to her parties only if they were very distinguished or else young and pretty. But Sophia, being naturally so friendly, never gave a thought to the fact that, without Hawthorne, she could be any the less welcome.

Annie Fields was everything that Sophia admired most in the world. Highest in Sophia's estimation came the woman who, like herself, devoted all her energies to furthering her husband's career. Mrs. Fields was the perfect hostess, queen at the Charles Street court even more truly than her husband was king. Hers was the fashionable taste which crowded the rooms with statuary, with paintings from floor to ceiling and with autographed photographs of notables. If she leaned toward the overdecorated in house furnishings, hers was the genuinely artistic touch when she combined people in groups, with here a lawyer, there a poet — in such a way that they struck sparks from each other like flint and steel. It took genius to keep a whole roomful of people striking sparks but never resorting to barbed shafts. In further proof of Annie's genius, each guest left her house feeling that, although he himself had been unusually brilliant all evening — so had the others!

Annie really loved her literary lions. Each night, after a social affair, she would record in her little blue-covered notebook the names of her guests and some of the witty things they had said. She could not help liking the most illustrious names the best. "Dickens to dinner — Edwin Booth and the Aldriches to tea . . ." Although an undiscriminating collector of art objects, Mrs. Fields was a connoisseur of people, and she liked to admire her collection and to gloat over the fact that it was without doubt one of the best in Boston.

It was not surprising that Sophia Hawthorne should have been lost in admiration of Mrs. Fields's social gifts. But Sophia also lost her heart. Annie Fields was beautiful, and beauty was something Sophia had never been able to resist. Only twenty-seven years old at this time, Annie's classic features were the delight of the photographer; her facial expression was no problem, for she had none. Annie's face in repose approached the Greek ideal, *athos* or absence of emotion — an attribute of a goddess. Annie seemed to be born to be looked at and to think nothing of it. An artist, of course, was entitled to see more than the camera, and Rowse (a year or two later) extended himself over Annie's eyes in a crayon portrait he made of her. But he too gave her an untouched look of one who is either very young, very heartless — or else immortal.

One look at Annie Fields and Sophia was carried back into her own girlhood. She remembered the beautiful Lydia Haven, the first bride among her friends, the first to die. "My Peri of a Lyd" Sophia had called her and now, sitting at her desk in Concord, Sophia wrote to Mrs. Fields. "Whenever I wish to escape from the chaos of an unfinished house, I wander off (in imagination) to Charles Street and sit down in one of those charming rooms with a dark-eyed Peri, who never lost Paradise." It was the first time, since Lydia's death, that Sophia, now fifty-two years old, had given this loved name to anyone. It made her feel young again and full of youth's enthusiasm to write like this to Annie Fields.

More than ever before, Sophia in 1861 felt the need of a close friend. Through her lack of sympathy for their efforts, she had almost closed the door between herself and her sisters. If, like Mary, she had been in Concord at the time of Frank Sanborn's threatened arrest, she might have felt righteous indignation. If, like Elizabeth, she had gone to Washington, she would surely have been touched with pity for Negro orphans. As it was, Sophia seemed perfectly unaware of the approaching War between the States until one of the workmen on Hawthorne's tower quit to join up. Annie Fields seemed to be the only person in the world able to understand how Sophia felt when she thought that Hawthorne's study was more important than the Civil War.

The friendship was bound to be one-sided, for there were infinitely more interests and more people in Mrs. Fields's life than in Sophia's. Mrs. Fields lived as though forever in the center of a lighted stage. But gratitude and affection such as Sophia's were impossible to resist entirely, and letters were soon to "Dearest Annie" while vague promises to visit Wayside when the lilies were in bloom filled the heart of "Dear Sophia" with pleasure, even when such promises were more often broken than kept.

CHAPTER TWENTY-TWO

Incendiary Concord

BOTH Mary and Elizabeth saw Sophia turn from them with regret. They loved her dearly and never for a moment considered her selfish but blamed Hawthorne — the man who had written the biography of General Pierce. All through the Pierce administration, antislavery had lost ground, and abolitionists were hot against him. Lydia Maria Child, for example, when moved to write verses castigating him, said that his name rhymed best with "curse." All this bitterness (which Elizabeth and Mary shared) was to be unknown to Sophia, when she returned fresh from her European experiences; but it was she who later seemed the stranger in Concord, while her sisters, actual residents of only a few months, seemed like original settlers. Outwardly calm, incendiary little Concord was seething with excitement over the slavery question.

Mary had arrived in Concord cold and angry to her heart's core, unable to weep for the loss of her husband and strained almost to the breaking point. It was three months before she could sleep quietly, her sister-in-law Ellen Peabody said. Sophia had urged her to go to Wayside, and she was grateful to find a shelter for herself and her three boys; but the old house seemed to be waiting for Sophia and her Nathaniel to return from Europe. They would soon come home, while Mary's heart seemed the more lonely because her own husband was gone past all returning. But there were the woods behind the house and the path that Hawthorne had made. Mary could escape there, and gradually she became less tense.

Brother Nathaniel Peabody had decided to make Concord his permanent home. Concord people were calling him "Dr. Peabody" now, by virtue of his skill in making homeopathic remedies, and he resembled his father in many ways — kindness being one of them. Ellen, his wife, though certainly not bookish, was a good housewife, social and pleasant. She was concerned for Mary and tried to distract her from her grief by asking in the neighbors to meet the sister-in-law from Ohio. These neighbors, whose sympathy had embarrassed Mary at first, were genuinely friendly, fervently antislavery, and anxious to know Mrs. Mann, whose husband had been so prominent in the cause. Mary found her initial bitterness lessening as these people offered her a chance to become identified with the cause which meant so much to her husband.

A frequent visitor to Wayside was Frank Sanborn, an ardent reformer, twenty-eight years old at this time but already experienced in Kansas affairs as a result of journeys there with Free-Soil settlers. He was now secretary of the Massachusetts Free-Soil Association. His friend John Brown had visited him recently. Sanborn was somewhat the sort of person Horace Mann had been in his younger days, Mary thought.

Sanborn was "sensible and manly and commands the respect of all who know him," Alcott said. He was a "graduate of Harvard and a scholar, in politics a republican," and these were points to commend him in Concord, so that it was no wonder that the school Sanborn had just established was "popular and prosperous and attracts scholars from the best families." Alcott, in his private diary, qualified his opinion of Sanborn with a word of caution, however. It might be that Sanborn was "something of a revolutionary in a quiet way — perhaps abetting Captain Brown and the Emigrant Aid measures. I think he is brave, and likely to do good service for freedom if necessary."

The education of her three sons would have been Mary's gravest difficulty in her widowhood except that friends of her husband's, Sumner, Dr. Howe and others, had done more than express condolences. They had seen to it that, in recognition of Horace Mann's work in behalf of education, money was given to his widow for the education of her sons. Mary could afford to send the boys to Frank Sanborn's to be prepared for Harvard.

She was well pleased with Frank Sanborn's teaching, but Alcott's warning that Sanborn might be "something of a revolutionary" proved true very shortly. Sanborn was sitting "in his quiet schoolroom at Concord," he said, on a Tuesday morning in October 1859, when word reached him of the attack on Harpers Ferry "by John Brown and his seventeen men," and of Brown's capture. "An infinite number of my letters were also captured," said

Sanborn; and now "slaveholding authorities knew" that he had indeed (in Alcott's words) "abetted John Brown." Sanborn destroyed papers which he feared might incriminate his associates — Dr. Howe, Wendell Phillips, T. W. Higginson and Gerrit Smith, the most deeply involved of them all. On Thursday, he sent his pupils off on a picnic but it was typical of him that he saw them off "with competent teachers in charge" before he took a chaise to Boston to get himself a lawyer.

Lawyer John A. Andrew, afterwards Governor of Massachusetts, told Sanborn that he "might be suddenly and secretly arrested and hurried out of the protection of Massachusetts law" and Andrew was right for during the coming winter the United States Senate voted the arrest of Sanborn.

There had been mixed feelings in Concord concerning the attack on Harpers Ferry. At Emerson's house argument raged, Alcott "defending the deed and the man," others saying that treason was treason no matter how right the cause. But when it came to the matter of arresting and carrying off the local schoolmaster, Sanborn, there was no division of opinion at all. Concord would stand for no such thing. By day, alert citizens would warn him of strangers in town such as sometimes turned up in search of fugitive slaves. By night, his whereabouts must be unknown. He must stay each night at a different house — and practically every house in town was offered him. Mary offered Wayside. It was kept quiet of course, and no one knew just when or how often Sanborn was there, enjoying the talk of an evening on matters educational and political with the well-informed Mrs. Mann.

Winter wore to a close, it was spring and no move had been made to arrest Mr. Sanborn. He had offered to testify in Massachusetts, the United States had refused, but nothing further was done. Judge Hoar, true son of revolutionary Concord, was heard to remark that he did not "overestimate the United States power" anyway, and Sanborn decided he was safe. He was in his own house late in the evening of April 3, 1860. Julia Leary, the Sanborn maid-of-all-work, had gone to bed and Miss Sarah Sanborn, who kept house for her brother, had gone up to her room. It was Frank Sanborn himself who answered a knock at the door. A young man presented a note, saying that the bearer was "a person deserving charity"; and Sanborn, leaving the front door open, held the paper to the hall lamp to read it. When he looked up, four men had crowded in upon him.

They had not finished reading the warrant for Sanborn's arrest when a fearsome apparition burst upon them and they automatically made way. It was Miss Sarah, who had been listening at the top of the stairs. Whether in curlers and wrapper or not, she dashed down the stairs and out the door, screaming for help at the top of her lungs. Across Sudbury Road, through the grounds of the Sanborn School and across Main Street she tore, arriving to pound on the door of Judge Hoar's house in a matter of minutes. Half of Concord heard her. The men had barely handcuffed Sanborn and carried him to the gate, fighting all the way, before church bells began to ring and townspeople, hustling coats over their nightclothes, came pouring into the streets. There had been nothing like it since the days of the British redcoats!

Sanborn braced his feet against the stone pillars of his gateway. They pried him loose and one of the men held his feet. But it was Miss Sarah into the fray again. She darted at the man who held her brother's feet and pulled his beard so hard he had to let go. A carriage stood at the gate, the door of which Sanborn managed to kick to pieces. And now an elderly Concord citizen beat the carriage horses with his cane; they bolted with the closed carriage which was to have been used to spirit away the schoolmaster. The crowd closed in upon Sanborn, and a lawyer asked him if he petitioned for a writ of habeas corpus. He said he did. Old Judge Hoar was not found among the crowd in the street. He was already at his desk making out the writ. One more Concord fight was over, and the citizens had had a wonderful time.

Everyone was there when they held a mass meeting in Sanborn's honor, when Sanborn's case was dismissed. Mary Mann was there of course, and likewise her sister, Elizabeth.

Mary now was thinking of making Concord her permanent home, and asked Mr. Sanborn if he thought there was a need in the town for a school for little children. Sanborn took only boys and girls in the higher grades and specialized in preparation for college. He told Mrs. Mann that a lower school should certainly succeed and together they talked over plans. Right next door to Mr. Sanborn's house and across the street from his school was a fine old white house with a homelike look to it. It was for sale and when Mary went to see it, she fell in love with it. Mary was fortunate in the fact that her husband's trusted friend and business adviser, Mr. Downer of Boston, was not only honest but shrewd. She now found that he had handled investments so well that, in spite of inroads made in behalf of Antioch, she could afford to buy a house. He approved her purchase of Number 7 Sudbury Road.

The new home was to be Elizabeth's as much as her own, Mary said, and Elizabeth was made happy by the idea. She would be at home for the first time in ten years, she told her friends — with all her things about her. Although she could hardly believe it herself, Lizzie was fifty-six years old now. Lately, she had been troubled by the idea that she had not lived up to her early promise. Now at last, "I may *do something* satisfactory to myself and friends which I have not done before," she said.

Mary's school was a success from the start. "Almost a kindergarten," Elizabeth called it afterwards, remembering innovations entirely original with her sister yet similar to those being tried out in Germany at the same time — but of which Mary knew nothing as yet. There were nature walks, for example, with the kindly Mr. Thoreau to teach the children names of birds and flowers and how to appreciate the outdoor world. The children were taught to sing and even to play games and work with their hands, a thing unheard-of in the usual school. This is not to say that fundamentals were neglected, however. Older brothers and sisters were in Mr. Sanborn's school, and Mary's scholars aspired to go there. They must read well, spell properly and know simple arithmetic backwards and forwards. The children did not expect to have lessons made into play. They were proud to work, since it showed that they were growing up. But a school where playtime came fairly frequently, as a reward for working, was a better place than they had supposed a school could be.

It had been suggested that Mrs. Mann write a life of her husband. At first Mary said that she was unequal to the task, but friends encouraged her, Mr. Sanborn said that he would help if she needed him — and Elizabeth went promptly to Boston, coming back with the news that Walker, Fuller and Company would publish the book. Mary began to assemble material. She wrote to old friends of her husband's, who sent her reminiscences, letters he had written — everything that might be of use and much that was not.

Elizabeth hurried to that beloved retreat, her own room; she turned over the contents of her now innumerable trunks of letters, papers and fragmentary diaries, and brought to Mary all the letters from "dear Mr. Mann" and all the letters about him which had comprised her share of "Cuba Journal." To her surprise, Mary found that she could read over what was almost a courtship between her sister and the man she loved and feel no bitterness any more. Certainly she had come close to losing him, but Horace Mann had been her husband, not Elizabeth's. Mary had made him happy as she was sure Elizabeth could never have done. There had been confidences between them, during their married life, far sweeter and more intimate than anything upon a written page.

At the time of Horace Mann's death, Mary had been handed a sheet of "last words" hastily scribbled down in his niece, Rebecca's, handwriting — incomplete, almost incoherent. Toward the middle of the page was a message: "To Mrs. Mann about money — You will have enough to make you comfortable for thirty years. Live where you like — and as you like." The words had sounded so cold when Mary first read them that they almost broke her heart. They referred to some insurance her husband had taken out for her, and they seemed to imply that she had wished to leave Yellow Springs for her own pleasure, when he knew — oh, how could he fail to know? — that it was only for his sake! Mary had hated the paper, but she had kept it; and now, reading it over, she saw that her husband was speaking of her to another — hence the seeming coldness. She felt that he must now understand how much she had always loved him.

At the top of the paper of "last words" were lines that certainly seemed to refer to Rebecca. "To me," the paper said, with the words underlined. "You have been to me the loveliest, tenderest [and the "tenderest" was crossed out] . . . dearest gentlest faithfulest daughter sister friend almost wife — goodbye . . ." Although Mary had struggled against it, these words had hurt her almost past bearing. But now she arranged all the many letters her husband had written to her and she read again of his terrible anxiety when their third child was born. She saw herself, again and again, called "dearest" and "dearly beloved" all through the years, and the proof of how dearly she had been loved seemed to heal her heart at last. Mary found that she could write to Rebecca now. "I have not been in a rational state," she would say, and she would tell Rebecca that she was sorry she had not seen her before leaving Yellow Springs. "When I do see you," Mary wrote, "I want you to come into my arms as if you were my own child."

Much material from her husband's letters Mary put into the biography, but everything personal must be left out. There would be a clue, in some cases, as to whom the letters were written, but the text would be exasperatingly sown with initials. May Alcott was employed to copy letters for Mrs. Mann, leaving out almost everything humanizing. It was the fashion of the period to write this way, and Horace Mann would appear about as much like himself as the statue of him, with his cloak draped toga-fashion, would resemble him when it stood near the statue of his arch-enemy, Webster, in front of the State House in Boston. Mary would have been embarrassed to write of her husband as a human being, and no one expected her to do it. She felt unsatisfied, however, and longed to set something down for her boys to read that might really bring their father back to life for them.

"A Journal of Remembrance" she called the intimate record begun as of January 24, 1860. She began it for her sons, but she soon found pleasure in it for herself as she tried to express her love for her husband. The journal began with poetry.

To Myself

I know that this was Life — the track
Whereon with equal feet we fared
And thou, as now, the day prepared
And daily burden for the back.
But this it was that made me move
As light as carrier-birds in air.
I loved the weight I had to bear
Because it needed help of Love;
Nor could I weary heart or limb,
When mighty love would cleave in twain
The lading of a single pain,
And part it, giving half to him.

To Him

Oh dearest, now thy brows are cold
I see thee what thou art, and know
Thy likeness to the wise below
Thy kindred with the great of old.
But there is more that I can see,
And what I see I leave unsaid
Nor speak it, knowing Death has made
His darkness beautiful with thee.

There were eleven poems in all, some of them "To Myself," some "To Him," but although it eased her heart to write, Mary felt that her lines never told all that was in her mind. When April came, she tried again — in prose this time, yet approaching close to poetry all the same: "How beautiful is this opening spring! How every breath of soft air speaks to me of my loved one! It is as if his breath passed over me and hushed my sorrow. . . ."

"He loved to hear me sing . . ." Mary wrote. "It was not long before my life passed out of myself and into him and I may as well confess at this remote time that it was not much longer before I had the prophetic vision that somewhere in eternity if not in time I should be one with him and he would be one with me. . . . I was not so unwise as to be sure that he could ever give himself up again to earthly love — I did not know that he might not consider it a profanation of his heavenly love, tho' I have since learned that love cannot profane. I understood him well enough to know that he needed earthly love and I preferred even the possibility of his finding it elsewhere than to obtruding mine upon him at the possible risk of giving him a pang of self reproach — for had I not given him my whole heart unasked?"

In the deep recesses of Mary's mind one question had always lingered. She had made it a point of honor never to try to usurp the place of Charlotte, her husband's first wife, yet hers was a demanding heart and she longed to know which of his two women her husband really loved the most. In 1863, she had a curious experience which meant so much to her that she added it to her *Journal of Remembrance*. A perfect stranger came to her and told of having communicated in some way with the spirit of Horace Mann. The message "has assured me that I am indeed the wife of his heart and though I never consciously asked for more than second place . . . I feel that this is precious testimony to me, and it explains many a word of love from him to which I never dared to give so much significance. I knew that I was the choice of his riper years as Charlotte was of his youth and I knew that my maturer experience gave me a different power of appreciating him from what hers could have been, young and inexperienced as she was — and I was satisfied — yet how dear are these words to me! I had not sought any such magnetic communication (for thus I interpret it) I should have no feeling of assurance that I was not self-deceived but this came to me so unexpectedly from a perfect stranger, so unsought and unwished for, for my entreaties had never conceived that form of response (being highly prejudiced against it) that I cannot set it aside."

The "entreaties" Mary had explained already in her journal. "If

I had not always talked with God, who could I talk to now when I call upon my husband and he does not reply. Now I can say beseechingly to my Father, 'Tell him! Tell him!' "

In her home with her sons, her school and her book, Mary was finding a deep satisfaction. She would have liked to see her sister Elizabeth equally content in that room of her own, but this was too much to ask. Elizabeth put her books upon her shelves. For a few days, she enjoyed the role of a woman happy in domestic duties as she arranged her belongings. Now that she had given Mary those letters from Mr. Mann, it would be a good time to sort out Dr. Channing's many letters to her and to complete one of those fragmentary diaries of her own. Lizzie shuffled her papers according to a new system every day while a dozen books she must write sprang into her mind. This was what she had always wanted — a place to write.

But almost at once, there was the matter of the forgotten followers of John Brown to claim Elizabeth's energies. John Brown's wife and daughters had come to Concord on their way to Virginia, staying with the Alcotts for a few days. Elizabeth had hurried about, collecting money, clothing, and hospital supplies for them to take to the prison "at Charles Town" — not only for John Brown but for the six men captured with him. It was Elizabeth who reminded everyone of these other men.

On December 2, 1859, John Brown had been executed, and from the white church steeples of New England, bells tolled. People laid aside their own affairs to go to church and to think, for a few moments, what it must be like to die as willingly and as bravely as John Brown had done — for the sake of the Negro slave. They prayed, not for John Brown but for themselves, because they were not yet brave enough to accomplish the defeat of slavery, together as a people — while Brown had attempted it almost singlehanded.

On December 16, four of Brown's men were hanged: Green, a fugitive slave; Copeland, a free-born Negro; Cook and Coppoc, young white men still in their twenties, one a law student, one a Quaker. But this time no bells tolled, although these men met death in the same cause and with equal courage. Elizabeth Peabody was shocked at the indifference of people who had so recently wept over Brown. Admiration soon flickered out, it would seem, and pity soon ran dry.

Two men were left — Albert Hazlett, who was identified only

inclusively and by only one man as having been at Harpers Ferry at all; and Aaron Dwight Stevens, who had received six bullet wounds while carrying a flag of truce. Vengeance must surely be satisfied by now, Elizabeth thought, and Hazlett would be released. Her sympathies were all for Stevens, most particularly because he had been so completely forgotten.

Aaron Dwight Stevens was twenty-nine, the oldest among Brown's followers. His service to the Free-Soil Kansas settlers was invaluable, for it was he who had organized several companies of mounted men and formed them into the Free State Volunteers to protect the homesteaders against the gangsters hired by slaveowning interests in Missouri and called "Border Ruffians." Aaron Stevens and his men had kept open the road by which Free-Soil settlers entered and staked claims in Kansas. Although financed and armed by the North, these settlers could not have made good their claims nor added their vote to make Kansas free without the help of the Volunteers. Within a year, the Territorial Legislature authorized a Free State Militia — James H. Lane, General; and Stevens, Brigadier General. "Colonel Whipple" they had called Stevens, however, when he commanded the Second Free State Regiment defending Tecumseh against the Ruffians.

It had all come out in the trial — why Colonel Whipple was really Aaron Dwight Stevens — and, reading the newspaper accounts, Elizabeth's heart had been touched by the wild, adventurous boy whose crime was one of ungovernable anger against injustice and abuse.

Stevens came of martial stock. He was born in Lisbon, Connecticut, and his great-grandfather had been an officer in the Revolution. His father had fought in the War of 1812 and Stevens, before he was twenty, enlisted in the war with Mexico. He was honorably discharged but, restless and adventurous, he enlisted again as a bugler in a United States dragoon regiment serving in the far West. In 1855, he saw a soldier inhumanly punished by a major for a slight offense. Stevens beat the major over the head with his bugle. He was court-martialed, and sentenced to be shot; but his sentence was commuted to three years' hard labor with a ball and chain fastened to his leg.

Stevens had escaped after serving one year. He became Charles Whipple, assuming his mother's surname, and offered his services in Kansas, promising to become a Free-State settler and to work for antislavery. The whole story was one which Elizabeth found tremendously appealing. Had she been born a man, it could all have happened to her, she thought; and she was angry when some of her friends pointed out that Stevens was really a deserter.

In March, 1859, Elizabeth set out for Richmond, Virginia, to appeal to the Governor for a reprieve for Stevens. "There has not been as much sympathy for John Brown's men as I think humanity demands," said Mrs. Alcott, who was one of the few who agreed with Elizabeth. And even Mrs. Alcott was too practical to put much faith in Elizabeth's effort. "Before this reaches you," she wrote her brother in Syracuse, "I fear Stevens will have closed his eyes on the injustice of this evil world."

The case against Stevens, by March 1859, had been shifted by the State of Virginia to the Federal Court, the Virginia court having shown signs of pity for him because of his many wounds. In spite of three bullets which were allowed to remain in his neck and shoulder, he had not died, however. President Buchanan, when appealed to by Stevens's lawyer, said that the case no longer interested the Federal Court — and Virginia eagerly resumed it. Charges of "treason and murder" against Stevens were dropped; he was accused only of "advising or conspiring with a slave to rebel or make insurrection." The penalty for this in Virginia was death. Stevens pleaded "not guilty." Hard as he had fought against slavery, to urge slaves to insurrection was one thing he could honestly say he had not done.

Elizabeth journeyed down to his assistance.

Miss Peabody, with her rusty black dress, her graying hair, was not a figure to impress a governor of Virginia, whose panic fear of slave insurrection had made him cruel past anything Lizzie ever imagined. But Wise, the governor who would have hanged Brown and all his men the day they were caught, retired at the end of 1859 and Letcher was governor by 1860. Miss Peabody hoped to find Letcher moderate, and inclined to mercy. When Brown and his men were trapped in the armory, Stevens had been shot down while carrying a flag of truce, she would remind the governor, and it was one of the leading citizens of Harpers Ferry who had dragged him, unconscious, within the armory. There was of course Stevens's record of service to Kansas settlers but this was not just the thing to bring up with a Virginian. Miss Peabody planned to remind the governor that Stevens had only obeyed Brown's orders at Harpers Ferry. There had been testimony to the effect that Stevens had urged John Brown to flee to the mountains, rather than to fight; had urged him to wait no longer for slaves from neighboring plantations who were not coming to him after all — whether he would lead them to freedom or not.

Governor Letcher listened in frigid silence. Miss Peabody looked to him like a typical antislavery agitator, and he hated them all. Many misguided women had come to Richmond to plead for John Brown's life, he told her — and they had failed. Miss Peabody was almost the only one, besides Stevens's sister, to speak a word for Stevens, but Governor Letcher did not find this pitiful nor in any way calculated to make him show mercy.

Stevens was "reckless, hardened and dangerous to society," Governor Letcher said. So Miss Peabody had felt it a duty to try to save this man? Well, Governor Letcher had also had a duty, and that was "to rid the world" of Aaron Dwight Stevens.

Elizabeth had been rebuffed many a time on her errands of kindness, but this was a matter of life and death and for almost the first time she saw that she was beaten. The light went out of her face and she was white with shock. There was nothing she could say, but her eyes were alive with anger and spoke for her. Governor Letcher saw himself accused and condemned — just as surely as he in turn had condemned Stevens and would see Stevens hanged on the sixteenth of March.

Wherever Elizabeth went in Richmond, her voice and accent as well as her appearance had proclaimed her a Northern woman. She had encountered angry, even threatening glances, and it was a shocking experience to her to discover so much suspicion and hatred among fellow Americans. Now as she traveled back to Concord, her first feeling was one of complacency because in Boston many were against slavery and the rest so tolerant. But were they? The long journey back to Concord gave Elizabeth plenty of time to think — and she was always honest with herself, whatever other faults she had.

There was the time back in 1835 when a mob outside the home of Elizabeth's friends the Jacksons threw mud at the windows because certain antislavery ladies were meeting there. Elizabeth had not been present, occupied as she was in trying to earn a precarious living, but Miss Martineau, the English social reform writer Elizabeth so admired, had spoken at the meeting. Attacks against Miss Martineau in the papers next day were so virulent that Elizabeth was humiliated for her fellow Bostonians, and tried to burn the newspapers so that Miss Martineau should not see them.

Well — that was a long time ago, Elizabeth reflected, and Boston thinking had changed. . . . In 1857, however, just two years previously, Elizabeth had written an antislavery pamphlet. She had tried in every way to get it published and had failed, for not a publisher would touch it. Again, however, Elizabeth was honest with herself and admitted that perhaps the pamphlet had had its faults. She had not forgotten how she had sent the manuscript of her pamphlet to Hawthorne, who was in Liverpool. She had been proud of it and had hoped he would show it to Sophia. When the pamphlet was returned without comment, she had assumed that it was a mistake and sent it again. This time Elizabeth got her reply.

DEAR E.

I read your manuscript abolition pamphlet, supposing it to be a new production, and only discovered afterwards that it was the one I had sent back. Upon my word, it is not very good; not worthy of being sent three times across the ocean; not so good as I supposed you would always write on a subject in which your mind and heart were interested. However, since you make such a point of it, I will give it to Sophia and tell her all about its rejection and return.

When Elizabeth returned to her room in Concord, she had shuffled through her papers, looking for the manuscript pamphlet. Perhaps she could change it and try again to get it published. She had not found it, but she had found the letter from Hawthorne. It was torn but on the other side there was a reference to the fact that her letters to Sophia concerning antislavery were of no avail. . . . "You agitate her nerves without affecting her mind." And the letter continued:

As you have suggested dropping your correspondence with Sophia, I hope you will take it in good part, some remarks which I have often thought of making on that subject. I entirely differ from you in the idea that such correspondence is essential to her peace of mind; not but what she loves you deeply and sincerely and truly enjoys all modes of healthy intercourse with you. But it is a solemn truth, that I never in my life knew her to receive a letter from you without turning pale, and . . .

Again came the torn portion of the letter.
Much water had gone over the dam since then, Elizabeth re-

flected. Surely John Brown's death had brought the end of slavery closer, and she wondered if Sophia had heard about it. Sophia was in England all through the winter and spring of 1859, and Elizabeth suspected that she never so much as read the papers. Whether she grew pale or not, Sophia ought also to know what new outrages were being committed under the more stringent Fugitive Slave Laws. Her niece, Una, whom Elizabeth adored, was fifteen by now and she should know the truth about injustice in her own country, so that she could grow up to take her stand for freedom. Fugitive slaves had been carried off from Boston to the eternal shame of citizens who thought as Elizabeth did. Sophia knew that. But now gangs of kidnapers had invaded the North, finding a new and lucrative form of slave trade open to them under cover of the iniquitous laws.

Sophia should remember, back in Salem days when she and her sisters were girls, seeing local colored people celebrating "Emancipation Day," with speeches, fish-fries, picnics and general gaiety. It had been harmless enough, but it had seemed silly to celebrate such a thing as freedom which those Northern Negroes might have taken for granted long since. And now suddenly it was touching and tragic! Kidnapers, armed with forged papers describing fugitive slaves who never existed, would seize one of those free-born Negroes and carry him off in the dark of the night — with no alarm given, so skillful were they — till his frantic friends and relatives missed him, much too late. With the new laws denying citizenship not only to slaves but to the children of slaves, prosecution was stopped before it was begun. Here was a profitable business for men of evil intent. The North was much nearer than Africa and the risk, the way the laws read, was negligible. Elizabeth told the story of a young colored girl, born free but captured and exposed for sale in the deep South, naked upon the block. She told it well, especially for Una.

Everyone was defying these wicked laws, Elizabeth said, and she told of that wonderful Negro woman who was organizing the underground railroad. She had heard about "the black woman Moses" from Mrs. Alcott, because the home of Mrs. Alcott's brother, the Reverend Mr. May in Syracuse, was a station on the railroad and Harriet Tubman had been there often.

To Elizabeth's long letter, Sophia replied, also at length — just upon the eve of her departure from Europe:

"I received the day before we left Leamington a long letter to me and to Una from you, dear Elizabeth, and one from Mary. It was impossible to show Una your letter to her.

"In yours to me, you apologize about writing to me so much about slavery and its painfulness. I do not wish you to refrain from writing to *me* your whole counsel upon slavery. . . . But I must guard Una from the ups and downs of sentiment and passion on her judgment and experience as long as I can. . . . She *never* reads newspapers. But as you wrote once that I probably never heard anything that was going on in America, even from newspapers, I told her when she wrote you to tell you that we saw the most liberal newspapers all the time. But we do not allow the children to read newspapers. Only grown persons should do that and even they must take care not to be demoralized by it. . . . The *Morning Star* of London is on the side of freedom in all senses and is the most sensible, moderate, wise, paper.

"I think the paper on John Brown in the *Atlantic Monthly* of last month is excellent, and I could give that to Una to read. . . .

"When you get so far out of my idea of right as to talk of its being proper to violate laws sometimes, because we 'can obey higher laws than we break' — this, dear Elizabeth, I used to hear in days past and I consider it a very dangerous and demoralizing doctrine and have always called it 'transcendental slang.' . . . I am just on the point of declaring that I hate transcendentalism because it is full of such immoderate dicta. . . .

"I wish the 'summer calm of golden charity' to reign on Una's 'sweet lips' during this blooming into Womanhood and tender spring green of judgment. And you would display before her great, innocent eyes a naked slave girl on a block at auction (which I am sure is an exaggeration for I have read of those auctions often and even the worst facts are never so bad as absolute nudity) . . .

"The story of the heroic woman who runs off slaves is very interesting. Your whole story is very interesting though I do not agree to some of your doctrines. Before I left America, I heard a gentleman who had travelled in Canada and seen herds of fugitive slaves there in a state of the most frightful bestiality and discomfort and he said he shuddered at the awful sin of allowing them to go to that cold region where they are far worse than animals, so frightfully degraded — so much worse than at the South. This is an undoubted fact somewhere in Canada — I hope the woman of whom you tell has a better colony than that. I cannot find words to describe their condition as that gentleman saw it. The cold makes them incapable of effort. And they become heaps of idle, torpid sin. I do not believe it is the way to overcome slavery for endurance is better for their souls than utter depravity of will and indulgence."

Small wonder that, back again in Concord, Elizabeth, after the first greetings to the Hawthornes upon their return to Wayside, found herself seeing less and less of them. In late 1860 Elizabeth spent most of her time in Boston, where she started a kindergarten like Mary's, and by 1861 Mrs. Alcott was saying: "Kindergartens are all the rage." It was a fortunate circumstance for Elizabeth, because her school now was successful enough so that she could afford an assistant now and then, and go at last to more of those antislavery meetings she loved to attend. Until now, she had been teaching school, selling books or peddling charts; she had never had the leisure to devote to the cause which Lydia Maria Child had, for example, or Julia Ward Howe, or Maria Chapman.

In January 1861 Elizabeth went to Tremont Temple to hear Wendell Phillips, James Freeman Clarke and Emerson on antislavery. She had no ticket, so she waited, outside the building where once she had helped Alcott with his school, for the main doors to open. A crowd was gathering and, from the ugly remarks she overheard, it seemed to Elizabeth that even now antislavery had few friends in Boston. She noticed several very serious young men standing about quietly. Many of them had been pupils of hers. It would be good to know if they were on the side of freedom, she thought, and at the same moment they saw her and came over to her. It pleased her to have them assume that of course she was sitting on the platform, and they offered to show her in by a side entrance. She had no ticket, she explained. She expected to sit in the balcony. It was an odd experience for Elizabeth suddenly to find herself firmly taken care of by boys whom she still considered mere children. They hustled her inside and made her promise to go out by no other door than the one they showed her — and to go quickly if they gave the word. This business of being looked after — it was like having a family of grown-up children, except that it now happened to her wherever she went, for she had a family of adult pupils numbering in the hundreds! Then she began to wonder why these boys had been quite so urgent with her — as though fearing for her safety.

The meeting opened well and Elizabeth began to feel that antislavery was making peaceful progress. Then Wendell Phillips stood up to speak and the crowd in the gallery began to yell. "All hell broke loose" (as Mrs. Child put it). "Throw him out," they yelled, "throw a brickbat at him!" They began to sing derisively, "Tell John Andrew, tell John Andrew, John Brown's dead!" Several hundred men and boys started down the gallery stairs toward the auditorium, while those at the back of the auditorium began to surge forward. And now Elizabeth saw her former schoolboys again. They were quietly closing in as a bodyguard around Wendell Phillips — and they were armed! Lizzie's breath caught but she was not afraid. If there had been shooting, she would not have left her seat — and she would have been a great deal of trouble, on that account, to those earnest young men who loved her dearly.

But Phillips had stepped forward to the edge of the platform and was speaking to a group of newspapermen down in front. Suddenly the crowd quieted down. Their curiosity had been aroused and they wanted to hear what Phillips was saying. He spoke magnificently. Phillips was always something of an actor and he needed to be. He was also logical and depended more on well-thought-out arguments than upon forensic effect. James Freeman Clarke followed Mr. Phillips, but few heard him, for again the tumult broke out. Emerson rose next, could not make himself heard, and gave over at last — having done what he could by being there and showing that he was not afraid to take whatever might come.

Before Elizabeth realized it, she had been spirited away with the other ladies after the speakers had left the platform. She found that Mrs. Child, at least, knew that they would all have an armed bodyguard not only at the meeting but to see them safely on their way home. It seemed to Elizabeth as if they had turned back the pages of civilized history — if men must go about with concealed weapons to protect themselves and others who wanted to indulge in free speech. Yet Elizabeth realized that she was excited rather than scared, that if she had been a man she would have gone out and bought a gun.

There is "a time to every purpose under the heaven," Elizabeth thought, and it seemed to her as if the time for the purpose of ending slavery must have come. In April of that same year, 1861, the news of the taking of Fort Sumter by South Carolina came as a shock but also as a relief. It was war but it was inevitable. Seventeen-year-old Horace Mann wanted to join the Massachusetts Volunteers and had to be told that he must spend at least a summer in Brattleboro getting over his cough before he would be strong enough to be of use. He got a job helping an old gentleman arrange a collection of ferns, for he was intensely interested in natural science. He was headed for Lawrence Scientific School at Harvard and would study under Agassiz. Julian Hawthorne was two years younger than his cousin, Horace Mann, and therefore out of reach of the war. But Elizabeth had a soldier nephew, so to speak, for her brother Nathaniel's daughter Ellen had married George P. How who became a Sergeant Major in the 47th Regiment of the Massachusetts Volunteer Militia.

The war went very badly, not only in Elizabeth's opinion but in the opinion of the North generally, of course. It was all the fault of the new President, Abraham Lincoln, and naturally Elizabeth Peabody went to Washington to see him, to tell him some of the things the Boston people were saying about him and perhaps give him a little good advice. Her first impressions of Lincoln were of his height and awkwardness. Mr. Lincoln took time to listen to her and she in turn revised her opinion of his fitness for his task. Elizabeth was always quick to admit herself in the wrong and now she would go home and tell Boston a few things! Meanwhile, it seemed that the President was doing his best at running the war and Elizabeth looked around for something that really needed her own services.

Miss Dix was organizing a nursing service. She had given it out that no beautiful women need apply. Elizabeth had no illusions. She could qualify as to looks. Elizabeth was fifty-seven, however, although Miss Dix was only two years younger Lizzie knew what she would say. There was no use going around and letting Dorothea Dix tell her she was too old!

Elizabeth soon found her work, of course — for she could be depended upon to champion the forgotten, even the unpopular, cause and help those from whom everyone else had turned away. This time it was the Negro children who haunted the streets of Washington, begging, some of them — many of them starving to death or dying of disease. They had been lost or abandoned when war had destroyed the plantation homes they knew — or when their parents had fled from their masters and, in the terrible confusion of war, disappeared. One look at their little pinched faces, their big appealing eyes, and Elizabeth's heart was lost.

She knew plenty of people in Washington. There was William Francis Channing. He was a Congressman now, but Miss Peabody had tutored him in Latin when he was a reluctant small-boy student. He still minded her when she told him to see about a home for colored orphans. His wife and the wives of Northern office-holders living in Washington formed a committee and promised to work hard.

Elizabeth went back home to find teachers for a Negro children's school to be connected with the orphanage. Her nieces, Ellen and Mary Peabody, whom she had helped to educate at normal school, volunteered at once — Ellen while her husband should be away at the war, and Mary for life, as it turned out, for she became a missionary teacher.

Next came the matter of funds. Fairs for the benefit of the Sanitary Commission — the name given the work of Miss Dix and her early nursing service — were already very much the thing. Large sums were raised again and again for doctors, nurses, hospitals and surgical supplies. Now Elizabeth organized fairs for Negro orphans — and she had her troubles. People who had just donated generously to the Sanitary Fair did not like to give again. But Elizabeth would not have been happy if her work had been easy. The government, through Congressman Channing, had given an estate and Elizabeth and her sister Mary organized fairs until they had raised, Mary wrote, $1100.00 to build a school.

With her boys and her home to take care of, her school and her book to write, Mary could not be off on missions of mercy in Civil War days the way her sister was. She could, however, write about Elizabeth's doings with her own light touch. At the Concord Fair, there was a literary atmosphere. Autographs and hand-written poems by local celebrities were sold, and there was even poetry by Mr. Browning, whose work was just beginning to be passionately admired in America. Mary had not too much use for Browning. "I wish Mr. Browning had more judgment," she said. "It seems to me he might be quite as poetic without being so erudite and poetry ought to be like the Scriptures, open to all true souls, whether learned or not." It gratified Mary, however, that "there was quite a rush for Mr. Browning's Sordello sheets which were put into hollywood covers and beautifully illuminated by Julian Hawthorne." She went on to describe the fair. "Men black as well as white made excellent music at the piano — and it did indeed seem a new order of things. How delightful it is to be no longer ashamed of one's own country!"

Mary might also have added, in her own thoughts at least, that by 1861 it was also delightful to be no longer so unhappy about the attitude of her own sister, Sophia. Once war had begun, Mrs. Hawthorne had given a gold piece to the first Concord recruit. At the Alcotts', where the women gathered to sew for soldiers, there came Sophia with her workbasket and her little gold thimble, setting her stitches with a neatness surpassing everyone's. It was in Sophia's delicate handwriting that the name Louisa May Alcott was written in indelible ink on a modest box full of garments when "Louisa got her summons" to go to Georgetown as a nurse. At all the fairs there were examples of Mrs. Hawthorne's decorative work: lampshades, bookmarks — and a painted vase.

As far as news of the progress of the Civil War was concerned, Mary followed it and commented with her accustomed touch of humor. "We are all in doubt about how it is exactly in Virginia," she wrote, "because they do not allow news to be published now till it has become an accomplished fact. But either Lee has outwitted Meade, or Meade has outwitted Lee! The rebels do not turn off their generals as soon as they have a little luck, but Lee and others learn a vast deal by experience which our generals do not have time to do."

Sophia had even less confidence in her own side. In July 1861 she said, "It is fearful to find that the President is not fit to be commander in chief. It [the paper] also said that our Balloon spy saw all the country round Washington covered with Rebel tents, and that their pickets were within three miles of Washington and that immense fortifications, batteries and ambuscades were in all directions and so on. That our soldiers suffered for food and clothes and got drunk a great deal. Indeed, there was not one pleasant thing in the paper."

Since she knew that her sisters would have scolded her for such an attitude, it was to Annie Fields that Sophia wrote: "I cannot believe that our Republic is going to wreck. Yet there is not quite virtue enough in us I fear." Sophia asked Annie to write, "telling me whether affairs are desperate in our country. In that case, shall we two families escape to old England?" The question was rhetorical but there was truth behind it. Sophia had become "enchanted," as Mary put it, with the Old World, "so as to think America vulgar." Always anxious to excuse her sister, "But it is very hard to resist the fascination of polished life," Mary added, "and keep the sentiment 'I am as good as you' which is Democracy in the rough. . . ."

On December 11, 1862, Louisa Alcott set out for the battlefront. "Fredericksburg is on fire by our guns," was the word going around Concord, and Sophia said that Louisa "goes into the very mouth of the war." On February 20, 1863, Louisa Alcott was back again, having by chance met Una Hawthorne on the train from Boston to Concord and having "laid her head upon Una's shoulder all the way, looking ghastly and uprolling her eyes, while she was like a sheaf of flame in Una's arms." Sophia's careful description of Louisa Alcott's illness would indicate that her so-called "fever" was diphtheria, and probably the only reason why Sophia, Una and the rest did not now have it was because at some previous time some "fever" of theirs had been a light case of diphtheria and so they had survived it long ago.

There had been times when Sophia had been annoyed with Mrs. Alcott for bringing her bad news of the Union armies; that "General Banks' army was entirely destroyed" and that "the rebels were hurrying to Washington" and that the governor had "ordered off every man capable of bearing arms." . . . "Mrs. Alcott is the most appalling sensationalist," Sophia had said. "She frightens me out of my five senses." But all that was forgotten during Louisa's illness. Abby, the only other Alcott daughter at home, came to the Hawthorne's to meals because "she too was drooping in the fevered air of Louisa's chamber." Every morning, Sophia went over to inquire, and for a few minutes Mrs. Alcott would come to sit with her "and pour out her griefs and fears."

By the end of July 1863 Hawthorne had finished his English sketches, entitled *Our Old Home*. The work of preparing it had seemed a heavy burden to him, and in spite of Sophia's loving efforts to make "his high estate in the Tower" a perfect retreat from the world, he had been troubled and saddened by the war. To Alcott he confided that he had longed to give up the book altogether and go about the country recruiting. But he saw so few people that Alcott was almost the only friend who knew for certain that Hawthorne was antislavery and pro-Union. And now Hawthorne had dedicated his new book to his old and dear friend Franklin Pierce!

Anger against Pierce was hotter than ever around Boston, every peace-loving but antislavery Northerner blaming him for the coming of the war — holding him personally responsible for the repeal of the Missouri Compromise; despising him for appointing Jefferson Davis to the Cabinet. No one knew this better than James T. Fields, and he wrote at once telling Hawthorne to remove the dedication. "The most good-natured, the most amenable man to advise," Fields had called Hawthorne. Hawthorne was not. He had a streak of iron in him. When he was so bitterly criticized for writing Pierce's biography, Hawthorne had remarked that, in standing by one old friend, he had lost almost all his others. But since that time, Pierce had been in Rome and during Una's illness he had proved a tower of strength to Hawthorne. Now Hawthorne would stand by him again and the dedication would stay.

Time and again, Annie Fields had promised to visit Sophia and had put off the date. Now she and Mr. Fields arrived to see what they could do about the dedication — but even Annie's charm failed of any effect. She wrote in her diary: "Friendship of the purest stimulates him and the ruin in prospect for his book because of his resolve does not move him from his purpose. Such adherence is indeed noble. Hawthorne requires all that popularity can give him in a pecuniary way for the support of his family."

Looking around Wayside, Mrs. Fields saw that "the woodwork, the tables and chairs and pedestals are all ornamented by her (Sophia's) artistic hand." Annie approved, much to Sophia's joy. But she would have been a little troubled, had she been able to see in Mrs. Fields's diary that "Mrs. Hawthorne is the stay of the family." Perhaps Mrs. Fields had seen with her own eyes something which, as yet, Sophia had not been able to bring herself to confide even to "dearest Annie." It was back in July of the previous year (1862) that Sophia first put into words a growing anxiety. Writing to her husband, who was at the seaside with Julian, "Of all the trials, this is the heaviest to me, to see thee so apathetic, so indifferent and hopeless, so unstrung. Rome has no sin for which to answer so unpardonable as this of wrenching off thy wings and hanging lead upon thine arrowy feet. Rome and all Rome caused to thee, what a mixed cup is this to drink."

Hawthorne's anxiety over Una in Rome was not the cause of his illness but Sophia could think of no other. He had no fever, for which she could give him aconite, no injury to be cured with arnica. There remained a journey for health such as she herself had taken, and Hawthorne was at the sea in hopes of regaining his strength. His weakness increased, however; and within a few months Sophia confided to Una that her own fears, too, were increasing. She tried for an optimistic note. "I am amazed that such a fortress as his stomach should give way. . . . The splendor and pride of strength in him has succumbed. But it can be restored I am sure. Meanwhile he is very nervous and delicate. He cannot bear anything and he must be handled like the veriest Venetian glass."

Hardest of all for Hawthorne to bear was the fact that his work, once a joy to him, had become an impossibly heavy burden. He had endured the years of consulship, even enjoyed some of them, had traveled (for the most part to please Sophia) and had come home to write, his leisure well earned at last. *Our Old Home* had been more or less of a pot-boiler but it was begun in enthusiasm — to end in weariness. Now his health was mysteriously gone just as the time had come to work on a "romance" — the kind of writing Hawthorne was best fitted to do and enjoyed the most. He began and then abandoned several stories and it seemed to him that he could do nothing but pace his small square tower as though it were a cage. He went out only to walk along the ridge behind his house, avoiding so much as a glimpse of friends and neighbors. They might see the trouble in his face and sympathize. Emerson, with his deep insight, might read the secret that haunted Hawthorne now: the fear that he was losing his mind. Sophia alone remained completely in Hawthorne's confidence. "The almost abnormal sensitiveness of her nature led her to see and understand," Annie Fields said.

Although Sophia was reluctant to confide her fears about Hawthorne's health even to Annie, Mrs. Fields had already noted changes. Hawthorne had been "slim, athletic," with "soft brown hair," and "rapid movement." Now, "though no less handsome, he was a large, slow-moving, iron grey man with marvellous dreamful eyes." Failing to understand Hawthorne's reserve, Mrs. Fields complained that she could never make him look at her. During her visit to Wayside, Mrs. Fields, who was always the object of so much masculine attention, was faintly piqued when Hawthorne hardly noticed her but "appeared to find a sense of genuine repose" when he listened to Sophia's "somewhat romantic rendering of every-day events."

At the beginning of the year 1864, Sophia wrote the Fieldses a difficult letter. She had to say that Hawthorne had been taken very ill — "more ill than ever in this life." He had just received a check for two hundred dollars for part of the *Dolliver Romance* which would appear serially in the Atlantic. And now he could not work! He was tortured by the fear that he would never be able to finish the story and the situation was like a nightmare. He had come before the public with a tale to tell and now he was like an actor who has forgotten his lines — only in Hawthorne's case there was no prompter who could help him from the wings.

The cause of Hawthorne's illness remained a mystery and he refused to see a doctor. In her desperation, Sophia's thoughts again turned to a journey for health, and she told Mrs. Fields that Hawthorne had agreed that a trip to Europe might help him. It was out of the question, financially, however. Sophia was not the only one who placed great faith in a change of scene, and the Fieldses proposed that Hawthorne should go to Washington with Mr. Ticknor, senior member of the firm. Hawthorne liked Ticknor. It seemed a good idea. Sophia went to Boston with her husband and left him at Mr. Fields's office, "at 135, safe in the little sanctuary" on Washington Street. He would spend the night at the Fields's home. Sophia had been asked to stay with him — but Hawthorne thought she should go home to the children.

Once back in Concord, it was a relief to sit down and write to her dearest friend Annie all about the recent months and the anxiety Sophia had tried to conceal. Mrs. Fields would be bound to see how Hawthorne had suddenly lost weight. She might hear him if he paced his room for hours in the night unable to sleep because of a strange gnawing pain. If this pain were only nervous indigestion, as Sophia hoped, then the pleasant company at Charles Street should give Hawthorne relaxation and sleep might return. The rest, during the train trip to Washington — the stimulating sights and people, once he was there — might give him back his old zest for living. That Sophia did not believe in an immediate, miraculous cure, was something she admitted only at the very end of her long letter. She would be hard at work setting her house in order, she said, "so that all may be quiet and leisure when he comes home."

Mr. Ticknor wrote to the anxious Sophia almost every day. In New York, Mr. Hawthorne was very tired but had hopes of a good night. In Philadelphia on April 7, Mr. Ticknor spoke of the dreadful weather — it was depressing — he had caught a cold. But Mr. Hawthorne seemed better. On the tenth of April, Mr. Ticknor died of pneumonia in a Philadelphia hotel.

"What an inscrutable Providence that her husband should die away from her," wrote Sophia, full of compassion for Mrs. Ticknor.

CHAPTER TWENTY-THREE

Insatiable Heart

HAWTHORNE returned to Wayside, his face "haggard, so white, so deeply scored with pain," that Sophia realized that she had never seen him so ill before. "He has more than lost all he gained by the journey by the sad event," she said. "From being nursed and cared for . . . led, as it were by the ever ready hand of kind Mr. Ticknor — to become nurse and night-watcher with all the responsibilities, with his mighty power of sympathy and his vast apprehension of suffering in others — his sense of the drear death in a hotel . . . as Mr. Hawthorne says himself, it told on him fearfully. There are lines ploughed on his brow which were never there before."

Mrs. Fields could have had no conception of Hawthorne's condition even after reading Sophia's letter. She invited Hawthorne to a "Shakespeare dinner" which she meant to make the most brilliant gathering of celebrities she had ever collected around her table. Sophia knew she should feel honored that Mrs. Fields considered Hawthorne practically indispensable to the occasion, yet it hurt a little to have to explain more than once that Hawthorne could attend "as easily as he could build Rome." He could not leave home. "He wants rest, and he says when the wind is warm he shall feel well." . . .

"I wish he were in Cuba or some Isle in the gulf stream," Sophia said. "But I must say I could not think him able to go anywhere without I could go with him. He is too weak to take care of himself — I do not like to let him go up and down stairs alone. . . . He is my world and all the business of it."

By the first of May, Hawthorne had recovered from the shock of his experiences in Philadelphia but his illness continued to progress. General Pierce came for a visit and could not help but be distressed over the change. Hawthorne now huddled like an old man in the greatcoat with capes which once he had worn with such careless grace. His step was faltering as though every motion were an effort, and his once beautifully shadowed, in-seeing eyes were now cavernous and haunted. General Pierce had a long talk with Sophia, and as usual the only cure seemed to be a journey. The kind of journey General Pierce proposed was such a pleasant one, and Sophia wanted so much to hope!

General Pierce had a luxurious carriage and a beautifully matched pair of horses that were the pride of his life. "I think the serene jog trot in a private carriage into country places, by trout streams and old farm houses — away from care and news, will be very restorative," Sophia told Annie Fields. There was another reason why Sophia tried to believe that this proposed journey would help her husband. He still refused to see a doctor and Sophia was desperate. She thought if she could get Hawthorne to Boston a way might be found to obtain medical help. Could Mr. Fields arrange for Dr. Holmes to see Hawthorne "in some ingenious way . . . as a friend — but with his experienced, acute observation to look at him as a physician?"

The interview was arranged. Dr. Holmes met Hawthorne as though by chance outside Fields's office. They strolled and talked, the doctor finding Hawthorne willing enough to speak of his pain, his extreme lassitude, his inability to work. There was hesitancy, however (which Holmes laid to shyness), when Hawthorne finally brought himself to mention the greatest fear that he had hitherto kept hidden. Could this inability to work mean the approach of insanity? Gently, Dr. Holmes assured him that there was nothing the matter with his mind. Hawthorne asked if the proposed journey would do any good and the doctor said that perhaps it might. They went together to a near-by drugstore, where Holmes ordered something for Hawthorne's "indigestion."

Sophia had expected a confidential report on this interview but she received not a word. It was Annie Fields who knew the outcome and wrote in her diary: "O.W.H. thinks the shark's tooth is upon him, but would not have this known. Walked and talked with him; then carried him to Metcalf's and treated him to simple medicine as we treat each other to ice cream." Holmes's words sounded heartless — but they were only hopeless. Of course no word was sent to Sophia, and Annie kept the secret well.

*   *   *

Back in Concord, Sophia again waited for letters from the man who was her world — and always had been. One came, written in a feeble hand yet telling of pleasant things. On the nineteenth of May, 1864, Sophia remembered that the next day would be her little daughter Rose's thirteenth birthday. They must make the day happy for her, ask her friends, perhaps, to come to tea. But Rose afterwards remembered that her mother "staggered and groaned . . . telling us that something seemed to be sapping her strength." In a hotel room in Plymouth, New Hampshire, Nathaniel Hawthorne had gone quietly to sleep. Sophia did not yet know that her husband was dead — that there would be no awakening.

Turning to the friend she loved so much, "I wish to speak to you, Annie," Sophia wrote. And Mrs. Fields kept the letter, writing in her own hand on the envelope, "The original of a precious and extraordinary letter by Mrs. Nathaniel Hawthorne while her husband lay dead."

In words straight from her heart, Sophia tried to sum up what her loved husband had been.

"A person of a more uniform majesty never wore mortal form. In the most retired privacy it was the same as in the presence of men. The sacred veil of his eyelids he scarcely lifted to himself — such an unviolated sanctuary was his nature, I his inmost wife, never conceived nor knew. So absolute a modesty was not before joined to so lofty a self-respect. . . .

"To me — himself — even to me who was himself in unity — he was to the last the holy of holies behind the cherubim.

"So unerring a judgement that a word would settle with me a chaos of doubts and questions that seemed perplexing to the ordinary apprehension. . . .

"When he awoke that early dawn and found himself unawares standing among the 'Shining Ones' do you think they did not suppose he had been always with them — one of themselves? Oh, blessed be God for so soft a translation — as an infant wakes on its mother's breast so he woke on the bosom of God and can never be weary any more. . . ."

Mrs. Fields thought that Sophia's mood of exaltation would die away, but it did not. Again, a little later, she wrote: "God has satisfied wholly my insatiable heart with a perfect love that transcends my dreams. He has decreed this earthly life a mere court of 'The House not made with hands, Eternal in Heaven'! Oh yes, dear Heavenly Father! I will be glad that my darling has suddenly escaped from the rude jars and hurts of this outer court — and when I was not aware — that an angel gently drew him within the Palace door that turned on noiseless golden hinges — drew him in because he was weary."

They carried Hawthorne to the top of a knoll in the beautiful Sleepy Hollow Cemetery in Concord and laid him to rest not far from the gentle Thoreau, who had preceded him by only two years. Emerson would one day be his neighbor in death as he had been in life; but, on this beautiful day in May 1864, Emerson walked the narrow cemetery paths with a feeling of deep regret because he had not known Hawthorne better.

Mr. and Mrs. Fields had come from Boston bringing a great sheaf of lilies of the valley, which they laid upon the coffin together with Hawthorne's unfinished manuscript, *The Dolliver Romance.* Fields looked about with satisfaction at the number of celebrities also out from Boston: Longfellow, Holmes, Agassiz — Mr. Fields made a mental note for the memoir he would write.

A large church funeral had not been Sophia's idea. Mrs. Fields had persuaded her that Hawthorne's fame required it, and Sophia acquiesced, but she asked to go home directly after the church service. At home, her orchard trees were in full bloom and they said to her believing heart that, just as surely as spring follows winter, so after death comes life eternal. What had Sophia Hawthorne to do with cemeteries?

But, in a sense, Sophia never returned to Wayside. She had lost too much. The passionately happy young woman who had come to Concord as a bride, who learned to live a whole life of health and happiness through her husband, was not capable of living fully after his death. Too much of her died with him. That "chaos of questions and doubts" of which she had spoken to Annie Fields assailed her now, and there was no one to speak Hawthorne's word of judgment. From earliest girlhood, Sophia had been encouraged to lean on others. With her marriage, she had freed herself of her mother's domination and from Elizabeth's — but she used borrowed strength to do it, and now that source of strength was gone.

Sophia was not aware of how much she suffered, and she considered it wrong to grieve, for that would imply a doubt of the goodness of God, the nearness of heaven and the inevitable reunion after death. She tried to go about much as usual, taking a basket of darning with her to spend an afternoon at the Alcotts', stopping in at the Emersons' for tea. There she often found her sister, Elizabeth — from whom she sometimes fled, for Elizabeth's talk about the war troubled and embarrassed her. Lizzie was talking about giving the Negroes a vote now. Sophia was "quiet as a clam" about it, while differing inwardly.

Mary Mann came often to Wayside, at least during the first few weeks after Sophia's loss. Mary was finishing her biography of Horace Mann, and she told what a comfort to her the work had been. She had a photograph of her husband, and also an engraving. Which one should she use as a frontispiece, she asked Sophia.

"Neither!" exclaimed Sophia emphatically, for neither the "gaunt photograph" nor the "heavy engraving" did him justice. And for more than a month Sophia devoted herself to doing a portrait of Horace Mann as she remembered him. She had always had a gift for catching a likeness; but in her girlhood, portraiture had seemed less romantic than the painting of imaginary landscapes. Now, during these first lonely days, her gift for portraiture returned to her, to give her comfort as nothing else could have done. Her success made her feel humble yet exalted. She prayed as she worked, "like the Angelic Fra," and when the picture was done she felt that she had captured Mann's "best expression" for her sister Mary.

The death of a cousin's child provided Sophia with another opportunity to make a portrait. This time, she altered a drawing she had made in her girlhood so that two angels looked down upon a child who resembled "Posy" Loring. Sentimental as the idea was, it gave great happiness to the child's mother — and to Sophia.[1]

But her children came first, and the idea that too much devotion might hamper a child's own efforts to grow was a heresy never proposed to Sophia except by her sister Elizabeth. Rejecting all of Elizabeth's ideas, Sophia found security only in following her own mother's pattern. Una's "Roman fever" gave Sophia the excuse to lay upon her daughter all the restrictions that had so hedged about her own girlhood; Una was given private tutors, urged to stay at home and study Greek and take piano lessons. When Una begged to be allowed to go to a school of "Gymnastics," Sophia could not seem to remember her own struggles for freedom.

The school was in Lexington, only a short distance away. It was run by a Dr. Dio, whose publicity campaign included an exhibition of weight-lifting at the Concord Athenæum. Everybody in Concord was there, and Julian Hawthorne obligingly went up on the platform and found himself unable to lift the dumbbells Dr. Dio had been so lightly tossing around. The "doctor" was something of a charlatan, but his campaign was a success. Physical education was just coming into favor and his school enjoyed great popularity — at least for a time. Una was aflame to go, Julian backed her up, and she herself thought of the one and only thing that would win her mother's consent. She got Dr. Wesselhoeft to say that gymnastics was just what she needed.

It was all arranged. And then Mrs. Hawthorne learned that Una would wear a tunic and bloomers which came just below the knee — like all the other girls. Sophia was horrified. Una's father would never have allowed such a thing, she said, and consent was withheld — till Dr. Dio promised that Miss Hawthorne's bloomers should come down to her boot tops. "You shall wear your trousers and tunic, dear," wrote Sophia, "and I shall not be distressed — if you cover up your legs entirely." When crossing the street from her room to the school, Una was to put the skirt her mother was sending her over the bloomers.

Sophia's misgivings continued. A clergyman, head of Una's table during meals at school, had let fall remarks concerning "woman suffrage." He approved! Sophia felt that she should go right over to have a talk with him, but meanwhile Una was to remind him that it was "men for the rostrum, women for the home, the penates," this being "the will of God," as any clergyman ought to know. "Do not become demoralized by him or Mrs. Stowe on these points," warned Sophia. She was thankful that the course at the school was but a short one, and that she would soon have Una safe at home again.

There was more trouble ahead, however. Upon finishing her course, Una planned to teach physical education! George Hillard, trustee of her father's estate, had advanced the funds for the school from money held in trust for Una. She was determined to pay back the sixty dollars and then earn her own living, preferably away from home. Mr. Hillard approved, she knew. With confident pride, Una wrote her mother that a class of ladies had been promised in West Newton, another in Dorchester, for the coming winter.

Once more an unhappy pattern from the past asserted itself and Sophia, beset with difficulties, took to her bed. She had put herself into a mood of renunciation over letting Una go to school in the neighboring town. Her letters had been full of assurances of unselfish happiness — together with requests for Una to be sure to come home every Sunday. All along, she had assumed that Una would be home for good at the end of the year. Why this "sudden" plan, she cried – blaming in turn every outside "influence." Never in the world would Una Hawthorne be allowed to "ride in the crowded horsecars alone in the dark." Why, oh why, did Una imagine that she needed to earn a living?

Elizabeth might, at this point, have come to Una's rescue with the reminder that all Peabody women had been teachers and that there was certainly nothing disgraceful about it. But Aunt Lizzie had sent her niece Una a volume of early English poets and a volume of letters – perhaps as a birthday present. The twenty-one-year-old Una never got a look at either book. Dating her letter March 5, 1865 (two days after Una's birthday), Sophia wrote to her sister Elizabeth:

". . . But a delicate young person who has not lived, who knows nothing of the mysteries of life – who is all question and all wakefulness about the hidden arcana, might most innocently become sullied in her thoughts by such plain revelations and might regret throughout her womanhood that she had stumbled upon them. It might rub the down and bloom from her maiden fancies." The letter was evidently intended to cover the return of the early English poetry, but it was only one of a series of arguments – for Aunt Lizzie never gave up.

"Delicacy" had been the watchword during Sophia's youth, and the difference between prudery and delicacy, between ignorance and innocence, was completely overlooked – so that Sophia's attitude, though exasperating, was understandable. Less easy to forgive was her use of her own ill-health to influence her children. "You can come home and have a class in gymnastics with poor me and poor Rose," Sophia said. Then there was Mrs. Mary Hemenway of Boston, recently widowed and drawn to Sophia by reason of their similar loneliness. She was wealthy, along in years, vigorous and healthy without any conceivable need for lessons in gymnastics, but Sophia said that Mrs. Hemenway would like to have Una teach her. Una could go to Boston once a week – she might even spend the night. To all this, Una replied unfavorably. Then her mother sent for her, pleading serious illness – and Una came.

Rose, the youngest child, seemed at that time to present no problem. She was beautiful, with red-gold hair and a passion for dancing. But when she was sixteen, Rose too was taken with a desire to go to Una's school. Remembering Una's strategy, Rose went to Dr. Wesselhoeft, with similar happy results. Certainly, gymnastics would be just the thing for her health. Then the blow fell. Aunt Mary Mann in 1866 decided to sell her house in Concord to a woman who wanted it for a girls' school. There was to be a teacher of gymnastics, and Sophia wrote in triumph of the "happy" turn of events. It was not that here was a chance for Una to obtain a position — Sophia still clung to the idea that Una must not earn a living because there was no need of it. The plan was that Rose could have gymnastic lessons at the school without leaving home. When Rose burst into floods of passionate tears, it was her nerves, her mother said — it proved that she should never go away to school. Both girls would be at home always, and Sophia felt a load drop from her shoulders. They would marry, perhaps, but that was in the dim future when some impossibly perfect young man would miraculously appear for each of them.

Although she never expected her son to take any responsibility, Sophia did not try to keep him at her side. He was a boy and that gave him the right to live away from home. He had entered Harvard at seventeen, the year his father died, but he had had only one year of what could be called preparation, with Frank Sanborn. He was too young to go to college, Sanborn thought, and it was a pity he passed his entrance examinations. Before his freshman year was over, Julian was off to Stockbridge "for tutoring in mathematics." The second year, and for part of the third year, it was the same. Sophia could not but exclaim, "The expenses are so great!"

It was a joy to Sophia to see her son grow to look more and more like his father. He was "Princely," she said. She could find no fault with him whatever, but it did seem a little strange to her that he could be in the Berkshires tutoring and still remain a student at Harvard. She asked him anxiously if it was all right, and with youthful optimism he assured her that it was. He had himself coached in a subject, took an examination at Harvard and passed — he then spent some time at college, where he was immensely popular and enjoyed himself thoroughly. If he got behind in his subjects he could easily be tutored again. But Harvard had other ideas, and in the autumn of 1866 young Julian Hawthorne was told that he had been absent too often. Although prostrated with grief, Sophia deferred taking to her bed until she had seen the president of Harvard personally. She was a touching figure in her black dress with her air of utter helplessness — but she was told that nothing could be done. "My heart has been used for a football by Harvard these nearly three years," said Sophia, exonerating Julian — who "bears this upsetting with his usual serene magnanimity — but it is very mortifying after telling all his friends that he was safely back."

"It was Mr. Edwin Seaver who led him astray. He is one of the faculty and he assured Julian that he was all right," Sophia explained to her sister, Mary Mann.

Unfortunately, Mary remembered a saying of her husband: "When a boy is inaccurate whip him!" And Julian remembered that he had never liked Uncle Horace.

"I do not agree to the whip," Sophia said and Mary was not surprised to hear it.

Sophia looked about for a tutor for Julian so that he might go on with languages, which he enjoyed. She could not bear to think of his student days as over and she had reason to suppose that she and the children were well off and that nothing need be said to Julian about earning a livelihood as yet.

There were those who said that Mrs. Hawthorne suffered delusions of grandeur, but actually Sophia had good cause to feel secure. If the European sojourn had been much less remunerative than Hawthorne had hoped, he had nevertheless sent money home regularly to Ticknor and Fields to invest. With the exception of a small sum to be paid annually to his sister Elizabeth, Hawthorne had left everything to his wife and children with their friend George Hillard to manage the estate for them. When Hillard had probated the will, the estimated assets came to $28,034.64. Taken in terms of the value of money in 1864, it was handsome. Sophia had always been a careful housewife and she was not given to understand that she need economize particularly.

Sophia had been taught to pinch pennies but no one had ever given her so much as the rudiments of instruction concerning investment of capital, rates of interest or the probable lifetime of royalty earnings. Hawthorne himself could not have told her very much, for he did not know how much his royalty earnings were supposed to be. Hillard was perfectly trustworthy but he would rather have been a poet than a lawyer, while business was the last thing in the world to interest him. Most of Sophia's and the children's money was invested in bank stocks. This was considered the safe, conservative thing to do. But as the Civil War dragged on, there were bank failures. Sophia read about them in the papers, never dreaming that here a portion and there a block of her capital was being wiped out. It was both painful and difficult for Hillard to make Sophia understand her position. She would have to live on less money, he told her. And Sophia replied that, with the cost of living rising so fast, she would have to have more, not less, to live on.

When Sophia's brother Nathaniel, his wife, daughter and grandchild arrived at Wayside in 1866, it was Hillard who would be obliged to write them a sharp note. They were to bring their bedroom furniture on this "visit," but Hillard was to tell them in so many words that Mrs. Hawthorne could not afford to support another family. It was difficult. Hillard's lot was not a happy one.

The business of being the widow of a famous man was something for which Sophia was ill-fitted. She was too sensitive, too sincere — nothing of the play-actor. Naturally enough, she wanted to keep for herself all her intimate memories of Hawthorne, for they were all she had. She wanted to present to the world an idealized picture: a sort of plaster saint in the Victorian manner — all perfection without a single human fault or failing. The Fieldses were able to help, for publicity was their sphere. But Sophia had been deeply grieved when Fields accepted, for the *Atlantic* for July 1864, Oliver Wendell Holmes's account of his last interview with Hawthorne. Fields, Sophia felt, should have protected Hawthorne's memory and should never have allowed such indelicate phrases to be used: "local symptoms, referred especially to the stomach, — boring pain, distention, difficult digestion with great wasting of flesh and strength. . . ." Sophia did not understand that here was a vivid description written with all the sympathy of a man who has lost a valued friend, but a man who is also a doctor and who sees no reason why accurate details should give offense.[2] Still more unforgivable in Sophia's eyes was Dr. Holmes's mention of Hawthorne's fear that he might lose his mind. She did not seem to notice that Holmes was completely reassuring on the point. Instead, she wrote in desperation to Mr. Fields. "Oh I wish Dr. Holmes would not say he feared it — Why not leave him intact as he is — oh do try to shield him, dear Mr. Fields."

Then Mr. Fields had suggested that Oliver Wendell Holmes write the life of Hawthorne! He ought not to have been quite so surprised at the reaction of Mrs. Hawthorne. "Never!" cried Sophia. Not one letter, one scrap of material, would she give to Holmes for this purpose. Two of Hawthorne's notebooks had been sent to Charles Street, and Sophia was greatly agitated to learn that Holmes had seen them. They must be returned at once! Since Mr. Fields had already asked Holmes to undertake the biography and Holmes had become enthusiastic over the prospect, Mr. Fields's position was now awkward. Sophia did not realize that she was also straining her friendship with "dearest Annie," her "dearest Lily," her "dear Moonlight." Mrs. Fields was particularly fond of Dr. Holmes, who came to all her parties, wrote her charming, flattering little notes which she kept among her personal treasures — just as she kept Sophia's letters with their varied and affectionate salutations.

Mrs. Fields was patient with Sophia. If Dr. Holmes was not to do a biography of Hawthorne, perhaps Sophia would write one herself. Her sister Mary had written of her husband very much to the satisfaction of her contemporaries, and Sophia could write — her letters had charm. Sophia refused without giving the idea a second thought. She had not forgotten Hawthorne's opinion of women writers, and she was not going to "walk abroad . . . stark naked." Sophia also remembered the day when Rose, aged about ten, had been caught by her father in the act of writing a story and had been severely scolded and told never to do such a thing again. Sophia was dedicated to her idea of what Hawthorne would have wanted.

Sophia's refusal was accepted without argument, and the Fieldses continued to search for some way in which immediate interest in Hawthorne could be kept alive and his books sold, for the sake of his wife and children. They had not told Sophia that this might be difficult. Was there not some unpublished romance? they asked hopefully. Sophia replied that there was nothing but a series of notebooks, such as they had seen, kept partly as journals, partly as a repository of ideas. Sophia said that she believed she could copy some passages, but as to publishing them — "the Veil he drew around himself no one shall lift," she said.

Sophia found a descriptive passage in a notebook kept by Hawthorne while in England which was sufficiently impersonal to be published without lifting any veils. She sent it to Fields, who was delighted and proposed a series of extracts from Hawthorne's notebooks to appear in the *Atlantic*.

In October 1865 Sophia was reading Hawthorne's notebooks and copying out passages with a pleasure she had never anticipated. The greatest joy of all was in store for her when she reread the journal of her early married life. Part of it she had written herself, a sort of daily love letter. The year at the Old Manse returned like a dream, with all the anxiety of financial stress forgotten and nothing left but the ecstasy of love fulfilled. Who could blame Sophia if she deleted certain passages, as when Hawthorne told of taking her in his arms at last after years of desiring her? She took pen and ink and blocked over, here a word, there a sentence. Sometimes she cut out whole pages and watched them curl up and burn in the marble fireplace. They were not lost, for never would she forget the words now turned to ashes. Her heart seemed to lift, and disappear with the smoke, in her longing to be with Hawthorne again, one with him in eternity as she had been in life.

"I live all day long with my husband," she wrote to Mr. Fields. He bought twelve of her articles, paying her a hundred dollars each.

But when the series appeared there were adverse criticisms, particularly from Sanborn in the *Christian Register*. "Hawthorne's notebook, doing so little justice to the genius of the writer, is again opened for people to gape at and wonder how such a man could write such commonplace things, and still more, how such a man's friends can wish to see them paraded before the world. His own delicate nature would shrink from it . . ." Had the Devil himself dictated the words, they could not have been better calculated to hurt Sophia. Every fear she had ever had concerning the publishing of the journals seemed realized.[3]

It had been Fields's intention to collect the *Atlantic* articles into a book, but now Sophia was terribly torn in her mind. Her instinct to avoid criticism and keep the beloved memory of her husband intact led her to suggest that no book be published. Then the fact that she seemed always to need money led her to beg Fields to publish the book and as soon as possible. In happier days, Sophia used to remind her husband of a little bird, contentedly building her nest — never flying far. She was pitifully like a small bird now, caught within a room — flying frantically against closed windows, thrown into a panic by those who meant her no harm.

"I am afraid your heart misgives you about the American notes," she wrote to Mr. Fields. "Do you prefer not to publish it? Is that the reason you delay so long? Or is it because you have a thousand books to publish *first*? I do not believe anyone can want money more than I do. . . ."[4]

CHAPTER TWENTY-FOUR
Final Flight

IN 1868 *Passages from the American Notebooks* finally appeared. Mr. Fields had suggested changes in words and phrases in accordance with his own taste for simpering prettiness and prudery. Words with too Anglo-Saxon a flavor were out. Latin derivatives must be used to smother the life out of a passage with their many syllables. Everything having to do with sex was either left out or changed. Some of these changes appealed to Sophia just as strongly as they did to Fields but every once in a while she stood out for Hawthorne's own expressions exactly as he wrote them down. Sophia, as editor, would be blamed or praised for the changes according to the temper of the times. At the moment, it made no difference, for the book was received for the most part with indifference. Hawthorne was too recently dead and his contemporaries too unaware of his permanent place in American literature. It was too soon for students of his style to appear and take delight in tracing methods and sources.

But Sophia was pinning great hopes upon the success of the book. What else had she to hope for? The Civil War was over but prices continued to rise, banks to fail. Sophia had no means whatever of forecasting her probable yearly income, and, although she knew she must practice economy just as she had always done all her life, she could not tell just how far her standard of living would have to be cut. Fields undoubtedly thought of her as foolish and unbusinesslike, but she needed desperately to know the answers to the questions she asked him.

"Can you let me have my account with you?" Sophia asked. "It would oblige me very much and be a great convenience; for I ought to know both my liabilities and my resources. . . . I heartily hope you have for me some money. . . .

"We used to be most woefully at fault in the days of Mr. Ticknor because for years and years he would never give Mr. Hawthorne his account, and we never knew whether we might live or die. Not all my efforts would persuade him to add up the sum, and Mr. Hawthorne himself would not ask, though he wished exceedingly to know about his affairs. Business is a terrific burthen to me, but if I am in doubt I can scarcely preserve my balance. Perhaps you ordered it to be sent long ago — and there was some mistake. . . ." [1]

Fields made no personal reply to this letter, but a statement was sent out from his office which showed a large, unitemized debt against the Hawthorne account — nothing due Mrs. Hawthorne. Sophia stared at the sum with a sensation of panic rising within her. She racked her brains to think where the money could have gone, and as far as she could remember she had charged nothing to her royalty account except $4.75 for Miss Austen's novels and $1.50 for a carriage for Una one stormy day in Boston.[2] "Have I then swallowed up all the rent of the $10,000 in your hands for the last year as well as the copyright income?" she wrote Fields in frantic disbelief.

Again, there seems to have been no answer from Fields.

Sophia's next inquiry was, naturally enough, about her *Passages from the American Notebooks.* Hillard had reminded her that she had no contract. A written contract was something which Ticknor and Fields had avoided in all their dealings with Hawthorne; but now, at Sophia's lawyer's insistence, something was prepared. "For this book, is the percentage to be, as it was for the others, in Mr. Hawthorne's time, fifteen cents?" Sophia asked. It was not. Mrs. Hawthorne would get twelve cents a volume and she would clutch at it as at a straw.

Anxiety made Sophia ill, just as it had always done when she was a girl, but she let the servants go and proceeded, with her daughters, to the business of baking bread, washing clothes, dusting high cornices and sweeping carpets. The days of high wages and scarce domestic labor were still to come, and laborsaving devices were consequently still undreamed-of. Sophia was right when she described her life as difficult. She was attempting feats not required even of Peabody daughters in their leanest days. Although she loved Wayside dearly, she began to think longingly of a little cottage somewhere where there would be only a few rooms to sweep and dust.

Physical fear was added to financial anxiety. There were returned soldiers about, some of them still under arms. A Concord bank was robbed, presumably by renegade soldiers such as sometimes stopped at the gate to ask for food. Sophia was afraid to be alone in the house, now that there was no strong Irish peasant girl to shout for help and wield a stick of firewood if necessary. When Hawthorne was alive neighbors had seemed near. Now, as Sophia carried her sewing to the Alcotts', the stroll along the road became a long one to her and she found herself wishing for city streets with close but impersonal neighbors. (Mrs. Alcott would be sure to have some terrifying story to tell of robbery and murder.)

No matter what economies she practised, there was never enough money and Sophia inquired anxiously to know how much Ticknor and Fields had received for her account as a result of the sale of the English rights to *Our Old Home*. Mr. Fields replied that he really did not know. He gave her his "impression" which was of a sum less than half the amount she supposed it was. And where did she get her own "impression"? It was only by word of mouth from her husband, now dead; and Hawthorne had it only through the word of Ticknor, now dead also. Sophia went back over old papers hoping to find some kind of proof. She found a receipt or two — and a mistake of seven hundred dollars in favor of Ticknor and Fields. They "acknowledged and rectified it" — and so the Hawthornes could pay the butcher's bill. They could clear up the account with the grocer too, and continue to eat for a while longer.

It was inevitable that the Fieldses' friendship should be strained to the breaking point. Sophia's nature was so naturally trusting and affectionate that she resisted her suspicions, but she could not help wondering about those large, unitemized sums debited against her. Gifts of port wine and oysters had been sent by Fields to the dying Hawthorne. Sophia had thanked Mr. Fields profusely, but now she wondered if they had simply been charged to her account. And how about the de luxe edition of Hawthorne's works sent to his widow; the portrait, the photographs and engravings of the author used in his books, copies sent to his widow? Sophia had understood that there would be no charge, and certainly it was Fields who had ordered the work done. Yet — how explain the sums expended?

Sophia remembered Fields's exuberance over the sales of *The*

House of the Seven Gables, his air of the benevolent benefactor.
. . . Upon the belated, but eventually gratifying, recognition of
The Marble Faun Fields had been like a jolly Kris Kringle: the
Hawthornes were not to stint themselves; they had plenty of
money. . . . She just did not understand business, Fields now suggested to Mrs. Hawthorne. And Sophia had to admit that it would
seem to be so.

There were no more invitations to Charles Street, no inter-
change of notes and letters with "dearest Annie." This, to Sophia,
was the hardest blow of all. She struggled hard for the friendship,
continuing to write long after her letters began to go unanswered.
It was hard to face the fact that the friendship had been all on
one side from the beginning and that, having given too much of
her heart to it, she was now more alone than ever before.

When Sophia had first begun to have her doubts concerning
the accounts at Ticknor and Fields, her sister Elizabeth had known
nothing about the business. Elizabeth was in Europe — the last of
the Peabody sisters to achieve that goal of their cultural ambitions.
She returned just in time to jump into the fray in behalf of her
adored Sophia. She saw at once that the loss of confidence in the
Fields friendship meant more to Sophia than the money involved
and so she wrote to Fields begging for some word of reassurance
for her sister. Fields ought "to make all clear and bright in the details of the past," Elizabeth said, and she asked for itemized yearly
statements in the future, saying with considerable wisdom that
when friends did business together they should be particularly
careful about accurate accounts.

The result of Elizabeth's letters was to bring forth certain statements from Ticknor and Fields which she found "full of errors" —
all in their own favor. Ticknor and Fields, however, explained
everything. Miss Peabody had been figuring a fifteen per cent
royalty on all of Hawthorne's works. The mistake was hers. Fifteen per cent had been paid on *The Scarlet Letter* alone. A subsequent verbal agreement had reduced to ten per cent the royalty on
all other works. This was indeed news!

Sophia had never heard of this agreement and Hawthorne had
always left the handling of money to her, at least in the matter of
household expenses. She would certainly have been told that she
was to expect less. Moreover, what reason could possibly have
been given, after the remarkable success of *The Scarlet Letter,* for

considering Hawthorne suddenly worth less to his publisher? Sophia simply could not believe the story — much as she would have liked to, for friendship's sake. The agreement, though verbal, had been made "before Hawthorne's attorney," Sophia was told. But Hillard was Hawthorne's only lawyer and Hillard knew of no such thing nor did he hold with verbal agreements.

"It has an ugly look," Elizabeth told Fields and she was so right that her efforts to repair the broken friendship were doomed from the start. "I do not suppose she will ever feel that affectionate confidence in your disinterested friendship that she once had," Elizabeth said with remarkable restraint.

Elizabeth's vigorous championship of her cause had resulted in one benefit to Sophia. There was unpublished notebook material about which Fields had shown only vague interest. Elizabeth wrote to George Putnam about it and he thought his publishing house would like to get out the book. Fields now bought it, giving Mrs. Hawthorne an advance — an almost unheard-of procedure for him.

Sophia had already decided what to do with the money. Hating the controversy over her affairs, emotionally overwrought because of the loss of a cherished friendship, she had decided upon a final flight. She would go to Europe never to return. Her slender income would go further abroad, she thought. Friends made during Hawthorne's consulship now seemed the only true ones, and almost any other country seemed more law-abiding and stable than her own.

As a result of the Fields misunderstanding, the idea that friends were against her was troubling Sophia's mind. She had made her decision and then asked for advice afterwards, and when this advice was contrary to her wish she was distressed. Ever since the death of Hawthorne, General Pierce had been a friend to the family, bringing presents to the girls on their birthdays, taking Julian on a vacation trip and talking to him about his future. But now he felt that Mrs. Hawthorne was taking too drastic a step. "The General has sent me word that he can neither advise nor help me," Sophia said. "We have lost him!" Hillard, when appealed to, was also opposed to the plan of her going abroad, lest Sophia and the children become homesick and find themselves without means to return or a home to come to. But Sophia felt that he, too, showed lack of friendliness.

Calling at Wayside at about this time, Frank Preston Stearns observed the widow of Nathaniel Hawthorne with the eyes of a journalist. She had grown gray but she was still a pretty woman, and he thought that in her girlhood she must have been lovely. Young Mr. Stearns knew Elizabeth Peabody and admired her — especially her gift for conversation. He found Mrs. Hawthorne almost as interesting, as she spoke of her life abroad before her husband's death. She might live by the wayside, Stearns said, but you could tell that "she had been accustomed to enter palaces."

One thing struck the young journalist, who was already planning a biography of Hawthorne. He sensed an elusive quality of tragedy. "Mrs. Hawthorne belonged to the class of womankind which Shakespeare has typified in Ophelia, tender-hearted, affectionate nature, too sensitive for the rough strains of life and too innocent to recognize guile in others."

It seems highly likely that some of the conversation which Stearns had enjoyed with Miss Elizabeth had been about Sophia and her trials. The young man's observations were probably true enough of Sophia just before she left Wayside forever. But once in New York and on her way to begin life in a new place, Sophia lost her Ophelia-like quality and became optimistic once more — just as she always had been. Her cousin, George Putnam, promised to publish her own travel notebooks and Sophia was delighted with the idea. She would try to make them impersonal enough so that she would not violate Hawthorne's principles about women writers. Another Putnam cousin, a lawyer, assured Sophia that she had a case against Ticknor and Fields, because of their reduction of royalty, and Sophia began to feel a return of self-confidence.

In Boston, Annie Fields made an entry in her diary which she dated October 27, 1868. "At night we heard, and we pray heaven it may not be true, that Mrs. Hawthorne has sailed for Europe, but has put her accusation against Ticknor and Fields into the hands of a New York lawyer." That Sophia had sailed was true enough. But she found she could not bring suit against friends she had once loved so much. Annie need not have bothered heaven about it.

The Hawthornes went first to Dresden because Elizabeth had been there and knew of comfortable, inexpensive lodgings. But the teachers who lived there and had seemed so inspiring to Elizabeth only bothered Sophia with their incessant talk. Although both Rose and Una had taken music lessons even when their mother was hard-pressed to find the money, neither was particularly musical and they had little in common with the other young lady boarders, who had come to study with Clara Schumann, who lived close by. For a time the art galleries were a source of delight to Sophia, but she took cold in the drafty marble halls and fell seriously ill.

Italy would have been the ideal, the logical place for Sophia to live — with its colony of Anglo-American artists and writers ready to receive the Hawthornes with open arms — but in Italy was still the dread Roman fever, and Sophia would not for the world have taken Una there again. England was decided upon as a better place to live than Germany and since Rose was beginning to show more than an ordinary talent for drawing her mother took her to London where she could study at the South Kensington Art School.

By November 1870 Sophia had made a home for herself at Number 5 Shaftesbury Terrace. The tiny house was a curious affair of two rooms to the floor, four floors in all, including the basement where there was a breakfast room, kitchen and scullery. There was no way to go from this floor to the next except by going outside and climbing "seven or eight steps into the front door." Here was a drawing room with a bow window and, through folding doors, a dining room. The rooms were not big enough for dinner parties, Sophia said. She did not seem to wonder just how the cook would have brought hot dishes outdoors, upstairs, and in again, even if the dining room had been larger. That was the cook's problem.

Above the dining room was Sophia's bedroom and Una's; above that an "atelier" for Rose, a bedroom for Rose and a cubbyhole for the cook, whose name was Louisa. The whole house cost five pounds a month rent, it faced south, was flooded with sunshine, and there was a tiny garden with an oval bed of flowers. Sophia felt pleased with the little house, the garden and the servant. Her meticulously kept account book shows how careful she had to be with her money; but now at last, by hook or by crook, she was making ends meet.

The cook, Louisa, received eleven shillings eightpence a month. She was indulged, however, to the extent of tuppence worth of beer every day, while occasionally a "helper" came in (and received four shillings fourpence for her services). Everything went into the account book, including sixpence for candy (once in a while) and sixpence for muffins (fairly often). A loin of pork cost five shillings sixpence, but they could buy a chicken for three and six, a haddock for only a shilling. So chicken and haddock appeared on the menu rather regularly. By means of such careful management, there was money enough for a month's vacation at Brighton, excursions to the amusement pier and souvenirs for the girls — a "stone locket" for a shilling, a shell pincushion costing sixpence.

Our Old Home had incensed the British for various reasons, among them Hawthorne's unflattering opinion of the beauty of Englishwomen. Real friends, however, had never held any of Hawthorne's opinions against him, and Sophia received more invitations than she cared to accept. She went out occasionally, wearing her black velvet dinner dress, looking very sweet, very ladylike — but increasingly frail. It was the climate again, she feared. Her house might face south, but London sunshine was unreliable and Brighton's sea breezes, instead of giving her strength, gave her a chest cold.

In February 1871 Una took over the keeping of the careful accounts.[3] Her mother was again dangerously ill, as she had been in Dresden. It was typhoid pneumonia, the doctor said, and he tried to tell the daughters as gently as he could that their mother had very little chance of recovery.

But Sophia fought her illness with courage and determination. She had been ill so many times before, and had always managed to pull through. Rose was to continue her painting and was not to worry. It seemed good, however, to have Una sitting by the bed. They spoke of Julian, who had found a position in New York. He had managed to be with them in Dresden, and now word had come that he was engaged to be married. Sophia had written him wishing him all the happiness which had been hers upon her own marriage. She could not have said more. It was pleasant now to lie still and reflect upon past happiness — and present peace.

All night long, Una sat beside her mother. Sophia seemed to sleep, but she still clasped her daughter's hand and Una dared not move for fear of disturbing her. Toward dawn, Una realized that her mother's strength was ebbing fast — that she was not sleeping but hovering upon the brink of unconsciousness. Should Louisa be sent running for the doctor? Should Rose be called? There was no time. But Sophia spoke once more, in a clear voice. "I only wanted to live for you children, you know. I never wanted anything for myself except to be with your father."

CHAPTER TWENTY-FIVE

Unconquerable Elizabeth

THE death of Sophia was a shock to both her sisters. They had not allowed themselves to think of her departure for Europe as a final parting but they saw now that they had known it all along. Sophia was the one who had always expected to die young and now she had done it — at least so it seemed to Elizabeth. Sophia was sixty-one when she died. And Elizabeth, at sixty-six, was in the midst of the most active, the most successful and the happiest period of her life.

It was at the age of about fifty-six that Elizabeth Peabody had begun, in 1860, an entirely new career. People had long since given up being surprised at anything Lizzie did, but that this career should prove successful was startling to some of her less than kind acquaintances. Her bookshop had been a place of enchantment, the ideal of every book lover. It was everything except solvent. As a publisher, Elizabeth had failed — but with distinction! Emerson's *Dial* and Hawthorne's early works were publications to be proud of, even when they lost money. As a teacher, Elizabeth had really failed spectacularly, accused by some of pulling down Alcott, but falling with him most certainly and standing by him amidst the ruins of his school. That success should come at long last, and in the teaching field, was the most unexpected turn of fate, even for the unpredictable Elizabeth.

As so often happened, quiet, unobtrusive Mary Mann was still behind her sister's efforts, working hard and contributing ideas which the more vocal Elizabeth would proclaim in the market place. This time, Mary's little school in Concord had given Elizabeth the new idea she needed, and with her faculty for finding in the written word additional grist to her mill she had seized upon the theories of a sensitive German educator, recently deceased. Friedrich Froebel had made little impression upon Americans up to this time; but Elizabeth read everything she could find about him and talked to everyone who could tell her anything at all. As a result of an unhappy childhood, Froebel had dared to advance the idea that little children need not be struck with iron-bound rulers for so much as wiggling in their seats. A little wiggling might be necessary to the development of their muscles and there should therefore be a time for exercise. Discipline need not be forgotten but it should not be the result of fear. Froebel advocated the use of the hands, and suggested that a child's senses were given to him to develop in the enjoyment of color, form and texture. The five senses were no longer to be repressed as though they were the snares of the devil. Froebel believed that the world of nature outside the schoolroom offered opportunities for education, and he discouraged introspection in the very young. Particularly in the matter of introspection, Froebel differed from Alcott; and Elizabeth Peabody was glad to see it. She had always hated to see Alcott's little scholars worrying about the sins of the mind instead of believing themselves the natural heirs to at least a little of the spirit of God.

All that Elizabeth had done since the death of her parents contributed now toward her success as founder of the kindergarten in America. As she had traveled about peddling Bem's Historical Charts, she had developed a wide acquaintance, particularly among private schools. Towards selling these charts, a logical step had been to write a history textbook to go with them. In 1859 E. P. Peabody had published a *Universal History; Arranged to Illustrate Bem's Charts*, and the subject was a large one, to put it mildly. She had found the task absorbing and congenial. She was proud of that book, whether it sold well or not, and with very little encouragement she would talk for hours about her adventures in research while preparing it. Her friends might have tried in vain to shut her off; it was a tribute to her conversational gift that, as a matter of fact, they constantly led her on — forgot meals and engagements while listening. Her historical lectures at normal schools were immensely popular, and she had appeared regularly year after year at a great many schools. Here was a readymade, ideal audience for Elizabeth when she now became the voice in the wilderness for kindergartens.

During those years of travel, Elizabeth had also solved the problem of baggage. Invited to the Newport home of the beautiful and accomplished Julia Ward Howe (whose little daughter Maud had been a pupil at the first kindergarten), Miss Peabody arrived with no baggage at all. Upon being asked about it, Lizzie explained. She was wearing her nightgown under her dress, and her toothbrush was in her pocket! Then she talked kindergartens, and nothing but kindergartens, all during the rest of her visit; and people who began by laughing at her ended by donating either money or services or both.

It was the Pinckney Street kindergarten — begun by Elizabeth in 1861 — that Maud Howe, later Maud Howe Elliott, attended.[1]

In 1866, Mary Mann had sold the house in Concord and moved to Cambridge to provide a home for her boys while they were going through Harvard. It was less expensive that way; and "the Ark," which the old house she bought was called, might easily be made to pay its way in rented bedrooms for other students. Mary got a good price for her Concord house and, although Sophia had considered her extravagant to put a furnace and plumbing into the Ark, that venture also turned out well. The new home was Elizabeth's also, just as the other had been; for the sisters were now partners in everything. Just before leaving Concord, they had written together and published *Moral Culture of Infancy and Kindergarten Guide*. The book attracted sufficient attention to warrant a second edition, and now Miss Peabody needed Mrs. Mann to help her with the kindergarten on Pinckney Street. (Eighty years later, Maud Howe Elliott would recall that "Miss Peabody was an angel" and that everybody in that first little class turned out to be very remarkable in later life.)

Mary and Elizabeth begun to make a little money with their school, but it was not for this that the kindergarten idea had taken possession of Elizabeth's soul. Not even the idea of making children happy in school instead of miserable seemed to Elizabeth of paramount importance. Her convictions went deeper; her dreams soared higher.

Elizabeth believed with all her fervent heart that education was the best means to bring about the answer to her daily prayer — that God's will should be done on earth as it is in heaven. If people only knew the right, they would never do wrong. Horace Mann had believed that a people taught to rule themselves could eradicate poverty, prevent war and see to it that dictators should rise no more. And William Ellery Channing had held that the child comes into this world free of sin. Evil, then, must be given to the child by means of evil environment. It must be corrected by education. Adding her own unquenchable faith to the teachings of the two men she had loved, Elizabeth conceived the idea that the kindergarten could correct evil environment — if placed in slum districts where the evil lay. Free public kindergartens were the answer; but until the public could be convinced of the value and allocate the funds, Elizabeth proceeded, with private donations, to lead the way.

The new pre-primary education could with justice have been called "the Peabody System" — except that it would not have been like Elizabeth to call it any such thing. She still found her greatest joy in the discovery of genius in others, and it was "the Froebel kindergarten" she was intent upon establishing. She therefore longed to go to Germany and study kindergartening at first hand. By 1867 there was money enough from the school to pay her passage and to pay for the modest kind of living she would require abroad. Mary urged her to go, and said it was about time Elizabeth put some of her own money to her own use, about time the oldest of the Peabody sisters achieved the distinction of foreign travel. It was no surprise to find Mary generous, eager to help. Elizabeth was in for a shock, however, when substantial gifts began to come from friends. She had raised many a fund but never before had she been the recipient of one! Part of the money was given in the name of social service — that kindergartens for the poor might be established all over the country, and teachers, of Elizabeth's choosing, be brought to the United States to give training courses. Some of the checks came with little notes: "Dear Miss Peabody, go and have a good time. . . ." These were the most heart-warming of all.

Among the most delightful friends of Elizabeth's later life was Charlotte Cushman, the actress. Sophia had met her first in Liverpool, and had succumbed to her charms, but with reservations. Was it all right to be friends with an actress? The stage was only beginning to be a respectable career for a woman, thanks in part to Miss Cushman herself and her irreproachable character. But Sophia knew what her mother would have said, and in turn had warned her daughters "not to like" an actor or an actress "too much." Elizabeth was troubled by no such scruples. One look at Charlotte Cushman and Elizabeth loved her. Miss Cushman had but to experience Elizabeth's zest for living — and they were friends.

During the Civil War, Miss Cushman had entertained the troops and had made money at it, a by-product of patriotism which Annie Fields seemed to think was to her discredit. Miss Cushman, however, cared not in the least what anybody thought. She got rid of her money in almost as many worthy causes as Elizabeth did. One cause was Elizabeth Peabody herself — a hundred dollars for tickets to a lecture by Lizzie on the kindergarten — and now Miss Cushman presented Elizabeth with clothes for her 1867 journey. They were striking garments, made of the finest materials and well suited to the handsome actress, part of whose business was to get herself looked at. On Miss Peabody, the clothes looked funny. But Lizzie didn't care. She had more than a touch of the dramatic herself, and she enjoyed the excessively lacy caps, the heavy satin "Balmoral" all aglitter with jet beads. Mary moaned and suggested that Elizabeth should wear her old clothes, but Lizzie only laughed and said it would never do to waste such good materials.

Elizabeth headed straight for Germany, with education on her mind, not sight-seeing. Nevertheless, she sailed down the Rhine and, mindful of what Sophia would want to hear in letters, she noted all the castles. She dutifully visited art galleries, and was somewhat taken with the rich colors, the bouncing big goddesses of Rubens. But Elizabeth liked people better than pictures or castles, and most of her letters told of some "rather fanatical and bigoted Lutherans" encountered in Hamburg or of "the transcendental Jews and their sympathizers, the friends of Carl Schurz" who were much more to her taste.

It goes without saying that Carl Schurz was a kindergartner, and so was his wife. They had come to America in 1852, formed a firm friendship with Miss Peabody in Boston, but established themselves in Wisconsin, where Mrs. Schurz had started a private kindergarten for her own children and their friends. Letters to their friends back in Germany now opened many a door to Miss Peabody.

In Berlin, Elizabeth visited the "Kindergarten Seminary" run by the Baroness von Marenholz Bülow, a pupil of Froebel. Here at last Elizabeth found what she had come abroad to seek. The apparatus amazed her — such lovely colored cubes; such peg boards and soft woolen balls! Then there was music. The children sang when they entered, they sang their prayers, and they played singing games

— old as the oldest folkways, yet new to Miss Peabody of Boston.
Elizabeth was as starry-eyed as the youngest pupil in the practice
school. . . . She set to work to persuade the best teachers to come
to America and spread the light, like missionaries to darkest Africa.

Madame Kriege and her daughter Alma set out for New York
while Elizabeth was still abroad. In New York City they found no
such enthusiastic welcome as Miss Peabody had promised, so they
journeyed to Boston, armed with letters to Mrs. Mary Mann. Here
their reception was more in accordance with their expectations;
but it would seem, on the surface at least, as though Mary had
been warming vipers when she welcomed the Kriege ladies. They
took over her school almost at once! In September 1868 the assistant hired to take Elizabeth's place withdrew, and an advertise-
ment in the *Transcript* extolled the virtues of the "pure Froebel
system" and the abilities of the Krieges, mother and daughter.
They would not only teach school; they would open a training
school for teachers as well. It would look as though the two Peabody sisters had lost a successful school, just as it was showing a
consistent profit. But Mary was as altruistic as Elizabeth, though
few people realized it. She had the cause of kindergartens just as
much at heart; and she knew that the German ladies must have
a place in which to show what they could do. So she stepped out
of the school, in order to write about kindergartening — since
publicity, now, was of utmost importance.

Elizabeth was heading for home by this time, after a year and
three months abroad. She had managed a quick trip to Rome by
means of one more unexpected gift. On her way through England,
she established an English Froebel Society — just by way of getting
her hand in before starting the Froebel Union in the United States.

She arrived at home in time to join the fray over Sophia's dimin-
ishing royalties, and to see her sister off for Europe. Elizabeth pictured herself as going back to Dresden or Hamburg in the not far
distant future, finding Sophia in a comfortable little apartment —
and visiting this dearest of sisters for months on end. . . . They
would have happy times, Elizabeth thought, still unable to realize
that she and Sophia never liked the same things.

Now, of course, Elizabeth had but one simple little problem on
her mind — to establish kindergartens from coast to coast. In the
beginning the difficulty was teacher training. Elizabeth went everywhere, and wherever she saw a sweet young girl with a look of

sufficiently saintly devotion in her eyes . . . "My dear," she would say, "you must take up kindergartening." There were plenty of young women in New England, widowed or left without matrimonial prospects by the Civil War — left behind and forgotten in the masculine trek westward — to whom the teaching of little children was the next best thing to marriage and motherhood. And if the most adventurous young men had gone West, every so often an enterprising young woman could go West herself, as a teacher — and then take her pick if she wanted to marry.

Only two student teachers had enrolled in Madame Kriege's first training class, but one of these graduates trained Miss Lucy Wheelock — who was to be, in turn, the founder of a famous school. In 1873 there was a kindergarten in St. Louis; and by 1878 Kate Douglas, afterwards Kate Douglas Wiggin, had established a free kindergarten in San Francisco. An important factor in the spread of the kindergarten was the exhibition of kindergarten work at the Philadelphia Exposition in 1876.

Wherever a teacher went to open a new field, there a new training school was started; and wherever there was a training school, Miss Peabody was considered indispensable. She must come to lecture at least once a year if the school was to have any standing at all. Fearful lest the material side be overstressed, spiritual aims were always her subject. The kindergarten was a force to set the feet of little children in the paths of righteousness so that they should never stray, and Elizabeth felt that she had at last found her vocation as she told this to these groups of earnest young women. She always ended her lecture by reciting parts of Wordsworth's "Ode on Immortality," and always there came into her mind the picture of Dr. Channing as he read her the poem for the first time. All their lives long, Miss Peabody's students would remember "the lovely expression of her face" and "the tender tones of her voice."

In 1870 Elizabeth Peabody established the first public kindergarten in the United States. To call it the first free kindergarten would be more accurate, because it was supported by gifts from public-minded people. For seven years the kindergarten was supported this way, and then the donors grew weary in well-doing. It was hoped that the Boston public school system would take over; but, although by this time kindergartens were a part of the New York schools, Boston was cautious. Elizabeth was by no means defeated. Her lectures, and Mary's writings, had won many influential friends for the kindergarten even in Boston. Mrs. Pauline

Agassiz Shaw, a wealthy woman, now shouldered the whole responsibility for the free kindergarten. With Miss Mary J. Garland as her assistant, she also established other free kindergartens for underprivileged children in different parts of the city.

Having read a little about Froebel, Miss Garland, a young Canadian, came to Boston in search of Miss Peabody. Like Miss Wheelock, she was told where to study and like Miss Wheelock, she later founded a famous school. All the leaders of the movement looked back the same way — to one woman. Elizabeth was often asked to pass upon graduates. It was the pride of many, and of Miss Wheelock in particular, to have a diploma signed by Miss Peabody.

Elizabeth had a slight stroke in 1877, and they warned her that she was now seventy-three and should not work so hard. But within a few weeks her brother Nathaniel announced that she had "recovered sufficiently to justify her venturing to Philadelphia in the interests of kindergarten instruction." Nathaniel remarked that his sister "bends or stoops a little" which was surely to be expected, but when he said that she looked "feeble" he was concerned with appearances only and could not see into her soul. There was nothing feeble about the spirit of Elizabeth Peabody, her will was unbending whatever the state of her back and it would take more than a stroke to so much as slow her down.

It was good strategy to have a big Froebel Union meeting in New York in 1878, because the Boston branch was already large and active. A good many of them could be depended upon to go to New York — Miss Peabody included of course. It was she who was organizing the meeting. But Mary had misgivings. Lizzie's eyesight had been failing lately and Mary had heard that those horsecars were driven scandalously fast in New York. There was no stopping Lizzie, of course, so her sister sent for Miss Wheelock, then a girl of nineteen. She was to take Miss Peabody to New York and see that nothing happened to her. Lucy Wheelock was flattered but anxious. Miss Peabody was not to go out on the street alone, Mrs. Mann said. At the meeting, she was positively not to wear that old dress of Miss Cushman's she was so fond of, but the new black silk which had just been made for her. Miss Wheelock promised to see to everything.

They stayed at Judge Peabody's, a cousin of Elizabeth's. All went well until the morning of the meeting and then Lucy Wheelock found that she had slept too long and too soundly. When she awoke, Miss Peabody was gone! She was off on her own in New York's fearsome traffic — whither, no one knew. But her sister Mary had known she would do it if she got a chance.

Miss Wheelock was frantic. But by breakfast time, there was Miss Peabody, serene and happy if a little out of breath. She had been to see the minister of the church where the meeting was to take place, because it had occurred to her that the room might not be properly made ready. There was that matter of the pitcher of water and the glass on the speaker's stand for example — suppose it should not be there! Yes, she had arrived a little early. She had pulled and pulled at the bell but nobody was up. A servant finally answered and after waiting awhile, Miss Peabody had seen the minister. It was all right about the church.

But in her excitement, Miss Wheelock forgot all about the new black silk dress — and when the meeting began Miss Peabody was wearing her old one just as she had intended to do all along. The elegant but conservative black silk went back to Boston still perfectly new and Miss Wheelock hardly dared to face Mrs. Mary Mann.

Mary was all this time just as much a part of the kindergarten movement as her sister. From 1873 until 1875, she and her sister brought out the *Kindergarten Messenger* with Mary, of necessity, doing most of the editorial work, since Elizabeth was so often away lecturing. Translations from German sources appearing in the magazine were almost all Mary's. The work was a Godsend to her, for in 1868 she had suffered one more loss, that of her oldest son. Writing in her "Journal of Remembrance" — "My beautiful Horace went to his father," she said. "Much as I prized him, how often I have felt, since he left me, that I did not estimate him at half his worth. . . ."

George and Benjamin Mann were both married and Mary realized that she should have been relieved to see them entering successfully into the adult world, but actually she missed their dependence upon her. She so loved to have someone to take care of! "I am left with nothing to do but amuse myself," she said. "I wish they had children but since they have not I must needs go after other people's children for that is the want of my nature. I visit kindergartens, and tell stories to the children, and think about it (the kindergarten) and write about it and wonder when the world will be better!"

The year was 1880 as Mary Mann sat at her desk writing these words, thinking about her life as a teacher; about her husband's great faith in education. Mary was ready to draw some conclusions. "It is not enough to cultivate the memory or even to enlighten the understanding. Out of the heart are the issues of life. . . . The introduction of the kindergarten is the first step, for the heart of the little child must be secured before it is corrupted by the world — and all other things can be added in due time. . . . When we look at the rapidity with which improvements and inventions succeed each other, may we not hope that a like rapidity will be discerned before long in the transformation of social conditions?"

So absorbed were both sisters in establishing kindergartens that it seemed as if, for once, Elizabeth could keep away from doubtful causes and avoid the clutches of impostors. But her heart was so pure and her impulses so generous that this was impossible, and if some magic spectacles could have been offered her enabling her to tell the true from the false she would have refused to use them, preferring to believe that every heart was true. Around 1883, Sarah Winnemucca Hopkins, or the "Princess Winnemucca," as she preferred to be called, put in her appearance around Boston and won over the susceptible Elizabeth. The usually more cautious Mary was also equally impressed. The "Princess" was an Indian woman with a true tale of grievances against the white race. The dramatic story of the Piutes, defeated, betrayed and driven into exile, appealed strongly to Mary Mann, and as the "Princess" talked, Mary seemed to see with her own eyes those tragic Indian women struggling down a long trail into a far country, their children dropping exhausted by the way, dying of hunger or disease.

Mary Mann had a good sense of plot and an interesting narrative style. She proceeded to write *Life among the Piutes; Their Wrongs and Claims*, and many people read her book with mounting excitement — and sent money to the cause as she suggested. Mary gave the Princess Winnemucca all the credit as the author, but the book was actually along the lines of a modern "true experience" story "as told to" some competent writer. Her reputation greatly enhanced by the success of the book, the Princess set about raising money for schools for Indian children — or at least that was what she said she would do with the funds when she saw how tremendously the idea appealed to Mrs. Mann and Miss Peabody.

Elizabeth hired halls and gave lectures with the Princess on the platform in full Indian regalia ready to tell her own story and sing a sad tribal song or two. It was a good show, people enjoyed it, and there was truth enough in the whole thing to fill the collection plates very well when they were passed around. The Princess finally returned to her people with a good-sized haul. Before she left, she made arrangements with Miss Peabody for further contributions to be sent to her.

Both Elizabeth and Mary continued to solicit funds and it was remarkable how well and how long they kept the cause alive. The American conscience was beginning to be troubled over exploitation of the Indians, and a dollar now and then made private citizens feel better. It was so much simpler than raising any sort of row with Congress. Elizabeth managed to send the Princess a hundred dollars a month for nearly six years! When the task of raising money became too much even for the indefatigable Elizabeth, the Princess complained bitterly. And then it was discovered that the schools she was supposed to be establishing had hardly been started! The money came too easily. The Princess could not tell exactly where it went.

People laughed at Lizzie over the affair of the Princess. It made no difference. Miss Peabody went right to Washington to see President Cleveland on behalf of the Piutes. Theirs was still a just cause, whether one representative proved worthy or not.

Miss Peabody was, of course, well over eighty when she went lobbying for the Indians. There was just one thing she had, so far, never found time to do — and that was to grow old.

CHAPTER TWENTY–SIX
Swifter than a Weaver's Shuttle

I HAVE an iron constitution and it stands much wear," said Mary Mann at the age of eighty. Her brother, Nathaniel, painted a different picture when he spoke of something never mentioned by Mary herself — her rheumatism. "Mary is not all the time confined to her bed but frequently takes her meals with her family and sits in her parlor an hour or so at a time. . . ." One of the reasons why Mary considered her illness too negligible to mention, one reason why she was content in spite of advancing age, was that her fondest desire had been gratified. When Mary was seventy-five, George, her second son, had a child. "I am living my life over again in this noble little grandson, whose 'dear Grandma' is the most beautiful music to my ears," she said. What other name could he have had save "Horace Mann"?

Whatever the years did to her body, Mary's mind remained clear and her sense of humor remained intact. She saw herself and her sister Lizzie pretty accurately. "We are rather dilapidated old ladies externally," she said, "but E. is one of those people who are immortally young in spirit and she circulates among her friends when she can get a helping arm, and continues to ply her pen assiduously." Elizabeth's pen was devoted to the cause of kindergartens as always these days, not to a description of Mary, which was a pity. A photograph of Mary Mann showed her not "dilapidated" in the least but exquisitely dressed as always in plain black with an outline of what she doubtless called "ruching" at the throat. Some of the longing, the anxiety, of an earlier daguerreotype was missing and her forehead was more serene. The shadows had increased around her deep-set eyes, but small steel-rimmed spectacles had not dimmed the twinkle. With the falling-away of flesh, the good bone structure of Mary's face was more evident, her Roman nose a dominant feature. It was an era of hideous photography but Mary Mann was still a charming woman, even in the picture.

Happy in spite of bodily pain, more self-assured than at any time in her life, Mary set to work to write her first novel — at eighty! She had always wanted to do it but she had never before had time. *Juanita*, her book was called, *a Romance of Real Life in Cuba Fifty Years Ago.* The book seemed to write itself, Mary said. It was the story of a beautiful slave girl, daughter of a Cuban-Spanish nobleman and a Moorish slave. Mary mentioned the Cuban custom of referring to a slave mistress and her children as a "holy family," a bitter Spanish jibe at both private morality and the Holy Church itself. Mary's heroine was free by law, her master supposed her ignorant of this and kept her enslaved — which she endured because of her hopeless passion for the son of the family. This young Cuban Spaniard, after becoming disillusioned concerning a girl of his own caste, at last returned the love of the slave girl. It was a daring book. It was an astounding book coming from a frail little lady of eighty, but Mary's only concession to public opinion came at the very end of her story when she had her star-crossed lovers killed in a slave insurrection before their intended marriage. The Morell family, under fictitious names of course, figured largely in the story, and Mary wove in many true incidents which gave her book life in spite of its somewhat stilted language.

How well Mary remembered the paralyzing homesickness she had suffered in that exotic island of Cuba as she thought constantly of the man she loved and had renounced! Now all the beauty she had seemed to miss came back to her and she wrote with joy of people and scenes she had known so long ago. She remembered only the hope in her heart when the first letter had come from Horace Mann at last — when she had learned that her sister Elizabeth was not in love with him and about to marry him. The voyage home had been a journey to meet him even though the way proved long.

Early in the new year the book was done. Mary laid aside the manuscript as she rested a little before embarking upon some new venture. Then suddenly she found herself upon one last voyage — this time, as her steadfast faith assured her, on her way to be united with Horace Mann forever. "My beloved, I will come and we will go on together," she had promised when first he left her. And on February 11, 1887, she kept her word.[1]

*   *   *

Her sister Elizabeth did not mourn for Mary. It would have been sacrilege. But she found herself strangely bewildered. After all, she was eighty-three herself, a ripe age, however young her spirit. The first thing she did after Mary's death was to lose the manuscript of Mary's novel. Now what was she to do, since Mary could not come and help her find it? But she reassured herself, as she scrabbled through her welter of pamphlets, letters, half-finished manuscripts of her own, begun and abandoned diaries, one after the other. "I am a very orderly person notwithstanding my habits," she said, just as she had said so long ago when she had found herself alone in Boston, Mary in Salem. It was curious how Elizabeth's habits always got the better of her orderliness when Mary happened to be away. When Mary returned — well, it was still more strange to reflect that Mary, who had so often gone away only to return, would not this time come back again. Elizabeth's eyes had a way of growing suddenly blurred, but it was just that these new spectacles were no good, she told herself angrily.

Mary had given the manuscript to the publisher herself, Elizabeth said, in an "Explanatory Note" which explained remarkably little. In any case, *Juanita* appeared in print in 1887 as though by a miracle. It was a good story and, had it appeared at the time of the antislavery agitation, it would have been widely read.

Although Sophia's death had not surprised Elizabeth, she had somehow counted on Mary to be a lifelong companion. In spite of Mary's illness, she was the younger and Elizabeth had felt sure that she, herself, would be the next to go. For some time she had been attending to matters long put off, as though preparing to go on a vacation. The first of these tasks was a book which had been written for pleasure just as much as Mary's novel was. *Reminiscences of William Ellery Channing* she called it, and she wanted it to be a fitting memorial to the man she had admired above all others. Elizabeth sent to friends for letters she had written; and masses of them came back to her, dating from the days of her girlhood. Of all the books she had ever written, Elizabeth probably enjoyed this one the most. Old people could be tiresome with their eternal dwelling upon the past, but Elizabeth was looking back for the first time in her life and she deserved the luxury. *Reminiscences of William Ellery Channing* was eulogistic, of course. Biographies were never otherwise, and when Elizabeth read over some of Mary's letters — written one summer in Newport when Mary was governess to the Channing children — there was nothing Elizabeth could use.

You could not say that Dr. Channing was "at times very facetious and tells conundrums"! You couldn't tell how the doctor ran after the butcher's boy to give him a letter to mail "but the butcher's boy rode by unmoved in spite of the Dr's beautiful voice," and Mary had laughed "to see the great little man kicking up his heels in vain." It would never do to admit that the sublime Dr. Channing spent half an hour "conversing about Macassa oil and its peculiar advantages." But Elizabeth could not help smiling a little, although Mary's flippancy still shocked her just as it had in other days.

It was still the prevailing fashion to use initials and dashes instead of people's names. However exasperating it might prove to succeeding generations, Elizabeth's public liked it, for it gave them a guessing game to play among their friends — and a game that they could win without too much effort, since Elizabeth's Boston was but an overgrown village where everyone knew all the neighbors. *Reminiscences* did fairly well, and this time the edition was not burned as *Record of a School* had been — to bring a loss instead of a profit.

When Theodore Parker became personally acquainted with Elizabeth (about 1843) he had said, "I never before knew in just what class to place her; now I see that she is a Boswell. Her office is to inquire and answer. 'What did they say? What are the facts?' A good analyst of character, a free spirit, kind, generous, noble — she has an artistic gift also. She may well be called 'the Narrative Miss Peabody.' " Here was Elizabeth, eulogized much to her surprise. And now she, in turn, proceeded happily to eulogize her friends. *Last Evening with Allston, and other papers* appeared in 1886. The story of her final call upon the artist was about all that was new in the book, but her essays, some from the *Dial*, some from the short-lived *Aesthetic Papers*, were new to what was by now a third generation of pupils — the kindergartners. There was an essay on Froebel especially for them. And again Elizabeth relived her past as she prepared an article on Brook Farm and her appreciation of Hawthorne's *Marble Faun*. She had lived in a Golden Age, and many of her contemporaries had been Olympians; some of them actually immortal. Whatever they were, Elizabeth still loved them all and took the greatest pleasure in presenting them in colors prettier than life, in stature heroic, every one.

There was one man whom Elizabeth had known well but about

whom she did not attempt to write. Perhaps this was because Alcott was still living and she felt she should not attempt, as yet, to tell of his life; perhaps it was because a eulogy of him would have come hard. Elizabeth still smarted, subconsciously, from her treatment at the Alcott dinner table where she was forbidden to converse — she to whom conversation was the breath of life. She had not by any means forgotten Alcott; when in 1879, the Concord School of Philosophy was started, Miss Peabody had been there.

When the School outgrew Alcott's study, and adjourned to the "Chapel," which looked like a large wooden box with gothic trimmings sprouting out of Alcott's garden, Elizabeth had been there, sitting on the hard seats. Alcott was the School and the School was Alcott. It was the vindication of his life and philosophy; it met for a session every summer for nine years, to his everlasting glory. But why Miss Peabody was not on the faculty from the first was a question most of the members asked each other and could not answer.

It was not that Alcott held it against Miss Peabody that she was closely connected with him at a disastrous turning point in his career. An entry in his diary for December 24, 1865, shows that they were good friends and that he fully appreciated her. "E. P. Peabody spends the day with me. Still the same sympathetic, serviceable, and knowing woman whom I have met from the first. The good purposes that she has furthered and brought to consummation during the last thirty years, who shall find out and celebrate? I think her one of the most generous souls that I have known, and a part of the life of New England."

Elizabeth herself had put her finger on the difficulty. There was discussion after each lecture in which she always eagerly took part. "I hated to have to refute one of his arguments," she said when she differed from Alcott. But she differed, and she refuted, every day.

Miss Peabody had finally been asked to lecture at the Concord School of Philosophy during the summer of 1882. She gave a paper on Milton, and she was as nervous about it as a young girl-graduate, much to her own surprise and consternation. She was even more surprised at her success. The paper caused a lively discussion and one of the things a Concord School session could use was liveliness. Elizabeth was booked in advance for the following year, to lecture on *Paradise Lost*, and everyone had a fine time discussing the personality of the Devil. Elizabeth also spoke on the "Philosophy of Education" and this lecture bore fruit — a second crop so to speak — when Lyman Abbot asked for an article for the *Christian Union* — "and promised to pay for it." One thing had not changed during the course of Elizabeth's long life. She could always get her work published, but her eternal struggle to get it paid for had never ceased.

While attending the Concord School of Philosophy, Elizabeth was a guest at the Emersons' each year. Mr. Emerson's pathetic loss of memory was something she could never bear to mention but when he was with her he seemed to remember a little better. Their long friendship was part of his past so that Miss Peabody helped that mysteriously closing door in his mind to remain open a little longer. And then, in 1884, Emerson was gone. Almost the whole program of the Concord School was devoted to him that year. There were fourteen lectures on his life and philosophy, and Elizabeth Peabody was asked to tell some of her personal recollections of the man whose tall, spare figure would no longer dominate the little platform in the chapel. "She was listened to with tearful interest," said Mrs. Anagnos, Julia Ward Howe's oldest daughter, who was there to write a record of the meeting.

Elizabeth looked about her at the subsequent meetings of the Concord School during the final four years of its existence and saw that she was now the last of her generation. The self-pity which so often descends along with white hair and arthritis upon those who have lived a long time was no part of Elizabeth's personality, however. She loved young people and hers was a cheerful, happy figure, photographed in the garden before the Chapel. Her ample figure resembled Queen Victoria's and she had much of a queen's dignity. Side curls like hers were no longer worn, but hers were thick and pure white, gaily defiant of time. Her near-sighted eyes had something of a squint, it must be admitted, but a lifelong habit of smiling had given them creases in the corners till they smiled of themselves. Her mouth had always been too small for the heavy chin, the square jaw and the fleshy face of General Palmer's great-granddaughter. It was firmer now, pleasant, but more than a little stubborn. She would no longer cry herself to sleep over Alcott's didactic attitude — she would refute him to her last breath. On the whole, Lizzie was wearing well; photographed among a modern generation, she looked well — like the good antique that she was.

During the last years of the Concord School, Miss Peabody had been observed to sleep sweetly in her chair on the platform during some of the longer lectures. At eighty-four she had a right to, and the younger generation, while they laughed, might have envied her. But no one could explain how she always awoke the minute the free discussion started. Pink-cheeked and rested from her little nap, she seemed somehow to have heard every word that had been said and her comments were illuminating and to the point.

When the Concord School of Philosophy finally came to an end, Elizabeth knew that some of the happiest experiences of her life were over. It had been "so delightful" she said, "to live with people who believe in you and are interested to understand your thought." But again, unlike most aging women, she did not complain or feel abused when the hurrying modern world rushed on ahead of her. She was right there herself, living in the future when she was in her eighties just as much as when she was nineteen. The cause for equal suffrage now claimed her enthusiasm, and it seemed to her that the franchise for women was another road leading straight to the perfectibility not only of man but of nations. Women, Elizabeth felt sure, would let conscience guide them. Vice, the demon rum and political corruption were all as good as licked. That women might be duped into voting for a political wolf in a public bene-factor's clothing never occurred to the pure-hearted Miss Peabody; but if anyone had brought up the point, she would have said that equal education would take care of that. She held Woman Suffrage meetings in her home, and she attended meetings elsewhere along with the equally ardent Julia Ward Howe.

There were those who laughed at Miss Peabody, of course. It is easy to be funny about the good and virtuous. Henry James's book *The Bostonians* was read and taken much more seriously than now seems possible, considering the incredible dialogue, the unconvinc-ing characters created so obviously for the sole purpose of proving the case against equal suffrage. The fashionable throng in Mrs. Fields's drawing room, where she still held court after the death of her husband, tittered among themselves as they spoke of Miss Birds-eye — so obviously Miss Peabody to the life. Mr. James denied it, of course, but his fictitious Miss Birdseye gave him away by proving to be the only character in the book even remotely alive. Shabby-genteel, ridiculously altruistic and even pro-women's-rights she might be — but she was also the salt of the earth.

"There were amusing traits of Miss Peabody given," wrote Annie Fields in her diary after a successful dinner party. Longfellow had said that, one evening after a lecture, Miss Peabody was given a lift in his carriage. It was dark and there were several passengers and she did not know he was there till someone spoke to him by name. Then she said, "Mr. Longfellow, can you tell me which is the best Chinese grammar?" Longfellow could not help her. He had kept up his Italian but he was not, so late in life, optimistically inclined to take up a difficult new language – nor was anyone else in that laughing group around Mrs. Fields's dinner table. But neither did anyone there realize that Lizzie had found one of the greatest secrets of staying young – the habit of always learning something new. Then there was the story about Miss Peabody's bumping into a tree while crossing Boston Common. "I saw it," she had explained, "but I did not realize it." This was perfectly rational transcendental talk, even if most of the people who could have understood it were now dead and Elizabeth Peabody had lived into another age. Could she have been as immortal as she seemed, she would soon have adopted a new lingo and would have explained about her subconscious – and the tree.

Born just four years after the beginning of the nineteenth century, Elizabeth Peabody now watched that century approach its end. She saw much around her to uphold her belief in perfectibility, at least in the material world. She now lived in a modern apartment in Jamaica Plain to be near Mary's son, her beloved nephew George. "Genteel" had been the word the advertisers used to describe houses in Boston when Elizabeth first took her family there in 1828. They were "modern" now, with "swell fronts" and steam heat. The electric streetcar ran close by Elizabeth's apartment, or she would never have consented to leave Bowdoin Street. She delighted in the trolleys even though she worried a little lest the motorman should forget to let her off at her corner. Naturally, she could not remember to signal to him because her mind was always on higher things. But motormen and conductors were such nice boys! They always took care of Miss Peabody, and she was sure she had seen them in kindergarten somewhere only a few years previously.

The street railway turned country into city, and friends of Elizabeth's turned country estates into city lots with profit. Then there were the railroads and the Lowell mills, bringing wealth to Boston families all of whom were Miss Peabody's old acquaintances – the women her former pupils more often than not. Elizabeth had no quarrel with wealth. She had attempted to acquire a competence herself, seeing wealth just around the corner time and again, all her life. She felt she knew just what to do with money if any of it should ever come her way, and so she had no hesitation in going to her wealthy friends and giving them the benefit of her ideas. Miss Peabody was a walking encyclopedia of worthy causes, and that she was sometimes something of a pest goes without saying. But no one could accuse her of insincerity, and many a wealthy friend envied her the happiness which was hers; not to be purchased anywhere at any price.

Elizabeth persuaded a businessman to leave some money in his will to one of her favorite causes. Then Lizzie got a look at some actuarial tables prepared by another early acquaintance of hers, Nathaniel Bowditch. She had never before heard of "life expectancy" but she went right back to the businessman's office and showed him that he had already outlived his allotted span and asked him to give away the money at once — it was long overdue. This time, however, Lizzie's enthusiasm carried her too far. The man refused to give a cent and cut the codicil out of his will.

With Robert Hallowell Gardiner, her former employer long years ago in Maine, Miss Peabody's luck was different and even more unexpected. In Mr. Gardiner's opinion, Miss Peabody was "wholly devoid of common sense." He remembered that nearly fifty years previously she "had imbibed many of the fallacies of the day and was for some time a member of a Communist Society in the neighborhood of Boston." (These were the gentle, religious-minded Brook Farmers, whom Elizabeth never actually joined.) But Gardiner contributed now to a cause which Elizabeth Peabody never in her life promoted. "Tired of aiding her abortive schemes . . . some gentlemen subscribed to an annuity for her," Gardiner said, and he was one of the "gentlemen." This was something that Miss Peabody deserved, but Gardiner was showing less than his usual intelligence if he thought he could buy her off, so that she would not again attempt to awaken his social conscience. It would not take Lizzie long to find someone who needed money more than Gardiner did, and then she would be right back to see him about it.

The twentieth century was upon the horizon and Elizabeth Peabody was almost ninety years old as she lay in her bed and listened to the bells ringing in the new year — 1894. She had seen a great deal happen in her ninety years and she was proud of the machine age with its miraculous telephone, its rails, its steamers. It would never do to wonder if man were as perfectible spiritually as materially. One must have faith and work hard. Was not the abolition of slavery a great forward step? But the fight for the emancipation of women had still to be won, and Elizabeth's newest and dearest project, world peace, required valiant effort if it were to succeed. A Universal Peace Congress had met at the Chicago World's Fair only the previous year and had proposed the idea of an international board of arbitration. Elizabeth would have been there if she had not somehow seemed just a little too tired to take the trip. She must organize some meetings now, and perhaps give a talk on this arbitration idea. But again, this New Year's Night, she felt very tired. It was the only thing she ever minded about old age.

During the first few days of January, there was no Miss Peabody out upon the icy Boston streets bound for the kindergarten for the blind near her home, or for a suffrage meeting, or to hire a hall for a World Peace symposium. People said that Miss Peabody must be getting a little sense about staying indoors in bad weather.

But on January fourth, the boy Mary Mann had adored, but who had forgotten his grandmother, was told that his Aunt Lizzie would not be in to see him any more. She would not be asking him those searching questions about his schoolwork which had been such a source of dismay at times. Aunt Lizzie had been so long a part of his world! Incredible as it seemed — they said that she was dead. They led thirteen-year-old Horace Mann to where a woman almost ninety lay in her coffin. Many years later he remembered that he looked at her, not in fear but in grave surprise. "Why, my Aunt Lizzie was beautiful!" he said.

They had the funeral for Elizabeth at the Church of the Disciples which her dear friend, James Freeman Clarke, had discussed in the shop in West Street when it was but an ideal in his mind. James Freeman Clarke was dead now, as were most of the devoted friends and latter-day disciples. The church was still liberal, however, for a woman was allowed to speak a eulogy for Miss Peabody along with Frank Sanborn and the other men. She was Mrs. Ednah Cheney, novelist, educator, friend of Concord School of Philosophy days. It did not so much matter what she said. A woman had spoken in church, Saint Paul notwithstanding, and Elizabeth would have been pleased.

All three of the Peabody sisters had at one time or another lived in Concord; Sophia in joy and in sorrow, Mary during the years of rebuilding her life after the loss of her husband. Elizabeth was there the least, perhaps, but now she came to stay. They laid her in the Sleepy Hollow cemetery, the only one of the sisters to be buried there. It was fitting, however, since through Emerson she had found Concord her "Mount of Transfiguration" not once but many times. Friends came forward asking to contribute to a monument to Miss Peabody, but a simple stone was selected.[2] The money which might have bought some marble monstrosity was used instead to found Elizabeth Peabody House on Charles Street, Boston.[3] Here Elizabeth Peabody's memory could live on among succeeding generations of teachers and of children. "Among children she was in her kingdom and of her kingdom," her friends remembered.

Freed from ancient fears of retribution after death, man could go forward to create a new devil in his own image by means of wars — with perfectibility expressed in perfect destruction. At Elizabeth Peabody House, and wherever devoted teachers look hopefully for signs of immortality in children, Elizabeth Peabody's own belief must prevail. A still small voice will still be heard and man will attempt perfectibility in God's image. A pure flame such as Elizabeth's can be covered deep in ashes — and be found alive and ready to rekindle a fire even after the longest night.

Notes

CHAPTER 1: *Cuba Journey*

1. Mrs. Clarke's famous boardinghouse is usually spoken of as being on Ashburton Place, but 3 Somerset Court is the address to which Sophia sent letters to her sisters. From *Nomenclature of Streets*, printed by the City of Boston in 1879, comes the explanation. In 1809 Somerset Court led from Somerset Street, west; in 1846 it was extended to Bowdoin Street and the name was changed to Ashburton Place.

CHAPTER 2: *I Hear the Drums*

1. Brigadier General Palmer was born in England in 1716, and died in Boston, 1788. He had three children, the oldest of whom was the invalid Elizabeth who finally married her cousin, Joseph Cranch, but died childless. The second daughter, Mary, never married, and it is from the third child and only son that the Peabody sisters of Salem are descended on their mother's side.

Quartermaster General Joseph Pearse Palmer, son of the old general, was born in 1750 and died in 1797. He and the dashing Betsey Hunt had nine children. Joseph, the oldest, was lost at sea and Edward, a third son, was drowned in the Connecticut River at the age of fifteen. Five sisters and two other brothers married and had children, providing the Peabody sisters with numerous cousins who figure prominently in all their letters. Through Mother Peabody's youngest sister Catherine, known as "Aunt Putnam," comes the story of the loss of Friendship Hall and its acquisition by Hancock. The story is colored by Palmer pride, yet the details are convincing. Two of Aunt Putnam's descendants, Frederic Tupper and Helen Tyler Brown, edited old diaries for *Grandmother Tyler's Book, the Recollections of Mary Palmer Tyler*, and it was published in 1925 by Putnam — the firm established by a son of Aunt Putnam, that "Cousin George" who was helpful to Sophia Hawthorne in later life. In *Grandmother Tyler's Book* is a genealogical chart from which I have drawn facts concerning Palmer ancestry, as well as the story of Friendship Hall. Descriptions of Friendship Hall are also from a letter written by Sophia Amelia Peabody when she was twelve years old and had made a visit to Quincy.

2. Elizabeth Palmer Cranch was childless. She adopted her niece Amelia, one of the sisters of Mrs. Peabody, when the Palmer family lost their fortune. The little girl was seven years old when she made the trip to West Point alone, carrying in a brown pocket handkerchief one frock, a cotton shirt and a pair of stockings. An acquaintance of the family took her to New York and, after some delay, put her aboard a barge going up the Hudson. It was evening when the bargeman set her ashore at West Point and told her to walk along the road till she came to her aunt's house. It grew dark, and the child saw no house, and at last her courage failed her and she began to cry. Her aunt heard the sound of crying in the darkness and found her.

3. Mary Palmer married Royall Tyler, a brilliant young lawyer and playwright who had been engaged to Abigail, the daughter of John Adams. Abigail Adams jilted Tyler, and Mary Palmer was always indignant at the insult, delighted as she was to marry him herself. She was born in 1775; he, in 1757.

4. In *Nathaniel Hawthorne and His Wife*, Julian Hawthorne states that Sophia Amelia Peabody was born September 21, 1811. According to the records of the South Church of Salem, however, she was baptized on October 1, 1809.

CHAPTER 3: *Kennebec Kingdom*

1. Spelling of Hawthorne: In 1825 the name was spelled "Hathorne." By 1831, Nathaniel was signing himself "Hawthorne." See *The American Notebooks by Nathaniel Hawthorne*, edited by Randall Stewart. Perhaps Hawthorne did this to insure the pronunciation that he liked, perhaps he thought it would look well as the name of an author.

2. The story of "Ebe" Hathorne at Mrs. Peabody's school was written for Mr. F. B. Sanborn, who was preparing *Hawthorne and His Friends*, and who applied to Elizabeth Peabody for any Hawthorne reminiscences he could use. Elizabeth wrote of her own mother also in Henry Barnard's *American Journal of Education*. (Elizabeth was nearly eighty years old when she wrote these family reminiscences, so if her dates were sometimes a little inaccurate, it was understandable.)

3. If a recluse is a person who never steps out of doors, then Mrs. Hawthorne was not, for she went from Salem to Sebago Lake and back when Hawthorne was a boy. If a person who never seeks friendship is a recluse, then she was, and so Salem thought her; so Elizabeth remembered her in after years.

4. Salem records, as printed in *Vital Statistics*.

5. Descriptions of the Kennebec country are from firsthand observations made on a special visit to the two towns of Hallowell and Gardiner. The gray stone Episcopal church, built by Robert Hallowell Gardiner,

still stands, looking very English indeed in its New England setting. A Gardiner mansion, in the same dark granite as the church, has replaced the white house with its classic portico and balanced wings which Elizabeth knew, and which later burned. Within a formal garden, in the midst of hayfields overlooking the Kennebec, it looks romantic and unreal, like the setting for a Jane Austen novel gone astray and awaiting in vain a cast of characters in nineteenth-century dress.

6. The Vaughan house remains as Elizabeth and Mary Peabody knew it, except that succeeding generations have made additions and alterations with a view to their comfort, and without that affectation which preserves everything old, no matter how unlovely and uncomfortable it may be. Astonishingly unchanged are the formal gardens behind the house with their charming little white summerhouses, the grassy paths still leading to the woodland walk. Here, the brook rushes over ledges far below, and only the gristmill is gone.

7. Needless to say, I have made every effort to identify "L.B." A search of vital statistics for Gardiner, Hallowell and neighboring towns reveals no suicides and few deaths of men having the right initials, and living within Elizabeth's generation. There is a suggestion in letters that the ladies of the Gardiner family admired Elizabeth for rejecting a life of ease in order to do good in the world. This implies that her suitor was wealthy, as was, for example, the Bridge family. Following the clue, "Bridge, my steamboat beau," I found in the Bridge genealogy the following account of one Levi Bridge:

"Like his ancestors, he was in his early life a man of varied capabilities and diversified activities. An unfortunate and severe mental affliction came upon him and for many years he was absolutely unfitted for the lines of business to which he devoted himself. He finally recovered but with diminished power and endurance. He never married and, having a tender heart toward the unfortunate, and especially children, his own misfortunes led him constantly to think of others."

This Levi Bridge was born in Winchendon, Massachusetts, and died in Cambridge, but he belonged to the "Maine branch" of the Bridge family and was associated in a charitable project with one of his Augusta cousins, which suggests that he visited Maine and knew them well. But he was born in 1784. Would the nineteen-year-old Elizabeth have known "the feeling of love" for a man who was thirty-nine when they met? It was an age when such marriages were considered suitable and she always found herself attracted to older men. Perhaps she recognized his temporary insanity as a flight from reality — hence, a "leaving of this world."

It is my hope that someone reading this book will be moved to look through old letters and records and solve this mystery, and I shall not be disappointed if this theory is exploded — just so long as the truth appears.

CHAPTER 4: *Eden in Miniature*

1. The *Dictionary of American Biography* is always entertaining, occasionally in error but rarely excessively eulogistic. In the case of William Russell, however, one would suppose that the gentleman wrote the article himself. The basis for my adverse opinion lies in letters from Elizabeth to Mary and from Mrs. Russell to Elizabeth among Mr. Horace Mann's collections of letters known as "Cuba Journal."

2. This quotation and the greater part of the material for the next chapter are from a diary in the Berg Collection: "Diary of Sophia Amelia Peabody Kept in Boston in 1829 when she was 20 years old."

CHAPTER 5: *New England Barbizon*

1. The collecting of early American illustrated books for children is a fascinating field, not as yet unduly exploited. To the few who are interested, Francis Graeter is a favorite artist, his woodcuts showing a good deal of merit.

2. Thomas Doughty was born in Philadelphia in 1793 and died in 1856. He was in the leather business and took up art when he was twenty-seven to achieve a notable but brief success. The British minister to the United States paid him $2500 for a landscape, a high price at that time. Doughty died in poverty in New York, however, ill and embittered by the loss of his popularity. His paintings were of high quality, and are now much prized. There are comparatively few Doughty canvases, and in *The History of American Painting* by Isham and Cortissoz (Macmillan), it is stated that this is because Doughty produced little. The number of pictures by Doughty which Sophia saw exhibited in Boston, at the Athenæum and elsewhere, contradicts this opinion. It seems to me that the reason why there are so few Doughty canvases is to be found in an item in the *Boston Evening Transcript* in 1830. All of Doughty's paintings and furniture were "lost aboard the Philadelphia packet *Flora* in the last gale." The *Transcript* proceeds to scold the Boston Athenæum for failing to purchase Doughty's "Fishing Party."

3. Because of evidence from diaries, the date of the costume and the painting technique, I feel certain that the portrait of Sophia reproduced in this book through the courtesy of Hildegarde Hawthorne is the one painted by Chester Harding in Boston in 1830, when Sophia was twenty-one. A detail engraving from the portrait, but with costume changed and features altered, was made later, and has been previously reproduced.

4. A portrait of Washington Allston by Chester Harding hangs in the Providence Athenæum. And in the reading room of the Massachusetts Historical Society is a portrait of Allston by Harding. The two are identical as to face and pose of head. There are slight differences in the costume and in the lower part of the canvas generally. The

Providence portrait was purchased "by thirteen friends through the efforts of Rev. E. B. Hall and presented to the Athenæum in 1859." According to the Athenæum records their portrait "was painted by Mr. Harding for his own use and pleasure as he [Allston] appeared a short time before his death." Mr. George B. Chase presented the Boston portrait to the Massachusetts Historical Society "in the name of Mrs. George Tyler Bigelow, an unfinished but admirable portrait of Washington Allston, purchased at the sale of the artist's effects." Of course Harding might have painted two almost identical portraits. But it is shown in letters in the Berg Collection that he gave Sophia Peabody permission to copy his Allston portrait. Sophia went to his studio to work, using his canvas and paints, presumably. There is no indication that she brought home her work, or that Elizabeth sold it for her, as she sold so many. Did she leave it unfinished?

5. King's Chapel was the Peabody sisters' church, their mother's and that of their grandparents, but, although it was never announced, Elizabeth always knew when Dr. Channing was to preach at Federal Street Church, and would be there accordingly.

6. George Flagg's father was Washington Allston's half-brother. George Flagg was born in 1816 and died in 1897. He was considered a child prodigy. In 1834 Elizabeth wrote to her sisters in Cuba that George had found a wealthy patron in New York, "Who gave him board and even a room to paint in, in his house. He is now going to send him to Europe and *support him there!* He has just painted the Execution of Lady Jane Grey for this gentleman." This gentleman was Luman Reid and Flagg became a popular genre painter, member of the National Academy of Design. Well known among his later works was "Laying the Atlantic Cable," "Landing of the Pilgrims," "The Little Match Girl," but one painting must have interested Sophia more than all the others. It was "The Scarlet Letter."

7. Salem, the town which Hawthorne both loved and hated, makes amends for past injustice by doing him great honor. At the Essex Institute are two interesting portraits of Hawthorne and a fine collection of his letters. But I went there in search of paintings by his wife. Inquiry in the Art Department had all the thrill of a treasure hunt, both for the Institute and for me. Listed under the name of "S. A. Peabody" were two canvases, but no one up to that moment had realized that "S. A. Peabody" was Sophia Amelia, wife of Nathaniel Hawthorne! There was still further suspense for me, personally. Suppose the paintings should be bad! One canvas was very poor, indeed. It was marked (in Sophia's hand) *"Copy of an English landscape."* She had not finished it and there is evidence of haste and distaste for the original. The other was more beautiful work than I had dared hope I should find her capable of doing! This second canvas is 18 × 21 inches, framed very simply in a broad uncarved gold molding. (Sophia always selected her own

frames.) The picture has a nineteenth-century air of elegance, artificial but charming. It is no farmhouse primitive full of bad drawing and rugged sincerity. Sophia's work was parlor painting and it must have looked exactly right in the fashionable rooms of her wealthy Salem and Boston friends. Essex Institute acquired the pictures from "Miss Amory."

Sophia was always careful not to take personal credit for her copies. This canvas is marked as follows: on the wooden stretcher, *Fourth picture Begun painting 9th 1832 painted in 70 hours*. And on the board backing the canvas, S. A. PEABODY is printed in ink but in letters resembling Sophia's delicate handwriting. I have not assumed that the picture is an original composition, however, without searching through the photograph collection at the library of the Metropolitan Museum of Art in New York for a Rosa or a Doughty, or some other landscape of the period, of which this might be a copy. I did not find one. The work is reminiscent, as a young girl's work is apt to be, but that is all.

Endless also is the search for further canvases by Sophia Peabody. Here is a list, gleaned from letters, of pictures she painted and which Elizabeth sold for her — or hoped to sell. Perhaps this will lead to the discovery of a valuable family treasure! Perhaps some museum may not mind having a rather obscure Italian landscape dis-authenticated but made far more valuable from a "human interest" standpoint by the discovery of S. A. PEABODY on the back.

"The Fall of Reichenbach." (Probably copied from Salvator Rosa.)
"Sappho."
"Temple of Paestum" and "Galileo's Villa" from Rogers's *Italy*. (A screen, or small screens, with ivory handles.) Signature should be S. A. H., or Sophia Hawthorne, perhaps. Other screens might have been signed S. A. Peabody earlier and sold for the benefit of the blind.)
"Flight into Egypt." (May have been bought by Theodore Parks or Mrs. Philbrick.)
"Landscape, by Salvator Rosa." (Exhibited at the Athenæum in 1834. Possibly bought by Mrs. Rodman of New Bedford.)
"Florimel, by Allston." (The original seems to have been owned by Miss Rawlins of Salem.)
"Jessica, by Allston."
Four original landscapes. (Whether all of these were finished is not clear, but it would seem so. It might have been one of these which was loaned to George Ripley and his wife, the former Sophia Dana, and which they kept, having understood that Elizabeth meant it as a gift.)

Sophia continued to paint and to sell copies of her paintings after she lived at the shop in West Street but, since the sisters were all living in the same place, letters are scarce and there is no record of her work.

CHAPTER 6: *"Dear Mr. M."*

1. Jared Sparks (president of Harvard 1849–1853) was working on the fourth of his twelve-volume *Writings of George Washington* at this time. Sparks was for a brief time a minister; his disposition was not improving, and Horace Mann called him "The Right Reverend Rude Rough" because of his remarks to Mary Peabody, who had expressed antislavery ideas.

The first Mrs. Sparks died in 1835 and in 1839 he married Mary Crowninshield Silsbee, Salem heiress. She had never been a favorite of the Peabody sisters or their friends. Lydia Haven described her as having "her head caught in a snarl of laces . . . rigged out in a gown that had the appearance of just kindling into a blaze" — her manners a "torrent of affectation."

2. In quoting Elizabeth's letter to Sophia from the Horace Mann Collection, I have taken the liberty of paragraphing. Postage was high, paper expensive, and Elizabeth always crowded every word she could get onto a page, paragraphing never, never hesitating to write at a different angle over lines already set down. Sometimes she cross-hatched in three directions. When she felt like it, she could punctuate, but when she warmed to her work, commas became dashes, as I have shown in this passage.

3. It took Elizabeth well over a year to find out what Lydia's husband had against Horace Mann but on June 10th, 1834, she wrote to Mary in Cuba: "Dear Mr. M. came and I contrived to make him tell me the history of his acquaintance with the Haven family. Mr. Mann said he never liked Judge Haven, that Mrs. Haven was patronizing because of her aristocratic family." Sam Haven had two unmarried sisters. "Catherine had charm, drawing you out in spite of yourself. Elizabeth died and Mr. Mann stopped coming — but took it up again and then the Judge and Sam began to question the motive of his visiting there, so he stopped going." Elizabeth proceeded to have a long talk with Catherine Haven, then Mrs. Frank Hilliard, and became convinced that "the past was all friendship." She next attempted to make Sam eat his words and admit that Mr. Mann was no philanderer. But Elizabeth had succeeded in proving that Mr. Mann was indeed "irresistible to women," and particularly to sisters!

CHAPTER 7: *Cuba Journals*

1. The first volume of Sophia's letters, called "Cuba Journal," disappeared and it was thought that Hawthorne burned it on that day in June, 1853, when he "burned great heaps of old letters and papers . . ." Both volumes were, however, given to Rose Hawthorne Lathrop and still belong to members of the Hawthorne family. They have been very kindly lent me by Beatrix Hawthorne Smyth, granddaughter of Nathaniel Hawthorne.

2. The letters from Elizabeth to Mary in Cuba, also known as "Cuba Journal," belong to Mr. Horace Mann, having come to him through his grandmother, Mary Peabody Mann. Mr. Mann thinks it was his Great-aunt Elizabeth herself who arranged them in more or less chronological order and sewed them together, not very skillfully, with coarse black thread. They, with their answers from Cuba, form a third volume and tell an entrancing story.

CHAPTER 8: *Temple School*
(*The material for this chapter is almost entirely from Elizabeth's "Cuba Journal."*)

1. The date when Elizabeth gave her first lectures, or "Reading Parties," is from letters to her from Lydia Sears, afterwards Mrs. Sam Haven. The first letter has only the year, 1827: "I am thankful you are going to have a historical school. I wish I could be your scholar. I am only afraid you will get tired to death doing so much." And the second letter says: "I feel as if I were losing the breath of life not to be at your Thursday afternoon sermons."

2. In *The Poets of Transcendentalism* George Willis Cooke includes thirteen of Ellen Sturgis's poems. Two of her lines were much quoted by her contemporaries:

> I slept and dreamed that life was beauty —
> I woke and found that life was duty.

When Elizabeth told of the duel over the beautiful Marian Marshall, she said that one of the principals was a Robert Hooper and that Ellen Sturgis was greatly distressed. Ellen married a Robert Hooper, who became a Boston physician.

3. The figures from Alcott's account book are given in *Pedlar's Progress: The Life of Bronson Alcott* by Odell Shepard. The description of Temple School is similar to that found in the introduction to *Record of a School*, and also in *Pedlar's Progress*, so I have used passages from the "Cuba Journal" which add to or which differ from other sources.

4. Sophia wrote a special account of her departure from Cuba just for Hawthorne. This interesting manuscript is the property of Mr. Manning Hawthorne, who has very kindly given me permission to use it.

Sophia felt that she had "inspired Hawthorne's genius" when he used the incident of a young girl who cleaned an ancient, discolored picture in his short story, *Edward Randolph's Portrait*.

5. My identification of Caroline Fernandez is from "Cuba Journal."

CHAPTER 9: *The House in Charter Street*

1. The original door of the house in Charter Street is now at the Essex Institute. The house is still standing and is known as the "Dr.

Grimshawe House," because Hawthorne made it the scene of *Dr. Grimshawe's Secret.*

2. Elizabeth considered that she lived in Salem at this time. In a copybook in the Berg Collection, she wrote: "In 1836 I went to Salem to live after leaving Mr. Alcott's school and house and lived on Charter Street for four years — except occasional visits and for one season at West Newton with Nath¹ about 1838. During these years Wellington died in N. Orleans and George returned from there to die after two years' lingering in paralysis (a word is illegible) as we learned after his death by consumption of the spinal marrow — It was during these years that we became acquainted with Mr. Hawthorne and these letters were written to me while I was away at Newton." The letters to which Elizabeth referred were dispersed and have reappeared in various collections.

3. My transcript of Elizabeth's letter to Alcott is direct from the Alcott papers and differs in only a word or two from that of Mr. Odell Shepard's in *Pedlar's Progress.* As Alcott's writing is most difficult to read, I am grateful to Mr. Shepard for his first translation.

4. Elizabeth loved to tell the tale of Hawthorne's first call and his subsequent first sight of Sophia. She was vague about the date, however, so it was a discovery to find in the Mann Collection the letter from Mary to George in New Orleans, with its date at the top.

5. Curiously enough, one of Hawthorne's many portrait painters gave him brown eyes. Mrs. Clifford Smyth tells me that her father, Julian Hawthorne, owned the portrait and used to point out the mistake and tell her that Nathaniel Hawthorne's eyes were really deep blue.

CHAPTER 10: *Year of Years*

1. Hawthorne's love letters have been privately printed by the Society of the Dofobs. They make delightful reading but no great pains were taken to decipher illegible words or to restore words inked out, probably by Sophia in after years.

CHAPTER 11: *The Shop in West Street*

1. Elizabeth herself was vague about the opening date of her shop and other sources give various dates. A letter in the Manuscript Room at the Boston Public Library, written by Sophia Dana Ripley, clears up the point.

2. In Barnard's *American Journal of Education,* Elizabeth wrote of West Street: "Those were very living days for me. Being so much occupied as I was at this time, I was obliged to deny myself to my friends, except on Wednesday evenings, and I may be said to have set the fashion in Boston of having regular reception evenings."

CHAPTER 12: *Wedding at West Street*

1. The Old Manse in Concord, Massachusetts, is open to visitors and they come streaming in of a summer's day, cars with licenses from far-

away states lining the driveway. At the Manse is a copy of the rare edition of "The Gentle Boy" containing Sophia's illustration and Hawthorne's dedication to her. In Hawthorne's study and in the dining room are window panes inscribed as I have quoted but these are facsimiles, the originals being put away for safe-keeping.

2. These lines are from "The Exequy" by Henry King, Bishop of Chichester, 1657.

3. Thomas Wentworth Higginson, in *Cheerful Yesterdays*, speaks of the colorful costumes at Brook Farm. Sophia wrote in letters of the fact that Hawthorne continued to wear his blue linen smock in the garden at Concord.

4. The Hawthorne Notebooks kept in part by Sophia are in the Morgan Library in New York. From these come the stories of the first quarrel and Sophia's great joy in the coming of spring. Many pages of Sophia's entries have been cut away and presumably destroyed but enough remains to give an intimate and charming picture — and also to make it reasonable to surmise that the missing pages concerned her miscarriage. In a letter to her mother, Sophia indignantly refutes Elizabeth's theory that she was never pregnant and had no miscarriage at all.

CHAPTER 13: *Again a West Street Wedding*

1. Horace Mann was the third of five children. A brother, Stephen, and a sister, Lydia, never married, but Mann's brother Thomas had nine children. Three of them died in the year 1825. In 1836 Thomas Mann died as did another of his children. Their uncle Horace then assisted in the education of his niece, Maria, who became "a teacher for half a century." He also helped Eliza, Sara Ann, Ellen, Thomas and Charlotte M., whose name and the date of her birth (1832) suggest that she was named for Horace Mann's first wife.

Horace Mann's sister Rebecca Pennell was left a widow with four children in 1824. Of these, Calvin, Rebecca and Eliza are frequently mentioned in letters of Mary Peabody Mann and were educated by their uncle, Rebecca and Eliza becoming teachers.

CHAPTER 14: *Paradise Lost*

1. This description of Sophia is from a pamphlet, *Some Reminiscences of Old Concord*, by Priscilla Rice Edes. Her misunderstanding of Hawthorne was probably a typical neighbor's attitude toward an author who never explained himself. She said, "So with love, beauty and no stint, his material desires satisfied, what need had he for spiritual philosophy?"

2. Putnam afterward turned *Mosses from an Old Manse* over to Ticknor and Fields.

CHAPTER 15: *Famous Husband*

1. The little red cottage in Lenox was on the Tappan estate. Before her marriage, Mrs. William A. Tappan had been Caroline Sturgis, a

transcendentalist poet like her sister Ellen Sturgis Hooper. Rose Haw-thorne Lathrop, in *Memories of Hawthorne*, writes of an unhappy situation. The Hawthornes had planted a garden beside the red cottage as they had at the Manse and they supposed that they were free to do so and also to use the fruit from the trees in their dooryard. Mrs. Tap-pan felt otherwise, stopping their servant to look in the basket she carried, questioning her concerning the Hawthornes' use of fruit and vegetables. Mrs. Tappan, born to wealth and having married wealth, regarded Sophia's seventy-five dollars' rent as a mere token payment — while Sophia learned that there is such a thing as too good a bargain. Rose Hawthorne Lathrop quotes one of Hawthorne's masterly letters covering the situation. He summed up his whole philosophy when he said to the Tappans, "I infinitely prefer a small right to a great favor."

The Tappan estate was known as "Highwood" in Hawthorne's time, but it now bears the name "Tanglewood," which Hawthorne made famous. It is the gift of Mrs. Gorham Brooks and Miss Mary Aspinwall Tappan to the Boston Symphony Orchestra. At Tanglewood, then, the great Berkshire Music Festivals are held with as many as thirty-eight thousand music lovers making the pilgrimage to Lenox each summer.

The red cottage, although considered by Hawthorne and his neighbors to be in Lenox, was actually just over the Stockbridge line. It was burned in 1891, but in 1948 it was rebuilt in exact replica (externally) through the generosity of the National Federation of Music. Within are prac-tice rooms for the use of the Berkshire Music Center, a school for ad-vanced music students conceived and conducted by Serge Koussevitzky.

CHAPTER 16: *Congressman's Wife*

1. In 1828, George Combe published his *Constitution of Man* which was widely read and highly praised in the United States. It was based upon "phrenology" but phrenology was not at that time a matter of colored charts and gypsy fortunetellers; it was a first groping effort toward a study of the different functions of parts of the brain and an effort at understanding mental strength and mental illness. Horace Mann was tremendously impressed by the *Constitution of Man*, and when Combe came to the United States to lecture, Mann sought his acquaintance. The two had much in common and became close friends, carrying on a correspondence until the death of Mr. Combe. When Mann planned his trip to Europe with his bride, Mary Peabody, he wrote to George Combe, who cordially invited him for a visit but pointed out the fact that Mann had omitted to tell him so much as the name of his fiancée, who she was or where she came from. Playfully Combe suggested that he be informed what fortunate woman had consented to become a Mann.

2. Mrs. Peabody named no names in the letter which I have quoted but Rebecca Stanley Mann, mother of Horace Mann, had died in 1837.

3. Daniel Drayton was the captain of the sloop *Pearl* taken into

custody in the lower Chesapeake on April 16, 1848, with seventy-six slaves aboard. Drayton was under indictment on the charge of stealing and transporting slaves, and Mann's first move was to show that the slaves had not been stolen but had run away. Dr. Samuel Gridley Howe, in a letter to Horace Mann published in the *New England Quarterly* for September 1943, said: "No man in the country will make more out of a bad case than you can."

Horace Mann did very well with his bad case. Among the points he made, he argued that the color of a man's skin was not proof that he was a slave. The criminal court decided against this! Mann argued that it was not larceny to induce slaves aboard a vessel with the promise of freedom and he showed that neither the owner of the *Pearl* nor her captain planned to sell the slaves. Again the lower court decision went against Mann but the circuit court reversed the decision.

Horace Mann was bitterly disappointed, however. He had argued that slavery was unconstitutional, and on this point the court did not uphold him. He had failed to change the course of history, singlehanded! (*Slavery; Letters and Speeches* by Horace Mann.)

CHAPTER 17: *The End of the Shop in West Street*

1. Lieutenant Greene is mentioned by Thomas Wentworth Higginson in *Cheerful Yesterdays* and by George Willis Cooke in his two-volume *Introduction to the "Dial."* Alcott was holding Conversations at this time, tickets for sale at the shop in West Street. One of his subjects was "Angelic and Demonic Man" in the course of which he described the blond, blue-eyed type like himself as "angelic" while his description of the black-haired, dark-eyed, energetic and "demonic" type exactly fitted Greene, who was sitting in a front seat. The incident amused contemporary Boston so much that it appears in nearly every volume of Reminiscences. In *Pedlar's Progress* Odell Shepard refers to Greene as "the Reverend William Batchelder Greene," and so he was — as Shepard shows, about as briefly as he was Lieutenant. It was as the dashing Lieutenant that Greene appealed to Elizabeth, although she made it clear that her account of his having graduated from West Point was hearsay.

CHAPTER 18: *Parting of the Ways*

1. Mrs. Peabody's very personal opinion of Webster was not without foundation in fact, as modern biographers freely admit. The whole family, and Horace Mann in particular, was indignant when Webster's statue was placed in front of the State House in Boston. It was with amused delight, therefore, that the grandson of Horace Mann pointed out to me the poetic justice of the fact that near the statue of Webster now stands the statue of Horace Mann, the great educator!

2. The name "Grace Greenwood" was a pseudonym but all her

friends called her by it. Mary Mann had a good reason to do so for Grace Greenwood's real name was Sara Clarke and confusion would surely have arisen in Sophia's mind had Mary's letters referred to any other Sara Clarke except the gentle artist, daughter of the garrulous boardinghouse-keeping Mrs. Clarke. Grace Greenwood was Sara Jane Clarke Lippincott, born in New York City in 1823. An early work, *Greenwood Leaves*, brought her popularity and later her travel letters from all parts of the world were published in leading newspapers. Her friendship for Mary Mann endured throughout Mary's lifetime.

CHAPTER 19: *College President's Wife*

1. In material recently sent me by Mr. Horace Mann, I found a letter from Elizabeth Peabody to Miss Rawlins Pickman which made necessary the changes in this chapter. Again, in February, 1950, Mr. Mann sent me further, recently discovered letters, and among them is one from Mary to Sophia describing the illness and death of Horace Mann. This will have to wait for some subsequent volume.

CHAPTER 21: *Pattern from the Past*

1. In the Berg Collection are Sophia's journals of her travels in Italy and also her handwritten manuscript for the book of travels she afterwards prepared.

2. Writing of this experience in his *Nathaniel Hawthorne and His Wife*, Julian Hawthorne says: "One day in the midst of some heavenly-minded disquisition from the dead mother of one of the onlookers the medium's hand seemed to be suddenly arrested, as by a violent though invisible grasp, and, after a few vague dashes of the pencil, the name of 'Mary Rondel' was written across the paper in large bold characters." . . . Nothing could give her any relief but "Nathaniel Hawthorne's sympathy," she said. According to Julian Hawthorne's account, there were several séances at which "Mary Rondel" always appeared, putting to flight other spirits and, in the opinion of other spirits, "a disorderly, mischievous person, an inveterate liar, and, in general, no better than she should be. Nevertheless, and whatever the frailty of her moral character — which, indeed she never attempted to defend — there was something so genuine, so human, and so pathetically forlorn about poor Mary Rondel, that nobody could help regarding her with a certain compassionate kindliness."

In the course of preparing this book, I referred to volumes of *Vital Statistics* of Salem, Massachusetts, in order to check the date of the death of Mrs. Hawthorne. I opened the book at random and read the following: "Sarah, d. illegitimate John Hathorne and Mary Russum, 1743. . . . Rondel . . . Runnel, Russum." How many troubled spirits did ancient Hathornes leave in their wake — or was there only one "disorderly, mischievous person," still up to her tricks and now opening people's books for them in the New York Public Library?

3. It was Julia Ward Howe whose witticism about the Storys' stone lions went the rounds in Rome.

4. Just before leaving Rome, Sophia bought for herself a "lapis lazuli brooch set in Etruscan gold." And in a photograph (one of the few ever taken of Mrs. Hawthorne) there is the brooch, just as described.

CHAPTER 22: *Incendiary Concord*

1. Alcott's opinion of Sanborn is from the Alcott journals, which are kept at the library in Concord, Massachusetts, and may be seen with the permission of Alcott's grandson, Frederic Woolsey Pratt.

2. Frank Sanborn tells the story of his arrest in his *Recollections of Seventy Years.*

3. Mary Peabody Mann's *Journal of Remembrance* in the Mann Collection of papers at the Massachusetts Historical Society is autobiographical throughout the first half of its ruled notebook pages, and her intention was to make it a diary after she had brought it up to the date when it was begun — September 5, 1864. This she did not do, being too busy living to write about it; and entries, almost without exception, were written in retrospect after all.

CHAPTER 23: *Insatiable Heart*

1. Mrs. Peabody's sister Sophia married Dr. Thomas Pickman of Salem. Their daughter Mary married George B. Loring and it was their child, Mary Loring, who was known as "Posy" and who died aged four-and-a-half years.

2. The letter telling of Sophia's distress over the Holmes article in the *Atlantic Monthly* is a recent acquisition in the Berg Collection.

3. Julia Ward Howe also wrote in disparagement of the Hawthorne notebooks but Grace Greenwood spoke with appreciation of the way in which they revealed an author's mind. Mrs. Hawthorne had never cared for Grace Greenwood but this was a straight road to her heart and they became friends.

4. The Fields correspondence in the Rare Manuscript Room of the Boston Public Library has been very ably discussed and excerpts from it printed in a series of articles by Randall Stewart in *More Books,* The Bulletin of the Boston Public Library.

CHAPTER 24: *Final Flight*

1. Mrs. Hawthorne was not the first nor was she the only person to question the curious bookkeeping of Ticknor and Fields. Gail Hamilton, popular fiction writer for Ticknor and Fields, had become

convinced that she too was cheated. She was writing a satire, *The Battle of the Books*, in which she championed Mrs. Hawthorne's cause as well as her own.

2. The whole of the Hawthorne side of the argument is in the Boston Public Library's rare manuscript collection, and Mr. Randall Stewart handles the Field controversy very clearly in his article for *More Books*, September 1946, entitled "Mrs. Hawthorne's Quarrel with James T. Fields."

3. The little account book kept with anxious care by Sophia and her daughters is in the Berg Collection. On May 24, in Rose Hawthorne's handwriting, is an entry: "Lot at Kensal Green £3,6,00." That is where Sophia Hawthorne is buried.

CHAPTER 25: *Unconquerable Elizabeth*

1. Literary friendships are among the greatest rewards of writing and my acquaintance with the late Mrs. Maud Howe Elliott was one of these. Mrs. Elliott asked me to call after she had read my young people's biography of her mother, Julia Ward Howe. We corresponded, but my call was delayed because of the war. In November 1946 I spent a morning with Mrs. Elliott at her home in Newport. The beautiful room in which we sat was lined with the work of her late husband, John Elliott, muralist and portrait painter. But across the mantel was a row of brightly colored birthday cards oddly at variance with the decorative painting above. Mrs. Elliott had just celebrated her ninety-third birthday. Certainly she remembered Miss Peabody and she told of that first kindergarten with its enrollment of gifted children. She told me, and gave me permission to use, the story of Elizabeth Peabody's appearing at Mrs. Howe's Newport home with no luggage.

I asked Mrs. Elliott what Miss Peabody looked like. She smiled and said, "I was a young girl then, full of my first parties and my first beaux. I thought of Miss Peabody as just one of Mother's old owls." Maud Howe Elliott had been a very beautiful young girl and in her ninety-third year she was slim, erect, with flashing dark eyes and pure white hair — an extraordinarily beautiful and gracious lady. Mrs. Elliott spoke of Hawthorne, whom she remembered perfectly, and of Sophia's humanizing and socializing effect upon him. It troubled her that she could not recall anything to tell me about Mary Mann, but the clarity of her mind and memory was amazing.

CHAPTER 26: *Swifter than a Weaver's Shuttle*

1. Horace Mann had been buried in Antioch, his monument in front of the college for which he gave his life. But upon looking over his papers, Mary must have found a request that he be laid beside his first wife, the beloved Charlotte, in North Burying Ground, Providence.

Mary had his remains brought home and friends contributed to an impressive monolith to mark his grave, Charlotte's name inscribed upon the south face — her grave to the right. The second ceremony had not been as hard to bear as she expected, Mary said. She had already learned to think of her husband as not dead, but in eternal life. In 1868, it was a cruel blow to have to lay her eldest son by his father's side. "Horace, son of Horace and Mary Mann" — only twenty-four years old. Mary placed her son's grave on the other side but left a place for herself close to the left of her husband's monument, and there they laid her.

2. I went early on a summer morning to look for the grave of Elizabeth Peabody. Hawthorne's grave was near those of other Concord immortals and I knew the location well. I asked an elderly man who was cutting grass if he could tell me where the superintendent's office was. He told me there was no such office, I must inquire at the town hall — which would not be open for an hour or more. Just on the chance, I mentioned Elizabeth Peabody — had he seen a marker? "Oh, Miss Peabody, the teacher?" he said. "Right down that main road and under the big pine."

He was right. On the roughhewn stone was mounted a fine bronze plaque with plain but beautiful lettering. Lizzie would have liked it. Near her were brother Nathaniel, sister-in-law Ellen, whose marriage to her brother she had championed, and small markers of children of a third generation, the life span of several of them being pathetically short.

3. The Elizabeth Peabody House was established in 1896 and dedicated on the 21st of April, Froebel's birthday. For six years, the work was carried on in a little house at 156 Chambers Street. The settlement house then moved to larger quarters at 87 Poplar Street and in January, 1913, the present building at 357 Charles Street was opened. Since 1896 a kindergarten has been carried on continuously along with many other activities.

The staff, aided by a large group of volunteers, now makes the Elizabeth Peabody House available to about a thousand people of all nationalities who enter its hospitable doors each week. The house has taken the lead, in Boston, in social service, and particularly in public health — so that the pioneering spirit of Elizabeth Peabody lives on at the Settlement which bears her name.

Sources and Acknowledgments

MANUSCRIPT LETTERS AND JOURNALS constitute the principal source of material used in the preparation of this book. The Henry W. and Albert A. Berg Collection, New York Public Library, has, among its extensive original manuscripts, 649 letters written by the Peabody sisters. The majority of these letters are by Sophia Hawthorne, and in the collection are several of her diaries. There are also many letters written to the Peabody sisters.

Mr. Horace Mann's private collection, consisting of the "Cuba Journal" and miscellaneous papers, includes 195 letters, 40 of which were written by Mary Peabody Mann and most of the remainder by Elizabeth Peabody. There are several diaries of Elizabeth's, begun and abandoned.

The Massachusetts Historical Society has daily letters of Mary and Horace Mann covering about three years. In this collection is, as far as I know, the only journal of Mary Peabody Mann.

In the Boston Public Library is "The Fields Correspondence," consisting of letters from Mrs. Sophia Hawthorne to Mrs. Annie Fields, and from Elizabeth Peabody to James T. Fields in connection with the controversy over the Hawthorne royalties. The Concord Free Public Library is the depository of the Alcott journals and other Alcott papers, owned by Mr. Frederic Woolsey Pratt. Among them are copies by Alcott of letters written to him by Elizabeth and Sophia Peabody. Other sources of manuscript material are Antioch College, Yellow Springs, Ohio; Essex Institute, Salem, Massachusetts; Morgan Library, New York City (sections of Hawthorne notebooks kept by Sophia Hawthorne), and New York Historical Society. Helpful assistance was given by Dartmouth College, Hanover, New Hampshire; Metropolitan Museum of Art, New York City; The Old Manse, Concord, Massachusetts; Providence Athenæum, Providence, Rhode Island; Sterling Library, Yale University, and Wayside, Concord, Massachusetts.

I want to thank especially the following people: Hildegarde Hawthorne and Beatrix Hawthorne Smyth, granddaughters of Sophia and Nathaniel

Hawthorne, were most gracious and helpful, as were also Julian C. Smyth, Manning Hawthorne and other direct descendants. In Mr. Horace Mann, I had the good fortune to meet the grandson of Mary Peabody Mann, one who remembered his great-aunt, Elizabeth Peabody, and could describe her to me. He not only loaned me his entire collection of family letters but wrote to me patiently in answer to my many questions. Dr. Harold Bowditch, through the study of his famous ancestor, Nathaniel Bowditch, has become an authority on Salem, while his genealogy studies helped me to identify members of the Peabody family. His connection with the Massachusetts Historical Society was of great value to me. Dr. John Gordan was helpful far beyond routine assistance in my research at the Berg Room. He gave advice on sources and on personalities of the period. Miss Margaret M. Lothrop, the present owner of Wayside, kindly allowed me to use her notes which she made for her monograph on Wayside. I wish to thank Mr. Frederic Woolsey Pratt for permission to examine the Alcott papers; Mr. Zoltan Haraszti, Keeper of Rare Books and Editor of Publications, Boston Public Library; Mr. Stephen T. Riley, Librarian, Massachusetts Historical Society; Miss Marion Barker of the Old Manse, and Miss Sarah Ripley Bartlett of the Concord Free Public Library. Mr. Walter How, descendant of Nathaniel Peabody, was helpful in discussing family background. I visited the late Maud Howe Elliott at her home in Newport and she recalled for me her memories of Nathaniel Hawthorne and Elizabeth Peabody.

Julian Hawthorne's *Hawthorne and His Wife* is so well known that I have omitted some incidents in it and have substituted others from the wealth of manuscript material to which I had access. Rose Hawthorne's *Memories of Hawthorne* gives a more intimate glimpse of her mother, but again I had sufficient new material so that very little is repeated. Permission to quote from *Grandmother Tyler's Book, the Recollections of Mary Palmer Tyler*, edited by Frederick Tupper and H. T. Brown, Putnam, 1925, has been given by the Vermont Historical Society.

While I have quoted letters in part, I have never consciously omitted anything that would change the meaning. Undated letters have been placed in proper periods by means of content, and it has been my intention to stick close to facts at all times, and to be as accurate as possible in my use of manuscript sources.

Index